BUSINESS LIFE AND
PUBLIC POLICY

D. C. COLEMAN

[*Photograph by Ian Fleming*]

BUSINESS LIFE AND PUBLIC POLICY

Essays in honour of
D. C. COLEMAN

Edited by

NEIL McKENDRICK

and

R. B. OUTHWAITE

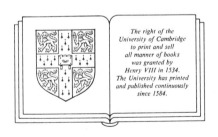

CAMBRIDGE UNIVERSITY PRESS

Cambridge

London   New York   New Rochelle
Melbourne   Sydney

Published by the Press Syndicate of the University of Cambridge
The Pitt Building, Trumpington Street, Cambridge CB2 1RP
32 East 57th Street, New York, NY 10022, USA
10 Stamford Road, Oakleigh, Melbourne 3166, Australia

© Cambridge University Press 1986

First published 1986

Printed in Great Britain by the University Press, Cambridge

British Library Cataloguing in Publication Data

Business life and public policy: essays in honour of D. C. Coleman.
1. Great Britain – Social conditions
I. Coleman, D. C.   II. McKendrick, Neil
III. Outhwaite, R. B.
941   HN385

Library of Congress Cataloguing in Publication Data
Business life and public policy.
'Bibliography of D. C. Coleman's published works': p.
Bibliography: p.
Includes index.
Contents: Piscatorial politics in the early Parliaments of Elizabeth I/G. R. Elton – Marriage
as business/R. B. Outhwaite – Age and accumulation in the London business community,
1665–1720/Peter Earle – [etc.]
1. Finance – Great Britain – History – Addresses, essays, lectures. 2. Businessmen – Great
Britain – History – Addresses, essays, lectures. 3. Great Britain – Politics and
government – Addresses, essays, lectures.
4. Coleman, D. C. (Donald Cuthbert), 1920–
I. Coleman, D. C. (Donald Cuthbert), 1920–
II. McKendrick, Neil.   III. Outhwaite, R. B.
HG186.G7B87 1986   332'.0941   85–31333

ISBN 0 521 26275 5

UP

Contents

Preface

This volume of essays, humbly offered by a few of his many pupils, colleagues and friends, celebrates the contribution to historical scholarship of Donald Coleman, a contribution happily still in full flow, despite, or perhaps even because of, his retirement in 1981 from his teaching post as Professor of Economic History in the University of Cambridge. The range and scale of that contribution can be glimpsed from the bibliography of his writings.[1] Its quality is no less remarkable. Essential features of the latter are its incisiveness, its humanity and above all its good sense. In work after work he has brought an acute economic perception to history without ever losing sight of the fact that the past was made by people not processes. These qualities are perhaps most vividly displayed in what is arguably his greatest work, the mammoth three-volume study, *Courtaulds: An Economic and Social History* (1969–80), where his alchemical touch transformed the all too frequent base metal of business history into an enthralling analytical narrative stretching over two and a half centuries. That great work confirmed his leading position among the world's historians of modern business, rivalling his eminence as an economic historian of the sixteenth and seventeenth centuries.

It is perhaps significant that Donald's working life began in the business world and his academic career rather late. In 1939, at the age of seventeen, he left Haberdashers' Aske's School for the City world of insurance. Two years later he enrolled at the University of London. Hardly had he done so, however, when he was called away by the war. The army occupied him for the next six years, and active service in, amongst other places, Italy nurtured a characteristic interest in that country's history and culture. Thereafter, in 1946, he exchanged what some might regard as one form of warfare for another by returning to the London School of Economics, where he was a prominent member of that mature and mettlesome student intake still remembered as the liveliest intellectual cohort of our time.

---

[1] See pp. 251–5.

Something of his general career there is recalled for us here by one of his teachers, Professor F. J. Fisher:

'In a recent tribute to Charles Wilson, Donald Coleman sketched a type of successful businessman that he claims often to have found in history. Imaginative and individualistic; shrewd and not easily swayed by the ideas and opinions of others; industrious and with great powers of application; ambitious, but for achievement and recognition rather than for money. With the substitution of academic for business achievement, that model would have fitted Donald as a student remarkably well. For Donald was never a conventional student. He entered upon serious academic study only after a decade of experience in the insurance world and the army. By then his adolescent doubts and indecisions were behind him: he knew what he wanted. He plotted his campaign of study with military precision. Those whose task it was to teach him were seen more as assistants, valuable or otherwise, than as leaders to be followed. Teaching him therefore was a challenge, but a challenge that was made the more welcome by the fact that, in the intervals of fighting in Italy, he had acquired a knowledge of food and drink that made him, in the world of hospitality, the teacher and the rest of us his students.

'Perhaps Donald's greatest achievement as a student was to finish an excellent doctoral thesis in the statutory minimum time of six terms – a feat no longer deemed possible despite all the aids to research that have become available. That thesis – on the economy of Kent in the early seventeenth century – was never published, although many others have raided it with profit. But it laid the foundation for much of his later career. The study of a single county over a short period was deliberately chosen as requiring the examination of a variety of economic activities and the use of a wide range of historical sources – an admirable training for any future teacher. Kent supplied materials for books on Sir John Banks, a financier who acquired estates in that county, and on the paper industry, one of the activities carried out there. But of more immediate importance was the fact that, since a good number of industries flourished in seventeenth-century Kent, Donald became the obvious candidate for appointment to a new lectureship in industrial history that had been established at the L.S.E. Thus he got his foot on the first step of an academic ladder, the top of which he was to reach in less than twenty years.

'That appointment was made in 1951 and in those days, when students were less cosseted than they are now, teaching duties at the School were light and, in any case, the demand for industrial history was small. Donald was able therefore to concentrate on writing and editorial work and he rapidly established his reputation through his books on Banks and on the paper industry, through a stream of important articles and book reviews, through his activities from 1952 to 1961 as English editor of the *Scandinavian Economic History Review* and, more especially, by his editorship from 1967 to 1973 of the *Economic History Review*. There are those who believe that, under his rigorous and even autocratic editorship, the *Review* reached a level from which it has since declined. And it was characteristic of Donald that one of his first actions as editor was to get an advisory editorial committee abolished, since he saw no need for its services.

'Donald's spectacular rise to eminence as a business historian did not, however, restrict him to that field. For one thing, as the historian of Courtaulds he inevitably became recognized as an expert on textile history just at a time when the generosity of Eric Pasold made a large sum of money available for its study. Inevitably, the Pasold Fund relied on Donald for advice, and since the recent death of its secretary and his close friend, Kenneth Ponting, his services to that body have increased.

'More importantly, the Courtauld volumes not only earned Donald in 1969 the personal title of Professor of Economic History at London, but were instrumental in producing an invitation to fill the Chair of Economic History in Cambridge, a post which he took up in 1971.'

Professor Leslie Hannah, a former Cambridge colleague and now occupying the recently established Chair of Business History at the London School of Economics, responded to our request for his views on Donald's achievements as a business historian with the following assessment:

'It was a chance development which drew Donald into a long and happy flirtation with a new subject in which his contribution was to be equal to that in his first chosen field. His biography of Banks and his study of seventeenth-century industry already entitled him to fame as a business historian, but the new venture into corporate history took him into fields and periods which were new. At Cambridge, Charles Wilson had already trodden that path, pioneering modern corporate history in Britain with his two volumes on Unilever. A number of other large British companies in the late 1950s and early 1960s were contemplating commissioning scholarly "official" histories. There was, of course, nothing surprising in this – many other institutions from monasteries to governments had hired their "official" historians – but academics tended to be especially wary in the case of commissioned histories of commercial organizations. The normal channel of invitation was from the chairman of a company to the professoriat of his *alma mater*: usually Oxford, Cambridge or the London School of Economics. Some projects fizzled out as it became clear that the paymaster viewed the corporate history in much the same spirit as the Communist Party of the Soviet Union viewed its historians, whereas the prospective piper was not prepared to play the company's tune. In 1961 the call came to Donald from Courtaulds, whose board, happily, proved willing to accept his terms of complete freedom to write a "warts and all" account, without censorship. A contract was duly signed, and Donald became the historian of that long-lived silk firm which was also the pioneer of rayon, a firm which was one of the largest and most successful textile enterprises in the world.

'Academics differ in their reaction to such windfalls. Not infrequently, an army of research assistants appears on the corporate payroll. Donald shunned this approach; the project became his own major research effort between 1962 and 1967. He had the valued assistance of Bernardine Gregory as secretary (her work going well beyond that to include tracking people and papers, and calendaring documents), but the bulk of the research he carried out personally. When the first two volumes of *Courtaulds: An Economic and Social History* appeared in 1969, it was immediately regarded as one of the finest, and certainly the most economically sophisticated, of corporate histories written by scholarly historians. The first volume traced the Courtauld family back to their origins as Huguenot refugees in the seventeenth century, through their success in the silk trade, to their commercial fortune as purveyors of that quintessentially Victorian necessity, mourning crêpe. The second volume continued the story into the twentieth century, showing Courtaulds' transformation into a large, public company developing rayon: the first artificial fibre. As the first mover in global oligopoly, Courtaulds dominated not only the European but also the American industry, until their American viscose subsidiary was expropriated in 1941 to help pay for lend–lease war supplies.

'Donald's taste for the new range of study opened up by the Courtaulds' experience did not wane when the work was completed. He was an active participant in business history conferences, speaking with the authority of a scholar who understood businessmen. (The conference organizer who mistakenly listed him as a representative of "Overhall Cavendish Ltd" – his Suffolk home being Over Hall – was paying an unconscious compliment to his developing intuitive understanding of the way contemporary businessmen ticked.) In the later 1970s, he and Sir Arthur Knight, the chairman of Courtaulds, played a leading role with Theo Barker, Leslie Pressnell and Peter Mathias in the establishment of the Business History Unit to promote research at the London School of Economics and at Imperial College, London. The Courtauld connection was also developed with the signing in 1976 of a contract to write a third volume of the corporate history, bringing the story forward from 1941 to 1965. That volume appeared in 1980. It was, the author recognized, more difficult to write the history of the recent past, and its judgments were more subjective and less securely based on statistical evidence than the two earlier volumes. Donald was acutely aware that he was praising the victors in the classic 1961 takeover struggle in which Kearton and Knight had defeated the predatory moves of I.C.I., and he well knew the danger of such a "Whig" interpretation of history. His devastating account of the years of conservative stewardship by the incompetent Sir John Hanbury-Williams, which had left Courtaulds open to the takeover threat, nonetheless rang true.

'While reflecting more generally on the lessons of the Courtaulds history, Donald gave birth to an entertainingly thoughtful seminar paper, "Gentlemen and Players", which eventually surfaced as a much quoted article in the *Economic History Review*. This *tour de force* was pure Coleman. Taking his categorization of businessmen from the "Gentlemen *vs* Players" cricket match, he mercilessly exposed some of the slack thinking which generalizations about poor entrepreneurship and amateurish management had easily slid into. He showed that the desire to escape from business to more prestigious gentlemanly pursuits had deep roots in English culture extending back at least to the seventeenth century; it was, then, implausible to explain Britain's recent economic decline in terms of such factors without squaring the explanation with Britain's evident dynamism during the Industrial Revolution. The increasing modern dominance of public-school and Oxbridge men in large-scale businesses – an easy target for critics of gentlemen amateurs – was not all loss. Yet there could hardly be a better example of it than the incompetent stewardship of Sir John Hanbury-Williams at Courtaulds. The real losses, he suggested came in the division between "practical men" and "gentlemen amateurs", which the British educational system engendered, limiting the growth of informed professionalism. Cautious and subtle, but providing a heavy weight of circumstantial evidence for the complex interaction of social values and business performance which it posited, the article remains a classic contribution to a debate whose inherent importance will maintain its irresistible fascination despite repeated failure to resolve the analytical issues from which the subject suffers.'

Donald's ten years in Cambridge were busy and productive ones. In addition to teaching in both parts of the History Tripos, he presided wisely and benignly over two Cambridge research seminars, looked after ten Ph.D. students, and served in various ways the Faculties of both History and Economics, not least by persuading appointments committees to admit a few outside Players into the ranks of the local Gentlemen. In other ways he also maintained and established links with the greater academic world, through for example his own service to the Economic and Social Research Council, the Business Archives Council and the British Academy. Despite these often heavy demands, he still found time to produce a steady stream of books, articles and reviews, to accept invitations to read papers in various parts of the world, and to act as a generous host in Pembroke College and elsewhere to that stream of distinguished visitors that Cambridge attracts. For many of the latter, memories of Donald and Ann at Over Hall will be vividly and warmly recollected.

Donald always seems at his happiest and most relaxed when presiding over such entertainments in his own Suffolk home. Looking out over his neighbour's vineyards it provides an apt location for him to bring together colleagues from London and from Cambridge, distinguished foreign scholars and aspiring young research students – even those academic neighbours who so rarely seem to socialize, theoretical economists and professional economic historians. For an intimate chat or a piece of academic gossip Donald made ample use of the pubs of Cambridge, but for formal entertainments he preferred his own home.

This may give a further clue to his reasons for retiring early. At the valedictory dinner given for him by the Cambridge History Faculty in the magnificent gallery at St John's, he explained to his colleagues his growing disenchantment with undergraduate teaching. Lecturing, he said, had become a painful duty he saw no reason to endure further. He modestly doubted if his own contribution in this sphere would be much missed. But to us it seemed there were other academic duties in prospect which speeded him on his way. The near certainty that he would become the Chairman of the History Faculty and the distinct possibility of becoming Master of a Cambridge college made the delights of retirement to Cavendish all the more appealing. He knew that there were many who wished him to accept posts in Cambridge which many men covet, but they held few charms for him. They would, he said, take him away from his scholarly work and saddle him with duties which would offer him little satisfaction. Position for its own sake was not an attraction, nor was power. What he wanted to do was to write. Secure in the grounds he had created in Suffolk, secure in Over Hall where entertaining is a pleasure not a duty, he happily cultivates his garden free from the demands of academic politics, and contentedly cultivates his scholarship free from the responsibilities of teaching and administration. Intimations of mortality made suddenly vivid by the death of his younger brother may have hastened his decision, but the prime compulsion seems to have come from the prospect of pursuing his scholarship in the uninterrupted peace of the place he likes best.

We were aware, as editors of this volume, that he is a hard act to follow. His scholarly range is enormous, stretching as it does from the sixteenth to the twentieth centuries, embracing not only general works on England and Europe, but also revealing particular interests and expertise in a whole number of specialist areas – the history of technology, industrial structures and change, the role and origins of economic ideas, and much more. Two principles, however, guided us in selecting contributions to this volume. One was that we should confine ourselves to that long period from the sixteenth century onwards in which he has principally operated: this meant we had to exclude from the volume contributions from medievalist colleagues who might have wished to contribute. The second is that amongst Donald's wide range of special interests two areas are prominent – the nature and making of government economic policy, and the economic and cultural milieu of the business world. Our collective efforts have been directed to these two areas.

Donald's generosity has always exhibited itself in many ways: he is as generous in imparting ideas and advice, particularly to younger scholars, as he is in dispensing hospitality. Ever economical, it is typical also that he almost invariably tends to combine these two activities. Those who know him well will recognize that fearsome snort of the nostrils which usually presages a verbal assault on yet another folly of *homo academicus*. The editors fondly hope that this modest collection, offered to him at the point when he *should* have retired from his Cambridge chair, does not provoke that familiar response.

NEIL MCKENDRICK
R. B. OUTHWAITE

List of contributors

B. W. E. Alford, *Professor of Economic History, University of Bristol*

Peter Earle, *Reader in Economic History, London School of Economics*

G. R. Elton, *Regius Professor of History, University of Cambridge*

F. J. Fisher, *Emeritus Professor of Economic History, London School of Economics*

Leslie Hannah, *Director of the Business History Unit and Professor of Business History, London School of Economics*

Julian Hoppit, *Fellow and Director of Studies in History at Magdalene College, Cambridge*

Neil McKendrick, *Fellow of Caius College, and University Lecturer in History, University of Cambridge*

R. B. Outhwaite, *Fellow of Caius College, and University Lecturer in History, University of Cambridge*

W. J. Reader, *Business historian, author of* Imperial Chemical Industries (*1970–5*), Metal Box (*1976*), Bowater (*1981*).

Barry Supple, *Master of St Catharine's College, and Professor of Economic History, University of Cambridge*

Clive Trebilcock, *Fellow of Pembroke College, and University Lecturer in History, University of Cambridge*

C. H. Wilson, *Fellow of Jesus College, and Emeritus Professor of Modern History, University of Cambridge*

J. M. Winter, *Fellow of Pembroke College, and University Lecturer in History, University of Cambridge*

1

Piscatorial politics in the early Parliaments of Elizabeth I

G. R. ELTON

In our period State action in economic and social matters can be seen as having four main ends in view: the maintenance of social stability and order; the encouragement and regulation of the internal economy; the encouragement and regulation of overseas trade and shipping; and the raising of revenue.

Thus Donald Coleman sums up a well-known problem and its usual conclusion.[1] His phrasing is cautious: 'state action' must be taken to include the legislation of Parliament, but the possibility that the initiative behind such laws might have come from unofficial quarters is not expressly excluded. Nevertheless, the mention of public order and public revenue does suggest that the author had it in mind here to equate the state with its government. That conviction – that Elizabethan economic legislation originated in official circles and reflected thinking there – is well entrenched in the literature; it goes back at the least to Archdeacon Cunningham, who decided that 'the more we examine the working of the Elizabethan scheme for the administration of economic affairs, the more do we see that the Council was the pivot of the whole system', as initiators and executors.[2] The only person who has dared to question the assumption was F. J. Fisher, though even he in the end resigned himself to the concept of government action, called forth in his view not by sovereign planning but by the haphazard pressures of the market and other circumstances.[3] In any case, he got a firm answer from Lawrence Stone who, restoring tradition in new clothes, rested his whole case tacitly on the conviction that legislative enactments reflected government policy while failed proposals indicated the defeat of government intentions by sectional interests in the House of Commons.[4] General accounts thus returned with relief to the supposition

[1] D. C. Coleman, *The Economy of England, 1450–1750* (Oxford, 1977), pp. 173–4.
[2] W. Cunningham, *The Growth of English Industry and Commerce*, 6th edn (Cambridge, 1907–10), vol. III, p. 53. He did not seem to know that most of the regulations he had in mind could only be enforced in the law courts and by actions brought by private informers.
[3] F. J. Fisher, 'Commercial Trends and Policy in Sixteenth-Century England', *Economic History Review* 10 (1940), 95–117.
[4] L. Stone, 'State Control in Sixteenth-Century England', *Economic History Review* 17 (1947), 103–20. Abandoning the traditional view, according to which regulations aimed

that manifestations of control and policy arose with 'government', and conversely that acts of Parliament can be used to find out what government was about.[5] Yet historians of Parliament are by now quite well aware that sixteenth-century statutes for problems of the common weal need by no means have come from monarch and Council. So far, the history of few such acts has been investigated, though one famous study, which, trying to distinguish the pressures behind the 1563 Statute of Artificers, cast much doubt upon the common conviction, apparently failed to weaken its hold upon the generality. Besides, it may not have got things quite right, and, this being a case where even a small discrepancy can throw a general chain of reasoning into confusion, the simplicities of tradition can reestablish themselves.[6] A look at some other measure of economic import may therefore help. I have chosen the 1581 fisheries act, which Ephraim Lipson regarded as an official attempt 'to stimulate native shipping by forbidding subjects to import foreign-cured fish'.[7] Is that what it was?

Sixteenth-century England ate a lot of fish, and a relatively large part of its population made a living out of this fact. When one considers the place occupied by cod and ling and salted herring in the menus of the time, it comes as a surprise to find how little serious work has been done on this theme.[8] Supplying England with the fish it needed especially in Lent and on other fast-days involved the despatch of regular annual fleets to the Iceland fishing grounds; it involved following the shoals of cod and herring as each year they travelled south from Scotland to the German Bight; it involved hundreds of small vessels exploiting the inshore fisheries off the English east coast from the mouth of the Tyne to the mouth of the Thames; it involved acquiring large quantities of salt which the more distant voyagers had to carry with them while the close-in fishermen stacked it on shore to deal with the catch unloaded there. It was widely, and correctly, thought that the safety of the realm, depending as it did on the maintenance

to forward prosperity, Stone claimed to have learned from the war just past that Tudor governments controlled the economy for reasons of national security.
[5] E.g. L. A. Clarkson, *The Pre-Industrial Economy in England 1500–1750* (New York, 1972), ch. 6.
[6] S. T. Bindoff, 'The Making of the Statute of Artificers', in S. T. Bindoff, J. Hurstfield and C. H. Williams (eds.), *English Government and Society* (London, 1961), pp. 56–94. According to Bindoff (p. 72), sect. 33, which exempted Norwich and London, did not enter the bill until at a very late stage of its passage through the Commons; yet, discussing the bill three weeks before the Parliament even met, the city council of York saw that clause included in it: *York Civic Records*, ed. A. Raine, vol. VI (1948), p. 50.
[7] E. Lipson, *The Economic History of England*, 6th edn (London, 1956), vol. III, p. 119.
[8] For a general introduction – no more – cf. A. Michell, 'The European Fisheries in Early Modern History', *The Cambridge Economic History of Europe*, vol. V, pp. 134–84. A very few points of direct relevance, as well as interesting details about the physiognomy and ecology of the herring, are found in J. T. Jenkins, *The Herring and the Herring Fisheries* (London, 1927).

of a large body of experienced seamen, called for a healthy fishing industry as a training ground for mariners. By the middle of the sixteenth century, English fishermen were retreating before the advancing enterprise of the Dutch, equipped with their superior vessels (the cod and herring busses), large enough to hold great quantities of fish salted on board – a considerable economy in the trade. From this grew an ever increasing reliance on Dutch fish, bought up in the Netherlands by English merchants – especially the members of the London Fishmongers' Company – who could undersell English fishermen increasingly forced back upon the scattered and uneconomic operations of individuals fishing the inshore grounds. There was a crisis in English fishing, and the Protestant dislike of popish fast-days did not help. And as many thought, there was a resulting crisis in the supply of experienced manpower to sail English ships and guard the island.

Thus, even before war forced the needs of the navy and of shipping upon government, the Elizabethan Parliaments several times concerned themselves with the protection and promotion of English seafaring interests. The legislation, proposed or enacted, pursued two separate but connected lines of thought: it tried to restrict English seaborne trade to native vessels, mariners and owners, and it tried to protect English fishermen against foreign competition. Most of what was done owed little to any initiatives by Queen or Council; instead, the acts testified to concern and agitation on the part of private interests. Since these interests included rivals as well as cooperators, the prehistory, passage and later fortunes of the statutes were never straightforward, as in particular the act of 1581 (23 Eliz. I, c. 7) well illustrates. Its history throws much light on the manner in which economic pressure groups used the legislative power of Parliament.

The sessions between the Queen's accession and 1581 provided a sort of run-up to the manoeuvres of the latter year. The act of 1559 (1 Eliz. I, c. 13) – to judge by its enacting clause, the only one of all these measures to stem from the Council[9] – tried to consolidate earlier legislation for the limitation of imports to English-owned vessels; ineffective from the first and limited to a trial period, it was not continued in 1571 and seems to have lapsed.[10] Markedly more important was the so-called great navigation act of 1563 (5 Eliz. I, c. 5), a comprehensive measure initiated privately in the Commons and much enlarged in the course of passage. It dealt with both the main concerns of all this legislation. Touching fisheries, it freed Englishmen from various constraints and from the payment of customs

[9] Cf. G. R. Elton, 'Enacting Clauses and Legislative Initiative, 1559–1571 [*recte* 1581]', *Bulletin of the Institute of Historical Research* 53 (1980), 183–91.
[10] The act was to endure for five years from the end of the 1559 Parliament and then to the end of the next one; it should thus have been renewed in 1566 when the expiring laws continuance bill (whose text is unknown) lapsed in the Lower House. The successful continuance act of 1571 (13 Eliz. I, c. 25) does not mention this navigation act.

but (for reasons which have not so far become apparent) expressly excluded Hull from these benefits;[11] it also contained the notorious clause promoted by William Cecil which made Wednesdays into fish-days – a clause which led to one of the few divisions recorded for these Parliaments.[12] A bill to repeal 'Cecil's fast', which probably reflected religious opposition rather than economic concerns, was introduced in the Lords in the next session but got no further than a first reading; the same fate befell efforts in the Commons to modify the ban on foreign fish imports and to protect the annual herring fair at Great Yarmouth in Norfolk, efforts which unquestionably involved commercial considerations.[13]

This is the first positive appearance in the story of the special herring interests represented by Yarmouth, and they gathered strength from then on.[14] Though the 1563 act was not due for renewal until the first dissolution of a Parliament after Michaelmas 1574 (it therefore called for action in the Parliament summoned in 1572 which after the session of 1581 petered out in repeated prorogations), the 1571 Parliament passed an act renewing and slightly amending it; the amendments all served the interests of the herring fishery. The time-limitation clause of this act took it out of the struggles over parliamentary recontinuation: after an initial time-limit of six years, its further existence was thereafter to be at the Queen's pleasure. Somebody in the Lords, confused as well he might be by these complexities, secured a first reading for a formal continuance bill in the session of 1576, but the law officers very likely drew his attention to the superfluity of his bill, of which no more was heard.[15] In fact, throughout the seventies the fishing interests of such outports as Yarmouth seem to have been in the ascendant. In 1571 they beat off a more determined effort to repeal the Wednesday fast, the bill passing the Commons but lapsing in the Upper House;[16] and in 1572 a bill hostile to Yarmouth was talked down on introduction, not being read even a first time.[17] Intended to permit the free sale of fish by all Englishmen to all comers except the Queen's enemies, it was put up by men of Suffolk and

---

[11] Sect. 3, which tried to balance this adverse discrimination against Hull by permitting the town to retain the tolls assigned to it under a repealed act of Henry VIII.

[12] C[ommons] J[ournal] I, 58; the clause passed by 179 votes to 97.

[13] L[ords] J[ournal] I, 6, 56; C.J. I, 77, 80.

[14] For the Yarmouth fishery cf. Robert Tittler, 'The English Fishing Industry in the Sixteenth Century: the Case of Yarmouth', Albion 9 (1977), 40–60. This article has nothing to say about the parliamentary transactions investigated here; it is also somewhat in conflict with A. R. Michell, 'The Port and Town of Great Yarmouth and its Economic and Social Relationships with its Neighbours on both Sides of the Seas, 1550–1714' (University of Cambridge Ph.D. dissertation 1978).

[15] L.J. I, 745.   [16] C.J. I, 89–90; L.J. I, 690.

[17] The bill is not noted in C.J.; we know of it from Thomas Cromwell's 'Diary' (Proceedings [in the Parliaments of Elizabeth I, vol. I: 1559–1581], ed. T. E. Hartley (Leicester, 1981), p. 363).

eventually demolished by one of the burgesses for Yarmouth – unquestionably William Grice, a man (as we shall see) of importance in this story. Yarmouth, he claimed, needed its special privileges in order to be able to maintain its harbour, a duty which in the last few years had allegedly cost it some £12 000.[18] Besides, Yarmouth paid a fee farm of £50 to the Queen in exchange for the privilege, and another £50 a year towards the upkeep of the fishing wharf. These claims to dedicated and expensive excellence prevailed, and Grice won the day.

As a matter of fact, the men of Suffolk seem on this occasion to have stepped out of line, for the next parliamentary session witnessed a most remarkable display of solidarity on the part of the coastwise fishing interests, a display which also shows how sophisticated the practice of lobbying the Parliament had become. A few days before the end of the session, perhaps in support of that superfluous renewal bill already mentioned, the seaports of England presented a certificate underlining the beneficent effects of the 1563 act whose fishing clauses, they maintained, had saved English shipping from disastrous decline: 'If the said law should no longer endure it would be in manner as utter decrying of all the whole fishermen within this realm.' This certificate was signed on behalf of twenty-eight ports (plus others unnamed) running round the east and south coasts from Newcastle to Devon, and including not only Yarmouth but also several Suffolk towns. Signed on their behalf, or so the document maintains; the actual signatures reveal something rather different about the lobby which promoted this appeal.[19]

Twenty-two men put their names to it, of whom three cannot be made out. The tally included eleven sitting members of the Commons, one ex-member and one man who later got elected to Parliament, four persons described as masters (that is, of the Queen's ships), one man from Dover (John Lucas – not a burgess in any Parliament), and one man about whom nothing relevant can be discovered (Richard Foxlyffe). Of the burgesses, five actually represented fishing ports, all of them on the east coast: Sir Henry Gates (Scarborough), William Grice (Great Yarmouth), Charles Calthorpe (Eye), Edmund Grimston and Thomas Seckford (Ipswich). Three not directly involved but all influential men in East Anglia added their names in support of their Yarmouth and Ipswich colleagues. Henry

[18] The figure may well be correct: in the half-century after 1549, harbour repairs at Yarmouth ran up a bill for £31 873 14s. 4d. (Tittler, 'English Fishing Industry', p. 55).

[19] P[ublic] R[ecord] O[ffice], SP 12/107, fos. 170–1. The named places are: Newcastle, Hartlepool, Whitby, Scarborough, Lynn, Blakeney, Yarmouth, Lowestoft, Goole (out of order). Dunwich, Aldeborough, Orford, Harwich, Colchester, Eye, Margate, Ramsgate, Broadstairs, Sandwich, Dover, Folkestone, Hyde, Rye, Hastings, Brighton, Portsmouth, Exmouth, Burport – a roll-call of fishing towns. All details concerning members of the Commons are taken from P. Hasler (ed.), *History of Parliament: The House of Commons 1558–1603*, 3 vols. (London, 1982).

Woodhouse, knight for the shire of Norfolk, was vice-admiral for both
Norfolk and Suffolk as well as Lord Keeper Bacon's son-in-law. One of the
Lord Keeper's sons, Nathaniel, who sat for Tavistock in 1576, was to prove
his standing in the shire by getting elected for it in the next Parliament.
And Robert Wingfield, though resident at Peterborough which he represented, belonged to the powerful Suffolk clan of that name. The really
impressive signatories head and end the list. At the top stood William
Wynter, the leading professional seaman in the House; although he sat
for the land-bound Duchy borough of Clitheroe, his real interests here came
through, and he was a splendid recruit for the campaign. At the tail there
appeared two of the Council's most influential men of business in the
Commons: Thomas Wilson (Lincoln), secretary of state, and Thomas
Norton (London), the famous and ever-active Parliament-man. Norton
revealed something about his character by adding the words 'to the latter
part' to his signature: apparently he did not wish it thought that he
supported the opening statement about a recent increase in the number
of sizeable fishing vessels, a detail of which he could hardly have known
from personal experience. The two people who sat in other Parliaments
were Wynter's son Edward (1584) and William Holstock, an official of the
navy who had represented Rochester in the previous House. A striking
mixture of fishermen's representatives, local men not technically connected
with the ports involved, and expert mariners drawn from outside the
House, the group attracted the sponsorship of the outstanding naval pundit
of the day and the support of two powerful government-men in the House.
The many ports on whose behalf they professed to speak could be content
with such unsolicited representation, but while the list of places put
forward included all the English seacoast except the west, from the Bristol
Channel to Cumberland (no fishing interests there), the signatories reveal
that the campaign originated in Norfolk and Suffolk: with the herring
interests.

Meanwhile these matters had also attracted the attention of one of those
learned propagandists and promoters who, one sometimes feels, abounded
in Elizabethan England, and whose writings have been too often treated
as plain statements of the truth, especially about matters economic. Robert
Hitchcock, described by the *Dictionary of National Biography* as 'a military
writer', became an enthusiastic convert to the patriotic virtues of fishing,
both near to home and on the Newfoundland banks. He wished to copy
the Dutch in building seagoing vessels of a large capacity, and he drew up
plans which, he claimed, would augment the number of English seamen
by 6000 and corner the world's fish supply for England. In order to achieve
this he proposed to set up a national organization based on eight leading
fishing centres and financed by a loan of £80000 raised from these

ports – London, Yarmouth, Hull, Newcastle, Chatham, Bristol, Exeter and Southampton: the profits of the trade, he argued, would soon cover these initial costs and maintain the scheme thereafter.[20] Hitchcock's enthusiasm inspired John Dee, ever willing to dream dreams and capable of outdoing anybody in the production of impracticable fantasies: in 1577 he published a proposal for a standing royal navy which would patrol the English fishing grounds in order to keep out foreigners. Dee singled out the Yarmouth herring fishery, allegedly so damaged by the Dutch that Norfolk and Suffolk had only some 140 ships left, all of them too small to support the ancient annual voyages to the Iceland fisheries. He envisaged a navy organized in six squadrons – one each to watch off the shores of Ireland and Scotland, one 'to intercept or understand all privy conspiracies by sea to be communicated', a fourth to be (apparently) permanently at sea against possible sudden attacks from abroad, another to control foreign fishermen, and a last one to clear home waters of pirates. The last in particular would be such a service to foreign princes that they would eagerly seek England's friendship: 'what liberal presents and foreign contributions in hand will duly follow thereof, who cannot imagine?' Who indeed? Unfortunately he concluded only with a confident 'dictum sapienti sat esto'; what was needed was rather his skill in the occult sciences.[21]

Hitchcock did not confine the dissemination of his notions to written memorials. As he tells it, he arranged a dinner at Westminster, a few days before the end of the 1576 session, to which he invited 'the burgesses of almost all the stately port towns of England and Wales'.[22] He read a summary of his programme to them and fired them with his own enthusiasm. Speaker Bell, burgess of King's Lynn, declared that 'a Parliament hath been called for less cause', and others offered to get their towns to equip suitable fishing fleets without national assistance. Others admittedly scoffed. It would be sensible, they said, to send off such armadas with crews drawn from the dregs of the people; if they were lost, as was likely to happen, 'it is but the riddance of a number of idle and evil disposed people'. Such sceptics, said Hitchcock, would soon change their minds when they saw the benefit in wealth and employment that his programme would bring. Indeed, these burgesses of the Parliament had not been the

---

[20] Robert Hitchcock, *A Politic Plat* (1581: *STC* 13531); reprinted in E. Arber, *An English Garner* (London, 1897), vol. ii, pp. 133–68. How well did he know the industry? Were Exeter and Southampton at all prominent in fishing and the trade in fish?

[21] John Dee, *General and Rare Memorials* (1577: *STC* 6459); reprinted as *The Petty Navy Royal* in Arber, *English Garner*, vol. ii, pp. 61–70. The anonymous advocate of reform, cited by Dee, was Hitchcock (*ibid.*, p. 65 and note).

[22] Arber, *English Garner*, vol. ii, pp. 167–8. Though the dates fit, it seems unlikely that the round-robin certificate mentioned above was produced at this meeting: the names of the signatories do not support such a conclusion, and the subject-matter also differs.

first to learn of Hitchcock's ideas. In 1573 he had sent a copy of his memorial to the Queen and a year later another to the earl of Leicester; during the 1576 session, twelve 'counsellors of the law and other men of great credit' had received copies, and one of them, Thomas Digges, had tried to raise the matter in the Commons – gaining great credit and a promise that, since the 1576 session was nearly at an end, the issue should be properly investigated in the next session.[23] Digges did not forget this promise, and in order to help him Hitchcock got his pamphlet printed as soon as it was known that the Parliament would reassemble in January 1581.

The first days of that session (which began on the 23rd) were preoccupied with attempts by extremer men in the Commons to set up a public fast – a thing sufficiently displeasing to the Queen to hold up business.[24] Since the Wednesday fast, which she also disliked, stemmed from a navigation act, one might have supposed that Digges would take the opportunity to revive the discussion of fishery, and he did so on the 30th, with a speech which would appear to have rehearsed the arguments of Hitchcock's *Politic Plat.*[25] Having listened to an exhortation which promised a stronger navy, larger army, employment for the workless and general economic improvement for the realm, all by means of a great and purpose-built fishing fleet, the Commons next day appointed all the privy councillors in the House as a committee to consider the possibilities; all members 'acquainted with that matter of plot [plat] and advice' – that is, all who had read Hitchcock – were urged to attend on the committee and press their points. A fair start, one might think, for a determined pressure group, but in fact also the end of the line for the propagandists: there is nothing to show that the committee ever met, and it certainly never reported any outcome of possible deliberations. For while Digges and his few enthusiasts were trying to persuade the realm to arm and reedify itself by means of fishing around Newfoundland and Iceland, preaching national unity against interloping (and better equipped) foreigners, it soon became apparent that the reality of fishing involved violent clashes between different English interests, more particularly a dispute in which the fishermen of Norfolk (and other parts) confronted the importers of foreign-caught fish and especially the London Fishmongers' Company. A related complication arose from the quarrel between the latter and the London butchers, who were accused of supplying meat on days supposedly set aside for the eating of fish.

[23] Hitchcock speaks of Leonard Digges, who never sat in Parliament; Leonard's son Thomas, however, did – for Wallingford (Berks.), as a Leicester client. Clearly the agitation roped in more than burgesses for port towns.
[24] J. E. Neale, *Elizabeth I and her Parliaments 1559–1581* (London, 1953), pp. 378–82.
[25] *C.J.* I, 121. It is interesting to note that Thomas Cromwell's 'Diary' passes this over in silence; he was interested only in the bills read that day.

The several interests involved submitted their memorials to the Parliament, for it seems likely that an undated petition of the Fishmongers belongs to this agitation.[26] In it they complained that repeated proclamations against the eating of meat in Lent and encouraging the eating of fish as a way to maintain English shipping had quite failed to stop people from preferring meat – the butchers flourished and the fishmongers decayed. Their fish 'watered [washed] for the market rests upon our hands unsold'. Complaints to the lord mayor had elicited answers 'with so little hope of reformation that we are forced to make great complaint to this high court of Parliament'. They asked that the butchers licensed to sell meat to persons for health reasons exempt from the Lenten regulations should be stopped from public selling during that time; the names of those licensed were listed but the petitioners knew that at least a hundred more practised their unlicensed trade in the suburbs. What was needed was 'a most plain and very penal law'. Quite probably the Fishmongers had a good case: it does not look as though the standard annual proclamations against supplying meat in Lent had had much effect,[27] while as late as 1600 a proclamation tried to enforce the Wednesday fast of the 1563 act in terms which suggest comprehensive non-observance.[28]

The Fishmongers received very qualified support from the wardens and assistants of Trinity House, Deptford, who, in addition to certifying on the eve of the debate that navigation acts were successfully increasing England's fishing fleet,[29] also submitted a list of proposals for the intended act of Parliament.[30] They agreed that the fish-day clause of the 1563 act was not being properly observed (except, they said diplomatically, at the Queen's court and in her navy), and they asked for stiffer penalties; they approved of the clause in an act of 1566 (8 Eliz. I, c. 13) which empowered them to license seamen to work Thames wherries between voyages and asked (superfluously, since it was not time-limited) that it be continued; but they also attacked the practices of London's dealers in fish. Especially they complained of the merchants' willingness to buy up 'putrified' Scottish fish at Lynn and Harwich, selling it for Iceland cod after washing and drying it, as well as of the Fishmongers' restrictive practices which confined the trade in imported fish to selected members of their Company

---

[26] P.R.O., SP 12/77, fos. 173–4.
[27] Not all those annual proclamations survive but those that do show that from 1561 onwards their terms remained unchanged: they had become a formula (*T[udor] R[oyal] P[roclamations]*, ed. P. Hughes and J. F. Larkin (New Haven, 1969), II, nos. 477, 489, 592, 600, 604, 638 – down to 1581). From 1577 the Council regularly and in vain added detailed regulations of its own (F. A. Youngs, *The Proclamations of the Tudor Queens* (Cambridge, 1976), pp. 123–5).
[28] *T.R.P.*, no. 800.
[29] P.R.O., SP 12/147, fos. 55–6 (26 January 1581).   [30] *Ibid.*, fos. 190–4.

even when other fishmongers were willing to buy. However, the real opposition to the London interests came from 'the coastmen with the consents of the masters of her Majesty's navy' (a revival, it would seem, of the pressure group of 1576), in a petition 'for the increase of navigation'.[31] This paper revealed the violent resentment felt in the outports and among practising fishermen against the London merchants. The petitioners wanted free trade in fish for all Englishmen, with customs duties paid only by such foreigners as bought from them, and they wished a stop to be put to the practices of merchants and fishmongers who bought up catches in the Low Countries for import into England, in rivalry with what the native fishermen had to offer. In addition they asked that alien importers of salted herring and other fish should pay double customs and be compelled to land their cargo at one or two appointed places where it could be effectively inspected for 'goodness and sweetness' before being sold.

It seems likely that this last paper (the foundation of the act to be passed this session) was promoted by the leaders of the 'coastmen', the fishing interests of Yarmouth: its terms are plainly reflected in the bill which we know originated with that town. As its Assembly recorded later, the new statute of navigation 'hath been obtained by special and great costs of this town'.[32] Yarmouth, in fact, on the very day that the Parliament opened instructed two of its leading townsmen to ride to London in order to convey to the town's burgesses in the House the instructions previously agreed upon, 'concerning the causes and estate of this town, and whatsoever they shall do therein the house [i.e. the Assembly] shall allow'.[33] Whatever the men of Yarmouth may have felt or said at the dinner organized five years before by Robert Hitchcock, they now mobilized their influence for the promotion of a narrowly self-interested bill in Parliament and forgot about the prospects of a great navy to protect the expansion of English fishing all over the northern Atlantic. Most surprisingly, they made no attempt to capitalize on Digges' initiative in the Commons: instead of presenting their case to the committee of privy councillors, their representatives in Parliament saw to the introduction of a suitable measure in the House of Lords where that bill was read a first time on 16 February.[34]

The likely reason for this manoeuvre throws light on the realities of Elizabethan parliamentary life – so very different from the picture of an ascendant Commons presented by Neale and his school.[35] Although

---

[31] Ibid., fos. 188–9.
[32] N[orwich] R[ecord] O[ffice], Yarmouth Assembly Books, vol. 4, fo. 22v. I owe all references to this source to Mr David Dean to whom I am grateful for permission to cite it.   [33] Ibid., fo. 18v.   [34] L.J. II, 34.
[35] The following analysis rests on the facts collected in Hasler, The House of Commons 1559–1603, vol. I, pp. 211–12, and vol. II, p. 226; the interpretation is my own.

Yarmouth professed much civic pride and enjoyed oligarchic government by its own burgesses, it had usually been willing to allow its high steward to direct its choice of members for the Parliament. After the execution of the fourth duke of Norfolk in 1572, that office fell to the earl of Leicester, and in 1581 the two burgesses for Yarmouth were both his clients. One of them, Edward Bacon, a younger son of Lord Keeper Sir Nicholas Bacon, owed his choice at a bye-election in 1576 to the earl whose influence overcame the desire of a majority of the electors to elect a strictly local man. But Bacon, a notable absentee from the Commons, mattered little; it was his fellow member, William Grice, who really watched over the interests of the constituency. Grice, also a client of Leicester's, occupied an ideally suitable position: a member of the Yarmouth corporation, he could be called a local man, but in reality he practised as an attorney in London and in that capacity had all the right legal and parliamentary contacts. In particular he knew that influential parliament-man, Thomas Norton, the most active draftsman of bills in the 1581 session when, according to his own testimony, he worked mostly in cahoots with the Privy Council.[36] Both of them had been among the men who signed the memorial of 1576, and later in the year they cooperated on Yarmouth's behalf in the quarrel with Hull which sprang from the fisheries act of 1581;[37] both men also sat on the two Commons committees appointed during the passage of that act. Yet despite this influential contact in the House of Commons, Grice put his bill into the Upper House, nor – to judge from the enacting clause – had Norton or any other Council draftsman anything to do with its composition. Rather than commit his concerns to the overworked and inefficient Lower House, Grice apparently utilized his connection with Leicester – who, it will be remembered, had been solicited by Hitchcock years before and may well have had a more than casual concern for England's navigation. If in this way Grice hoped to secure a rapid passage for his bill he was reasonably successful, though a mysterious ten days' delay between the second reading on 22 February and a further second reading with an order to engross on 2 March suggests that the Lords found themselves lobbied by interests hostile to the coastmen-fishers and thus hesitated a while before proceeding with the bill. However, by 4 March they had passed it and sent it to the Commons.[38]

We do not know the terms of the bill as first read in the Lords; all that survives is the engrossed version passed by that House and amended in the Commons.[39] Its preamble denounces the 'merchants and fishmongers of

---

[36] Cf. M. A. R. Graves, 'Thomas Norton, the Parliament Man: An Elizabethan M.P., 1559–1581', *Historical Journal* 23 (1980), 17–35.

[37] N.R.O., Yarmouth Assembly Books, vol. IV, fo. 26v.

[38] *L.J.* II, 36, 40, 43.   [39] Original acts in House of Lords Record Office.

divers places of this realm' (read London) for their willingness to buy great quantities of fish caught by foreigners. Not only is the fish inferior to what Englishmen bring home from their Iceland voyages, but the practice moreover results in the export of much money and the impoverishment of the realm. In addition to these 'unnatural dealings', the eating of meat 'on the accustomed and usual fish days' has caused a crisis in English shipping; more than 200 vessels – 'good and serviceable ships' – have had to drop out of the Iceland fisheries, and a great many seamen fit for the defence of the realm in time of war have been lost. The preamble thus reflects both the grievances of the fishermen of England and the national concerns of the propagandists, but (as the body of the act showed) it was the former that mattered. The remedies proposed were embodied in three clauses and two provisos, and since the three clauses came straight from the memorial of the 'coastmen' it may be conjectured that they constituted the original bill, the provisos being added during the hold-up over the second reading as a result of further representations received in the House.

The main clauses prohibited, under penalties of forfeiture, all import of foreign fish by natives acting in person or through agents: such imports were reserved to aliens who in addition to the normal duties were to pay sums equal to any impositions levied on English ships in their own home ports. Provided that the foreigners importing their fish into England paid all the customs due, English shipowners were permitted to carry such cargoes. That is to say, the original bill simply aimed to stop the flooding of the home market with fish bought abroad, in part by barring Englishmen from trading in it at all and in part by rendering such fish much more expensive than English catches, but it allowed English vessels a share in the carrying trade so long as the higher costs fell on the foreigner. The two provisos did not touch this core of the measure. The first gave the act some very necessary teeth by providing penalties for attempts at deceitful evasions, that is to say, those standard practices of bogus manifests and pretended ownership which so regularly defeated all efforts to protect English trade against foreign competition: natives stood to incur fines of £200 for every breach of the law, while aliens committing frauds would forfeit their ships as well as their cargoes if these on inspection were declared unfit for sale. Since nobody would wish to be saddled with forfeited loads of rotten fish, this last provision must be read as an ominous opening for chicanery: it must have been dangerously easy to acquire good fish for free after a word with the inspector. The other proviso, however, broke ranks and conceded a point to the London Fishmongers: it totally prohibited the sale of meat in Lent by any butcher, poulterer or victualler. It seems likely that the acceptance of this additional clause (also, we conjecture, added during the passage of the bill) caused the reference to meat-eating on fish-days to be inserted in the preamble. In a manner quite familiar from the histories of bills in Elizabethan Parliaments, a straightforward measure promoted by one identifiable interest was amalgamated with a different though cognate issue raised by quite another.

In this form the bill reached the Commons, on 1 March;[40] it was read a first time that afternoon, for in expectation of an early prorogation or dissolution the House at that time also sat after dinner in order to get as many bills through as possible.[41] Even so, the bill did not turn up again until the 15th, but in view of the pressure of unfinished bills it would be rash to assume that this delay reflected organized opposition to it. In any case, the interval was not entirely wasted. When the bill came up for second reading it was accompanied by three provisos presented to the House which were read twice on the same day and thus incorporated in the bill. Quite evidently, these provisos dealt with various doubts or reservations felt after the first reading and thus made passage easier.

One exempted all fish imported from Iceland, Scotland and Newfoundland, with their adjoining seas, as well as fish taken and salted anywhere by the Queen's natural subjects. On the face of it this might be thought a wrecking clause; that it proved acceptable to the promoters confirms that all along the real purpose of the bill lay in the protection of the one fishery not included in the exception. Thanks to this proviso the act in effect safeguarded the North Sea herring grounds and banned only supplies obtained in the Low Countries. The second proviso weakened the act further by permitting everybody (including presumably Dutchmen and London Fishmongers) at present engaged in the import of staple fish and ling 'for the better furnishing of this realm withal' to continue to operate for three years after the end of the session. Though time-limited, this marked a notable concession to precisely the people whom the bill had meant to bar altogether from the trade; and it also recognized some virtue in the merchants' standard argument that English fishermen could not supply all the fish the country needed.[42] From these facts it may be inferred that the proviso originated with the London interests; it too may well have proved acceptable to Yarmouth because it remained silent on the topic of herrings, the trade in which continued to be ruled by the main clauses of the act. (Herrings were not 'staple fish'.) The last proviso, on the other hand, constituted a frontal assault on the London Fishmongers (though

---

[40] The diary entry (*Proceedings*, p. 542) defines the contents of the bill at first reading in the Commons as 'restraining the buying of any salt fish or salt herring from beyond the sea, and buying it of any strangers, and against the killing of any flesh between Shrovetide and the Tuesday before Easter, and against the selling of flesh to any not having licence to eat'.

[41] *C.J.* I, 131.   [42] See below p. 18.

it took care to speak also of other like bodies, none being involved) by declaring void any ordinance that had made or would hereafter make to inhibit trade in fish within the realm; for every breach of the statute, offenders were to be fined the prohibitive sum of £100. Thus when the bill was committed after second reading it had been quite noticeably narrowed in its effect but also explicitly turned against the London Company which would lose control not only over outsiders but even over its own members.

The timely production of these provisos left the committee with little to do, and most of its amendments concerned minor drafting points.[43] But the committee did one drastic thing: it deleted the clause against the killing and selling of meat in Lent. Thus the proviso added in the Lords in response to the Fishmongers' memorial went out again, leaving the bill with no joy at all for this much disliked privileged body. When, however, the bill was reported on the 17th and read a third time, further problems arose and it was recommitted; we do not know what held it up or was done to it now (nothing significant, to judge by the Original Act), but on the following day it finally passed the Lower House.[44] The Lords accepted all the changes made and read the amended bill three times on the 18th, the last day of the session;[45] at the assent, the Speaker especially singled it out with two other bills as worthy achievements of the session, which at least demonstrates that its hesitant and disputed passage had not gone unnoticed.[46] However worthy, it really had caused quite considerable difficulties especially in the Commons, a fact which indicates that Grice had been wise to start it in the Lords, though even there there had been hesitations. In the end, Yarmouth got the essence of what it wanted, at the cost of relinquishing any larger purpose or national interest in the act. Its grandiloquent title – 'For the increase of mariners and for the maintenance of navigation' – better described the ambitions set out in the preamble than the import of the much amended enactment. A more accurate title would have been 'For the protection of the east coast fisheries and against the Fishmongers' Company of London'.

A little more may be learned from a look at the two committees that reviewed the bill. The ordinary bill committee appointed on second reading consisted of fifteen members, and it says something about the bill that not one of them was a privy councillor. The most likely explanation is that the government wanted to keep clear of the conflict of interests involved in the measure. Instead, the chair was taken by Owen Hopton, lieutenant of the Tower and knight of the shire for Middlesex, and it may not be without

[43] A paper schedule of amendments made in committee is attached to the Original Act.
[44] C.J. I, 134, 136.
[45] L.J. II, 53.   [46] Proceedings, p. 546.

significance that round about this time he was involved in a rather prolonged dispute with the city of London.[47] Grice and Bacon, burgesses for Yarmouth, naturally sat on the committee, as did other representatives of port towns: Edward Lewknor (New Shoreham, Sussex), John Cowper (Steyning, Sussex), Edward Grimston (Ipswich, Suffolk), Charles Calthorpe (Eye, Suffolk), John Shirley (Lewes, Sussex). Two Londoners were included but cannot be regarded as intended balances in the interest of the merchants: both Thomas Aldersey and Thomas Norton were regular and active committee-men in all the Parliaments they sat in, as were two otherwise rather surprising members – Sir Thomas Sempole (Lincs.) and Robert Newdigate (Berwick). Sir Thomas Scott (Kent) may be thought to have had an interest, but Thomas Onley (Brackley, Northants.) and Giles Estcourte (Salisbury, Wilts.) must be regarded as makeweights. The two Suffolk men well balanced the self-interest of Yarmouth, and the presence of three men from Sussex reminds one of the deep involvement which that shire had with the cod fisheries at Scarborough and the herring fishery at Yarmouth.[48] The committee thus presented quite a typical mixture of members of the Commons directly interested in the bill, active men of business experienced in committee work and usually employed during a session in supervising the efficient management of bills, and a handful of extras who were there to make up numbers and gain experience. An office-holder of modest distinction made a reasonable figurehead.

However, it is notorious that members appointed to committees did not by any means attend with assiduity – the chief reason for the constant increase in the size of committees. Here the second body becomes of interest. Appointed only two days after the first, it contained only four of the fifteen members of its predecessor – Sempole, Aldersey, Grice and Norton: three men of business and one interested party. It is a reasonable guess that they were the committee members who actually attended on the 15th, or at any rate had on that occasion done the real work. To them were added five new men: Sir Walter Mildmay, chancellor of the Exchequer and privy councillor; Sir Henry Radcliffe, who sat for Portsmouth, a town concerned with navigation; and three more of the experienced men of business – Francis Alford (Reading, Berks.), Robert Wroth (Middlesex), and Thomas Cromwell, the diarist, a resident of King's Lynn though he sat for Bodmin in Cornwall. The accident that the bill necessitated the appointment of two committees within three days thus enables us to see something of the manner in which such bodies were selected and went about their work. Since Hopton's committee had (apparently) left raw edges in its drafting,

[47] *Calendar of State Papers Domestic, 1581–90* (1865), p. 83.
[48] C. E. Brent, 'Urban Employment and Population in Sussex between 1550 and 1660', *Sussex Archaeological Collections* 113 (1975), 35–50.

it seems to have been thought wiser to get that influential man, Mildmay, to preside on the second occasion; but the work would really seem to have been done by Grice, burgess for the promoters, and his friend Norton, with the assistance of other 'men of business'. Aldersey belonged to the Haberdashers' Company and Norton to the Grocers', so that the Fishmongers had no representative and apparently no friend on either committee. It is no wonder that Yarmouth got what it wanted, despite the clear signs that opposition to its plans existed in both Houses.

The act thus unquestionably favoured the interests of those engaged in sea fishing and went counter to those of men engaged in the buying and selling of foreign fish. Despite its origin in the Lords, it owed absolutely nothing to any initiative from the government who did not even bother to put a privy councillor on the bill committee, and it did nothing for larger policy or the active promotion of English industry and trade. Its most surprising feature remains to be mentioned: it carried no limitation in time. As we have seen, earlier navigation acts all included clauses designed to bring them up for reconsideration at some fixed point in the future, and this was particularly the case with the much more important statute of 1563. Great Yarmouth, on the other hand, meant to hide behind a permanent act, so that any persons attacked or affected by it would have to promote a full-scale repeal it they were to recover the ground lost. An attempt had, in fact, been made in the Lords to prevent so total a victory for one side. Among Burghley's papers there survives a draft proviso which, arguing that the act might not turn out so useful to the common weal as its promoters claimed, meant to appoint a committee on whose advice the Queen could by proclamation suspend it.[49] The projected committee can only be called crazy: six spiritual and six temporal peers, one knight for every shire, and one citizen or burgess for any one constituency in every shire. Such a body could never have been assembled, and it is no wonder that the idea got no further than Burghley's files, but its existence demonstrates that someone felt apprehensive about the effect of the act. Why no one saw to the addition of that familiar device, a time-limitation clause, must remain a puzzle; by putting the issue before the whole of a future Parliament, it would have achieved much more readily what, it seems, this select body of parliamentarians was intended to do.

Was the act successful? To judge from the fortunes of the Yarmouth herring industry in the fifty years after 1581, legislation proved as helpless as in such matters of commerce and industry it usually was.[50] Perhaps this

[49] P.R.O., SP 12/147, fo. 197.
[50] Tittler ('English Fishing Industry'. 52) speaks of stagnation or decline, Michell ('Port and Town of Great Yarmouth', pp. 27, 37–8) more convincingly argues that Yarmouth was prosperous in the reign of Elizabeth, with a flourishing fishing industry backing up notable developments in maritime trade. Either way, the statute made little or no difference.

disappointing result sprang from inadequate enforcement, and someone might look into the history of the various conflicting interests as well as at the king's remembrancer's memoranda rolls in the Exchequer after 1581, for that is where any action brought under the penal clauses of the act would have had to be initiated. The results are not likely to be impressive: esoteric penal legislation in economic matters tended in this period to sit silent upon the statute book. What is certain is that Yarmouth's parliamentary triumph did not silence its adversaries for long. Immediately after the session, the town decided to recoup some of the costs incurred over the bill: 'for that the same is to the benefit of the whole coast', it was resolved to send an emissary up and down the shores of Norfolk and Suffolk to acquaint neighbours with this splendid act and 'see if they will extend any benevolence towards the charges aforesaid'.[51] So far as the evidence goes, Yarmouth merely learned the advantages of getting your money in advance. At least two rival ports started suits to limit the benefits obtained by Yarmouth. With Hull, it would appear, the town came to some sort of terms quite quickly;[52] the dispute with Lowestoft dragged on.[53]

The interest most affected did not allow the grass (or seaweed) to grow long under its feet. By early October 1581, Yarmouth had to take steps to resist the counter-agitation of the Fishmongers' Company. A member of the town oligarchy was despatched to London to agree action with Norton and Grice, still looking after Yarmouth's interests, after coordinating things with the London agent for the smaller ports of Norfolk (Blakeney and Wells).[54] They had reason to act, for the Fishmongers had put forward a memorial to the Council which constituted a comprehensive denunciation of the act and a demand for its rescission.[55] It therefore looks as though the Company may have been caught by surprise in the 1581 session, and it is not beyond the parliamentary possibilities that such surprise could be engineered more readily by introducing a bill into the Lords rather than the Commons. At any rate, the Fishmongers now turned up, after the event, with the kind of powerful arguments that would surely have influenced opinion decisively in one House or the other.

As they saw it, Parliament had been persuaded to pass the act by statements which looked plausible enough so long as they were not questioned. (A familiar line to take: but why then had they not been questioned in Parliament?) It was alleged that English fishmongers, for private gain, brought in inferior foreign fish. But (the inferior apart) this was a longstanding practice, at its height when the English Iceland voyages were still going strong; without it, fish supplies would prove insufficient

[51] N.R.O., Yarmouth Assembly Books, vol. IV, fo. 22v.
[52] *Ibid.*, fos. 26v, 27v, 34v.   [53] This is being investigated by Mr Dean.
[54] N.R.O., Yarmouth Assembly Books, vol. IV, fo. 32v.
[55] P.R.O., SP 12/148, fos. 127–33.

and prices be driven up. Indeed, that was exactly what had happened since the passing of the act, thus fulfilling the real ambitions of 'the coastmen, the solicitors and procurers of this law...for their own private lucre and gain'. People now ate meat on fish-days because it was cheaper; and Flemish fish could cure this, being as good as but much cheaper than what could be got from Iceland. That English merchants buying foreign fish had to export money for this purpose was simply untrue: it was well known that they either exported trade goods or used the exchange. (Accusing an adversary of denuding the realm of specie in return for unwanted imports had been a standard tactic for a century or more.) Nor was it the case that these foreign imports were driving out native supplies caught by native labour: English fishermen had never been able to satisfy the needs of the realm, whereas now (thanks, one presumes, to section 1 of the act) they were in fact selling a lot of their catch especially of Yarmouth herring to customers abroad – engaging in a trade profitable to themselves and leaving England short of fish. The Fishmongers forcefully questioned the assertion that 'unnatural dealings' and failure to observe fish-days had cut the Iceland fleet by 200 ships; they doubted whether there had ever been as many as that engaged in the trade, but if there existed as many as that or more they would easily sell all they caught. In their view the decline of the Iceland fishery arose from quite other causes: to judge from the fact that ships regularly returned from there with small catches and much of their salt unused, the grounds were being fished out, and in any case English fishermen had decided that inshore fishing with small boats was both safer and more profitable. There was also the fact that general trading into various countries had so much grown in recent times that shipowners preferred to use their vessels 'to traffic from place to place for a good hire and freight, which is certain unto them, than to venture upon these casual Iceland voyages, not knowing whether they shall lose or win thereby'.

The document contains less self-contradiction than such papers usually do, and its major points sound convincing enough. English trade had expanded without shipbuilding keeping pace, so that there were fewer seagoing fishing vessels available. Even supposing, however, that the reasons advanced by the coastmen had more substance, the Fishmongers argued that the statute passed could not be expected to mend matters. English merchants who had employed English ships to export English manufactures and had used fish as a return cargo were now forbidden this sensible practice (did foreigners really like fish-scented English cloth?). Alien merchants had jumped at the chance of taking over. 'It hath never before been seen...in any common weal that any subject hath been forbidden to bring in any victual, and strangers permitted': a good point.

However, while the Fishmongers could legitimately and successfully controvert the economic arguments of their adversaries, they had to resort to more highflown and woolly assertions when they turned to the true nub of their grievance. That cursed act had declared their Company's ordinances void – as we have seen, in a proviso added by the Commons. Perhaps the Fishmongers had at first been willing to let the act pass without any very energetic protest, believing it to be of little import or effect; and this thrust to the heart came too late for them to mount a campaign in the Parliament. In their view, the clause had had disastrous consequences. 'It is well known that a multitude living without government grow to disorder and abuse,' they said; and since the act the common weal had promptly suffered from ill-ordered persons' dealings whose chief effect had been to push up the price of all fish. 'Wherefore we pray...that we may have liberty to put in execution only amongst ourselves such ancient orders as have been confirmed unto us according to the law and long time used, liked and allowed of to be good and wholesome for the common weal.' Let all members of the good Company 'brought and trained up in the buying and bringing in of fish' once more import the necessary victual from anywhere, provided 'it be in English bottoms', paying the old duties and customs to her Majesty, 'the statute aforesaid notwithstanding'.

The argument that freeing the trade from restrictions had increased prices supposes the existence of large numbers of Englishmen from outside London competing for the available stocks or unusual self-restraint by the Londoners in the days of their monopoly. Neither point seems very probable at first sight. Nevertheless, the Fishmongers' general case had real merit; as we have seen, not everybody believed that Yarmouth herring merited advantages which hindered much fishing and the trade in fish elsewhere. However, the offending act stood unlimited in time and more was therefore needed to overthrow it than would have been required if it had had to come up for renewal at some fixed point in the future. This memorial, in fact, was the opening shot in a long campaign of agitation, with bills in Parliament and such like, which cannot here be pursued. It was only in the Parliament of 1597 that Yarmouth's victory of 1581 was apparently reversed, and even then most of that victory survived. The act of 39 Eliz. I, c. 10, repealed the earlier statute as ineffective: English suppliers had not been able to satisfy England's need for fish and only foreigners had benefited. So the Fishmongers had said from the first, and it is probable that they were right. However, the repealing act went on to re-enact the bulk of what it had just wiped off the book. The only part of the 1581 act to disappear was its first clause which permitted free trade in fish by all Englishmen but prohibited the import of foreign fish by English merchants. All the rest, including the voiding of the Company's ordinances, came back by the other door. It was only when this act, now time-limited, was considered for the expiring laws continuance act of the next Parliament (43 Eliz. I, c. 9) that the Fishmongers secured the removal of that offensive provision – incidentally proving how much easier it was to amend an act needing renewal than to repeal a permanent act in all the details objected to. What was left of the Yarmouth fisheries act of 1581 after the session of 1601 was, thus, a law which generally penalized aliens engaged in the fish trade with England but kept the trade open provided English vessels were used – a true navigation act of the kind to which that title is commonly given.

The efforts of Yarmouth and its associated coastal ports around the shores of England to exploit fish and fish-days for their sectional interests thus in effect foundered, but they did so less on the superior strength of their opponents, the London merchants, than on their inability to serve the needs of the realm. Meanwhile, the Dutch took the herring in English waters and sold it back to the English.

2

~~~~~~

Marriage as business: opinions on the rise in aristocratic bridal portions in early modern England*

R. B. OUTHWAITE

In case it should be thought that an essay on marriage is an anomaly in a volume of studies devoted largely to the worlds of economic policy and business, let us begin with a remark on courtship in general made by the eminent American sociologist, W. J. Goode:

> All courtship systems are market or exchange systems. They differ from one another with respect to who does the buying and selling, which characteristics are more or less valuable in that market, and how open or explicit the bargaining is.[1]

Few would deny that market systems come squarely within the province of the economic historian and there can be little doubt also that amongst the upper classes in sixteenth- and seventeenth-century England the bargaining was extremely open and explicit. Irrespective of the role of romance in either initiating or concluding courtship, marriage negotiations at this social level almost invariably took on eventually the appearance of business transactions. Negotiators corresponded on behalf of their courting clients like solemn commercial diplomats, agreements were eventually formalized in private treaties – the marriage contract – and financial considerations seem frequently to override sentiment. Pecuniary obsessions sometimes spilled over into the marriage itself. Nowhere is this better illustrated than in the letter which Eliza Spencer wrote in 1610 to her husband of perhaps ten years' standing, William Lord Compton, who had just got his hands on the fortune of Eliza's father, city magnate Sir John Spencer, reputedly the richest commoner in England.

My sweet life,
    Now I have declared to you my mind for the settling of your state, I supposed that that were best for me to bethink or consider with myself what allowance were meetest for me. For considering what care I ever had of your estate, and how respectfully I dealt with those, which both by the laws of God, of nature, and civil polity, wit, religion, government, and honesty, you, my dear are bound to, I pray

* I am grateful for the comments and criticism offered by my co-editor Neil McKendrick, Julius Kirshner and Charles Wilson, and by Lloyd Bonfield, whose expertise in this area is such that he ought really to have written this chapter. The deficiencies are my responsibility.
[1] W. J. Goode, *World Revolution and Family Patterns* (New York, 1963), p. 8.

and beseech you to grant to me, your most kind and loving wife, the sum of £1600 per ann. quarterly to be paid.

Also I would, beside that allowance for my apparel, have £600, added yearly (quarterly to be paid) for the performance of charitable works, and these things I would not, neither will be accountable for.

Also I will have three horses for my own saddle....

Also I would have two gentlewomen, lest one should be sick or have some other lett....

Also I will have six or eight gentlemen; and I will have my two coaches, one lined with velvet, to myself, with four very fair horses; and a coach for my women, lined with sweet cloth, one laced with gold, the other with scarlet, and lined with watched lace and silver, with four good horses.

Also I will have two coachmen, one for my own coach, the other for my women.

Other demands, all prefaced by 'also', went on to include spare horses and coaches, a horse for her gentleman usher, the provision of two footmen, twenty gowns of apparel, £2200 in pin-money, £6000 to buy jewels, £4000 to buy a pearl chain, and all this 'besides my yearly allowance'.

Now seeing I have been and am so reasonable unto you, I pray you to find my children apparel and their schooling, and all my servants, men and women, their wages.

Also I will have all my houses furnished, and all my lodging chambers to be suited with all such furniture as is fit....

And, this 'loving wife' finally added, 'I pray, when you be an earl, to allow me £1000 more than now desired, and double attendance.'[2]

Financial considerations intruded because marriage amongst the upper classes involved more than the union of two freely consenting marriageable parties; it also involved a complex and sizeable interchange of income and property between the families of these parties. Marital eligibility was thus well tempered with economic and social considerations. The bride's father supplied her with a dowry, her 'portion', usually a cash sum, which on the occasion of her marriage went to the groom's family; initially it went to the groom's father but increasingly as the seventeenth century progressed it went to the groom himself. In return for this portion, the groom or his family allotted the bride a 'jointure', land or an annuity from land which was to be possessed by the bride during, but only during, her widowhood.[3] For parents this transaction was perhaps always unequally weighted, in favour of sons and against daughters, for the portion represented a permanent loss of income for the bride's erstwhile family whilst the jointure, even if widowhood occurred, represented only a temporary loss

---

[2] The letter is printed in *The Court of King James the First; by Dr Godfrey Goodman*, ed. J. S. Brewer, 2 vols. (London, 1839), vol. II, pp. 127–32. For some of the background to it, see L. Stone, 'The Peer and the Alderman's Daughter', *History Today* (Jan. 1961), 48–55.

[3] L. Stone, *The Crisis of the Aristocracy 1558–1641* (Oxford, 1965), pp. 176–8, 632–49.

to the groom's family. Jointured property usually returned to the groom's family or heirs at the death of the widow or, as was sometimes specified, on the occasion of her remarriage. This complex interchange became, indeed, more unequally weighted as the period progressed.

It was H. J. Habakkuk who in 1949 first drew attention to the changing relationship between the size of the portion and that of the jointure between the sixteenth and eighteenth centuries.[4] The ratio moved, he argued, from about five to one in the earlier period to ten to one by the late seventeenth century. It was Lawrence Stone, however, who in the 1960s provided the first statistical series illustrating what was happening to the level of aristocratic bridal portions.[5] He showed how portions provided by English peers moved from an average of around £500 per daughter married in the early sixteenth century, to a figure of £2000 in the last quarter of that century, and to a staggering £9700 in the fifty-five years after 1675. Professor Stone does have his critics and many of them tend to fasten obsessively on the fallibility of his statistics. There was some carping about these figures in the anonymous review of *The Crisis of the Aristocracy* which appeared in the *Times Literary Supplement* of 7 April 1966, but its author, J. P. Cooper, reserved most of his complaints until the mid-1970s when his long essay 'Patterns of Inheritance and Settlement by Great Landowners from the Fifteenth to the Eighteenth Centuries' first appeared in print.[6] One grouse was that Stone had underestimated the size of portions in and before the early sixteenth century and had therefore overestimated the rate of increase in the sixteenth century as a whole. Cooper provided moreover an alternative set of figures of portions contributed by peers.[7] Table 2.1 reproduces these two series and indexes them, making the base years the period 1525–49 when both Stone and Cooper more or less agree on the average size of the portions mentioned in wills, family settlements and marriage contracts. From that period onwards there is little major disagreement between the two sets of figures. The Cooper series does suggest a slower mid-sixteenth-century rise and a faster late-sixteenth one, but both agree that by the last quarter of that century portions had roughly tripled, and, more interestingly, that they then rose fourfold in the following hundred years. By 1675–1729 both scholars believe that portions were some twelve or thirteen times the level they had been in the base period 1525–49. It is hard to believe that this marked rise in bridal portions was simply the product of increasing aristocratic

[4] H. J. Habakkuk, 'Marriage Settlements in the Eighteenth Century', *Transactions of the Royal Historical Society* (1950), 15–30.
[5] Stone, *Crisis*, pp. 644–5, 790–1.
[6] In J. Goody, J. Thirsk and E. P. Thompson (eds.), *Family and Inheritance: Rural Society in Western Europe 1200–1800* (Cambridge, 1976), pp. 192–327.   [7] *Ibid.*, p. 307.

Table 2.1. *Marriage portions offered by peers*

Date	Stone			Cooper		
	Average £	Number	Index: 1525–49 = 100	Average £	Number	Index: 1525–49 = 100
1300–50				1200	11	160
1351–1400				950	15	127
1401–50				1100	16	147
1451–1500				700	28	93
1475–1524	500	10	71	750	34	100
1525–49	700	28	100	750	51	100
1550–74	1300	21	186	850	32	113
1575–99	2000	20	286	2250	23	300
1600–24	3800	45	543	3550	34	473
1625–49	5400	85	771	5050	73	673
1650–74	7800	22	1114	6250	38	833
1675–1729	9700	23	1386	9350	51	1247

prosperity, the first explanation that comes to mind. Without entering into debate about the ebb and flow of the fortunes of the aristocracy, let it be said that there is general agreement amongst scholars of this subject that bridal portions generally ran ahead of aristocratic incomes and that they became particularly burdensome to estates in the later seventeenth century, when the peerage comprised about 160 titled families compared with the 54–55 families of the sixteenth century.

How does one explain this increase in dowries? Explaining variations about the trend is somewhat easier than explaining the trend itself. Some girls always enjoyed bigger portions than others. Generally speaking the larger the family, and especially the larger the number of daughters, the smaller the portions they received. Cases exist also where fondness for a particular daughter is revealed in a larger than average dowry. Stone suggests, moreover, that the 'physical and mental defects of a girl had to be compensated for if she was to be married off', a remark he supports with Sir John Oglander's couplet on Elizabeth Hobart:

> Neither well proportioned, fair, nor wise,
> All these defects four thousand pounds supplies[8]

– a remark which, if nothing else, proves that Oglander was almost as desperate a rhymster as he was supposedly a declining gentleman.

What we cannot do, however, is to extrapolate from the particular to the general. No one has yet explained the continuous sixteenth- and seventeenth-century rise in dowries in terms of decreasing family size,[9] or increasingly doting fathers, or a general rise in mental and physical defects amongst upper-class Englishwomen. Clearly there are other factors explaining the trend, whilst particular circumstances and qualities explain variations about the trend and, incidentally, variations in the portion-to-jointure ratio.[10]

Amongst those attempts to explain the trend, two are outstanding, those

[8] Stone, *Crisis*, pp. 640–1.
[9] Indeed Stone at one point argues the reverse (*ibid.*, p. 647): 'Under conditions of universal marriage for girls, an important factor in upsetting the balance may have been an increased number of children born per marriage, or an increased proportion who survived to a marriageable age, or both. There was certainly a steady increase in population in the late sixteenth and very early seventeenth centuries, which may have been caused by one or other of these factors. Either would produce a larger number of daughters to be married off and a larger number of younger sons, but only a very small increase in the number of heirs male with whom the daughters could be mated. If this in fact occurred it would in itself go far to explain the increase in the size of portions.'
[10] Habakkuk, 'Marriage Settlements', p. 26: 'If the bride was young and beautiful, if her husband was much in love with her, if there was a prospect of her becoming an heiress, if she was of a social status superior to his, the husband might accept a portion which, in relation to the jointure he settled on her, was below the standard ratio. In the reverse of any or all of these conditions he might be able to demand an abnormally large portion. But the standard ratio was clearly recognized as the basis for the bargaining.'

of Habakkuk and Stone, and indeed all historians of this subject remain deeply indebted to them. Habakkuk's 1950 essay on 'Marriage Settlements' was the earliest attempt at a general explanation, and this, his first major sortie into the field, was both characteristic and uncharacteristic of him. It was perhaps characteristic that in attempting to find an answer his mind should turn first of all to the rate of interest, and uncharacteristic in that he discussed a severely limited range of causal influences. The answer, he thought, lay in the operation of two forces. One was 'a relative fall in the number of eligible potential husbands' (to which we will return); the other, less plausibly presented, was a more calculatingly avaricious attitude towards marriage within the landed classes. 'The greater the importance attached to wealth as an object of marriage', he wrote, 'the more necessary it would be for a landowner who wished to secure for his daughters good marriages to the eldest sons of landowning families to provide them with large portions.' The argument embraced also the importance of 'friendship' and political connection.[11] Attachment to wealth, however, is not necessarily an argument for endowing daughters generously, and whilst the kin network would be widened via a daughter's marriage, a landowner's personal influence was not necessarily likely to be greater with his son-in-law than with his sons. Cooper, indeed, made the point that 'whenever circumstances permitted, fathers were liable to be more generous to their sons than their daughters', a remark clearly at odds with Habakkuk's views.[12]

Stone's explanation is far from limited, embracing as it does the operation of perhaps a dozen or so causal influences.[13] Stone picking is called for to sort out the more plausible from the less plausible influences supplied by this generously prolific mind. Several examples of the less plausible make an appearance. His argument, most insistently pressed in The Family, Sex and Marriage, that the Reformation upset the marriage market is one: 'The marriage market was flooded with girls who had hitherto been consigned to nunneries', he writes, 'but who now had to be married off at considerable cost, to their social equals.'[14] Apart from the fact that the total population of female inmates was only about 1800,

---

[11] Ibid., pp. 24–5. Habakkuk returned to this subject briefly in his 'Preface' to M. E. Finch, The Wealth of Five Northamptonshire Families, 1540–1640 (Northamptonshire Record Society, 1956), pp. xi–xix, where he widened the range of causal influences to include the 'competition of heavily endowed mercantile brides' and the 'growth of the long-term mortgage'.

[12] Cooper, 'Patterns', p. 215. Habakkuk himself acknowledged that landowners with large numbers of daughters to provide for were likely to suffer ('Marriage Settlements', pp. 28–9).

[13] Offered first of all in Crisis (1965) and, more recently, in The Family, Sex and Marriage in England 1500–1800 (London, 1977).

[14] Stone, Family, p. 43; Crisis, p. 646.

many of them presumably very elderly and not a few, one suspects, otherwise undesirable, the effect would principally be a once-and-for-all effect. The Cooper index raises doubts that there was much dowry inflation in the period of the dissolution of the religious houses and the trickle of aristocratic daughters who might after 1540 have been so consigned can hardly explain the later substantial rises in portions.[15] Another example can be found in his observation that 'a change in the conventional estimate of life expectancy' may have had an effect in the latter half of the seventeenth century. But, as Stone himself acknowledges, 'We do not know how far these theoretical arguments, which anyway appear very late in the century, seriously affected the thinking of practical men.'[16] It is thus an argument which hardly has the ring of conviction about it.

Other historians have nibbled at the subject. Roger Thompson offered the ingenious suggestion that the migration of large numbers of males from England to America and elsewhere lay perhaps at the root of the problem.[17] It raises, of course, a number of difficulties: the rise in portions began well before emigration got seriously underway in the 1620s; the stream of emigrants cannot, even in the seventeenth century, be correlated with the rise in portions; also the majority of migrants would be well below the elite group examined here, and even if there were substantial numbers of gentlemen amongst them, they were most likely to be impoverished younger sons, too poor to marry anyway. Any contribution made by migration was likely to be a post-1620 phenomenon and marginal, rather than a long-lasting and central one.

J. P. Cooper's contribution to the debate was that of the intellectual Luddite: a determined historical model-wrecker. It was, I think, M. M. Postan who divided historians into two camps: those who approach facts determined to find patterns within them, and those who approach the facts equally determined not to do so. Cooper was firmly in the second camp. One of his conclusions, buried in a wholly characteristic mire of obfuscation,[18] has a certain negative value for us. He thought it unlikely that amongst the great landowners rising portions for daughters came at the expense of decreasing provision for younger sons. Great landowners, he suggested, were equally generous to all their younger children, irrespective of sex. Thomas Wilson's complaint that younger sons got what the cat left on the malt heap was truer of provision amongst the less than

---

[15] The Cooper series in Table 2.1 suggests that there was comparatively little rise before the late sixteenth century (1575–99), too late for the dissolution to have been an immediate cause.

[16] *Crisis*, p. 649.

[17] R. Thompson, *Women in Stuart England and America* (London, 1974), pp. 21–52.

[18] So much so that one is almost tempted to say that there is no such thing as a J. P. Cooper 'conclusion'.

great landowners. Although the social cut-off point remains somewhat obscure, this finding naturally qualifies another possible explanation.[19]

Clearly historians are not in agreement on many aspects. Habakkuk, for example, firmly ruled out the decline in the rate of interest as an important causal factor, whilst both Stone and Cooper allowed it to play a part.[20] Rising portions could conceivably be linked with declining interest rates if dowries were viewed as capital sums which could be traded for life annuities (so that a larger capital sum was necessary to produce a given income), or if portions were raised by borrowing. Apart from the objection that the rise in portions clearly long antedated the first reduction in the statutory maximum rate of interest in 1625, Habakkuk argued that portions were not spent on life annuities but on land and that the nominal rate of return on the purchase of land remained fixed at 5 per cent throughout the period. Others have quibbled with these judgments. Christopher Clay has argued that the nominal rate of return on land purchase was much more variable than Habakkuk supposed: that whilst it may have risen from the first to the second half of the seventeenth century, when it lay generally just above 5 per cent, the nominal rate fell generally from the 1690s to levels of less than 4 per cent by the mid-eighteenth century.[21] Peter Roebuck, admittedly examining a slightly lower-placed social group than the titular peerage, has recently argued that 'there were no strong conventions regarding the utilization of portions, which met a variety of needs according to the circumstances of those who received them'.[22] Habakkuk was inclined later, as a result of Mary Finch's convincing arguments, to suggest that much more important than the rate of interest was the increasing ease of borrowing on mortgage. Before the Court of Chancery developed a general equity of redemption for mortgagors between 1615 and 1630, landowners were fearful of raising loans in this manner; thereafter they gradually lost some of these fears.[23] Clearly the difficulties of borrowing could have suppressed the size of portions before the early seventeenth century, and the growing ease of doing so, coupled with declining interest rates, may thereafter have exercised some influence. The cost of borrowing generally fell; portions spent either on land or

[19] Cooper, 'Patterns', pp. 212–21. Cf. Habakkuk's 'Preface' to Finch, *Five Northamptonshire Families*, p. xviii: 'There is no evidence in these studies of any trend in the provision for younger sons analogous to the increase in daughters' portions.'

[20] Habakkuk, 'Marriage Settlements', pp. 22–3; Stone, *Crisis*, p. 648; Cooper, 'Patterns', p. 222.

[21] C. Clay, 'The Price of Freehold Land in the Later Seventeenth and Eighteenth Centuries', *Economic History Review*, 2nd Series 27 (1974), 173–89. This follows from his findings that the number of years' purchase was generally around eighteen from 1650–90 and that it rose thereafter, though in fluctuating fashion, to twenty-seven in the 1750s.

[22] P. Roebuck, *Yorkshire Baronets 1640–1760* (Oxford, 1980), p. 328.

[23] Finch, *Five Northamptonshire Families*, pp. 32–3, 168–9 (and 'Preface', pp. xvii–xviii).

annuities would need to rise to maintain a given income; and larger debts could be carried in comparative safety. Nevertheless in this complex area doubts remain, and the rise in dowries before the early seventeenth century remains largely unexplained.

These varying monetary arrangements obviously do not exhaust the list of likely economic causes. It is possible, for example, to view the portion as a sort of capitalized life annuity, the price a father paid to persuade some other male to relieve him of the obligation to support his daughter for the remaining term of her natural life. Whether or not it was sensitive to varying rates of interest, or to prevailing views about life expectancy, remains uncertain. What is more likely is that the portion reflected the costs of filial subsistence, and perhaps current rather than past or future costs. We lack however a suitable price index to measure such costs. Attempts to trace movements in 'real portions' by comparing them, as Stone does, with movements in the Phelps Brown price index are obviously unsatisfactory since one thing we can be sure of is that peers' daughters did not partake of the same 'basket of consumables' as Oxford building workers, overweighted as that basket is with basic agricultural commodities. Using the Phelps Brown 'industrial index', as Cooper does, may be slightly more satisfactory, in that industrial prices continued to rise through the 1670s, whereas agricultural prices subsided from the mid-seventeenth century.[24] Obviously both indexes lack coverage of the sort of commodities, many of them imported luxuries, which upper-class girls increasingly coveted. Quite clearly, however, the period from 1475–1524 to 1625–49 when average portions increased at least seven-fold was an inflationary one: the general price index rose nearly six-fold, the industrial one nearly three-fold. It would be surprising if portions escaped this inflationary experience. Comparing 1625–49 with 1675–1729, however, reveals a modest 17 per cent increase in the industrial index and a mere 3 per cent rise in the general one. Over the same period portions doubled. It is possible that some of the rise in dowries down to 1625–49 partly reflects a combination of inflation plus expanding material appetites, but the continued rise thereafter suggests that the responsibility may well lie elsewhere. One corroborative argument has come from Stone. He has suggested that the widening in the portion-to-jointure ratio that occurred before about 1620 was partly illusory. The actual income derived from the jointure was frequently greater than its nominal rental value, and that portions increased to take account of this. 'Real', and more significant, increases in the ratio occurred after 1620.[25]

It is at this point that we must widen the discussion to take in a range

---

[24] The calculations below are based on the Phelps Brown index numbers reproduced in Stone, *Crisis*, p. 790, and Cooper, 'Patterns', p. 307. [25] Stone, *Crisis*, pp. 645–6.

R. B. OUTHWAITE

Table 2.2. *Mean age at first marriage of those peers' children who married*[26]

Cohort born	Men	Women	Age difference
1550–74	25.28	20.26	5.02
1575–99	25.71	19.70	6.01
1600–24	25.99	20.67	5.32
1625–49	27.37	21.95	5.42
1650–74	26.88	21.54	5.34
1675–99	28.07	22.74	5.33
1700–24	30.16	23.51	6.65

of demographic and social considerations. Life, as Roger Thompson has pointed out, was difficult for the nubile girl in Tudor and Stuart England. Although nature produces about 105 male babies to every 100 female ones, higher infant and child mortality rates among boys rapidly eroded the number of males. It was not just disease which whittled away the numbers of the physiologically weaker boys but also cultural patterns which put premiums on risk and valour. Boys got drowned in greater numbers, fell off or under horses, or injured each other in mock or real combat. Girls, then as now, were more carefully watched and were trained moreover in those virtues of docile obedience that kept them out of trouble. By age twenty the sex balance was probably already tilting against them. Matters were made worse by the tendency for men to marry later in life than women. As Hajnal pointed out, the larger the difference in the age at which men and women customarily marry the less chance the younger female sex will have of finding a partner because more of the older sex will have died.[27] Table 2.2 reproduces the mean ages at first marriage for the children of English peers. It reveals that whilst males gradually postponed their marriages, so also did females, with the result that the crucial age difference between them did not widen significantly except for those born in the late sixteenth and early eighteenth centuries. Nevertheless these developments did nothing to improve the marriage chances of girls. The imbalance would be corrected somewhat by higher female than male death rates within the early years of marriage, resulting from deaths in childbirth, and by the tendency of widowers to remarry. But not all widowers who remarried coupled themselves to hitherto unwed girls. Forty per cent of the second marriages of peers, Stone tells us, were with

[26] Drawn from T. H. Hollingsworth, 'The Demography of the British Peerage', Supplement to *Population Studies* 18 (1964), table 17, p. 25.
[27] J. Hajnal, 'European Marriage Patterns in Perspective', in D. V. Glass and D. E. C. Eversley (eds.), *Population in History* (London, 1965), p. 129.

widows.[28] The latter clearly had their charms, which must include jointures and any other property they were lucky enough to possess.

There prevailed then a demographic structure which generally produced a sex balance unfavourable to marriageable girls. Certain events in the sixteenth and seventeenth centuries may have worked to make the situation even more unfavourable. Habakkuk thought that the increase in portions probably derived from 'a relative fall in the number of eligible husbands among the landowning families' and drew attention to the losses of landed sons in the Civil Wars and campaigns against Louis XIV. He also argued for a 'longer term movement of younger sons into government service and the army and navy', professions which may have lessened either their capability of, or eligibility for, marriage into the landed classes.[29] Thompson's leakage of young men to the colonies can perhaps be brought back into the reckoning, for even if the proportion of gentlemen of all types was no more than a few per cent, the overall dimensions of this outward flow was sufficiently large to have aggravated the problem. Gemery has recently suggested that the number of New World emigrants between 1630 and 1699 may have reached 378 000, whilst the Wrigley and Schofield 'back-projection' method of estimating external losses places the figure for the same period at more than half a million.[30] Thompson has pointed to Gregory King's explanation of adult male losses 'by wars, the sea, and the plantations, in which Articles the Females are very little concentrated'. King also thought these hazards outweighed those of childbed.[31] Some appreciation of this can be gained from Table 2.3, which reproduces estimated survival rates to both age fifteen and age fifty of the children of English peers. Survival rates to age fifteen were consistently better for females than males, corroborating what was said earlier, with a particularly marked discrepancy for the cohort born 1625–49. Survival

[28] Stone, *Crisis*, p. 621.
[29] Habakkuk, 'Marriage Settlements', p. 24. Stone, however, disagrees with much of this. He argues, 'Younger sons, even of the peerage, were hardly in the running, since the limited size of their inheritances normally made it impossible for them to provide jointures which could begin to match the portions offered with their sisters. This concentration on heirs male is a reason for thinking that the death of many heirs to landed estates in the Civil War, and the subsequent decline – if decline there was – in the proportion of younger sons who married had very little effect on the situation in the seventeenth century. The death of an heir male merely meant his replacement as an eligible husband by his younger brother, and since younger sons were in any case rarely able to compete in this expensive marriage market, any trend towards bachelordom could not have affected the situation' (*Crisis*, p. 648). If we are concerned, at this stage of the argument, with the total pool of marriageable partners, then obviously younger sons do matter. Stone later lost some of his doubts whether there was a trend towards celibacy: *Family, Sex and Marriage*, pp. 43–4.
[30] E. A. Wrigley and R. S. Schofield, *The Population History of England 1541–1871: A Reconstruction* (London, 1981), p. 224 and sources there cited.
[31] Thompson, *Women in Stuart England*, pp. 31–2.

Table 2.3. *Rates of survival per 1000 males and females born*[32]

	To age 15		To age 50	
Cohort born	Male	Female	Male	Female
1550–74	722.9	750.0	361.4	426.5
1575–99	715.6	754.2	348.8	450.0
1600–24	693.3	720.7	297.1	398.6
1625–49	646.8	693.8	288.9	351.7
1650–74	621.1	642.6	257.4	349.0
1675–99	667.3	677.0	322.9	376.0
1700–24	673.7	686.0	338.8	380.6

rates to age fifty were again consistently better for females than males, with the discrepancy being particularly marked for those born in late Elizabethan and Jacobean England.

At this point we must introduce another causal element into the explanation – the means by which status was transmitted. Here again there are marked differences for males and females. A man's status was a peculiar mixture of birth, occupation and personal success, but above all it was largely within his own grasp. A woman's status, on the other hand, was derived from that of her husband. A man could, within limits, marry a girl of a lower social status and not lose his. For the woman, however, circumstances were very different. Stone, as so often, presents the situation neatly: 'the emphasis on patrilinear descent meant that it was still not considered decent to marry your daughter to a mere merchant's son, even though your son and heir might at a pinch marry his sister'.[33] For a girl born into an elite group, marriage to a member of that elite was the only way in which she could safely perpetuate her status. The implications for marriage in a status pyramid are obvious and are described in Fig. 2.1. 'A' females can only hope to retain status by marrying 'A' males, a situation made impossible for all, if only because demographic conditions produce more marriageable females than single males anyway. To make matters worse for these 'A' girls, some 'A' males will deliberately marry 'B' females for money. The rules of status transmission raise the possibility that the leakage of willing 'A' males to level B will be greater than the leakage of willing 'A' females to level B. Though obviously a lot of 'A' females will have to marry at level B, neither they nor their parents may like it. 'I can't bear when a woman of quality marry one don't know

[32] Adapted from table 52 in Hollingsworth, 'Demography of British Peerage', p. 67.
[33] Stone, *Crisis*, pp. 647–8.

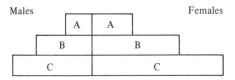

Fig. 2.1. A status pyramid with unequal marriage cohorts

whom', moaned one eighteenth-century monarch, echoing a well-established point of view.[34]

A number of social developments exacerbated the problem of upper-class females. One was the propensity, already observed, of upper-class males for celibacy. Hollingworth's estimates for celibacy amongst children of English peers are reproduced in Table 2.4. This evidence suggests that the

Table 2.4. *Proportions (per 1000) of males and females remaining unmarried*[35]

Cohort born	Males	Females
1550–74	25	90
1575–99	139	42
1600–24	229	128
1625–49	150	179
1650–74	179	151
1675–99	219	238
1700–24	200	263

proportion rose to nearly 23 per cent for those males born 1600–24 (and marrying a generation later), and it never fell below 15 per cent thereafter. Stone also has talked of 'a distinct trend towards bachelordom among owners of medium to large country houses' in three sample areas in the late seventeenth and eighteenth centuries.[36] This tendency was probably most pronounced amongst younger sons, who frequently could not afford to marry and especially to marry girls of their own social rank.[37] Such girls, or their parents, would anyway prefer to trade their portions for suitably sized jointures. This, Stone assures us, is the meaning behind that late-seventeenth-century complaint that 'women in this age, like hens, desire only to lay where they see nest-eggs'.[38]

[34] R. Trumbach, *The Rise of the Egalitarian Family* (New York, 1978), p. 98.
[35] Taken from table 11, Hollingsworth, 'Demography of the British Peerage', p. 20.
[36] Stone, *Family, Sex and Marriage*, pp. 43–5.
[37] Stone observes that the younger sons of peers 'throughout married mostly among the gentry' (*Crisis*, p. 627).   [38] *Ibid.*, p. 598.

Another exacerbating element was that of increasing competition from girls with wealthy fathers in other social groups.[39] Competition came, for example, from the daughters of professional men and merchants. Whilst these competitive draughts had long been felt by the daughters of landed men, for their inheriting brothers had long sought financial bliss in the arms of daughters of London aldermen, these draughts became stronger with the rapid expansion of commerce and the professions in the second half of the seventeenth century. Sir William Temple complained in the late seventeenth century that 'within less than fifty years, the first noble families that married into the City for downright money...thereby introduced by degrees this public grievance which has since ruined so many estates, by the necessity of giving great portions to daughters'.[40] City widows also exercised a certain fascination, partly because the 'custom of London' gave them a third share of their husband's estates, and partly because these often sizeable estates were conveniently liquid.[41] Moreover the number of widows probably increased as mortality rose in seventeenth-century England. An increase in competition from mercantile daughters because of increasing commercial wealth, and from wealthy widows generally because of rising mortality, could well have forced portions up in the second half of the century.

There is a further competitive pressure to consider. It was Hollingsworth who first drew our attention to that rise in mortality and contraction of fertility in Restoration England which resulted in the English peerage failing to reproduce itself. It was Christopher Clay, however, who first

[39] This has been noted by several authors: Habakkuk, 'Marriage Settlements', p. 23; Stone, *Crisis*, pp. 639, 647. Hollingsworth's data on the extent of marital social endogamy suggest that between the late sixteenth and the mid-eighteenth centuries the percentage of males marrying into aristocratic families fell more sharply than that of females ('Demography of the British Peerage', pp. 8–9):

Endogamous marriages of children of peers

Cohort born	Per cent of males marrying into nobility	Per cent of females marrying into nobility
1575–99	37.6	29.5
1600–24	41.3	31.2
1625–49	38.0	33.0
1650–74	36.6	30.8
1675–99	33.3	32.0
1700–24	23.2	27.3

[40] Cited in Habakkuk, 'Marriage Settlements', p. 23.
[41] And more than a third share if the marriage was childless. See Stone, *Crisis*, pp. 628–9; Cooper, 'Patterns', p. 225.

pointed out that one of the consequences of this would be an increase in the frequency of female and indirect succession.[42] As family size fell one could expect some rise in the proportion of families who produced only surviving daughters.[43] At any social level experiencing these demographic tendencies the number of heiresses would rise. Stone has recently written that 'it is astonishing to discover that the proportion of the squirearchy and above who died leaving no son to inherit was twenty-five per cent, rising to over forty per cent as the practice of contraception reduced family size after 1650'.[44] Whilst both the Stone and Cooper statistical series of portions deliberately exclude those of heiresses, they cannot exclude the competitive pressures such heiresses exerted in the marriage market. If marriages with heiresses attracted frequent contemporary comment it may not be because they 'were being sought more systematically':[45] the answer may lie in an increasing supply rather than an increasing demand.

Attention has been concentrated here on aristocratic dowries because they are the best-documented examples we possess. There is some evidence, however, of steep increases in portions among lesser social groups. Stone, for example, argues that in the late sixteenth century 'prices were being forced up by competition from the squirearchy, the most prosperous of whom were now offering £2,000 or more with their own daughters'.[46] Cooper prints a table showing a rise in portions proposed by knightly families: from an average of £286 in the period 1501–50 they rose to an average of £859 in the years 1551–1600.[47] It was probably the scale of the problem which varied; not its fundamental nature. Girls were becoming an increasing financial liability amongst the landed classes in early modern England. How far down the social scale such tendencies were revealed, and how far things changed in the course of the eighteenth and early nineteenth centuries, are problems which await investigation.

Perhaps one should revert briefly to a theme touched upon at the beginning – the role of romance. Habakkuk asked whether there was at this elite social level 'an increasing subordination of marriage to the increase of landed wealth' and thought on balance there was: that calculations of material interest were playing an increasingly important part in matrimony.[48] These views are perhaps at odds with Stone's argument that parentally arranged marriages gradually declined; that increasingly from 1660 onwards children made their own marital choices and did so frequently on the basis of personal affection.[49] Case histories

[42] C. Clay, 'Marriage, Inheritance, and the Rise of Large Estates in England, 1660–1815', *Economic History Review*, 2nd Series 21 (1968), 517–18.
[43] Cooper, 'Patterns', p. 301. [44] Stone, *Family, Sex and Marriage*, p. 66.
[45] Habakkuk, 'Marriage Settlements', p. 27. [46] Stone, *Crisis*, p. 638.
[47] Cooper, 'Patterns', p. 311. [48] Habakkuk, 'Marriage Settlements', pp. 24–6.
[49] Stone, *Family, Sex and Marriage*, p. 272.

supply a bewildering variety of examples, but a number of generalizations can perhaps be offered. Parental influence was exerted most forcibly where the property stakes were greatest, and was probably always more powerfully exerted over girls than boys. Arranged marriage was also not incompatible with love and affection. Children always had rights of veto over the choices made for them and parents increasingly recognized their duty to pay attention to the wishes of their children. The conflict between parents and children was perennial and served in most cases to limit the range of choices available; but 'love', one could say, is frequently 'the art of the possible'.

In conclusion, the rise in the nominal value of portions down to the early eighteenth century must be seen as a compound phenomenon. Rising agricultural prices and increasing land values in the period 1520 to 1640 helped eventually to swell aristocratic incomes: average gross income per peer, Stone estimates, rose by 150 per cent between 1559 and 1641,[50] a rate of increase well below that experienced by portions which over the same period may have risen twice as fast. Even allowing for the possibility that inflation may have encouraged expenditures to rise more rapidly than income, there is obviously something left to explain. From the mid-seventeenth to the mid-eighteenth century, moreover, price inflation virtually ceased, whilst dowry inflation continued with portions doubling over this period. Other economic influences should be brought into the explanation. From the 1620s borrowing for the landed classes became easier, less risky and less expensive, enabling them to raise inflated portions by mortgaging their estates if other means of payment were not available. Over the whole long period, however, the impulse persuading fathers into offering larger dowries would appear to have been competition in the marriage market and those varying forces – demographic, social and economic – which led periodically to relative surpluses of status-seeking nubile women. This tendency was present in the sixteenth century and was accentuated in the seventeenth when male survival rates deteriorated, emigration and male celibacy rose, and competition from widows, heiresses and trade fortunes increased.

Explanations cast along these lines must, however, consider the objections recently raised by Eileen Spring. She objects to the emphasis on rising *female* portions, arguing not only that 'daughters were of no more consequence to landed estates than younger sons' but also that 'portions [expressed as a proportion of estate income] did not rise under the strict settlement'.[51]

[50] Stone, *Crisis*, p. 762.
[51] E. Spring, 'The Family, Strict Settlement, and Historians', *Canadian Journal of History* 18 (1983), 385, 387. See also her 'Law and the Theory of the Affective Family', *Albion* 16 (1984), 1–20.

Her swingeing attack on both Habakkuk and Stone contains numerous insights of value but also, it must be said, much rather poorly supported assertion. Her evidence that younger sons and daughters were treated alike derives partly from Cooper and partly from Trumbach. Cooper, however, admitted that 'Most of these examples are of provision by those who could afford to be generous', whilst Trumbach's sample comes entirely from the period after 1690.[52] Even *if* younger sons were generally in sixteenth- and seventeenth-century England being equally generously provided for, it might be possible to argue that they were benefiting from the forces which inflated their sisters' portions. The evidence for a rise in bridal portions, expressed in terms of current prices, is overwhelming and it is clear that this rise continued into the period when prices and rents were stagnating and when the strict settlement was establishing itself.[53] Spring's attempts also to argue that 'There would thus seem to be little reason to think that an excess of females marked the aristocratic marriage market' rests on an inappropriate statistical foundation: mortality within marriage matters much less than mortality before it.[54] The argument presented in this chapter, that there were imbalances in the marriage market, rests on a more appropriate empirical base and on a firm bed of supportive contemporary comment. The complaint of Moll Flanders that 'The market is against our sex just now' operated at social levels other than her own. And it is, of course, with markets that we began.

[52] Cooper, 'Patterns', p. 218, and Trumbach, *Egalitarian Family*, pp. 88–9. Habakkuk, in contrast, noted that amongst Miss Finch's Northamptonshire landed families 'There is no evidence... of any trend in the provision for younger sons analogous to the increase in daughters' portions' (note 19 above).
[53] L. Bonfield, 'Marriage Settlements, 1660–1740: The Adoption of the Strict Settlement in Kent and Northamptonshire', in R. B. Outhwaite (ed.), *Marriage and Society* (London, 1981), pp. 101–16, shows that as early as the period 1660–80 nearly two-thirds of settlements in these two counties were of the 'strict' type. On rents, see M. G. Davies, 'Country Gentry and Falling Rents in the 1660s and 1670s', *Midland History* 4 (1977), 86–96, and J. Broad, 'Alternate Husbandry and Permanent Pasture in the Midlands, 1650–1800', *Agricultural History Review* 28 (1980), 82.
[54] Spring, 'The Family', p. 386.

3

Age and accumulation in the London business community, 1665–1720*

PETER EARLE

Adam Smith tells us in *The Wealth of Nations* that the capital of a society 'is the same with that of all the individuals who compose it' and that any growth in a society's wealth is the sum of the accumulations made by such individuals.[1] Such an emphasis on the accumulation of the individual may read strangely to us who have been brought up in a world of corporations and bureaucracy, but it makes perfectly good sense when seen against the background of the economy of the seventeenth and eighteenth centuries, an economy which was composed overwhelmingly of individual sole traders and small family businesses. It follows that, if we want to understand why the wealth of England expanded in the early modern period, we will need to investigate the conditions which encouraged or discouraged accumulation by individual men and women. The most obvious place to make such an investigation is amongst the London business community. Here, in the largest city in western Europe, was concentrated the great majority of the 'middle sort of people', the merchants, tradesmen and shopkeepers whose eager search for profit provided the enterprise which kept much of the rest of the English economy going. Great landowners might be individually richer, but they would be unlikely to match the rate of accumulation of these London businessmen whose whole ethos was directed towards the augmentation of their fortunes.

This London business community has been rather unevenly studied. Far more has been written about merchants and financiers than about the shopkeepers, wholesalers and manufacturers who made up the majority of London businessmen. This is understandable. London was famous as a centre of international trade and of finance and, perhaps more significantly, merchants and financiers have left far better business papers for historians to analyse than have the other members of the London business community. Nevertheless, this concentration on one sector of the

* My thanks are due to Dudley Baines and D. D. Hebb for their comments on a draft of this article and to Anne McGlone for advice and assistance on computing.
[1] 1961 edn, vol. I, pp. 358–9.

community, albeit the richest, is unfortunate since it conceals the fact that in many respects the whole of the business community shared the same attitudes and ambitions and ran their businesses in very similar ways. At first, it might seem surprising that there should be very much in the way of shared experience between, say, a wealthy Levant merchant worth £20 000 and a haberdasher or tavern-keeper worth a few hundred pounds. But, in fact, they have much in common, a fact which is perhaps inevitable when one considers the nature of business in this period. The most striking characteristic in this respect is that the vast majority of businessmen were sole traders and employed only a handful of people in their enterprises. Partnerships were unusual and partnerships of more than two people very unusual,[2] while the few joint-stock companies, though deservedly famous, were hardly representative.

It is clear that most sole traders had the same economic ambition and went about achieving it in the same way, however humble or prestigious their actual occupations. That ambition is simply stated. The object was to make money, the more the better, ideally to make sufficient money to withdraw from the bustle of the market-place and live the leisured life of the rentier in later years. Nearly all sole traders went about this process in a similar way, a fact which makes a comparative study of their life cycles illuminating. Nearly all started as apprentices to a London livery company and set up in business in their mid-twenties. From then on, they were on their own. Success was a matter of individual accumulation, a matter of turning over stock at a profit and of making sure that at each stock-taking that stock was rather bigger than it had been in the previous year. Relative success in this process was clearly very much a result of individual competence, a certain amount of luck and the accidents of trade, but it was also a result of other factors which can to a certain extent be statistically demonstrated. It will be the object of this chapter to attempt to throw some light on this process of accumulation by analysing some of these factors making for business success in the period, 1665–1720.

The main records which will be utilized are the same that were used by Richard Grassby in two path-breaking articles published in 1970.[3] These are the records of the London Court of Orphans, an institution whose function was to supervise the division of deceased citizens' estates between all children under the age of twenty-one and those over twenty-one who

---

[2] Of the 375 businessmen in the sample discussed in this article, 341 had no partners, 32 had one partner and 2 had two or more partners.

[3] 'The Personal Wealth of the Business Community in Seventeenth-Century England', *Economic History Review*, 2nd Series 23 (1970), 220–34: 'English Merchant Capitalism in the Late Seventeenth Century: The Composition of Business Fortunes', *Past and Present* 46 (1970), 87–107.

had not been advanced in their fathers' lifetimes.[4] The Court lost its compulsory powers in 1693 and virtually disappeared in the 1720s when its records cease. But up till 1720 sufficient citizens still used the Court for its records to provide a valuable basis for an analysis of business activity. The records used here are two-fold. The Common Serjeant who administered the Court kept a Common Serjeant's Book in which summary valuations of the personal estate of the deceased are listed, together with in most cases the number of orphans (and often their names and ages) between whom the customary one-third part of the estate was to be divided. Other useful information in the Common Serjeant's Book includes the description of the deceased as testate or intestate and sometimes a summary of his will. The second type of record consists of copies of the inventories from which the summary valuations were made. These seem to have been made by professional valuers (certainly the same names turn up very frequently) assisted by men of the same occupation as the deceased who were able to value stock in trade, tools, equipment and other specialized possessions. The inventories are fuller than most that were prepared for probate purposes and are nearly all produced in a consistent manner, starting usually with domestic goods (often listed in great detail) and continuing with shop or trade goods, leases, plate, apparel, linen, cash, debts owing to the deceased and since received, debts owing and not received, debts owing by the deceased, and finally postmortem debts, such as the cost of funerals and of the process of having estates valued and administered by the Court of Orphans itself. There are over 3000 of these inventories starting in 1666 after the Fire and continuing into the 1720s. Between them they provide an incredible range of information about the domestic and business life of mainly middle-class Londoners.

Historians are now well aware of the general problems of using inventories and there is no need to discuss such problems in great detail.[5] Richard Grassby has also noted some of the particular problems of the Orphans' Court inventories.[6] Use of the Court was not compulsory after 1693 and was by no means universal before that date. Bachelors, childless men or old men with grown-up children will not be represented. Valuations as usual present difficulties. The impression that one gets from the inventories is that domestic goods were valued at very low 'clearance sale' prices, shop goods at wholesale prices and stocks and shares at market

---

[4] For general information on the Court see Charles Carlton, *The Court of Orphans* (Leicester, 1974), and Grassby, 'Personal Wealth'. The records of the Court are in the Corporation of London Record Office (C.L.R.O.).

[5] For a useful summary of some of these problems see Ursula Priestley and P. J. Corfield, 'Rooms and Room Use in Norwich Housing, 1580–1730', *Post-Medieval Archaeology* 16 (1982), 93–7.

[6] 'Personal Wealth', pp. 220–1; 'English Merchant Capitalism', p. 89.

prices. Debts were of course valued in full, with the result that the 'domestic' side of the citizen's life appears undervalued relative to the 'business' side of his life. Another major problem arises when one wants to assess the total personal wealth of the citizen. It is clear that many debts owing to the deceased would never be recovered by his executor, who was normally a widow inexperienced in business. However, since the inventories do not treat doubtful and desperate debts in a consistent manner, there is no way of being certain how great a proportion of the deceased's supposed assets should be written off as unrecoverable. Grassby's answer to this problem was to assume that debts not yet received when the accounts were closed in the Common Serjeant's Book were never received.[7] This is a reasonable approach, but one that seriously underestimates the fortunes of many men, especially overseas merchants and wholesalers whose assets would clearly take a long time to recover. One even finds such easily recoverable assets as East India Company and Bank of England stock in the lists of 'debts not yet received' in the inventories. Since the major object of this study is to analyse the structure of the wealth-holding of living citizens rather than the proportion of that wealth which eventually passed to their families, the opposite solution to the problem has been adopted. All debts, received or unreceived, have been counted as assets and, as a result, wealth levels will be rather higher than in Grassby's analysis.

Since many of the inventories are tens of yards long and life is short, it was decided to sample them for the analysis presented here. The method of sampling which was adopted was designed to overcome one of the major problems of inventory analysis, ignorance of the age of the deceased. This was done by linking the data from the Court of Orphans with the data in Boyd's Index of London Citizens, which is kept in the library of the Society of Genealogists. Percival Boyd's Index is an astonishing compilation. It was prepared in the 1940s and consists of proformas on which he entered any relevant genealogical information which he could find on 60000 citizens of London, most of whom flourished between the late sixteenth and late eighteenth centuries. He drew on parish registers, monumental inscriptions, wills, marriage allegations, livery company records and, of course, on the Common Serjeant's Book, which provides invaluable information to the genealogist since it gives an approximate date of death, the names of widows and the names (and often ages) of the children of deceased citizens. The sample drawn from linking these two sources was of all citizens who had a date of birth in Boyd's Index[8] and an entry in volumes 2 to 6 of the

---

[7] 'Personal Wealth', p. 221.
[8] The commonest source used by Boyd for birth dates seems to have been the applications for a licence to marry in the diocese of London (Guildhall Library MS 10,091). These give ages of bride and groom.

Common Serjeant's Book. This provided an original sample of 450 people which has now been whittled down to 375. Some turned out not to have an inventory, or to have an inventory which was not drawn up in the normal consistent way. Some of Boyd's information was sufficiently ambiguous to make it seem wiser to leave that particular citizen out of the analysis.

The sample thus consists of 375 citizens of London whose age at death is known and whose inventory survives in the records of the Court of Orphans.[9] In order to provide a few more variables for analysis, two other data sources were searched for information. Since the livery company of the whole sample was known, the records of the companies were searched for apprenticeship bindings and freedom records.[10] Many company records have vanished and many are very poorly indexed, but it was still possible to find the apprenticeship binding records of 230 of the sample (61 per cent). Such sources give a useful extra dimension to a life-cycle analysis since they provide information on age at apprenticeship and freedom, county and place of origin and the occupation or status of the apprentice's father. Finally, a search was made for the wills of the 225 men in the sample who were described as testate in the Common Serjeant's Book. Only the records of the Prerogative Court of Canterbury were searched, but this produced 177 wills (47 per cent of the whole sample and 79 per cent of those described as testate).

What can be said of the typicality of this sample of London businessmen? It is, of course, not random and is likely to suffer from the usual statistical problems of a sample that is produced on an availability basis. It does, however, have a very fair spread of occupations, levels of wealth and age cohorts, and, for this reason, seems a sufficient basis for generalizations about the London business community which are likely, at the very least, to be more acceptable than those based on the very few sets of business papers which have survived or on the throwaway comments of literary contemporaries. In the accompanying tables, some characteristics of the sample are set out from which the reader can judge for himself the biases which the process of sampling and the sources themselves may have produced.

[9] More information on the sample will appear in my forthcoming book, provisionally entitled *The Middling Sort of People* (to be published by Methuen).
[10] The records of the Apothecaries, Barber-Surgeons, Fishmongers, Grocers, Haberdashers, Joiners, Merchant-Taylors, Tallow-Chandlers and Vintners were searched in Guildhall Library and the records of the Clothworkers, Drapers, Goldsmiths, Mercers, Salters, Skinners and Stationers in their respective Halls. For general information on the location and contents of these archives see Guildhall Library, *Guide to the Archives of City Livery Companies* (1982).

Table 3.1. *Decade of death of cases in sample*

	No.	%
1665–9	23	6.1
1670–9	112	29.8
1680–9	76	20.3
1690–9	52	13.9
1700–9	78	20.8
1710–19	34	9.1
Total	375	100.0

Table 3.2. *Age at death of cases in sample*

Age at death	No.	%
Under 30	17	4.5
30–9	107	28.6
40–9	131	34.9
50–9	83	22.2
60 and over	37	9·9
Total	375	100.0

Table 3.1 shows the decade in which the sample died and calls for little comment, except perhaps to note that the 1670s are rather heavily represented and that one is beginning to run into a shortage of cases by the 1710s. Table 3.2 shows the age at death. Purely from the point of view of the analysis which is to be done here, the distribution of ages at death is very convenient since, although there are not very many old men, the whole range of ages of men in their prime is well represented, which will enable estates to be analysed on a life-cycle basis. But the distribution has an alarming demographic tale to tell, showing as it does an appallingly high level of mortality. Everyone in the sample must have reached the age of twenty-four, which was the minimum age for attaining the citizenship, while the median age at death was only forty-four. This high mortality, which was particularly concentrated in the 1670s and 1680s, is not a fluke of the sample but a reflection of high mortality throughout England in this period. For London, these two decades represent the nadir of a long-term curve in the life-expectancy of middle-class adults, a subject which will be discussed in more detail in the final section of this chapter.[11]

[11] See below pp. 58–62.

Table 3.3. *Region of origin of sample*

Region	No.	%
London and Middlesex	91	38.5
Southeast	49	20.8
East	14	5.9
Midlands	34	14.4
Southwest	11	4.7
West	21	8.9
North	9	3.8
Outside England	7	3.0
Total known	236	100.0
Unknown	139	

Table 3.3 looks at the region of origin of those cases for whom it can be determined from apprenticeship bindings or other sources of information. The most striking aspect of the table is the very high proportion of the sample, nearly two-thirds, who came from the home counties and southeast England. Historians who have analysed London apprenticeship records have discovered that throughout the seventeenth century there was a tendency for more and more apprentices to come from London and the home counties and for fewer to come from regions which had previously been important catchment areas, such as the north, west and midlands.[12] The sample reflects this trend, though it probably exaggerates it.

Table 3.4 examines the status of the fathers of the sample as given in the same sources. The distribution is broken down into six groups, the balancing group 'Others' being mainly composed of provincial traders and artisans. Not surprisingly, there is a high number of citizens of London amongst the fathers since so many of the apprentices came from London and Middlesex. But in nearly a quarter of the known cases the fathers were described as gentlemen, a trend which was much commented on by contemporaries and which has been confirmed by other analyses of

[12] See S. R. Smith, 'The Social and Geographical Origins of the London Apprentices, 1630–1660', *Guildhall Miscellany* 4 (1973); W. F. Kahl, 'Apprenticeship and the Freedom of the London Livery Companies, 1690–1750', *Guildhall Miscellany* 1 (1956). In general, see John Wareing, 'Changes in the Geographical Distribution of the Recruitment of Apprentices to the London Companies, 1486–1750', *Journal of Historical Geography* 6 (1980), and the further references on p. 241 of that article.

Table 3.4. *Status of fathers of sample*

Status of father	No.	%
Citizen of London	76	36.0
Gentleman	47	22.3
Yeoman	30	14.2
Husbandman	4	1.9
Clergyman	12	5.7
Others	42	19.9
Total known	211	100.0
Unknown	164	

Table 3.5. *Personal fortunes of sample*

Fortune	No.	%
Insolvent	14	3.7
Under £500	90	24.0
£500–999	47	12.5
£1000–1999	61	16.3
£2000–4999	90	24.1
£5000–10 000	38	10.1
£10 000 and over	35	9.3
Total	375	100.0

apprenticeship bindings.[13] In general, it should be noted that few apprentices were the sons of men of very low status such as husbandmen or labourers. This had been fairly common in the sixteenth century but, by the period of this study, most apprentices were the sons of men of the middle classes in the broadest sense of the term.

Table 3.5 tabulates the personal fortunes (gross assets less liabilities) of the men in the sample and, as one would expect, indicates that London businessmen tended to be rather well off compared with most of their contemporaries. The median fortune for the whole group was £1717 and the range ran from a negative £2023 to a positive £122 349; from the

[13] Smith, 'Social and Geographical Origins', pp. 195–206; Kahl, 'Apprenticeship', pp. 19–21; Richard Grassby, 'Social Mobility and Business Enterprise in Seventeenth-Century England', in D. Pennington and K. Thomas (eds.), *Puritans and Revolutionaries* (Oxford, 1978).

gloriously insolvent linen-draper Andrew Kendrick, who passed his time in unpaid-for splendour between his house over the shop in Cheapside and his farmhouse in Hertfordshire, to the very wealthy immigrant from Danzig, Peter Vansittart.

What did the citizens included in the sample do for a living? By this period, there is no longer a very good match between the livery companies to which citizens belonged and the occupation or occupations which earned them their livings. The degree of match varies considerably between the companies; generally speaking the more socially distinguished the livery company the less likely were its members to practise the occupation described in its title. Mercers, Clothworkers, Salters and Fishmongers rarely practised those trades; Poulterers, Pewterers and Plumbers usually did. This problem means that it is necessary to determine occupation from the inventories, which is generally quite easy, though it sometimes involves leaping from a mere hint to an inspired guess.

The sample was drawn from fifty-nine different livery companies of which the following, representing 68 per cent of the sample, have the most cases:

Haberdashers (31)	Salters (20)	Goldsmiths (12)
Vintners (26)	Drapers (19)	Stationers (10)
Mercers (25)	Grocers (17)	Distillers (10)
Clothworkers (23)	Apothecaries (16)	Skinners (8)
Merchant-taylors (20)	Fishmongers (12)	Coopers (8)

There was an even greater variety of occupations, a total of 172 being distinguished, ranging from Levant merchant to market-gardener and from surgeon to dealer in nets and lines. In Table 3.6, these occupations are broken down into a number of groups.

While these groups help to give some idea of the range of occupations, they often conceal more than they reveal. Textiles includes men engaged in the manufacture of cloth or in its preparation for export as well as rather wealthy linen-drapers and rather poor dealers in thread and yarn. Victualling includes wealthy cheesemongers and tavern-keepers with poulterers and sweetmeat manufacturers. Construction includes large-scale builders with jobbing carpenters and so on. Just for the record, the largest component in the accessories group are booksellers, printers and publishers and in the services total apothecaries and money-lenders.

Occupational distribution really defies easy analysis in a place with such a wide variety of occupations as London and, in any case, it would often make more sense to group occupations on the basis of the nature of the business rather than on the particular goods and services which it produced or sold. Merchants are an easily definable group in this sense since they are people whose main business is overseas trade. Wholesalers would be

Table 3.6. *Occupations of sample*

Merchants	43	Wood and leather	20
Textiles	91	Construction	13
Victualling	102	Accessories	18
Metal	33	Services	55

another group, as would retail shopkeepers, but these two groups are very difficult to distinguish via inventories. Manufacturers and artisans are two further groups that are different in concept but often very difficult to distinguish in detail.

The best that one can really say is that most occupations known to have been practised in London were well represented in the sample. There are several haberdashers and linen-drapers, tavern-keepers and apothecaries, pewterers and coal merchants, booksellers and builders. There are silk-weavers and undertakers, upholsterers and clockmakers. There is a portrait-painter and a map-printer, a wharfinger and a dealer in whalebone whose main business was the manufacture of foundation garments. London was a place of many trades. The two main groups which are not well represented are the professions, other than apothecaries, and the trades of the river. There are no shipbuilders, watermen or rope-makers in the sample. This is unfortunate, but a sample which included every possible occupation would have to be very large indeed.

In this section, an attempt will be made to analyse what determined the chances of success in the London business world. What sort of people became rich and what sort of people failed to make much progress towards those 'easy circumstances' which Defoe described in *Robinson Crusoe* as one of the major characteristics of the middle sort of people.[14] It is clear that such an analysis will only be able to produce broad pointers since important personal characteristics such as intelligence, determination, thrift and faith cannot be distinguished from the sources.

Most businessmen in this period followed a similar career pattern. School would be followed by apprenticeship, usually begun at some age between fourteen and eighteen, the median age of the sample studied being just over sixteen. Apprenticeship lasted between seven and nine years, seven years being much the commonest, and was followed after some delay by the taking of the freedom of the City, typically at the age of twenty-four. It was now that business life proper started, sometimes immediately,

[14] 1972 edn, p. 6. Defoe is much the best contemporary commentator on the London middle classes, particularly in *The Complete English Tradesman* (1726–7).

sometimes after some years in which capital was accumulated from a journeyman's wages. This period in his early twenties was the time when the young businessman received one of the most vital components of his future success, his portion, a crucial variable which our sources do not reveal. If his father was already dead, he would normally receive his portion at the age of twenty-one, either from the Court of Orphans or from the executors of his father's will. If his father was alive, he would probably receive his portion at freedom, though it is clear that fathers were often reluctant to release assets to start their sons. Because of the very low expectation of life in the middle and late seventeenth century, it seems clear that many, possibly the majority, would actually have received their portions at the age of twenty-one, a fact which would be likely to cause some tension in the last years of apprenticeship since independent servants would fit uneasily into their masters' households.

The early years of the young businessman's career were generally considered the most crucial. It was now that he learned his trade in earnest; it was now that he must save every penny that he could in order to build up his trading capital. It was also the period when he would be looking around with the help of his 'friends' for a wife, a choice which would make a vital contribution to his life chances. A good wife contributed to business success in three main ways. She would keep household expenditure to a respectable minimum. She might also make a valuable unpaid contribution to the running of the business. Finally, or perhaps primarily, she would bring the second major injection of capital to the business in the form of her portion or dowry. Young businessmen were exhorted by the writers of conduct books to delay their marriages, to discover in the words of the publisher John Dunton 'whether my trade wou'd carry two, and then to proceed upon a safe bottom'.[15] Several men in the sample ignored such advice and married within a few months of attaining their freedom, some following the classic path of marrying their master's daughter, but the majority seem to have accepted the wisdom of their elders since the median age at first marriage of the sample was twenty-seven. Men in this class typically married women much younger than themselves. The median age of the businessmen's wives was twenty-one.[16] Teenage brides were common and it is clear that these wives of the London middle sort did not live under the same constraints as the rural and small-town women studied

---

[15] *The Life and Errors of John Dunton* (1818 edn), p. 61.
[16] For a general discussion of the age at marriage in London see Vivien Brodsky Elliott, 'Single Women in the London Marriage Market: Age, Status and Mobility, 1598–1619', in R. B. Outhwaite (ed.), *Marriage and Society: Studies in the Social History of Marriage* (1981).

Table 3.7. *Father's influence on son's fortune*

	Status of father			
Fortune of son at death	Elite livery[a] %	Humble livery[b] %	Gentleman %	Yeoman %
Less than £1000	24	44	17	33
£1000–1999	0	31	17	10
£2000–4999	47	19	43	40
£5000–9999	19	0	8	17
£10000 and over	10	6	15	0
Total	100	100	100	100
No. of cases	21	16	47	30

[a] Elite livery = Clothworker, Dyer, Mercer, Draper, Salter, Fishmonger, Scrivener.
[b] Humble livery = Weaver, Feltmaker, Baker, Butcher, Pewterer, Saddler, Bricklayer, Carpenter, Plasterer, Tiler.

by the Cambridge Population Group whose median age at marriage in the same period was twenty-six.[17]

We will now leave the young married couple to build up their business and consider what factors were likely to make that process a success. Once again it is clear that innate qualities will be important, though these themselves may well be the product of upbringing and education. It should be clear from the brief discussion above that, in a world of individualist sole traders, the status and wealth of the young businessman's father were likely to play a paramount part in his success. The sources do not unfortunately enable us to trace wealth levels between generations directly, but it is possible to cross-tabulate the fortunes at death of the sons of four groups of fathers whom one can reasonably divide into two sections, one likely to be well off and one likely to be not so well off. In Table 3.7, this exercise is done for the sons of fathers described as gentlemen and yeomen and for the sons of fathers who belonged to elite and humble livery companies.

Scrutiny of the table demonstrates that the expected relationship does exist, but that it was not a particularly strong one. Sons of gentlemen and

[17] F. A. Wrigley and R. S. Schofield, 'English Population History from Family Reconstitution: Summary Results, 1600–1799', *Population Studies* 37 (1983), 157–84.

Table 3.8. *Influence of livery company on fortune*

| | Livery company | | |
Fortune at death	Elite[a] %	Middling[b] %	Humble[c] %
Less than £1000	20	40	57
£1000–1999	15	16	17
£2000–4999	32	29	12
£5000–9999	12	9	10
£10000 and over	21	6	4
Total	100	100	100
No. of cases	99	153	123

[a] Elite livery = Clothworkers, Drapers, Mercers, Fishmongers, Salters.
[b] Middling = Dyers, Haberdashers, Merchant Taylors, Grocers, Vintners, Goldsmiths, Ironmongers, Leathersellers, Apothecaries, Scriveners, Stationers.
[c] Humble = All others.

sons of the members of elite livery companies die richer, but not staggeringly richer than the sons of yeomen and of members of humbler livery companies. One would certainly expect such a relationship to exist, since at almost every stage the wealth and contacts of the father was likely to have affected the son's chances. The rich father could pay for a better education, could afford the apprenticeship for prestigious and profitable occupations such as overseas trade, could provide a larger portion for his son and could attract a richer woman to be his son's wife. Status alone may, however, not be the most satisfactory way of looking at the influence of the father on the son's life chances. There were, for example, rich yeomen and poor gentlemen and, of course, mean and purse-tight fathers of all classes were not unknown in the seventeenth century.

The influence of the father's wealth and contacts on the son's fortune at death becomes much clearer when we look at livery company and occupation, two important career choices which were made by the father or guardian in consultation with the son. Table 3.8 looks at the fortunes of men belonging to three groups of livery companies: the elite from which most merchants were drawn, the middling group from which most shopkeeping and professional people were drawn, and the humble which catered mainly for artisans. The borders between the groups are somewhat arbitrary, but it is clear from the table that there was a fairly strong relationship between fortune at death and livery company. The choice of

Table 3.9. *Influence of occupation on fortune*

	Occupation			
Fortune at death	Merchant %	Draper etc.[a] %	Haberdasher[b] %	Artisan[c] %
Less than £1000	5	17	50	60
£1000–1999	2	17	15	25
£2000–4999	19	49	25	7
£5000–9999	34	3	2	6
£10000 and over	40	14	8	2
Total	100	100	100	100
No. of cases	43	29	40	52

[a] Draper etc. = Draper, woollen-draper, linen-draper, mercer, silkman.
[b] Haberdasher = Milliner, laceman, haberdasher, yarnseller, threadman, ribbon and button seller, fringe and lace seller, hatter, tailor, outfitter, salesman.
[c] Artisan = Working goldsmith, silversmith, wiredrawer, jeweller, cutler, pewterer, clockmaker, loriner, plumber, brazier, tinsmith, joiner, turner, coffin-maker, box-maker, bricklayer, carpenter, glazier, mason, plasterer, horner, combmaker.

livery company was also, as S. R. Smith has shown, related to social origin.[18] Sons of gentlemen went into companies like the Fishmongers and not into companies like the Butchers or Bakers.

To join a distinguished livery company was not, however, sufficient in itself to guarantee fortune. This was much more likely to be determined by the actual occupation in which one was engaged and the amount of capital with which one started. In most cases, the choice of the particular master to whom a boy was apprenticed was tantamount to a choice of occupation. Most people ended up in the same occupation as their master.

In Table 3.9, an attempt is made to cross-tabulate fortune at death with occupation. The problems of grouping occupations was discussed above and this table in fact only covers 44 per cent of all cases in the sample. The groups were chosen on a basis that would have made sense to contemporaries: merchants; drapers and silkmen; haberdashers and other dealers in clothing or smallwares; and artisans.

The distribution in the table is what contemporaries would have expected and was reflected in the level of apprenticeship premiums which were paid for young men to be trained in these four groups of occupations.[19]

[18] Smith, 'Social and Geographical Origins', p. 200.
[19] The premiums below are all drawn from cases heard before the Mayor's Court and are in the series Mayor's Court Equity and Mayor's Court Interrogatories in C.L.R.O.

The premiums for merchants' apprentices in the 1670s ranged from a low of £100 to a high of £860 asked for a Levant merchant's apprentice in 1679. The usual range was between £200 and £500. A witness in a court case of 1653 said that the typical premium for a woollen-draper was £100 to £120 and similar figures were paid for mercers' and drapers' apprentices in the 1670s. In the same decade, a boy apprenticed to a milliner was asked to pay £30 and to a yarn-seller £40, figures which reflect the range of premiums paid by apprentices in the haberdasher type of business. Artisans paid similar premiums; four coopers received £10, £25, £30 and £35; working goldsmiths received £20, £25, £30, £40, £50; cutlers £10, £25, £30, £35; while a humble boxmaker got only £8 with his apprentice in 1679.

Such payments illustrate why so few husbandmen or labourers were the fathers of London businessmen, but the apprenticeship premium was only the beginning of the father's financial responsibilities. Apprentices were expected to be clothed according to their status and the initial cost of their wardrobes was normally a charge on their parents or guardians. Clothes suitable for a merchant's apprentice might well cost his father £40 or £50, for a milliner's apprentice £20, while the wardrobe of the boxmaker's apprentice mentioned above cost only £7, but even this nearly doubled his premium.[20] Then there were other costs such as freedom fees and the entry fines that merchants would have to pay before they joined a trading company. All this before actually setting up in business. We have no setting-up costs for the middle of the seventeenth century, but a hundred years later the figures given by Campbell in *The London Tradesman* give some idea of what fathers might expect to have to pay to see their sons started in business.[21] Once again, the figures reflect the distribution demonstrated in Table 3.9. For merchants and silkmen, Campbell merely says that setting-up costs were unlimited. For the other occupations represented in Table 3.9, the *lowest* setting-up costs are given in Table 3.10. Such figures would have been a little lower in the middle of the seventeenth century when most of the sample discussed here started in business, but they do indicate the importance of having a wealthy and well-connected father if one wanted to make a success of business. On the other hand, such universal truths should not disguise the fact that it was quite possible for a young man from a less privileged background to do well – possible but not all that likely.

One group from a privileged background who attracted much attention at the time and have been much discussed by historians were the sons of gentlemen.[22] We saw in Table 3.7 that they were likely to do quite well

---

[20] These figures are drawn from the same series as in note 19.

[21] R. Campbell, *The London Tradesman* (1747).

[22] See, in particular, Grassby, 'Social Mobility'.

Table 3.10. *Starting-up costs*

Drapers etc.		Haberdashers etc.		Artisans	
Linen-draper	£1000	Haberdasher	£100	Boxmaker	£20
Mercer	£1000	Hosier	£500	Pewterer	£300
Laceman	£1000	Salesman	£100	Turner	£50
		Threadman	£500	Tallow-chandler	£100

Source: R. Campbell, cited in note 21, pp. 337ff.

in business, as we would expect. Their median fortune was £3200, just under double the median of the sample as a whole and over £1000 more than the median for the sons of yeomen. What occupations were considered suitable for the sons of gentlemen? The answer is that there was a fairly wide range of occupations considered suitable, some fairly humble, though none of the gentlemen's sons in the sample seems to have sunk quite so low as to make things with his own hands. There were ten who became drapers or silkmen, eight merchants, six money-lenders or bankers, three tobacconists, two each were apothecaries, grocers, haberdashers and cheesemongers, and one each was an ironmonger, jeweller, leatherseller, tavern-keeper, silversmith, bookseller, salter, druggist and looking-glass manufacturer. The sons of gentlemen thus permeated the London business world fairly thoroughly, though they tended to be concentrated in such profitable occupations as overseas trade, linen-draping and finance.

What conclusions can we draw from this discussion of the influence of fathers on their sons' chances of accumulation? We have seen that, in general, the higher the status of the father the greater the wealth of the son. In this respect, the decline of social restraints on the movement of the sons of the gentry into trade is an important factor to take into account when considering the growth of business wealth in London. Such restraints seem to have been weaker in practice than they were in theory ever since the late sixteenth century, and, by the early eighteenth century, the idea that gentility and trade were incompatible seems to have virtually disappeared.[23] This meant that, in a period of indifferent profitability in agriculture, landed wealth could effectively be translated into business capital by providing apprenticeship premiums and portions for the younger sons of the landed classes. This flow of capital into London is impossible to measure, but it has to be seen as at least a partial reversal of the

[23] See, for instance, Smith, 'Social and Geographical Origins', pp. 200–1, and the interesting analysis of Edward Chamberlayne's *Angliae Notitia* in Helen Sard Hughes, 'The Middle-Class Reader and the English Novel', *Journal of English and Germanic Philology* 25 (1926), 366–70.

traditional flow of business wealth out of London into the purchase of land. Such a reversal was strengthened by the perhaps increasing reluctance of businessmen to make major land purchases from the late seventeenth century.[24] Business wealth thus increasingly stayed in London and would be available to provide larger portions for the growing percentage of apprentices who were the sons of Londoners. London was thus getting more like Amsterdam, where land purchase did not cause a continual haemorrhage of business capital.[25] The way was now open for the rise of business dynasties in the eighteenth century as gentry capital and existing London wealth combined to create an intergenerational accumulation of wealth in the business community.[26]

So far we have concentrated our analysis of the chances of business success on the status of the businessman's father and on the choice of livery company and occupation which the prospective businessman made in conjunction with his father or guardian and friends. That analysis paints a picture which is more or less what we would expect. The other major determinant of the personal fortune left by the businessmen in the sample which will be discussed here is the age at which they died. In a world of sole traders or small partnerships, we would expect life expectancy to have a paramount effect on the level of fortune achieved by the individual. If business was profitable at all, and there would seem little point in engaging in it if it was not, then businessmen should get progressively richer the longer they lived or at least up to that point in their life-cycles when they started divesting themselves of assets to provide portions for their sons and daughters.

Table 3.11 cross-tabulates age at death with fortune and it can be seen that, in general, the distribution satisfies the common-sense hypothesis above. Naturally, the fit is not perfect, since the sample includes men with a wide range of occupations and a wide but unknown range of initial capital stocks. So we find some men dying young and rich, and some dying old and poor. However, this mixed nature of the sample cannot obscure the general principle. Businessmen got richer as they got older.

There also seems to be a relationship between age at death and

---

[24] H. J. Habakkuk, 'English Landownership, 1680–1740', *Economic History Review* 10 (1940), 2–17.

[25] See, for instance, the observation of Sir Thomas Culpeper (1669): 'The Dutch master us in trade. We always begin young men here; there it holds from generation to generation.' J. Thirsk and J. P. Cooper (eds.), *Seventeenth-Century Economic Documents* (Oxford, 1972), p. 73.

[26] Cf. Nicholas Rogers, 'Money, Land and Lineage: The Big Bourgeoisie of Hanoverian London', *Social History* 4 (1979), 437–54, and Donna T. Andrew, 'Aldermen and Big Bourgeoisie of London Reconsidered', *Social History* 6 (1981), 359–64.

Table 3.11. *Influence of age at death on fortune*

	Age at death				
Fortune at death	Under 30 %	30–9 %	40–9 %	50–9 %	60 & over %
Less than £1000	76	53	38	31	14
£1000–1999	12	20	18	15	5
£2000–4999	12	20	26	23	35
£5000–9999	0	5	10	11	30
£10000 and over	0	2	8	20	16
Total	100	100	100	100	100
No. of cases	17	107	131	83	37

Table 3.12. *Influence of occupation on age of death*

	Proportion dying			
Occupation	Under 40 %	Under 50 %	Under 60 %	No. of cases
Merchants	19	46	78	43
Drapers etc.	32	68	87	29
Haberdashers etc.	47	82	97	40
Artisans	42	71	96	52

occupation which is illustrated in Table 3.12. The number of cases is rather small to carry much weight, but it is interesting to note that the two poorer groups, artisans and haberdashers, tended to die young, thus making it even more difficult for businessmen engaged in such low-grade occupations to make it to the top of the accumulation ladder. If this relationship is real and not just a freak of the sample size, there are interesting implications for the environmental causes of the high mortality in this period.

To demonstrate that businessmen got richer as they got older may be to state the obvious, though it seems to be an obvious fact that has not often penetrated the consciousness of economic historians. The relationship does, however, have some important implications, not least in throwing doubt on other analyses of wealth from inventory sources which have no control for age at death. Leaving that aside, there seem to be some important points which can be made here. The main point is that the

Table 3.13. *Mortality before and after 1690*

	Proportion dying	
	Before 1690	After 1690
Age at death	%	%
Under 30	6	3
Under 40	42	24
Under 50	78	57
Under 60	92	87
No. of cases	211	164

accumulation of the individual will affect the accumulation of the society. If men get richer as they get older, then periods of high mortality will not just be periods of indifferent accumulation for individuals but, other things being equal, they will also be periods when the wealth of families and of the nation as a whole will grow more slowly. This can be illustrated by comparing the experience of those members of the sample who died before and after 1690, two periods of very different mortality experience. The median age at death in the first period was 42.6 and in the second 47.8. The breakdown by age-groups is shown in Table 3.13. This differing mortality experience is reflected in the accumulation of wealth of cases who died in the two periods. Men who died before 1690 left a median of £1353; men who died after 1690 left a median of £2076. Other factors may well be involved in this large difference, which is reflected in all age and wealth groups, but age at death is clearly an important factor to take into consideration when attempting to explain the undoubted growth in London's wealth after the Glorious Revolution.

It has been suggested that the connection made here between the effect of mortality on the accumulation of the individual and on the accumulation of families and of the nation as a whole is an illusion, since the early death of the father simply means that the children inherit earlier and the total accumulation of father and children together will be the same. This would only be true under the extremely unlikely conditions that, first, the children inherited all their father's capital and, secondly, they increased that capital at the same rate as their father had. There are a number of reasons why this is unlikely to happen.

In the first place, it would be unusual for all the father's capital to pass to the son or, since it comes to the same thing in this discussion, to the children. There are several possible leakages. Transfer costs at inheritance were very high, including funeral costs, legal fees and debts which could not be collected by executors. And few people would leave what was left of their estates entirely to their children. The one-third which was the portion of widows by the custom of London might find its way back into the accumulation system and ultimately to the children, but there would inevitably be leakages in the process. Bequests outside the family would of course be lost completely. Even in the long run, after the children had inherited from their mother, it seems unlikely that much more than a half to two-thirds of a man's fortune would actually pass to his children.

Secondly, it would be unusual if the son was able to increase the capital that passed to him at the same rate as his father had. The high mortality of the period before 1690 led to a median age at death of 42.6 for the men in the sample. This meant that their eldest sons were unlikely to be more than fourteen when their fathers died, with the result that the eldest son's inheritance would not be employed in business for some ten years after his father's death. Naturally, the younger brothers and sisters would have to wait considerably longer. No doubt their money would be put out at interest by executors or trustees, but this would be at a much lower rate of return than might be expected from an active businessman.

The effect of this can be illustrated by a numerical example. We will assume that in 1660 a man aged twenty-four starts up in business with a capital of £1000. He dies in 1678, aged forty-two, and has accumulated during his business career at a compound rate of profit of 10 per cent.[27] When he dies, all his accumulated fortune passes to his only child, aged ten, whose guardians invest it at the maximum rate of interest of 6 per cent until he starts in business himself at the age of twenty-four, after which he accumulates at the same rate of 10 per cent as his father. In 1710, fifty years after his father started up in business, the son will be forty-two and ready to die himself. If neither his father nor himself had spent a penny in the meantime, his accumulated fortune would be £69 891. Now let us assume that the father lives till 1696 when he is sixty, gives his only child a portion of one-third of his fortune in 1692 when he is twenty-four and leaves him the remainder when he dies. Both father and son accumulate at the same rate of profit of 10 per cent. When the son is forty-two in 1710, he will be worth £117 392. Such are the joys of compound interest.

It may be unrealistic to assume that the difference between the rate of profit and the rate at which guardians could put out a child's money was as much as 4 per cent, but then it is also probably unrealistic to assume that an inexperienced man with a small capital will get such a good return

[27] This is probably somewhat higher than the actual rate of profit in this period. See Richard Grassby, 'The Rate of Profit in Seventeenth-Century England', *English Historical Review* 84 (1969), 721–51.

on his business as an older man with a larger capital. It is also probable that domestic expenses, though lower absolutely, will be higher relatively for the young man so that he does not in fact have nearly so much working capital to turn over at compound interest.

Such simple examples can only suggest possibilities, but it does seem that, whatever the actual numbers, the relationship between age at death and total accumulation is a realistic one and not simply an accounting illusion. The implications of this relationship can be considered further by looking at the long-term mortality experience of the London middle classes. Only crude estimates can be made in the current state of research, but these can be very suggestive. Two approaches have been attempted here. The first, which is illustrated in Table 3.14, is based on Boyd's Index of London Citizens, which was discussed above. The age at death of all citizens for whom Boyd gives both a date of birth and a date of death or probate was calculated and the proportions dying under various ages were tabulated by twenty-year birth cohorts from 1550 to 1729. It is assumed that, whatever the biases which may be incorporated in Boyd's Index, those biases are consistent throughout the period under consideration. It should be noted that the percentages presented here do not reflect expectation of life at birth, since the whole sample must have reached the age of twenty-four to be included, being all citizens of London.

Table 3.14 demonstrates that life expectancy was rather good for London citizens born in Elizabethan and Jacobean times. It began to deteriorate for the cohort born between 1610 and 1629 and then reached a nadir for the cohort born between 1630 and 1649. This birth cohort seems to have experienced particularly severe mortality in their thirties and forties, in their very prime as businessmen. This unfortunate group of citizens is very heavily represented in the sample which has been discussed in this chapter. Nearly half (46.9 per cent) the sample were born between 1630 and 1649 and it is the early deaths of this cohort in the 1670s and 1680s which helps to keep the median fortune of the pre-1690 period relatively low. For those born from 1650 onwards, the life expectancy of Boyd's citizens begins to improve again, reaching a level similar to that of Elizabethan times for those born in the 1690s and improving even on that for the last birth cohort in the table, those born between 1710 and 1729.

Supporting evidence for this improvement in life expectancy following the high mortality period between 1665 and the 1680s is illustrated in Fig. 3.1. This is based on the Bills of Mortality. The method used was to calculate deaths per thousand for two groups of 'middle-class' parishes distinguished by Jones and Judges in their article 'London Population in the Late Seventeenth Century'.[28] Middle-class parishes were defined on the

---

[28] *Economic History Review* 6 (1935), 45–63. See also the introduction to D. V. Glass (ed.), *London Inhabitants Within the Walls 1695* (London Record Society, 1966).

Table 3.14. *Age at death from Boyd's Index*

| Proportion dying | Birth cohorts of citizens born | | | | | | | | |
	1550–69 %	1570–89 %	1590–1609 %	1610–29 %	1630–49 %	1650–69 %	1670–89 %	1690–1709 %	1710–29 %
Under 30	4	2	2	2	7	7	2	4	2
Under 40	17	16	15	14	29	24	17	13	9
Under 50	33	33	30	33	52	41	36	33	22
Under 60	52	47	53	58	68	60	60	51	43
Under 70	71	71	75	79	84	82	81	73	71
Under 80	93	91	91	94	96	96	94	92	91
No. of cases	178	315	411	443	823	536	252	154	118

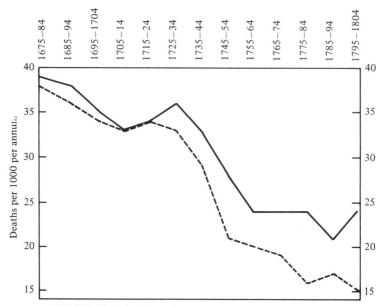

━━━ LONDON BRIDGE GROUP = St.Andrew Hubbard, St.Benet Gracechurch, St.Botolph Billingsgate, St.Dionis Backchurch, St.Dunstan in East, St.Gabriel Fenchurch, St.George Botolph Lane, St. Leonard Eastcheap, St. Magnus, St.Margaret Pattens, St.Mary at Hill.

━ ━ ━ GUILDHALL GROUP = Allhallows Bread Street, Allhallows Honey Lane, St.John Evangelist, St.Lawrence Jewry, St.Martin Ironmonger Lane, St. Mary le Bow, St.Mary Magdalen Milk Street, St.Matthew Friday Street, St. Michael Bassishaw

Fig. 3.1. Middle-class mortality in London

basis of their high proportions of 'substantial householders' assessed for personal estate of the capital value of £600 and upwards in the Marriage Duties assessments of 1695. The two groups of parishes are clustered round the Guildhall and at the northern approaches to London Bridge. Their total populations were taken as those of the 1695 data from 1676 to 1704 and then are assumed to have changed evenly decade by decade until they reached the figures given in the 1801 Census. This is probably a rather unrealistic assumption, but it should be acceptable for the crude analysis attempted here.

If Fig. 3.1 is taken at face value, it shows a virtually continuous decline in mortality in both groups of parishes from the late 1680s to the early 1780s, with the exception of a quite serious hiccough in the two decades 1715–34. This last period includes the well-known time of general high mortality in the late 1720s. One would be reluctant to put too much reliance on the exact figures of deaths per thousand in Fig. 3.1. The Bills of Mortality do not have the best reputation amongst demographers and both the 1695 and 1801 population totals are probably underestimates. However, it seems reasonable to accept that the trend is accurate, even if the death rates themselves are suspect. One is given confidence by the fact that the experience of both groups of parishes moves very much in tandem and that the larger individual parishes within the groups consistently mirror the experience of the groups as a whole. It is, of course, possible that the decline in deaths per thousand which is illustrated in Fig. 3.1 was entirely accounted for by a fall in infant and child mortality and that there was no improvement in adult mortality, which is our main interest here. This, however, seems inherently unlikely, especially in view of the improvements in adult mortality demonstrated in Table 3.14. It seems reasonable to accept that Fig. 3.1 reflects changes in the mortality of adults, even if it does not exactly measure them.

It is then possible to discuss the long-term mortality experience of the London middle classes on the basis of the information in Table 3.14 and Fig. 3.1. Those who were born in Elizabethan and Jacobean times and became citizens of London had a very reasonable chance of living into their fifties, and nearly half of them might expect to live to a hypothetical retirement age of sixty. But then, in the reign of Charles I, the chances of children destined to become London citizens deteriorated very seriously, so that less than half reached the age of fifty and less than a third reached the age of sixty. From the Commonwealth onwards matters improved and, by the reign of George I, had improved very considerably. Now, over three-quarters could expect to reach the age of fifty and well over half might expect to reach the age of sixty. Boyd's data run out at this point, but the middle-class death rates presented in Fig. 3.1 suggest that the improvement was continued and that a middle-class Londoner born in the reign of George II would have very good life chances indeed for a man living in the high-mortality metropolis of a pre-industrial state. Support for these general propositions comes from parallel studies. The work of Wrigley and Schofield presents very much the same long-term cycle of mortality experience for England as a whole, though without the rather dramatic improvements for the eighteenth century shown here.[29] Hollingsworth's study of the demography of the English peerage does however show that another privileged group in English society shared the same very strong improvements in life expectancy in the eighteenth century as shown here for middle-class Londoners.[30] Various reasons can be suggested for this

[29] E. A. Wrigley and R. S. Schofield, *The Population History of England, 1541–1871: A Reconstruction* (London, 1981).
[30] T. H. Hollingsworth, 'The Demography of the British Peerage', supplement to *Population Studies* 18 (1964), 56. Expectation of life for males aged 25 increased from 25.6 for those born 1650–74 to 37.1 for those born 1775–99.

striking upturn in mortality chances, apart from factors likely to affect the
population as a whole such as the changing incidence and virulence of
particular diseases. General environmental factors are likely to be important,
such as greater cleanliness in street, house, clothing and person, and more
balanced diets. Smallpox inoculation has had much claimed for it, while
a recent article suggests that access to better nursing was an important
factor in preventing more privileged groups from succumbing to diseases
which we today would consider to be fairly trivial.[31] But, whatever the
reason, the fact of greater life expectancy seems to be certain.

When one considers the strong and intuitively obvious relationship
between age at death and personal accumulation which was demonstrated
earlier in this chapter, the implications of the mortality cycle discussed
above are quite interesting. One begins to suspect that one good reason for
the apparent wealth, enterprise and general exuberance of Elizabethan and
Jacobean London was that the more privileged members of the citizen class
were living long enough to accumulate large personal fortunes. Richard
Grassby suggested that, when inflation is taken into account, the fortunes
of London freemen in the period 1586–1614 were as high as, if not higher
than, those of the early Restoration period.[32] This fact would have
surprised Sir Josiah Child, but need not surprise us when we consider that
it was not easy for the individual businessman to translate undoubted
economic growth into massive accumulation if God chose to strike him
down in his prime.

For the eighteenth century, the implications are greater still, since the
middle classes were living even longer than they had in Elizabethan times.
Because they lived longer, they accumulated more and were more likely
to be able to transfer their capital to their heirs when they were adults
rather than children. Since the children of eighteenth-century businessmen
were more likely to follow their fathers in a business career, this meant
that there was a cumulative increase in the wealth of the business
community. Further implications follow from the probability that older
businessmen do not behave the same as younger businessmen. It seems
probable that older men will invest more of their capital outside their
immediate businesses and will indeed tend to play a rentier role in the
business world. If this is true, then more older businessmen will mean more
investment. It also seems probable that the older and richer the individual
member of the middle class, the more absolutely he will spend both on his
day-to-day living expenses and on the durable possessions with which he

---

[31] Stephen J. Kunitz, 'Speculations on the European Mortality Decline', *Economic History
Review*, 2nd Series 36 (1983), 349–64; see also P. Razzell, *The Conquest of Smallpox*
(Firle, Sussex, 1977).
[32] 'Business Wealth', p. 225.

graced his dwelling house. If this is true, then more older businessmen will mean more consumption.[33]

What do we discover when we read about the eighteenth century? We find that the London business community was becoming increasingly wealthy, that something called a financial revolution was taking place and that a new consumer society was being created, overwhelmingly composed of members of the middle classes.[34] Many writers have suggested many reasons for these developments. Here it is only necessary to conclude that one important and hitherto neglected factor may be that the members of the London business community were living ten or twenty years longer than their grandfathers.

[33] I hope to establish both propositions relating to investment and consumption, using the same sample, in my forthcoming book, *The Middling Sort of People*.

[34] P. G. M. Dickson, *The Financial Revolution in England* (London, 1967); Neil McKendrick, John Brewer and J. H. Plumb, *The Birth of a Consumer Society: The Commercialization of Eighteenth-Century England* (London, 1982).

4

The use and abuse of credit in eighteenth-century
England*

JULIAN HOPPIT

It is a commonplace that in eighteenth-century England all businessmen
made frequent use of credit. The financial underpinning of economic
activity at the time has increasingly been seen in terms of its widespread
use. It was business historians, such as Professor Ashton, who first stressed
its significance.[1] The rather atomized picture of credit generated by
business histories gradually became more organized, partly to qualify the
insistence of both Lewis and Rostow that a rapid expansion of fixed capital
formation was a central feature of the growth process.[2] As Crouzet pointed
out, 'This new view of the capital structure of eighteenth-century business
leads us to reconsider the problem of financing industry, this time
emphasizing the importance of *trade credit* (or book debt).'[3] Such borrowing
and lending often took place within well-established lines, so that by 1800
something approaching a system of credit can be said to have existed.[4]
Recent work has confirmed that many firms had more of their assets tied
up in credit than in capital and that, particularly in the second half of the
century, in many areas there existed a developed network for working
capital.[5] So successfully has credit been championed that historians looking

* Neil McKendrick, John Morrill and Brian Outhwaite have generously read and commented
  on a draft of this chapter.
[1] T. S. Ashton, *An Eighteenth-Century Industrialist: Peter Stubs of Warrington 1756–1806*
  (Manchester, 1939), ch. 8.
[2] W. A. Lewis, *The Theory of Economic Growth* (London, 1955), ch. 5; W. W. Rostow, *The
  Stages of Economic Growth* (Cambridge, 1960), ch. 4.
[3] F. Crouzet, 'Editor's Introduction' to his (ed.), *Capital Formation in the Industrial Revolution*
  (London, 1972), p. 44, and in the same volume, S. Pollard, 'Fixed Capital in the Industrial
  Revolution in Britain', pp. 145–61. See also P. Mathias, 'Capital, Credit and Enterprise
  in the Industrial Revolution' reprinted in his *The Transformation of England* (London,
  1979), pp. 88–115.
[4] The complexities of such networks have been most forcefully described by B. L. Anderson,
  'Money and the Structure of Credit in the Eighteenth Century', *Business History* 12
  (1970), 85–101, and 'Provincial Aspects of the Financial Revolution of the Eighteenth
  Century', *Business History* 11 (1969), 11–22.
[5] P. Hudson, 'The Role of Banks in the Finance of the West Yorkshire Wool Textile
  Industry, c. 1780–1850', *Business History Review* 55 (1981), 379–402; M. Miles, 'The
  Money Market in the Early Industrial Revolution: The Evidence from West Riding
  Attornies, c. 1750–1800', *Business History* 23 (1981), 127–46; L. Weatherill, 'Capital

at other aspects of eighteenth-century England have also stressed its significance. Professor Pocock, for example, has partly described the early eighteenth-century debate between Court and Country ideologies in terms of their discussion of it.[6] And Professor Brewer has taken it further, from the history of political ideas to the history of politics itself, arguing that the politicization of shopkeepers and tradesmen in mid-century was helped by their struggles with credit.[7]

It is not the intention of this chapter to argue that this attention has been misplaced. Rather it is to suggest that credit had negative as well as positive features, and that both must be considered when its role is being assessed. Credit cannot be presented as an homogeneous factor to be worked into growth models – it took too many different forms, was resorted to for a wide range of functions and, in many cases, is not measurable.[8] Most businessmen had to use it, but found it difficult always to use it successfully. Because of the conditions attached to it credit could hurt those who tried to wield its power. What I want to do in this chapter is simply to explore some of the risks attached to it. This is done first by looking at the ways contemporaries judged its difficulties, then by demonstrating those problems in practice by looking at some specific uses of it, before finally looking at the ways in which creditors and debtors tried to settle their differences when they did have problems.

Trade credit was simply the result of borrowing and lending on largely personal security. Such loans might generate interest, as when bills of exchange were used, or they might not, as was often the case with book debts. Central to the relationship between the debtor and the creditor was mutual confidence. Because the loan was backed by nothing but personal security, which is just the belief that it will be repaid, '*Confidence*... is the soul and essence of credit.'[9] Confidence is easily created and just as easily destroyed. This meant that credit was tied to both economic and personal expectations. It was bound hand and foot to risk-taking and speculation. Logically then there is nothing surprising about its growing importance in

and Credit in the Pottery Industry Before 1770', *Business History* 24 (1982), 243–58; J. M. Price, *Capital and Credit in British Overseas Trade: The View from the Chesapeake, 1700–1776* (Cambridge, Mass., 1980).

[6] J. G. A. Pocock, *The Machiavellian Moment* (Princeton, 1975), ch. 13.

[7] J. Brewer, 'Commercialization and Politics', in N. McKendrick, J. Brewer and J. H. Plumb, *The Birth of a Consumer Society: The Commercialization of Eighteenth-Century England* (London, 1982), especially pp. 203–16.

[8] This presumably explains why it is all but ignored by those adopting a quantitative approach to the eighteenth-century economy. See the lack of discussion of it in R. Floud and D. N. McCloskey (eds.), *The Economic History of Britain since 1700*, 2 vols. (Cambridge, 1981), vol. I.

[9] J. Steuart, *An Inquiry into the Principles of Political Oeconomy* (1767), ed. A. S. Skinner, 2 vols. (Edinburgh, 1966), vol. II, p. 442.

eighteenth-century England, for the expanding economy provided a fertile seedbed for its creation.

Businessmen use credit when they lack the funds to make payments immediately. In the eighteenth century that inability arose from at least two main difficulties: the lack of sufficient cash and the delays in production and distribution that resulted partly from imperfect communications. Minted coins were always being melted down, exported and counterfeited.[10] Consequently, a reliable currency in small and large denominations was lacking right through the century. Trade tokens helped fill the gap at one end, bills of exchange at the other. But bills (and other paper instruments) were also used because they helped cover the varying speed with which returns on expenditure could be expected. Poor and slow transport meant that money for goods sent to a market would return only after a delay – which might amount to weeks or months for the home trade, and months or years for overseas ones. Moreover, the quality of communications and the state of the markets were very variable so that the speed of returns was uncertain and unpredictable. Credit was vital in allowing businessmen to cope with this, enabling them to balance income with expenditure. Every businessman in the eighteenth century was beset by such variability, just as they all lacked ready access to a pool of cash. In such circumstances the ubiquity of credit was hardly surprising. Trade credit was crucial to the functioning of exchange and spun a vast web over the economy. At any one time any business owed and was owed money for goods caught up in the process of exchange. All businessmen were creditors and all businessmen were debtors.

If the extent of credit is clear, its contribution to economic life is not. Businessmen struggled less to find credit than to use it well. Contemporary observers were struck by three interlocking problems when it was being used extensively: overtrading, synchronization and interdependency. These contemporary criticisms can be described briefly before testing them by looking at the problems some businessmen got into in their credit dealings.

Overtrading was the result of too much credit being used in relation to the capital base of the business. William Petty believed that traders should not rise 'into debt above halfe the stock they set up with'.[11] Quite where the line should be drawn naturally varied from business to business and

[10] T. S. Ashton. *An Economic History of England: The Eighteenth Century* (London, 1955), ch. 6; J. Styles, '"Our Traitorous Money Makers": The Yorkshire Coiners and the Law, 1760–83', in J. Brewer and J. Styles (eds.), *An Ungovernable People* (London, 1980), pp. 172–249.
[11] *The Petty Papers, some Unpublished Writings of Sir William Petty*, ed. Marquis of Lansdowne, 2 vols. (London, 1927), vol. I, p. 249.

from trade to trade. But Defoe was in no doubt that 'Credit is a Gulph which is easie to fall into, hard to get out of.'[12] Because it was relatively easily created many businesses expanded quickly on the basis of it. But this would only work if the pace of the returns from the investments that it was tied to was sufficiently swift to repay the advances on time. Having become deeply enmeshed in such networks any businessman was confronted by the problems of trying to synchronize the payments being made to him as a creditor with those he had to make as a debtor. The more elaborate his usage, in terms of the numbers, amounts and distances involved, then the more difficult this became.[13] It might take only a small incident to upset the timing. Yet that incident might have had little to do with the individual who came under pressure because of these difficulties of synchronization. The acute interdependence of businessmen in such dealings made any individual's chances at least partially dependent on the success of those both within and without his immediate circle of trading contacts. Interdependence is of course a timeless fact of business life, but it was particularly damaging in the eighteenth century because of the articulation of many loans by bills of exchange. Successive endorsements of bills and the centrality of trust and confidence meant that the collapse of one businessman could bring down many others like a line of dominoes toppling over. Switching metaphors, contemporaries saw credit as a chain in which businessmen were the links 'and where there is one bad Link, that will occasion a Separation and Breaking of the Whole'.[14]

In times of expansion credit provided the bedrock for the growth of a business. In times of stagnation and decay that bedrock turned to a quicksand, through which only the fortunate and the skilled could pick their way. While these problems were ever present they were most visible when the system suffered strain and dislocation. At such moments the difficulties of overtrading, synchronization and interdependence affected both healthy and struggling businesses.[15] All three maladies can be clearly seen by looking at the economic difficulties of 1788.

Between 1770 and 1800 England suffered five financial crises, all

---

[12] D. Defoe, *Defoe's Review*, reprinted in 23 books (New York, 1939), book 6, vol. III, no. 7. The Quakers cautioned against overtrading; see *Extracts from the Minutes and Advices of the Yearly Meeting of the Friends Held in London* (London, 1783), p. 247.

[13] See M. Postlethwayt, *The Universal Dictionary of Trade and Commerce*, 2 vols. (London, 1757), vol. I, p. 574; J. Lacy, *Letter* (London, 1730?), p. 4.

[14] *A Speech Without Doors, in Behalf of an Insolvent Debtor in the Fleet Prison* (London, 1731?), p. 13. Also, D. Defoe, *The Complete English Tradesman* (London, 1726), p. 198; Defoe, *Defoe's Review*, book 6, vol. III, no. 7; W. Playfair, *Better Prospects to the Merchants and Manufacturers of Great Britain* (London, 1793), p. 6.

[15] See Ashton, *An Eighteenth-Century Industrialist*, ch. 8; T. S. Willan, *An Eighteenth-Century Shopkeeper: Abraham Dent of Kirkby Stephen* (Manchester, 1979), ch. 7.

marked by a sudden and pronounced surge in the numbers of bankrupts.[16]
The year 1788 saw one of those crises. Between 1783 and 1787 an
average of 510 businesses went bankrupt each year. But in 1788 the
number was 705, a rise of 38 per cent.[17] It was the textile sector and more
especially the expanding cotton and linen industries that were particularly
badly hit. Between 1783 and 1787 some 22 per cent of bankrupts came
from the textile sector, yet in 1788 the proportion was up to 29.7 per cent.
The crisis particularly involved the emerging Lancashire cotton industry
and its trading connections in the capital. In 1788 a little over 20 per cent
of textile bankrupts came from Lancashire compared with just 10.7 per
cent in the previous five years; the proportions from the metropolis were
41.2 and 34.3 per cent respectively. Why was the crisis particularly located
in these areas?

In mid-1787 there were already storm clouds gathering on the horizon.
From London the Saltes wrote to Samuel Oldknow that 'the times and the
Trade are both very precarious & no man has much encouragement to
venture far. We think they will be worse. Everything is over done & in
consequence every article sold for loss or no Profit.'[18] But this in itself did
not amount to a crisis. It was a depression, probably caused by the
over-expansion of the cotton industry in the mid-1780s following a
speculative impetus stimulated by the ending of the American War and
the expiration of Arkwright's patent.[19] By 1787 the supply of cotton goods
had outrun the growth of demand. Producers were forced to cut both
output and prices and wait for the situation to improve. It may have begun
to do so by early 1788, but in April and May 1788 the depression turned
into a crisis. On 2 May *The Times* printed the first of many reports about
the crisis, noting the destructive rumours which questioned the solvency
of a major firm on Cheapside. As Steele had warned, 'Credit is undone in
whispers.'[20] Bankruptcy proceedings were soon started against 'a capital
house in the Manchester branch, and dockets are struck against some

[16] J. Hoppit, 'Financial Crises in Eighteenth-Century England', *Economic History Review*, 2nd
Series 39 (1986), 39–53; T. S. Ashton, *Economic Fluctuations in England, 1700–1800*
(Oxford, 1959), ch. 5.
[17] Figures are drawn from the *London Gazette*. The full data are presented in J. Hoppit, 'Risk
and Failure in English Industry, c. 1700–1800' (University of Cambridge Ph.D. thesis,
1984), p. 240.
[18] Quoted in G. Unwin, *Samuel Oldknow and the Arkwrights* (Manchester, 1924), p. 90. See
also the letters from Richard Arkwright, Junior, of 21 June 1787 on p. 93 and from
Oldknow to his brother in October 1787 on p. 97. See also Gloucester Record Office,
D149/F161, 17 April 1788, for a similar appraisal of the demand for woollen cloth.
[19] P. Colquhoun, *An Important Crisis in the Calico and Muslin Manufactory in Great Britain,
Explained* (London, 1788), pp. 2–3; S. D. Chapman, *The Early Factory Masters* (Newton
Abbot, 1967), pp. 72–124; M. M. Edwards, *The Growth of the British Cotton Trade
1780–1815* (Manchester, 1967), pp. 10–12, 40–2; *Manchester Mercury*, 20 May 1788,
p. 4.   [20] *The Spectator*, ed. D. F. Bond, 5 vols. (Oxford, 1965), vol. II, p. 350.

others'.[21] Manchester itself was soon 'in the utmost confusion'.[22] In July Samuel Salte complained that 'We really hardly know who to trust. Houses are stopping here that were never suspected & we hear the same complaints from different parts of the country.'[23]

Early in May 1788 the *London Chronicle* suggested that the crisis had been caused by the abuse of the East India Company's monopoly, by speculation arising from the commercial treaty with France in 1786 and, finally, by the 'common but pernicious expedient of drawing and re-drawing'.[24] The first two causes were important but it is the last which is most significant in relation to the problems of credit in the eighteenth century.[25] It was unequivocally true that much of the expansion down to 1787 and 1788 had been so funded. Bills of exchange and accommodation notes had been written out too freely and the volume and costs of their creation were too great to be supported by the actual returns being generated by trade. In short, there was simple overtrading.[26] It was in these conditions that the problems of synchronizing credit and avoiding the domino effect were greatest – problems clearly illustrated by looking at a couple of case studies.

At the height of the storm in May 1788 the partnership of Abraham Wilkinson and George Cooke, merchants trading from Wallbrook in the City of London, went bankrupt. They had begun in business on 1 May 1783 looking to trade with newly independent America – Wilkinson put up £1500 and Cooke £2830.[27] But, as they discovered, many others had had the same idea and between 1783 and 1785 their market in Carolina was generally over-stocked with goods from Europe. There was a widespread misjudgment of how many goods America could soak up.[28] With their troubles mounting Wilkinson and Cooke were left with two options: they could withdraw, still solvent, and accept substantial losses, or they could press on, raising additional funds to tide them over what they hoped was just a short-term difficulty. They pressed on. 'About the beginning of 1785', George Cooke told the bankruptcy commissioners, 'Several large cargoes shipped to Mr Wilkinson at Charlestown becoming due about this time I found it necessary to apply to my friends for assistance to enable

---

[21] *The Times*, 3 May 1788, p. 2. A docket initiated bankruptcy proceedings against a firm.
[22] *London Chronicle*, 8–10 May 1788, p. 450.
[23] Unwin, *Samuel Oldknow and the Arkwrights*, p. 102.   [24] 1–3 May 1788, p. 426.
[25] On those first two causes see Unwin, *Samuel Oldknow and the Arkwrights*, p. 96; Edwards, *The Growth of the British Cotton Trade 1780–1815*, p. 11; Colquhoun, *An Important Crisis in the Calico and Muslin Manufactory in Great Britain, Explained*, p. 11.
[26] L. S. Pressnell, *Country Banking in the Industrial Revolution* (Oxford, 1956), pp. 453–5.
[27] This capitalization was low, perhaps very low, by the standards of the time. J. M. Price, *Capital and Credit in British Overseas Trade: The View from the Chesapeake, 1700–1776*, ch. 3.
[28] On 11 May 1785 a merchant in Philadelphia wrote that 'Trade in general is still continuing dull.' P[ublic] R[ecord] O[ffice], C105/19.

me to keep up my payments punctually.' He took on board more and more credit. But this had unforeseen consequences because 'this first introduced a circulation of paper which I have never since been able to get rid of'.[29]

Cooke raised the bulk of the credit in London. Of the 108 creditors who proved debts against the firm, eighty-six (79.6 per cent) came from the capital, accounting for 89.3 per cent of the total debts of £121629. Yet the role of the provincial creditors may have been disproportionately important because all but three of them came from textile-producing areas and, indeed, the majority of them were directly involved in the developing but, in 1788, troubled Lancashire cotton industry. It may well have been the calico printer from Bury owed £1568, or the merchant from Liverpool owed £2266, who chased repayment most vigorously, bringing about the final collapse of the firm. What is clear is that with a glutted market Wilkinson and Cooke were overtrading; by taking on board so much credit a losing trade was turned into a disastrously unprofitable one. It was the ease with which they had raised it after 1785 that created the enormity of their failure. In June 1795, when the bankruptcy proceedings were brought to an end, they had repaid creditors just one shilling and sixpence in the pound on all their debts. Many creditors would have been very shaken by this.

Creating credit in the early part of the Industrial Revolution was often straightforward because of the ease with which bills of exchange could be written out, accommodation notes fabricated, fictitious bills produced and personal security established. It was often possible to manufacture short-term loans by drawing and redrawing bills or by making them out with non-existent names on them. These techniques had frequently been used in the expansion leading to the crisis of 1772 and once again became commonplace in 1787 and early 1788.[30] Many businesses were involved in this abuse of credit in 1788, but perhaps the most significant was the firm of Livesey, Hargreaves, Anstie, Smith & Hall, calico printers and bankers from Clitheroe and London.[31] They failed in late April 1788 and were in the *London Gazette* in June. Their bills were soon contested in the courts and many were found to be fraudulent.[32]

[29] P.R.O., B3/5162. All details about the firm are drawn from this source.
[30] For 1772 see A. Smith, *An Inquiry into the Nature and Causes of the Wealth of Nations*, ed. E. Cannan (Chicago, 1976), vol. I, pp. 328–37; *London Chronicle*, 28–30 April 1772, p. 412; 2–4 July 1772, p. 12: 16–18 July 1772, p. 58; Daniel Defoe remarked on these practices as well, *Defoe's Review*, book 6, vol. III, no. 22. Attempts had been made earlier in the century to prevent the forgery of bills and their misusage. In 1733 7 Geo. II. c. 22, tried to stop forgery and in 1775 (15 Geo. III, c. 51) and 1777 (17 Geo. III, c. 30) there were attempts to stop them being created for small amounts. J. M. Holden, *The History of Negotiable Instruments in English Law* (London, 1955), p. 142.
[31] Pressnell, *Country Banking in the Industrial Revolution*, pp. 91–2, 454–5.
[32] *Ibid.*: J. K. Horsefield, 'Gibson and Johnson: A Forgotten *Cause Célèbre*', *Economica* 10 (1943), 233–7; P.R.O., B3/1847, fo. 180.

With the collapse of Livesey & Co. came many others. Gibson & Johnson, bankers in the City who discounted Livesey & Co. bills, stopped payment on 1 May.[33] Attempts were made by Richard Arkwright and others to keep both firms afloat, since if they sank many others would be pulled under with them.[34] But despite these efforts both firms went bankrupt. Gibson & Johnson failed with debts up to perhaps £300000 (it is difficult to be accurate here because of the fraudulent bills they handled). If all the debts claimed and proved against them are considered, they had 198 creditors who were owed on average £1500. By February 1800 they had all been repaid thirteen shillings in the pound which, given the considerable expenses involved in the commission, was a very good return.[35] But only the strong could support the considerable delays in repayment that the bankruptcy created. As late as the summer of 1794 only five shillings and eight pence in the pound had been repaid.[36] Richard Arkwright was better able than most to put up with the discomfort, but even he must have been very worried given that he was owed £32534.[37] Others, with fewer reserves, were in an even less happy position. A factor from Cateaton Street had to prove his debt against Gibson & Johnson from the Fleet Prison, where he had presumably been imprisoned for debt.[38] A clothier from Devizes proved a debt for over £2000 but was himself already a bankrupt.[39] With so many creditors involved, and with so many large sums tied up, the fall of Gibson & Johnson felled many others. The complexity of the credit networks centring on the bank ensured the effective transmission of disturbances to parts of the economy that were far removed from the tornado that hit the cotton trade in the spring of 1788.[40]

In various ways the difficulties of 1788 have thrown up evidence which points to the problems of overdependence on credit. Unless the volume of credit given and taken was kept under control then overtrading, the poor synchronization of credit and debt, and a liability to the impact of secondhand collapses might all be experienced. Of course, these issues were most acute in crisis years but they were constant problems, part of the fabric of enterprise at the time. Why did some businessmen make too much use of such devices? Contemporaries advanced three main reasons: because of the youth of the businessman, because of risk-taking and speculation, and because creditors and debtors did not know one another

---

[33] P.R.O., B3/1847.
[34] *The Times*, 5 May 1788, pp. 1–2. James Jenkins went to the meeting of the creditors of both firms 'on behalf of my friend Rutt, who suffered severely by their [Livesey & Company] failure'. London Friends Meeting House, J. Jenkins MS, 'Records and Recollections 1761 to 1821', fos. 281–2.
[35] P.R.O., B3/1845–8.   [36] P.R.O., B3/1847.   [37] P.R.O., B3/1845.
[38] P.R.O., B3/1847.   [39] P.R.O., B3/1848.
[40] On the links between Gibson & Johnson and other country banks see Pressnell, *Country Banking in the Industrial Revolution*, pp. 436–7. They were also heavily indebted to other London banks who, in turn, would have had country connections.

well enough. These can be looked at before turning to see how the risks of credit were further heightened by the laws that existed to settle differences between creditors and debtors.

Young men setting out into the business world usually had restricted amounts of capital at their disposal. Their parents would have provided some, and friends and relations may have lent more. But these were only occasionally substantial sources of funds. Borrowing on credit was an alternative, enabling the young businessman to do more trading or manufacturing than would otherwise have been the case. The threshold of entry into business was thereby lowered.[41] More than this though, with their lack of experience young men were liable to be too attracted by business opportunities and unable to assess accurately the risks involved. As Adam Smith saw, 'The contempt of risk and the presumptuous hope of success, are in no period of life more active than at the age at which young people chuse their professions. How little the fear of misfortune is then capable of balancing the hope of good luck.'[42]

It was not just the young and inexperienced who misjudged opportunities. As the eighteenth-century economy grew, so business opportunities gradually multiplied. But to businessmen trying to seize these possibilities they often emerged suddenly rather than slowly – with the end of a war, the expiration of a patent, recovery from depression, a shift in demand following a good harvest, or a change in fashion. These openings could not be accurately predicted and the finances accumulated beforehand to enable a rapid response to their appearance. Credit allowed businessmen to stretch out and grasp what they hoped were golden opportunities. In a very real sense it was venture capital. Risk-taking and speculation were often only possible with an expansion of credit relative to the capital base. In 1718 London merchants were sternly warned from the pulpit that 'it is this *hastening to be Rich*, and endeavouring to make great Fortunes in a little time, by most immoderate and excessive Gains, that makes a few Men become the Ruine of many Families, and contract so great Debts, that it is easier to resolve never to pay *any*, than to think of satisfying *all*'.[43] The economy could not have grown had businessmen not speculated and taken risks. But it is possible that because credit could be easily acquired there was often an incomplete appreciation of the scale of the problems to be overcome.

It was not just the debtor who was to blame in such circumstances. The

[41] *The Remembrancer: Addressed to Young Men in Business. Shewing how they may Attain the way to be Rich and Respectable* (London, 1794), pp. 5–7.
[42] *An Inquiry into the Nature and Causes of the Wealth of Nations*, vol. I, p. 122. Also, *The Management and Oeconomy of Trade, or the Young Traders Guide* (London, 1783), pp. 19–21.
[43] W. Fleetwood, *The Justice of Paying Debts. A Sermon Preach'd in the City* (London, 1718), p. 12. On similar lines see *Defoe's Review*, book 6, vol. III, no. 7.

creditor provided loans in the hope of expanding his trade and increasing his profits. Just as the debtor had to find credit quickly when opportunities dawned, so creditors had to find debtors. In those circumstances there would have been less care taken over the choice of borrower. In theory, 'In giving credit, the capital or means of the person credited should be first considered; next to that is to be considered the purpose for which the credit is wanted; and last of all, the character of the man to whom it is to be given.'[44] Again, 'every Man ought to know the Person with whom he deals, or to whom he gives Credit'.[45] Adam Smith, incisive as ever, felt that creditors should look at the 'fortune, probity, and prudence' of prospective debtors.[46] But when businessmen were in a rush these maxims could not always be religiously observed. In other words, at certain times personal security, which was the only security available in trade credit, was not taken. Loans were unsecured and, therefore, very risky. Loans would be given to little-known characters, usually because they were too far away to allow a quick assessment of their credit worthiness. The problem of distance was obviously greatest in overseas trade, and in the eighteenth century this was most often the case in the rapidly expanding colonial trade.[47] But not only was credit being given to unknown faces and abilities, it was also being given 'long' – and long credit was especially difficult to control.[48]

Vital though trade credit was in the eighteenth century it was always possible for debtors to fail to meet their obligations. Creditors were well aware of just how easy it was for a good debt to become a dubious or a bad one. As a further example of the problems and risks of credit it is important to look at the ways creditors sought to prevent the appearance of such assets in their ledgers. In particular this involves an examination of the laws creditors had at their disposal. Persuasion and bullying were obvious starting-points for creditors demanding repayment, but words alone were not enough. Creditors needed the weight of the law to warn against the reckless contraction of debts, to enforce repayment from a reluctant debtor or to distribute the assets of an insolvent one. But in the eighteenth century creditors found that the laws they might call upon were often inadequate, confused and chaotic. Many of the uncertainties of credit were born of the failure of the law to provide acceptable powers for

---

[44] J. Montefiore, *A Commercial Dictionary: Containing the Present State of the Mercantile Law, Practice and Custom* (London, 1803), under 'Credit'.

[45] *The Case of Bankrupts and Insolvents Considered* (London, 1734), p. 42.

[46] *An Inquiry into the Nature and Causes of the Wealth of Nations*, vol. I, p. 118.

[47] In 1731 5 Geo. II, c. 7, tried to improve the situation with regard to America, though problems remained.

[48] J. Vanderlint, *Money Answers all Things: Or, an Essay to Make Money Sufficiently Plentiful Amongst all Ranks of People* (London, 1734), p. 66.

creditors and debtors to settle their differences. Inevitably, it was weakened because of the worries this caused.

Creditors and debtors battled out their differences therefore not only by tugging at the money that bound them together but by trying to alter or avoid the laws that existed to mediate that struggle. While creditors sought access to as much power as possible over the person or possessions of the debtor, the debtor sought as much freedom and independence of action as possible, either because he had no money at all or because if left unmolested he would in time repay in full. Logical arguments could be mounted to support the demands of both debtors and creditors.

There was never any question that creditors deserved the protection and power of the law to help secure their assets, especially from fraudulent and dishonourable debtors. It was often said that if the laws were inadequate in the eyes of creditors then not only would they charge more for their loans but they would also give less of them.[49] Three aspects concerned them: did the law provide enough power to enforce repayment from a debtor who was able but unwilling to do so; did the law provide a fair means of dealing with the estate of an insolvent debtor; and were the processes cheap enough? In reclaiming debts economies of scale operated, which meant that small debts were especially troublesome. Indeed it was in the areas of small and medium-sized debts that there was most dispute over the law.

From the 1670s onwards there was constant pressure exerted by creditors for the creation of more summary and cheaper means of redress for such small debts. Creditors called for what were known as Courts of Conscience or Courts of Requests. Such local courts offered creditors cheap and readily available means of enforcing repayment from debtors owing less than forty shillings. Creditors saw such courts as offering a vital support for the credit given out to retail customers or domestic outworkers.[50] London had the first Court of Conscience as early as Henry VIII's reign, but it was not until 1689 that the second appeared and it was to be another fifty years before they began to spread generally through the country.[51] Although businessmen vigorously demanded these courts from the late seventeenth century their calls were mostly repulsed until the 1740s.

In February 1674 the House of Commons gave leave to bring in a bill for a Court of Conscience for Southwark. In April permission was extended

---

[49] Guildhall Library, MS 14973; *Select Committee on the Insolvent Debtor Acts, Parliamentary Papers*, IV (1816), pp. 360, 365, 367–8, 374, 430, 466.

[50] Daniel Defoe noted the dangers of such credit, *Defoe's Review*, book 6, vol. III, no. 9. Gentlemen were notoriously tardy in repaying shopkeepers and wholesalers. See J. Brewer, 'English Radicalism in the Age of George III', in J. G. A. Pocock (ed.), *Three British Revolutions: 1641, 1688, 1776* (Princeton, 1980), p. 348.

[51] W. H. D. Winder, 'The Courts of Requests', *Law Quarterly Review* 52 (1936), 369–94.

for a bill that created a court or courts over London as a whole.[52] This attempt, which got nowhere,was frequently repeated down to the accession of Anne. Exeter and York also pushed for courts, but all of these efforts failed. Only Bristol and Gloucester, Newcastle and Norwich succeeded, perhaps because they contented themselves with private acts.[53] Despite the considerable head of steam built up by creditors and their champions there was insufficient force to overcome local and legal opposition. In 1675 the proposal had been rebuffed, for example, by the opinion that Courts of Conscience contravened common law – because there were no juries and the adjudicators were untrained – and social hierarchy – a court would compel 'persons of quality to submit for small debts to a company of shopkeepers'.[54] It was also true that London and other towns had ancient courts that might provide the same services as the proposed Courts of Conscience. Until 1748 the House of Lords was usually hostile to the proposals for Courts of Conscience because it was felt that they drove nails into the coffins of ancient local courts such as the Hundred or County Courts.[55]

By the middle of the eighteenth century resistance was being overcome, not because more sophisticated arguments were being used but because the problems of small-scale credit had grown, despite the attempts by Parliament to improve the security of such credit in other ways. In 1696 a statute suppressed sanctuaries and privileged places in London, places where debtors escaped both their creditors and the rule of law. It was popularly held that creditors could not use the law against debtors in such areas.[56] The debtors claimed, when the sanctuaries came under renewed assault, that such places were essential 'to avoid perishing in Prison' at the whim of a creditor.[57] Such arguments had some force, so that although sanctuaries were attacked by two more statutes Parliament limited the

---

[52] C[ommons] J[ournal] IX (1667–87), 312, 317.
[53] On these attempts see *C.J.* IX (1667–87), 361, 396, 397, 731; X (1688–93), 53, 77, 85, 274, 277, 356, 545, 780; XIII (1699–1702), 7, 10–11, 36, 46, 79, 127; Guildhall Library, MS 3778a/3; *Reasons Humbly Offered in Favour of the Bill (now Depending in Parliament) for the More Easy and Speedy Recovery of Small Debts, within the City of London, and the Liberties Thereof* (London, 1689?).
[54] *Calendar of State Papers Domestic, 1675–1676* (1907), p. 86. William Blackstone agreed on the point of law: *Commentaries on the Laws of England*, 4 vols. (Oxford, 1766–9), vol. III, pp. 81–2.
[55] W. S. Holdworth, *A History of English Law*, 3rd edn, 17 vols. (London, 1924–72), vol. I, pp. 190–1; *Lords Journal* XXV (1736–41), 411.
[56] 8 & 9 Will. III, c. 27; E. P. Thompson, *Whigs and Hunters* (London, 1975), pp. 248–9. Defoe thought there were 20000 shelterers in sanctuaries in 1709, *Defoe's Review*, book 13, vol. V, no. 145.
[57] *The Deplorable Case of the Poor People in the Mint* (London, 1722?). Even Quakers sometimes used sanctuaries, see London Friends Meeting House, MS 'The Third Book of the Monthly Meeting of the People Call'd Quakers at Horselydown', entries for 9 July 1691 and 20 October 1691.

powers of creditors to put small debtors in prison.[58] It was hoped that a new balance was being struck: debtors could no longer avoid the law but the law was no longer as harsh as it had been. In a sense this arrangement can be viewed as an alternative to Courts of Conscience. But in fact it failed not only to deal with the principal complaint that creditors had of the law – its cost – but also, given the survival of some sanctuaries, in its aims. The continued attractiveness of Courts of Conscience is clearly evidenced by the expansion of personnel at the London court in 1740.[59]

Despite the best efforts of Parliament, by the middle of the eighteenth century Courts of Conscience appeared to be the only means of tackling an ever-growing problem. Resistance crumbled under the pressure of reality. All of London, the main ports and manufacturing areas soon had courts. These quickly proved their worth.[60] Both Birmingham and Liverpool were successful in 1751. In the 1770s the main textile-producing areas were provided for – Lancashire, the West Riding and Exeter. All in all, between 1748 and 1800 some fifty-one statutes were passed establishing or modifying Courts of Conscience. Slowly then, creditors got what they had long wanted. But until they did they felt less secure in giving out credit for small amounts.

Creditors and debtors battled out their differences over greater sums as well. In 1700 the powers available to creditors who believed their debtors were not bankrupt were extensive. A creditor could chase a debtor either by proving his debt and getting the debtor thrown into jail (*mesne process*), or he could go to court and get judgment on the property of the debtor. The second and more popular course of action saw the debtor imprisoned only if even after the court's decision he refused to repay. If he were without funds then such might be his fate.[61] The Dickensian picture of Marshalsea was common enough in the eighteenth century.[62] Creditors found it relatively easy to threaten their debtors with the prospect or reality of imprisonment. To their way of thinking it was a lever or deterrent ultimately available to ensure the honest contracting of debts and their repayment. But creditors could not always know if debtors had the money

---

[58] 9 Geo. I, c. 28; 11 Geo. I, c. 22; 12 Geo. I, c. 29.

[59] 14 Geo. II, c. 10, allowed the number of beadles serving the Court of Request at the Guildhall to be linked to the increasing volume of business the court handled.

[60] *Queries Humbly Submitted in Behalf of the Bill for Explaining and Amending the Act for Recovery of Small Debts within the Tower-Hamlets* (London, 1752?).

[61] J. Innes, 'The King's Bench Prison in the Later Eighteenth Century', in Brewer and Styles, *An Ungovernable People*, pp. 251–61; P. J. Lineham, 'The Campaign to Abolish Imprisonment for Debt in England 1750–1840' (University of Canterbury, New Zealand, M.A. thesis, 1974); I. P. H. Duffy, 'Bankruptcy and Insolvency in London in the Late Eighteenth and Early Nineteenth Centuries' (University of Oxford D.Phil. thesis, 1973), ch. 2.

[62] J. Howard, *The State of the Prisons* (Warrington, 1777).

to pay, and throwing them in jail would only increase the unlikelihood of repayment. Unsurprisingly, debtors and their advocates were quick to stress this.[63] Parliament was forced to recognize an old dilemma: creditors had to be well protected, but there was no point in the jails being full of destitute and penniless debtors. Yet though they were prepared to pass legislation to clear the crowded jails every now and then, they were unhappy at the prospect of treating these debtors – who usually owed less than £100 – as bankrupts. They feared too great a use of credit at the base of economy and society. Right through the century Parliament assiduously protected established distinctions between small debtors, larger debtors and bankrupts (substantial debtors who were insolvent).

Between 1700 and 1800 Parliament passed thirty-two acts to clear the jails of debtors or to remedy the machinery to do so, a clear indication of the uncertainties of the available legal framework. Creditors may have been able to throw recalcitrant debtors into jail, but as soon as the prisons were full so Parliament emptied them, making little distinction between honest and dishonest debtors. Such a contradiction points to Parliament's indecisive handling of competing interests and a failure to consider the body of laws about indebtedness as a whole. 'The very circumstance of passing an Act of Insolvency [to clear the jails]...proves to a Demonstration, that there is an Error somewhere.'[64] As with the Courts of Conscience, what mattered was not that creditors and debtors disagreed and struggled to pin down or evade one another – that was to be expected – but that creditors had a source of dissatisfaction which they believed increased the cost and decreased the quantity of credit they gave.[65] They certainly felt less secure than they wanted.

In conclusion, it is clear that while credit was ubiquitous in eighteenth-century England it was fraught with difficulties and problems. Because it rested on personal security and confidence it was easily created when the conditions were right. It is hardly surprising then that it came to saturate economic life, lubricating the expanding manufacturing and trading sectors. But precisely because it could be widely used, and precisely because the economy was providing an ever-expanding range of opportunities, there were manifest dangers of it being overused because of the vicious

---

[63] Arguments on the debtors' side had a long heritage by the eighteenth century. See D. Veall, *The Popular Movement for Law Reform 1640–1660* (Oxford, 1970), pp. 145–51; Lineham, 'The Campaign to Abolish Imprisonment for Debt in England 1750–1840'.

[64] A. Grant, *The Public Monitor* (London, 1789), p. 21. For a concise discussion of the issues see J. B. Burgess, *Considerations on the Law of Insolvency, with a Proposal for Reform* (London, 1783), pp. 160–81.

[65] *Select Committee on the Insolvent Debtor Acts*, p. 463; *The Case of the Merchants and Traders in and about the City of London, on Behalf of Themselves and the Traders of the Kingdom* (London, 1707?).

short-term fluctuations of economic life at the time. With credit inextricably linked to confidence it is unsurprising that its availability fluctuated more widely and wildly than actual fluctuations in economic activity. Credit and insecurity went hand in hand (an insecurity heightened by the problems that surrounded the laws dealing with indebtedness). Finally, because of the form that credit took it was very difficult to control in a rational and calculated fashion. Time after time, eighteenth-century observers echoed Davenant's warning that 'Of all beings that have existence only in the minds of men, nothing is more fantastical and nice than Credit; it is never to be forced; it hangs upon opinion; it depends upon our passions of hope and fear; it comes many times unsought for, and often goes away without reason, and when once lost, is hardly to be quite recovered.'[66]

I have shown in this chapter that using credit was risky and difficult in eighteenth-century England. Credit creation in a buoyant economy with savings is not difficult. Using it, when cash is in short supply and delays in exchange plentiful, is to be expected. The issue, rather, is to see how well it was used. From such a perspective its role, while general, was ambiguous. The widespread use of credit in eighteenth-century England can no more be ignored than its widespread misuse and abuse. It was both a cause and an effect, linking into and dependent upon the developing economy which, ultimately, rested on productivity gains. It depended on patterns of income and wealth inequality, propensities to consume, hoard or invest, the nature of emerging opportunities and more. It is well worth bearing in mind Defoe's belief that 'CREDIT is a Consequence, not a Cause; the Effect of a Substance, not a Substance; 'tis the *Sun-shine*, not the Sun.'[67]

[66] C. Davenant, *Discourses on the Public Revenue, and on the Trade of England* (London, 1698), in *The Political and Commercial Works of Charles D'Avenant*, ed. C. Whitworth, 5 vols. (London, 1771), vol. I, p. 151.
[67] D. Defoe, *An Essay upon Publick Credit* (London, 1710), p. 9.

5

Convicts, commerce and sovereignty: the forces behind
the early settlement of Australia

C. H. WILSON

The problem of the origins of modern Australia is one round which
controversy has bubbled for more than three decades. The older school of
Australian historians did not doubt (in the words of W. A. Sinclair) that
'the prime intention was to find a destination for convicts sentenced to
transportation'.[1] Coglan, Shann, Fitzpatrick, O'Brien, Shaw and Manning
Clark were in broad agreement.[2] The wider debate was initiated by
K. M. Dallas, in 1952; it turned on less obvious reasons which may have
motivated the despatch in 1787 of the First Fleet.

Dallas suggested that alongside the shortage of jail space there were
complex economic and strategic reasons for a settlement at Botany Bay.
England needed a new naval base to strengthen the trade routes of her
eastern commercial empire; also a port where naval and merchant ships
could refit and revictual. The China tea trade was expanding after the
reduction of the import duties on tea in 1784. The tea ships used the narrow
straits near Sumatra, always menaced by pirates and now, as the Dutch
were drawn into the strategic embrace of France, menaced by the
Franco-Dutch alliance. It would be safer for them to sail round Tasmania
and up the east coast of Australia, thence through the islands east of New
Guinea. Lucrative smuggling and privateering expeditions were nosing into
the rich Spanish trades linking the Philippines, Mexico and South America.
For all these, Botany Bay could provide a valuable port of call for fresh
water, food and supplies. Dr Dallas expounded this theory brilliantly in
Hobart University, but his audience consisted mainly of local historians:
it did not set the Derwent on fire.[3]

---

[1] W. A. Sinclair, *The Process of Economic Development in Australia* (Melbourne, 1976), p. 38,
note 2.
[2] T. A. Coglan, *Labour and Industry in Australia*, 4 vols. (Oxford, 1918); E. O. G. Shann, *An
Economic History of Australia* (Cambridge, 1930); B. C. Fitzpatrick, *The British Empire in
Australia* (1914) (Foreword by G. Blainey, Melbourne, 1969); Eris O'Brien, *The Foundation
of Australia* (Sydney, 1950); G. J. Abbott and N. B. Nairn, *Economic Growth of Australia
1788–1821* (Melbourne, 1969) collect essays of varied opinions together conveniently.
[3] K. M. Dallas, 'The First Settlement in Australia: Considered in Relation to Seapower in
World Politics', *Papers and Proceedings Tasmanian Historical Research Association*, 1952.

Another fourteen years elapsed before his theory was taken up and developed by Professor Blainey, of the University of Melbourne, in a book of great imaginative force and penetration, *The Tyranny of Distance*.[4] Blainey expanded Dallas's suggestion and added a further argument: the Treaty of Paris which wound up the Fourth Dutch War in 1784 gave the British the right to take their ships through the Dutch East Indies. The port of Penang in the Malay Peninsula was founded in 1786 as a port of call for the East India Company's trade to China, suggesting that an Australian port would offer 'a base for excursions to the opposite end of the Dutch trading realm'. England commanded no port between St Helena and India, nor between India and the Pacific. France had Mauritius; the Dutch had the East Indies; Spain held the approaches to Cape Horn and with it the eastern approaches to India. Like the Dutch in the seventeenth century, eighteenth-century England was rich in her eastern trades; but now her sea lanes were disturbingly vulnerable. Such reflections were common talk amongst imperialist–mercantilist propagandists in the 1780s – the 'rocking-chair colonizers' as Professor Blainey described them.

Their theories, he suggested, were arguable. They *may* have influenced the choice of Botany Bay; but the official documents offered no explicit proof of it. He accordingly looked for supporting reasons why, nearly twenty years after its discovery by James Cook, the British government decided to bestow upon this faraway deserted shore the honour of becoming a repository for its unwanted convicts – even though it was 'so remote that it thrust as many disadvantages on the English tax payer as on the convicts themselves'.

A possible explanation lay in Britain's need of additional supplies of strategic resources vital to survival in war. They included flax (for the making of canvas and sail cloth), hemp (for the making of ships' cables) and timber (for masts and spars). Britain depended on the Baltic for these supplies; but the Baltic had been a strategically precarious region since the seventeenth century. Even then, its dominion was intermittently threatened by the Dutch. From 1780 it seemed (Blainey argued) that it might be threatened by the formation of the 'Armed Neutrality' by the North European powers. (In the Second and Third Dutch wars, Britain had tried to use North America as a substitute supplier of naval stores: but without conspicuous success.)[5] More than a century later, with France, the Netherlands and the former American colonies all on the wrong side of the diplomatic fence, North American supplies were out of the question. New hopes therefore focused on Australia.

[4] Melbourne, 1966.
[5] See my *Profit and Power* (The Hague, 1978), pp. 44, 72, 138.

A rope cable made of South Seas flax (Lord Sydney noted in a submission to the Commission on convict transportation) would be stronger than one made of European hemp. A supply of such excellent flax, he argued, 'would be of great consequence to us as a naval power'.[6] The trees which Cook, Sir Joseph Banks and their shipmates had seen growing by the side of seas and rivers in New Zealand and New Holland could replace the Baltic planks and spars, North American masts, Ukrainian top masts, perhaps even main timbers of Sussex oak. Norfolk Island, a thousand miles off the coast of New South Wales, might help to provide timber and supplies for the Royal Navy; he could have added, for the ships of the merchant navy too.

Supplies of flax would also be serviceable for maintaining stores of raw material for the linen industry – and particularly timely, since the Irish, Scottish and English linen industry produced not only fine wares for the rich but (like its rivals on the Continent) supplies of cheap cloth for the masses, as well as providing useful part-time peasant employment.

But Australian flax was to prove difficult to work. There were no experienced workers. On the mainland, aborigines pulled up the growing crop and found it handy for making fishing lines. The pines on Norfolk Island were disappointing. They went rotten under the bark; a dangerous liability in heavy weather. The dream of a surrogate Baltic faded. With Norfolk Island went another insubstantial, mercantilist Cloud Cuckoo Land.

All this Blainey conceded before his critics got to work; this did not take long. The tradition of Botany Bay and Australia's convict origins was deeply rooted. As time passed, the First Fleet with its unhappy band of compulsory pilgrims became converted (or inverted?) into a kind of enlarged latterday *Mayflower*. What had to some seemed a shameful tale, to others became transformed into a romantic myth as men became aware of the settlement's debt to convicts like Francis Greenway – convict but architect of genius, creator of churches, hospitals, government buildings, a Conservatorium of Music, respected confidant of the Governor himself. Another, Simeon Lord, who arrived in the colony in August 1791 with nothing beyond his seven-year sentence, became an entrepreneur, rich and respected, and ended a magistrate. It was all too good to be untrue, too good to be lost. Professor Bolton (of the University of Western Australia) did not let it die. His reply to Blainey was crisp and dry.[7] He was ready to see a little (but not much) truth in the strategic argument for Botany Bay as an imperial base. He agreed that the Franco-Dutch threat to British

---

[6] Blainey, *Tyranny*, p. 27.
[7] G. C. Bolton, 'The Hollow Conqueror: Flax and the Foundation of Australia', *Australian Economic History Review* (March 1968).

eastern trade had grown and accepted that propaganda (e.g. that of Matra and Young) may have rallied support for Australia as an attractive settlement – but *after* the convicts were installed, not *before*.

From Monash University, Melbourne, the response of Professor A. G. L. Shaw was even less sympathetic.[8] He stuck firmly to the old orthodoxy; the prime concern of the British government during the years of decision from 1786 to 1788 was to find a convict settlement, preferably at a very great distance from the British Isles and, indeed, from everywhere. It did not lie in flax, hemp or timber. From Canberra the magisterial cadences of Professor Manning Clark betrayed scant patience with any arguments about imperialist or mercantilist motives. Insofar as there was a government policy at all, it was the work of upper-class politicians anxious to remove a nuisance from beneath their noses before the smell became unendurable. At best, the supporters of Botany Bay as a jail were idealists dreaming of a new society acceptable to the well-born Enlightened and based on the perfection of the human race. But it was a long way off.[9]

To these, and others, Blainey returned a short answer.[10] He had never *dismissed* the convict problem: he had only suggested that the British government's motives were multiple. They included strategic and economic security. If flax and timber meant nothing to the men in London, why was Arthur Phillip instructed to cultivate flax? Why was Norfolk Island settled at all? If the convict problem provided the sole motive pointing to an overseas jail, why did it point to one at such a vast distance? True to his broad theme, he reiterated his conviction that here as elsewhere distance *was* a tyranny – and whatever the great men in London may have thought, it is difficult to think of a Governor of New South Wales who did not endorse his sentiments. London itself was always nervous about the cost of Australian settlement. Major Ross, commander of the military garrison and Deputy Governor, shared these feelings. In July 1788 he wrote to Lord Nepean at the Home Department: 'this country will never answer to settle in....it will be cheaper to feed the convicts on turtles and venison at the London Tavern than be at the expense of sending them here'.[11]

There is a flat contradiction here between what some men believed and other men did. It may be argued that this is the essence of history. But when the motives behind colonizing a vast continent – 'the greatest island' – are in question, it is worth asking whether there is any new, or concealed, evidence which may suggest a solution to the enigma.

[8] A. G. L. Shaw, 'The Hollow Conqueror and the Tyranny of Distance', *Historical Studies, Australia and New Zealand* (April 1968).
[9] Manning Clark, 'The Choice of Botany Bay', *Historical Studies, Australia and New Zealand* (1959–61).
[10] 'A Reply...', *Historical Studies, Australia and New Zealand* (April 1968).
[11] See John Cobley, *Sydney Cove 1788* (London, 1962), p. 188.

The First Fleet made landfall at Botany Bay on 18 January 1788. Its commander, Captain Arthur Phillip, R.N., by agreement with the authorities in London, had settled on Botany Bay in the light of the favourable comments made by Cook and Banks when they had disembarked there (from 28 April to 6 May 1770). But Phillip was disappointed with Botany Bay. It took him only three days to decide to move north to Port Jackson. Henceforth this superb, spectacular harbour, and in particular Sydney Cove, which he named after the figurehead of the operation, Lord Sydney, was to be the centre of settlement.

The First Fleet's general plan of operation derived from Cook. Cook's voyage derived from those of generations of earlier explorers: Portuguese, Spanish, Dutch, French, English. His genius lay in his careful study of their operations and in the personal judgment, tenacity and courage with which he directed his own voyages. That they became possible at this time was also due to the successive inventions of navigational aids: the compass, astrolabe, cross-staff and other forms of the quadrant. Theoretically a navigator could know where he was not only when in sight of land but when out of sight too; the exact measurement of longitude still eluded him. The search for Australia was peopled by the ghosts of lost navigators whose claims to discovery were often as doubtful as the instruments they used.

It seems likely that the Portuguese had reached the *terra incognita*. A Spanish expedition from Peru under the command of de Quiros had reached the New Hebrides in 1606. The Dutch had done better. Willem Jansz, skipper of the *Duijken* (*Little Dove*), sailed from the Dutch Indies in 1606. Like his contemporaries, he was looking for gold and spices. Ten years later another Dutch commander, Dirk Hartog, in the *Eendracht*, sailed east from the Cape of Good Hope and reached the island (still named after him) near Shark Bay on the west coast of Australia. Here he fastened on a pole an inscribed pewter dish recording his discovery. Later Dutch explorers sailing from the west filled in the outline of the north, west and south coasts, from the southern side of the gulf of Carpentaria to the Pieter Nuits' archipelago, 900 miles eastwards along the south coast. It was left to Abel Tasman, a captain in the service of the Dutch East Indian Company, to execute two vast, masterly sweeps round Australasia (including Van Diemen's land, later, in 1855, renamed Tasmania), New Zealand, Fiji and Tonga.

Not for nothing was Australia's first European title 'New Holland'. The names of the Dutch explorers inscribed on the map were never erased. Like the (later) explorers, the Dutch were animated by the spirit of curiosity and adventure: but the basic motives of their sponsors were commercial. An early Dutch sketch of a section of the west coast calls it 'The Golden

Province': red sand near the coast was believed to promise deposits of gold. The optimism was premature: even hopes of spices were never realized. Van Diemen, head of the company in the Dutch Indies, would have gone on trying: his masters at home were not prepared to lay out more money. William Dampier, buccaneer, the first Englishman to set foot on the mainland, was inclined to the same view: 'The hodmodods of Monomatapa, though a nasty people, yet for wealth are gentlemen to these [aborigines].'[12]

The third group of European explorers (and least familiar in English history) were the French. If the legends of de Gonneville, said to have sailed from Honfleur in 1503, have any basis in fact, France must be ranked among the prime contenders for the area. The French were also the last rivals to worry the English seriously by their presence in the seas round Australia, Van Diemen's Land and New Zealand, remaining indeed until the middle of the nineteenth century.[13] Of all the European rivals for the prize of Australia, the French were the most formidable. By the strange courtesy that persisted even amongst the most determined rivals of those times, more French names are left on the map than those of any other nationality except British. They decorate the maps of Western and southern Australia, and of Tasmania, like candles on a Christmas tree. Yet the English school of historians paid only passing attention to their achievements; even now, little serious attempt has been made to assess in any detail how the British rated the threat from France in this area.[14]

Professor Sinclair concluded his brief résumé of the Botany Bay controversy: 'It is unlikely that the last has been heard of this question.' That was in 1976.[15] It is only a matter of months since it has been opened up again by Professor Leslie Marchant's survey of French eighteenth- and nineteenth-century exploration of the eastern and southern areas.[16] His research sheds new light on French exploration of Australia, though his immediate interest in this new study is concentrated on Western Australia. But his text is superbly illuminated with facsimiles of the maps drawn by the cartographers who sailed with the French expeditions: sketches, drawings, paintings by the botanists, naturalists, geographers, engineers, zoologists and astronomers who made up the passenger lists of the French explorers (as of Cook's); biographical details of the principal commanders,

[12] A. W. Reed (ed.), *Captain Cook in Australia* (Wellington, Melbourne, 1969), ch. 2 *passim*.
[13] See below pp. 91–2.
[14] Reed, *Captain Cook*, has a valuable chapter on early discoveries in Australia but it contains only a passing reference to the controversy over the de Gonneville legend and nothing on eighteenth- or nineteenth-century French explorations. They are, however, admirably covered in the chapters on Australia, especially vol. VII, of the *Cambridge History of the British Empire* by Prof. Sir Ernest Scott (Cambridge, 1933).
[15] Sinclair, *Economic Development in Australia*, pp. 37–8.
[16] Leslie Marchant, *France Australe* (Perth, 1982).

their strengths and foibles, blow-by-blow accounts of the quarrels and jealousies which punctuated their voyages (much more than they did Cook's). Shipwrecks and deaths from sickness and misadventure seem more frequent in the French expeditions; morale less high; objectives less clearly formulated, targets less carefully identified. Yet the navigational achievements were remarkable: they rested largely on the skill of tough and experienced sailors from the ports of Normandy and Brittany.

French exploration was also inspired by double motives: the old haunting curiosity about the South Seas and the South Land, conjured up two centuries earlier by Gonneville, was now combined with the practical end of providing for the trade with India some more effective link beyond Mauritius. During the eighteenth century when this island – first occupied by the Portuguese, then the Dutch – became the Île de France, it was a crucial centre for French naval and privateering operations against English trade routes to and from India. Meanwhile the vision of a deep-water port to supplement Port Louis and a colony to link Île de France with the Pacific never faded. These were the targets of Bouvet de Losier (1739), Marion Dufresne (1772), Bougainville the elder (1764), Kerguelen-Tremarec (1772) and St Allouarn (1772). They were all bold navigators and their imaginations were whetted by readings in the Utopian fiction of writers like Charles de Brosses and Cyrano de Bergerac.

With the exception of St Allouarn, the pre-Revolutionary explorers achieved little by way of occupation or settlement: St Allouarn reached the west coast of Australia and on 30 March 1772 an ensign from his ship, the *Gros Ventre*, landed at Turtle Bay and took possession in the name of the King of France. A parchment recording this was buried in a bottle at the foot of a tree, with two French coins. St Allouarn then left for Timor and Mauritius, where he and his ensign died soon after landing, apparently from the effects of their voyage.

St Allouarn had no immediate successors. France still believed in prescriptive right as the proof of territorial ownership, at least in regard to territory claimed as French. Turtle Bay had been 'acquired': that, in the French view, was enough. The British view was that possession demanded 'effective occupation'. The King of France's gesture was not disputed; it was simply ignored. Not until 1785 did la Pérouse set out on a potentially more important expedition with his two ships, *La Boussole* and *L'Astrolabe*. La Pérouse was to be the first European encountered by Arthur Phillip at Botany Bay.[17] After la Pérouse left, his expedition was totally lost. Among those sent to find and rescue it (without success) was the Chevalier Bruny d'Entrecasteaux. In 1792 he got as far as Esperance on the south

---

[17] See below p. 87.

Australian coast with his ships, the *Recherche* and the *Esperance*, the last under the command of the Breton, Huon de Kermadec. Then followed what in the light of later history was the most significant aspect of their voyage – their arrival in Tasmania and the reconnoitring of its vast estuaries and inland seas.

An interval followed before further voyages were sponsored by the Directory and Napoleon. The principal commander of the expedition that finally sailed in 1800 in the *Géographe* and *Naturaliste* was Nicolas Baudin, touchy, querulous, jealous of his naval rank (he was originally a merchant seaman from the Breton Île de Ré) and uncertain of his authority. His second-in-command, Jacques Hamelin, was, like Baudin, a merchant seaman by origin but a more assured commander of men. With them sailed the renowned scientist of the Revolution, François Peron. Peron's team of scientists and their intellectual (and political) preoccupations acted as a constant needle on Baudin's temper.

Nevertheless, with the help of Jacques Hamelin, a young officer, Louis de Freycinet, Hyancinthe Bougainville (the younger) and a gifted carto-grapher, Rosily, Peron and his team made important progress in elucidating the geographical, botanical and zoological conundrums of the west and south Australian coasts. They then moved on to the greener pastures of Van Diemen's Land with its excellent harbours, abundant food, wild life, timber, water, scientific specimens, friendly natives (including relatively attractive girls) – 'The work done on Tasmania is...a highlight of the Baudin expedition.'[18] After that Baudin ran into Matthew Flinders, busy making his own survey of the south Australian coast; then he headed for Port Jackson and five months of refitting and nursing his diseased crews back to something like health.

That marked the end of French imperialist–scientific exploration of Australia until the post-Napoleonic period. But for the English the successive French landings, on the western and Tasmanian coasts especially, had caused renewed anxiety.[19]

The revolt of the North American colonies, the Franco-American alliance and the shift of Dutch sympathies towards France created a disquieting diplomatic and strategic prospect not only in Europe but in the Eastern and Southern Seas too. Under the constitutional arrangements in force, Lord Sydney, at the Home Department, was responsible for colonial as well as

[18] Marchant, *France Australe*, p. 182.
[19] After Napoleon, French interest in Australia (and New Zealand) revived. It took, outwardly, the form of admiring emulation of Britain's ingenuity in removing a slice of the problem of criminality for treatment to a colonial settlement. France, of course, faced the same problems of finding suitable ways of colonizing these faraway lands as Britain.

domestic affairs. From 1785 it was his task to ponder the consequences of the loss of the North American sources of naval stores and the disposal of convicts who had earlier been conveniently assigned to Maryland and Virginia as compulsory labour. At home crime and punishment had grown in parallel as the population of Britain increased. Fears grew as violence erupted on the streets of London. The Wilkes riots (1768) had been bad enough. The Gordon riots of 1780 were even more serious. Sydney was under pressure to produce formulas to deal with both sets of problems: but it was obvious that neither was susceptible to instant remedy.[20]

Overseas, the risks from the expansionist ambitions of rival European powers were more than the feverish imaginings of the English jingos. Amongst the vulnerable areas were the east and south coasts of Australia (as the continent was soon to be named). Since Cook's first voyage, they had been almost forgotten. The news of the Count de la Pérouse's expedition that set sail from France in 1785 jolted English fears and memories. Was there a French plot to link up with the Dutch, or even Spain or Portugal, for a move east or south? Would there be fresh territorial claims like those of St Allouarn a few years earlier? Could the French override Cook's own claim? Who could tell? The background to popular reaction to such problems was nevertheless consistent: the ancient hostility to France had proved strong enough to defeat the efforts of the Tories to formulate an Anglo-French trade treaty in 1713. From then until Cobden's free trade treaty in 1861 – still a surprising achievement to most people on both sides – Anglo-French trade relations were a source of friction rather than fraternity.[21] British 'mercantilist' ideology in the eighteenth century had for its goal the defeat of France in a 'war of trade'.[22] In that never-ending battle of wits and force, defence and offence were permanently entangled and inseparable, suspicion and vigilance unceasing.

The first Europeans to encounter Phillip at Botany Bay were la Pérouse and his expedition. The immediate alarm proved false: la Pérouse was a naval officer of the old regime. His attitude to Phillip and his officers proved to be exquisitely courteous. He entertained them to dinner. They returned his hospitality. His attitude to straying convicts who offered him their services was strictly proper. They were bundled back to Sydney Cove. He was, as ever, chivalrous, grateful for help and he reciprocated whenever he could. But undoubtedly his most helpful (if tragic) act was to leave

[20] For the criminal and penological problems see O'Brien, *Foundation of Australia*, and R. M. Hartwell on 'The British Background' in Abbott and Nairn, *Economic Growth*.
[21] See Professor Coleman's 'Politics and Economics in the Age of Anne: The Case of the Anglo-French Treaty of 1713', in D. C. Coleman and A. H. John (eds.), *Trade, Government and Economy in Pre-Industrial England: Essays Presented to F. J. Fisher* (London, 1976).
[22] Steven Watson in vol. XII of the *Oxford History of England* (Oxford, 1960), pp. 16–20.

Botany Bay – for ever. Baudin, a decade later, was less easy; but he caused
no really serious problem. The decencies were preserved.[23]

Older writers assumed that French exploration represented the ancient
French threat of expansionism.[24] Professor Marchant takes a less melo-
dramatic view. The French (he thinks) were less predatory and more
enlightened in the pursuit of geographical and scientific knowledge than
English historians allow. A central problem nevertheless remains: were the
English justified in their mistrust of their 'ancient enemy'? Marchant
himself emphasizes the French view of 'prescriptive right' to new territories.
By this token, the French did not need to *occupy* Botany Bay; only to claim
it. And so far, the English had done no more. The English certainly had
good reason to respect the potential threat posed by the professional
fighting qualifications of the French naval officers who were always placed
in charge of their explorations. Louis de Bougainville had been an efficient
aide to Montcalm in France's campaign against Britain in Canada. Kerguelen
had proved an able commander in the Seven Years War. So had Dufresne;
he had also been involved in the exercise to get Bonnie Prince Charlie out
of Scotland. Hamelin was later to take charge of the naval force assembled
on the French coast to invade Britain. Later still he was to be Director
General of the Naval Ministry. French interest was visibly moving eastwards
in the 1780s towards Van Diemen's Land and Botany Bay. St Allouarn's
parchment claim at Turtle Bay; la Pérouse, the scourge of British Canada,
in person at Botany Bay; d'Entrecasteaux and Huon Kermadec in
Tasmanian waters looking for shipbuilding timber; Baudin and Hamelin
refitting in Port Jackson – it all added up to a disquieting picture for Royal
Navy officers like Phillip and his successors as Governors, all seasoned
warriors in the Anglo-French struggle. What *were* the French up to? Was
Australia destined to become another Canada?

In 1787 when the First Fleet set sail, another war with France seemed
imminent. But developments *after* 1788 are not irrelevant either; they
complete the historical framework in which the First Fleet was despatched.
Amongst the officers of the First Fleet was Lieutenant Philip Gidley King.
King, later Governor, was not personally hostile to the French: but he was
probably the one who harboured the deepest suspicions of French
ambitions. Phillip quickly gave him his first promotion (to Lieutenant
Governor) at Norfolk Island. From the start King was preoccupied with the
problem of defence and the production of 'mercantilist' material. Norfolk
Island, a thousand miles to sea east of Sydney, he saw as the colony's outer
rampart – the first manifestation of what was to become the standard

---

[23] See G. W. Rusden, *History of Australia* (Melbourne, 1897), *passim.*
[24] See, for example, Leslie Marchant's opinion of Ernest Scott's *Terre Napoleon* (1910) in
his *France Australe.*

'screen of islands' policy, in vogue down to the Second World War. After King's departure, his successor at Norfolk Island received a rude shock. A large formation of nine ships appeared off the coast and even fired a gun to leeward. True, they also hoisted English colours but this only deepened fears of a French or Dutch invasion. (La Pérouse had likewise been taken on first sighting as a Dutch or French invader.) The visitors proved, in fact, to be the English East India Company's China fleet seeking refreshment. But such incidents showed how tense the Anglo-French relationship was. Norfolk Island was disappointing: the timber was poor, hemp and flax would not grow. For a time whaling was to save the settlement, but only at the cost of an illegal trade in liquor smuggled in by American whaling skippers. It survived as a prison until 1856. 'Mercantilist' development had to be sought elsewhere.

Meanwhile, as the Revolution pursued its way in France, Anglo-French relations in the Southern Seas reflected the transition of diplomacy from the traditional balance-of-power phase to the more sharply ideological. The change was to colour English domestic politics (as well as the European scene) for several decades. The outward courtesies that marked Anglo-French colonial relations in Phillip's day wore thin in the 1790s and after. For this there were other reasons besides ideology.[25]

In the same year (1798) that the straits between Van Diemen's Land and the south coast of Australia were navigated, Captain William Reed in the *Martha* charted King Island at its western end, and brought back an impressive cargo of seal skins and oil. A great fishery arose in the next few years: whales, sea-elephants and seals produced growing quantities of skins and oil. These swiftly became a new source of economic rivalry between the nations. Thirty years later they still made up half of Australia's exports. In an ecstasy of enthusiasm, the editor of the *Australian Quarterly Journal* (the Rev. Charles Wilton) declared in 1828 that the *soil* of Australia would never be an adequate source of wealth; but her 'almost interminable length of coast swarming with whales' should be a gold mine. 'Merchants of Australia, open your eyes, use your reason.'[26]

The new commodities entered the market. As objects of competition, timber, hemp and flax were joined by whales: and whaling and sealing meant shipbuilding. The new diplomacy and changing economy decided King, now Governor of New South Wales (1800–6), on firmer measures. Van Diemen's Land and the Bass Strait were on the direct route between New South Wales and Britain. The French explorers had advanced eastwards along that route. They were followed by French and American sealers and whalers. Now it was time for King to move south and west.

[25] See Rusden, *History of Australia*.
[26] *Australian Quarterly Journal* 1 (1828), 86–94.

H.M.S. *Cumberland* was despatched to the straits, ostensibly on a mission
of geological enquiry; but its commander carried secret instructions to look
out for French ships and forestall Baudin by taking control of Bass Strait.
At King Island they met. The English lieutenant landed, with three marines,
proclaimed the island to be British, ran up the Union Jack (upside down,
for he was in a great hurry), fired a volley, led three cheers and retired:
to the astonishment of the French. The *Martha* then went across the straits
to Port Phillip, another promising whaling centre.

At Hobart, on the estuary of the River Derwent, was another infant
settlement, Risdon Cove.[27] It was commanded by a young (and uncertain)
Superintendent, Lieutenant Bowen. Bass and Flinders, who had visited it
in 1798, had rhapsodized over the beauty of its valleys, its long grassy
slopes, the riches of its timber, the fertility of its soil and the profusion of
its vegetation. So did Bowen, adding for good measure that he had seen
'with his own eyes' the flax plant growing at Risdon Cove.[28] King, an
earnest observer of economic potential, was impressed. When he reported
the anti-French mission to King Island to Lord Hobart in Whitehall, he also
reported Bowen's discovery and settlement of Risdon Cove. In view of the
expected French presence, Governor King had given Bowen very explicit
instructions. His objectives were 'to prevent the French gaining a footing
on the East side of these Islands; to divide the Convicts: to secure another
place for procuring timber, with any other natural Productions that may
be discovered and found useful: [to assess] the advantage that may be
expected by raising grain; and to promote the Seal Fishery....'[29]

King underlined these instructions to Bowen in greater detail, especially
regarding timber. 'You will also inform me whether the general timber in
that country is fit for the purpose of being sent to England for the
construction of the King's ships, particularizing...the different species,
length of trunk and diameter; also whether it grows mostly crooked or
strait, and notice the facility of getting it on board ships....'[30]

Bowen was also commanded 'to Counteract any Projects or Plans' the
French in the neighbourhood might be harbouring; especially to thwart
any attempt to 'form an Establishment anywhere...', informing the French

---

[27] I am indebted for what follows to Margeret Glover's paper *History of the Site of Bowen's
Settlement, Risdon Cove* (Occasional Paper No. 2, National Parks and Wildlife Service,
Tasmania, 1978) and to material in the Risdon Centre.

[28] *Historical Records of Australia* (Sydney, 1914–   ) series III, vol. I, pp. 198–9; Bowen to
King, 27 September 1803.

[29] *Historical Records of Australia*, series I, vol. IV, pp. 144–5, 248–9. The most recent upholder
of the 'convict' motive, Miss M. Gilten, 'The Botany Bay Decision, 1786: Convicts not
Empire', *English Historical Review* 97 (1982), suggests that strategic economic motives
died – if indeed they had ever existed – with the disembarkation of the First Fleet.
Whoever may have forgotten them, Governor King certainly did not.

[30] *Historical Records of Australia*, series I, vol. IV, pp. 152–3.

Commanding Officer of 'His Majesty's right to the whole of Van Diemen's Land...'. But there was to be no 'Act of hostility if it can be avoided...'. Equally, on no account should Bowen suffer 'His Majesty's Flag to be insulted'. Anything of that kind to be reported 'in the most Early and Circumstantial detail...'.[31]

Bowen's was not a successful appointment. He was early required to depart, and was succeeded by David Collins, formerly Judge-Advocate at Sydney, as Lieutenant Governor. Under Collins, and again under careful instructions from King (and later from Governor Macquarie), the Hobart settlement made good progress. Its whaling flourished. So did timber-cutting. The Huon pine (named, ironically, after the French explorer of Van Diemen's Land in 1792, Huon Kermadec) proved 'the world's best boat-building timber'.[32] The richest supplies were to be found on the Gordon River, West Tasmania, where they were worked by convicts from the penal settlement at Sarah Island on the nearby Macquarie Harbour. In contrast to Norfolk Island, this settlement built an astonishing number of excellent ships. The largest was the barque, *William IV*; it sold for £1375. (Its inhabitants also mined coal, burned lime, tanned hides, murdered their guards and attempted escapes which ended as gruesome orgies of murder and cannibalism.) Shipments of Huon pine soon began to arrive at Hobart.

Away to the southeast of Hobart was another penal settlement, later called Port Arthur, after Colonel George Arthur, its formidable founder. Port Arthur had coal mines employing over 500 miners, sawmills, craft workshops for carpenters, tailors, brickmakers, bootmakers, an asylum, a Gothic church of charming simplicity designed by a convict architect, a hospital, a penitentiary, above all a Panopticon, all built (like the rest of the settlement) by convict labour. It would have delighted Jeremy Bentham. It was a severe regime but managed (unlike Sarah Island earlier) with meticulous discipline and conscience. Its picturesque remains still stand, in an idyllic setting of lake and sea, forests and lawns, a green and tranquil memorial to the earnest philanthropic-cum-mercantilist aspirations of a past age; a Benthamite precursor of Saltaire and the later English Victorian model-industrial villages.[33] King's optimism over economic development in Tasmania seemed not ill-founded.

The rest of the story may be briefly despatched. After Baudin, French activity round Australia was suspended; it revived only after 1819, as the Bourbon monarchy restored French morale. The early 1820s saw new proposals to establish a colony in southwest Australia. The organization

---

[31] *Ibid.*, pp. 153–4.
[32] Hans Julen, *The Early History of the Tasmanian West Coast* (Launceston, 1976), pp. 7–8.
[33] Ian Brand, *Port Arthur* (Jason Latrobe, 1975), gives a well-balanced account. For Arthur see the very full account in the *Dictionary of National Biography*, vol. II (1885), pp. 132–5.

behind the plans of Jules Blosseville – navigator, scientist, prison reformer[34] – and the voyages of Duperrey, Bougainville and Dumont D'Urville in the mid-1820s, was the French Naval Planning Department. Its Head was still Rosily, former ensign with Kerguelen in 1772, now old, proud of his half-century of service to France and still a diligent enthusiast for colonial ventures in the South Seas. 'The French Government', ran a naval ministry memorandum in the early 1820s, 'has for a considerable time been searching for a place to establish a colony.' Its eyes were fixed on southwest Australia.[35] These schemes revived anxiety in England. Anglo-French diplomatic relations deteriorated correspondingly. As the French navy began to expand once more, a British official was despatched to King George Sound (southwest Australia) to occupy it on behalf of the Crown (1 March 1826). He returned three years later to complete his task by formally taking possession of the whole of Western Australia.

Effectively, that was the end of the French attempts at an Australian connection.[36] Their interest now moved away to New Zealand, where French progressives envisaged a possible new home for convicts. The naval ministry had its own ideas. New Zealand was more accessible than Western Australia. It contained excellent anchorages for warships. Why should it not become 'a colony of war like Botany Bay'?[37]

Professor Marchant's research makes it clear that in many respects French exploration closely resembled British, with an equal component of scientific enquiry. His *France Australe* is less convincing when arguing that it provided no legitimate cause for British anxiety. Marchant's quotations from French naval sources indicate clearly that French objectives were, at least intermittently, colonialist and expansionist. Like the British navy, the French navy was an instrument of trade defence. Like its rival, it was, equally, designed for offence when necessary. Especially in the troubled years before, during and just after the Revolution – for Britain unstable years, domestically as well as internationally – it was natural for the English to suspect France's motives in her ambitious southern explorations. The mutual respect and courtesies which Marchant rightly notes between the French and English commanders were certainly not unimportant. They did something to soften the barbarities of war by making it easier to accomplish codes of conduct in wartime. But they did nothing in themselves

---

[34] He visited the penal colonies of British Australia and was impressed both by their organization and by the commercial activities to which they had given rise.

[35] Marchant, *France Australe*, pp. 235–6. The memo seems to have been the work of either Rosily or Duperrey.

[36] Admiral Dumont d'Urville put in an appearance at Raffles Bay, the new colony in the far north, in 1838, but his stay was brief and Anglo-French contacts were marked by all the traditional courtesies. M. Barnard, *History of Australia* (Sydney, 1962), p. 195.

[37] Marchant, *France Australe*, p. 250, quoting French naval sources.

to identify or mitigate the underlying causes of hostility. The issues of peace or war were decided elsewhere: by politicians, princes, governments representing or purporting to represent the ambitions, interests and passions of the people. Whichever decision was taken, the professional gladiators immediately identified themselves with the national cause. Meanwhile the greatest and most decisive contests for maritime supremacy were yet to be fought. Professor Marchant has a point in arguing that the British always suspected the worst, even when it was not necessary: but that their fears were realistic can hardly be doubted in this long period of continuous Anglo-French rivalry for profit and power.[38]

Two explanations have been put forward for the despatch of the First Fleet to Botany Bay: traditionally, it was assumed that its mission was solely to establish a penal settlement; in more recent times, the framework was broadened to cover England's need for maritime security and additional supplies of timber, hemp, flax and other naval stores. The crisis over convicts and the crisis over trade and naval stores all arose from the loss of the American colonies. There is no necessary conflict between the two interpretations.

To take the transportation of convicts first. Transportation in itself was nothing new, nor did it occasion any general disquiet. What was new and disturbing was transportation to Botany Bay. In America there was an established body of settlers to whom convicts could be assigned as labour: in Australia there were only aborigines. Especially significant was the scramble, confusion and muddle of the embarkation itself; this brought the whole project to the brink of disaster and, for once, united the Governor and Lieutenant Governor (Phillip and Ross) in detestation of the convict 'system'. On everything else they disagreed.

What was the justification for a new act to legalize transportation to Botany Bay? Edmund Burke declared that there were 100000 convicts waiting to be properly dealt with. Eris O'Brien dismisses this as 'hyperbole', and prefers John Howard's figure of *c.* 4500. If Burke was anywhere near correct, transportation was absurd; if Howard was right, it was rash, grossly extravagant and unnecessary. Howard himself denounced those who 'adopted the expensive, dangerous and destructive scheme of transportation to Botany Bay'.[39] The First Fleet consisted of two warships, six transports and three supply ships. They carried some 560 male convicts

---

[38] Being mainly concerned with Western Australia, Marchant pays only passing attention to the extension of French exploration along the south coast to Van Diemen's Land and up the east coast. British anxiety over this area is vividly reflected in Australian historical sources with which Professor Marchant is not principally concerned in his study.

[39] *Memoirs of John Howard the Philanthropist* (London, 1818), p. 533.

and 190 women and children. Phillip repeatedly demanded their dossiers; they were repeatedly promised, but never supplied. The exact number of convicts, male and female, cannot be calculated: nor, in an age of indiscriminate punishment, could trivial offenders be distinguished from violent criminals. Some eighty naval and marine officers, surgeons, a lawyer, surveyor and other specialists, plus naval petty officers, marine non-commissioned officers and ranks to the number of approximately 200 men were also aboard. There were no convict overseers or prison staff nor (as far as can be judged) any free settlers beyond a handful of paid artisans. The voyage of the eleven ships lasted eight months and covered over 15 000 miles. Forty-eight persons died on passage and over a hundred within four months of disembarkation. The cost in food, stores, clothing, etc., was enormous. Yet compared with its successor, the expedition was rated a technical success. Certainly, but for Arthur Phillip's firmness in command things could have been very much worse.

The alternative explanations of the expedition suggested by Dallas and Blainey derived from the sheer inadequacy of traditional explanations to fathom this apparently inexplicable enterprise. Surely there must have been more urgent or serious economic or strategic motives to justify the removal of a few hundred convicts, many guilty of only petty offences, to the ends of the earth? Certainly shipbuilding timber, canvas, ropes, etc., were much in the minds of the propagandists like Sir George Young, Matra, even Lord Sydney. They were written into Arthur Phillip's commission. Philip Gidley King, who sailed as his second lieutenant and became Lieutenant Governor of Norfolk Island and finally Governor of New South Wales, took the 'mercantilist' arguments for the development of Australia very seriously.[40] Nevertheless, the practical results of the mercantilist projects, though of some local interest, did not prove more than modest. Australia's economic future lay elsewhere.

How, then, to explain this grotesque enterprise? Did it arise solely from irrationality, ignorance or incompetence? Almost certainly not. There exists another aspect of the problem which is at once legal, technical and arcane, while at the same time so obvious that it has been largely overlooked by lawyers and historians, perhaps because it never provoked a war or even a legal suit. Security reasons and common prudence dictated secrecy regarding it before the event. After its successful accomplishment, it was taken for granted. It has therefore left behind it little documentary evidence. It is, quite simply, the validity of the English claim to the possession of Australian territory under 'international law' as it stood in the mid-1780s.

[40] See above p. 90.

The early settlement of New South Wales has sometimes been described as if it was undertaken for (even by) the convicts as a civil project.[41] This is quite misleading. Phillip's commission as Governor was awarded for 'loyalty, courage and experience *in military affairs*' (my italics). It covered the eastern half of modern Australia, including towns, 'garrisons, castles, forts and all other fortifications...military works...etc.'. He was to act 'according to the rules and discipline of war'.[42]

Although Phillip reported to Lord Sydney and Sir Evan Nepean, at the Home Office, the occupation of Australia was a naval and military operation. Juridically, the central ceremony was enacted on 26 January 1788, at Sydney Cove, only a week after the Fleet had 'hauled in' for Botany Bay. A flagstaff was erected. 'Possession was taken for His Majesty' (as Lieutenant King wrote). 'The Union Jack was run up, the marines fired volleys, the Governor, principal officers and private soldiers drank the Royal health and success to the new Colony.'[43]

Two weeks later the Governor's commission was solemnly read before the entire company. The convicts, male and female, sat on the ground. The marines marched and 'a band of music played'. The Governor's judicial powers, military and civil, were firmly set out. Letters patent constituted the courts of law. All this was legally of vital importance, and underlined graphically by the French presence. Any claim which Cook might have made to Australian territory (and he had made one) could have been challenged according to England's own conventions by the French as defective in view of subsequent years of British absence and inaction. By the 1780s it was almost universally agreed that 'discovery' by itself was not enough to constitute title: it needed to be followed by 'effective occupation'. Essential to prove this was a recognizable machinery of state capable of enforcing law and order. In turn that implied the existence of a community, not merely a garrison subject to military or naval law.[44]

In short, the command of the First Fleet was completing the legal business which Cook had necessarily left unfinished. After his departure all had been forgotten in a hurricane of international war, revolution and riot: but the spirit if not the letter of Cook's *Secret Instructions* survived. The discovery and occupation of the Great South Land would 'tend greatly

---

[41] For example, *Chambers' Encyclopaedia* (London, 1895), vol. I, p. 593.
[42] See Cobley, *Sydney Cove*, p. 13. The best summary of Phillip's outstanding achievements will be found in J. J. Auchmuty's introduction to *The Voyage of Governor Phillip to Botany Bay* (Sydney, 1970).
[43] The marines took a strictly military view of their duties: they were not there to oversee convicts at work. Barnard, *Australia*, p. 55.
[44] See Oppenheim's *International Law*, ed. H. Lauterpacht (London, 1935), vol. I, pp. 555–62; G. Schwarzenberger, *International Law* (London, 1957), *passim*; *Chambers' Encyclopaedia*, vol. III (London, 1950); D. P. O'Connell, *International Law* (London, 1970), pp. 408–28.

to the advancement of the trade and navigation' of Great Britain. The diaries kept by a number of the naval and marine officers strongly suggest that they were fully aware they were making imperial history, not merely founding a jail. D'Entrecasteaux, Kermadec, Baudin and their squadrons were still energetically exploring the south coast and Van Diemen's Land.[45] The timeliness of Phillip's actions was apparent in 1802 when King (by then Governor) was to read to Baudin the terms of the British claim to New South Wales and Van Diemen's Land 'which could not be breached by France without threatening the peace recently arrived at'.[46]

It has been customary to regard the pleas of Cook's former midshipman, Matra, and Admiral ('Formosa') Young as rhetorical imperialist bluster. Were the discoveries of the 'wonderful Cook' (cried Young) 'to be relinquished by this Nation to her faithless neighbours...'? Cook's discoveries were not given in vain.[47] They might have been had news not arrived at that moment of la Pérouse's embarkation for the Pacific and South Seas with two warships. It was this which gave special urgency to the need to set the indisputable seal of law on Cook's 'claim', reviving as it did all the traditional fears of French aggression.[48] For was this not the bold la Pérouse who, in the war only just concluded, had destroyed the Hudson's Bay Company's fort in Canada? Only this can explain the scramble to get the First Fleet off on its long journey.

The Governor's powers, and the battalion of marines, gave the authority, force and firepower to support and justify the British claim. But how to provide the semblance of a settled community? To persuade a trading company, or individual merchants or settlers, to take an interest in a project which involved a journey of 15000 miles (and possibly back again) to a colony which at that moment had neither ports, nor trade, nor anything to sell, nor the means to buy, was out of the question. The East India Company was actively hostile to it. There were no takers. The only hope lay with the proposal for a convict settlement. Few wanted it. Sydney was apathetic; influential political and reforming figures like Burke and

[45] See the general introduction to *Sydney's First Four Years, being the Diaries of Captain Watkin Tench*, ed. L. F. Fitzhardinge (Royal Australian Historical Association, 1961). For a new view of the 'imperial' argument for New South Wales in relation to British trade in the east, see Alan Frost's *Convicts and Empire* (Melbourne, 1980). The *Nouvelle Biographie Générale* (Paris, 1889) has convenient summaries of the French explorations before and after the disembarkation of the First Fleet.

[46] See Rusden, *History of Australia*, vol. I, p. 304.

[47] Quoted by Prof. Sir Ernest Scott in *Cambridge History of the British Empire*, vol. VII, ch. 3, p. 57.

[48] See E. A. Benians, *ibid.*, vol. II, ch. 1, p. 27. See, for la Pérouse's voyage, the *Nouvelle Biographie Générale*, vols. 29–30 (Paris, 1889), pp. 513–17. La Pérouse was instructed to follow up, and complete, Cook's plans. Economic enquiry was prominent among his objectives (whaling, sealing, furs, minerals, trade routes and, in general, 'ouvrir au commerce de nouveaux debouches', including the southwest coast of Australia).

Howard (and later Bentham) resolutely hostile. Phillip himself wanted to see Australia a free settlement (as he continued to plead), not a prison. So did his deputy, Ross. But without the convicts the Governor would have had no one to govern, no one to dig, or sow, or build, or fell timber.

The British decision to go to Botany Bay provokes some analogies with the later decision to move into Africa. Both remain puzzles unsolved. In both cases government seemed to be concentrating its efforts on an area of doubtful importance to British prosperity. In neither case were ministers fully aware of the forces at work, nor in control of what happened. In both cases assumptions, conscious and unconscious, were concealed: and there were 'many things too well understood between colleagues to be written down'.[49] Botany Bay itself was a package deal which promised to kill two, possibly three, birds with one stone. This was too much for the politicians to resist. So, after scandalous delay, and eventually in disgraceful confusion, they bustled off the First Fleet: then, so far as possible, they put it out of their minds.

The French threat to Australia remained so long as Napoleon lasted, and, as regards New Zealand, longer. But Arthur Phillip had ensured that New South Wales was not to be another Canada (nor a Falklands). After 1815 a new Europe emerged: a new Australia too. The constraints of the original settlement were broken, the Blue Mountains breached. Wool, pastoralism, mining, immigration, free settlers, capital, burgeoning cities – all combined to exorcise the ghosts of the old regime. With it slowly faded the penal system itself until it became, like Pierce the Pieman and Ned Kelly, merely a relic of that gruesome folklore still dear to Australians.

---

[49] R. Robinson and J. Gallagher (with Alice Denny), *Africa and the Victorians: The Official Mind of Imperialism* (London, 1961), pp. 17, 19–20, ch. 1 *passim*, 470–2. In evaluating the shortage of documentary evidence for the strategic importance of an Australian settlement, it has to be remembered that utmost secrecy was also essential where there was the slightest likelihood of a naval engagement. Nelson thought that, in such matters of security, the French arrangements were if anything more rigorous than the British.

6

'Gentleman and Players' revisited: the gentlemanly
ideal, the business ideal and the professional ideal in
English literary culture

NEIL McKENDRICK

Amongst the high seriousness, and indeed high solemnity, of much recent
sociological writing, there has been one set of findings which must have
brought a smile to the face of most of its readers. This was Liam Hudson's
assertion of a significant statistical correlation between the educational
background of medical specialists and the parts of the body they specialized
in.[1] The smile must surely have broadened with each revelation. Specialists
from English public schools tended to specialize in the parts above the waist
rather than those below, on the surface of the body rather than its innards,
on the living rather than the dead, and on the bodies of men rather than
those of women. Specialists educated in the state system, on the other hand,
tended to get the less status-packed parts of the poorer, less prestigious, sex.
This is not, of course, to suggest a systematic social and educational
hierarchy with Etonian surgeons operating solely on the brain surface of
living males while their colleagues from the comprehensive school system
delved dutifully into the nether regions of dead females. There is no
suggestion either of an educationally predictable hierarchy of talent or
expertise. The article is simply an amusing demonstration of the interaction
between social and educational background and the subtle workings of
career choice. Beyond the lighthearted observation there lies a very
important point.

For status, prestige, class values, social and even aesthetic preferences
powerfully, if not always obviously, influence our career choices. Inherited
assumptions, educational imprinting, subtle social indicators of preferred
occupations, accepted modes of social ascent, profoundly affect the
adoption of distinctive national attitudes to work and to leisure, to risk
taking and to the search for security, to money and how to acquire it. Our
national culture both reflects and arguably determines these values.

---

[1] Liam Hudson and B. Jacot, 'Education and Eminence in British Medicine', *British Medical
Journal* 4, 162 (1971), 111, quoted in Alistair Mant, *The Rise and Fall of the British
Manager* (London, 1977), p. 7.

It is an area which Donald Coleman highlighted in his influential and suggestive article 'Gentlemen and Players' published in 1973.[2] As befitted a social and economic historian who had done so much to put business history on the map of educationally acceptable disciplines, he was concerned to discuss the relationship between entrepreneurial excellence, or even adequacy, and some of the cultural values of our society. In doing so he did much to illuminate and explain distinctive attitudes to British management. He pointed the way towards the need for enquiry into difficult qualitative problems. He implied the need for the business historian to try to grasp the significance of such elusive concepts as the claims to effortless superiority of the English gentleman, the skills (real or imaginary) of the educated amateur generalist, the so-called 'worship of inutility' of the English educational syllabus, the values of a society dominated first by the gentlemanly ideal and later moralized by the professional ideal.

His characteristic choice of the traditional 'Gentlemen *vs* Players' cricket match as a symbol of the persistence of certain English values through the nineteenth and twentieth centuries neatly encapsulates a set of problems which has increasingly preoccupied a very wide range of academic disciplines. Economists concerned with measuring differential performance between the national branches of international companies have pinpointed and precisely quantified the contribution of behavioural and attitudinal characteristics of different cultures.[3] Sociologists have endeavoured to understand 'the way in which nationality predisposes our thinking' and have sought to identify previously 'invisible cultural differences'.[4] They have even tried to measure these differences and to explain them in terms of the mental building programmes which are developed in early childhood by the expectations and values of the family and are reinforced by our schools, universities and national institutions, and which cumulatively determine our distinctive national culture.[5] Literary critics have sought to explain the influence of powerful schools of critical interpretation from Ruskin to Leavis by way of Carlyle, Morris and T. S. Eliot, and have drawn

[2] D. C. Coleman, 'Gentlemen and Players', *Economic History Review*, 2nd Series 26 (1973), 92–116.

[3] C. F. Pratten, *Labour Productivity Differentials with International Companies* (Cambridge, 1976). See also Ronald Dore, *British Factory, Japanese Factory* (London, 1973) and David Grannick, *Managerial Comparisons of Four Developed Countries, France, Britain, the United States and Russia* (Cambridge, Mass., 1972).

[4] Geert Hofstede, *Culture's Consequences: International Differences in Work-Related Values* (London, 1980), p. 9.

[5] *Ibid.*, p. 11. For a discussion of the concept of the dimensions of culture, see A. Inkeles and D. J. Levinson, 'National Character: The Study of Modal Personality and Sociocultural Systems', in G. Lindzey and E. Aronson (eds.), *The Handbook of Social Psychology*, vol. 4 (Reading, 1969).

attention to the influence of 'the rise of English' as an academic profession on our attitudes to economic progress.[6] Literary historians have started to chart in more detail the way in which the capitalist or the businessman is portrayed in literature.[7] Social historians have drawn attention to the rise of the professions and the impact and import of their supportive ideologies.[8] Historians of education have examined the influence of the public schools and universities – probing the problem of technophobia and the cult of the classics.[9] Political and ecclesiastical historians have pointed to the influence of anti-semitism[10] and antipathy to non-conformists in forming our attitudes to entrepreneurial achievement.[11] Historians of the family have looked at the effects of the values instilled by different sects and different classes on the need for achievement[12] and the withdrawal of status respect[13] identified in particular social subgroups. Business historians have increasingly heeded the need to incorporate such findings in their work. On to the narrative history of the firm and the biographical history of the individual entrepreneur have been grafted the influence of the adversary culture and the importance of literary, ideological and social assumptions in controlling the supply and the quality of entrepreneurial talent.[14]

Unfortunately those who have flocked to pronounce on the economic consequences of English culture have not always taken advantage of these scholarly findings to refine their theories and qualify their verdicts.

[6] Terry Eagleton, *Literary Theory* (London, 1983); Chris Baldrick, *The Social Mission of English Criticism* (Oxford, 1983): and D. J. Palmer, *The Rise of English Studies* (London, 1965).

[7] Neil McKendrick, 'Literary Luddism and the Businessman', General Introduction to P. N. Davies, *Sir Alfred Jones, Shipping Entrepreneur Par Excellence* (London, 1978), pp. ix–lvi; John McVeagh, *Tradefull Mercants: The Portrayal of the Capitalist in Literature* (1981). McVeagh's treatment is the most comprehensive. For more detailed coverage of shorter periods see later notes.

[8] Harold Perkin, *Professionalism, Property and English Society Since 1880* (Reading, 1981); and E. C. Hughes, 'Professions' in the special edition on the professions in *Daedelus* 92 (Fall 1963).

[9] Michael Sanderson, *The Universities and British Industry, 1850–1970* (London, 1972); and G. Roderick and M. Stephens, *Education and Industry in the Nineteenth Century* (London, 1981).

[10] For a general discussion see Stephen Aris, *The Jews in Business* (London, 1970).

[11] For a critical summary of the literature see M. W. Flinn, 'Social Theory in the Industrial Revolution', in Tom Burns and S. B. Saul (eds.), *Social Theory and Economic Change* (Edinburgh, 1967), pp. 9–34.

[12] D. C. McClelland, *The Achieving Society* (Princeton, 1961).

[13] E. E. Hagen, *On the Theory of Social Change, How Economic Growth Begins* (Boston, 1962).

[14] Neil McKendrick, 'General Introduction to Business History', in R. J. Overy, *William Morris, Viscount Nuffield* (London, 1976), pp. vii–xliv; Neil McKendrick, 'In Search of a Secular Ideal', General Introduction to Clive Trebilcock, *The Vickers Brothers Armaments and Enterprise, 1854–1914* (London, 1977), pp. ix–xxxiv; Neil McKendrick, 'The Enemies of Technology and the Self-Made Man', General Introduction to Roy Church, *Herbert Austin, The British Motor Car Industry to 1941* (London, 1979), pp. ix–l; and McKendrick, 'Literary Luddism and the Businessman'.

Those preaching the effects of literary and educational Luddism are easy to find in contemporary Britain. Those diagnosing the causes of the British disease and peddling simple cures have been too quick to see a direct causal linear link between literary antagonism to the businessman and economic decline. It could be persuasively argued that despite Britain's relative economic decline (and few could doubt that Britain's position has declined in the economic league tables and in the tables which measure so many of the social amenities which wealth can buy – health, housing, education, social services and the arts) Britain's economic performance has improved in absolute terms during the years when adversary values have been dominant. It could be equally convincingly argued that the case for this unchecked advance of literary opposition to capitalism, technology, industry and commerce in general, and to the businessman in particular, has been both overstated and misunderstood.

It has certainly been stated widely. Martin Wiener's book, *English Culture and the Decline of the Industrial Spirit, 1850–1980*,[15] focused fresh attention on the problem and stimulated a host of imitators who stressed:

> that one of the main reasons for Britain's failure to keep pace with competing economies is that, for more than a century, our elite culture has been anti-entrepreneurial, anti-industrial and, in a professional sense, anti-productive – esteeming the tasteful consumption of wealth, but disparaging its creation and creators. In that culture, talking and writing have consistently ranked higher than making or selling; knowledge without obvious utility higher than knowledge with it. Hence the paradox of an industrial society rich in Nobel prize winners, but starved of technological innovation: rich in talented civil servants but starved of trained managers: rich in theorists of the business cycle, but starved of thrusting businessmen. And hence, of course, the creeping de-industrialization which now threatens to turn the relative economic decline of the last 100 years into absolute decline.[16]

In fostering and disseminating the elite culture, in promoting the view that the world of industry and commerce is 'a nasty vulgar place', English literature in general, and its treatment of men of business since the middle of the nineteenth century in particular, have been found to carry a heavy responsibility.[17]

I want to suggest a note of caution. I want to suggest that the roots of literary antagonism to the men of business are very long. One can find accusations that the pursuit of profit blinds them to the public good as early as William Dunbar's advice 'To the Merchants of Edinburgh' written at the end of the fifteenth century:

---

[15] M. J. Wiener, *English Culture and the Decline of the Industrial Spirit, 1850–1980* (Cambridge, 1981).

[16] David Marquand, *The Times*, 3 September 1981, p. 10. This is a representative example from a host of such commentators.

[17] Wiener, *English Culture*, *passim*.

Singular proffeit so does yow blind
the common proffeit gois behind.[18]

I want to suggest that far from the twentieth century representing a peak
of such attacks on the businessman, there is a decline in attention to him
in the literature of the last fifty years, reflecting a relative indifference to
business capitalism and a preoccupation with other values. I want to
suggest that one needs to look for a far more complex and subtle interaction
of business, literature and society than a simple graph of the rise and fall
of literary Luddism.[19] The economic consequences of cultural responses to
industry require even more careful treatment. Peaks of hostility to the
businessman can reflect times when his place in society, his power and his
influence are seen to be at their most influential. They can, of course, also
reflect widespread concern that economic decline is the result of his
entrepreneurial and human failings. Troughs of apparent indifference can
reflect times when his power and influence are in eclipse.

I want to suggest that the case for using literature as one of our finest
storehouses of recorded attitudes is a strong one as long as it is used as
sceptically and as critically as any other historical evidence. Literary
attitudes are often partial, particular to a single class or interest group,
prone to reflect specific political connections and social obsessions, and
open to mimetic distortion as a result of literary convention, passing
fashion, the needs of the readership, the demands of the critics or the
pressure of public opinion. But few sources can tell us more about
prevailing social attitudes and preferred social values. I yield to no one in
my belief in the importance of what Trilling has called 'the rise of the
adversary culture' but I feel that its influence is in danger of being
misunderstood.[20]

It is, therefore, of more than usual importance to establish with some
precision what the literary reaction to the men of business really was. Too
many of the bold generalizations made on this subject reveal a remarkable
lack of knowledge of the evidence. Some of the authorities quoted do not
even seem to think that such lack of evidence weakens their case.
G. K. Chesterton warmly endorsed Cobbett's denunciation of commercial
practices in spite of, or almost because of, Cobbett's lack of evidence: 'It

[18] William Dunbar, 'To the Merchants of Edinburgh', quoted in *Social and Documentary Poetry, 1250–1916*, ed. David Wright (London, 1976), pp. 147–9.
[19] I am using 'literary Luddism' in its general sense of anti-industrial, anti-entrepreneurial and anti-technological rather than in the sense of actual machine-breaking. See McKendrick, 'Literary Luddism and the Businessman'. For an earlier discussion see F. R. Leavis, *Nor Shall My Sword: Discourses on Pluralism, Compassion and Social Hope* (London, 1972), ch. 3, pp. 75–100.
[20] See Irving Kristol, 'The Adversary Culture of Intellectuals', *Encounter* 50, 4 (October 1979), 5–11.

is a perfectly sound criticism on the anonymous tyrannies of trade that we have no possible means of knowing' that such criticisms 'are *not* justified'.[21]

In such circumstances it is more than usually necessary to establish exactly what the literary precedents are. As John Selden cautioned us in his *Table Talk* of 1689: 'We commonly are at what's the reason of it, before we are sure of the thing. The *reason* of the thing is not to be enquired after, till you are sure the thing itself be so.'[22] This is particularly true of all those generalizations about the hostile nature of the literary response to industry from the middle of the nineteenth century to the present day, and of the explanation of the consequences of that hostility.

Martin Wiener is merely the most recent in a long line of respected authorities who have made this mistake.[23] The fact that even Donald Coleman has contributed to this view by writing 'Look for the businessman in English fiction and either you will not find him at all or he will vary from the sinister to the absurd'[24] is evidence of its persuasive and pervasive nature. Even the most distinguished authorities have been misled for want of evidence of the literary record. Few commentators seem to realize how easy it is to compile a benign business anthology. Yet a catalogue of commercial virtue and business worth is firmly in position in England's literary heritage alongside the catalogue of commercial vice and business villainy. In the sixteenth century Thomas More's 'accursed plague' of capitalists with their socially divisive pursuit of profit, is balanced by Francis Bacon's 'Merchants of Light' with their life-enhancing contribution to civilization and material progress. Shakespeare's Shylock is balanced by his Antonio, his true *Merchant of Venice* (1596) – although revealingly this acceptable face of commerce is never shown actually conducting trade while Shylock (the despicable face of commercialism) is imprinted on our memories as the incarnation of the loan-shark by his insistence on his pound of flesh. Other voices at the turn of the century were less ambiguous. Indeed Thomas Deloney, Thomas Dekker and Thomas Heywood seem almost to compete to endorse the commercial spirit, the commercial career and the beneficial consequences of commercial activity.

Deloney's *Jack of Newberry* (1597) exemplifies and approves the self-made

[21] G. K. Chesterton, Preface to William Cobbett, *Cottage Economy* (first published 1822, reprinted with preface by G. K. Chesterton in 1916; Oxford, 1979), p. x.

[22] John Selden, *Table Talk* (1689), p. cxxi.

[23] Wiener, *English Culture*, p. 157. The mistake seems to me to be largely one of chronology and emphasis. Much of Wiener's argument seems to me to be perceptive, persuasive and important, but his lack of awareness of the literary response to business and industry before the middle of the eighteenth century seriously weakens his case. His lack of attention to the implications of the literary neglect of businessmen in the last fifty years weakens it further.

[24] D. C. Coleman, *What Has Happened to Economic History?* (Cambridge, 1972), p. 11.

success story in the Dick Whittington mould, and it is significant that it was at this time, too, that the Whittington legend first appeared in print (1605). This is even more significant if one accepts the reading which makes commerce rather than a cat the source and symbol of his spectacular success. For if Dick Whittington's cat is interpreted, as it is by some, as a corruption of the French word *achat*, then trade in the form of a judicious purchase becomes the origin and explanation of his social climb – a far more convincing cause and effect than the *Puss in Boots* version of pantomime fame.[25]

In the decades each side of 1600, other literary spokesmen were only too willing to explain and justify success and civic virtue in terms of trading ventures and commercial enterprise. Dramatists like Dekker and Heywood were not dealing in ambiguities. Their message of commercial approval is loud and clear. Dekker's Simon Eyre in *The Shoemaker's Holiday* (1599) is allowed to prosper unabashed as a consequence of a shrewd trading purchase and his success and standing are dramatically symbolized by the fact that the King is made to visit *him* rather than he being made to visit his monarch. The same point is made so boldly by Thomas Heywood that it even appears in the title of his play *If You Know Not Me, You Know Nobody* (1605). The title echoes and underlines the central importance in the play of the merchant Hobson's reply to Queen Elizabeth, 'Knowest not me, Queene? Then thou knowest nobody, Bones-a-me, Queene, I am *Hobson*.'[26] In the same play, the greater merchant Gresham also seeks and receives royal endorsement for his commercial values and financial schemes. Gresham is not only allowed to prosper exceedingly and unashamedly from commerce, but he is explicitly admired and commended for doing so. In one striking passage he reduces to powder a pearl which no other nation, let alone any other merchant, could afford to buy. To confirm his personal power and wealth he then drinks the powdered pearl. And, as if that is not enough, he makes this flamboyant gesture (a defiant response to the material loss incurred in one of his rare failures) whilst wearing slippers *each* of which cost £30000. Yet this is not part of the familiar literary attack on conspicuous consumption and vulgar display but part of a demonstration of national pride and civic virtue. For Gresham is not only presented as more successful than any other foreign merchant but he is also presented as a symbol of beneficent commercial wealth and power. Gresham College and the Royal Exchange were the tangible proofs of his responsible use of that wealth and power. The Royal Exchange occupies a central role in the play. In John McVeagh's words,

---

[25] Paul Harvey, *The Oxford Companion to English Literature* (Oxford, 1932); see the entry under 'Whittington'.

[26] Thomas Heywood, *If You Know Not Me, You Know Nobody* (1605). part II, act I, 317. Quoted in McVeagh, *Tradefull Merchants*, p. 13.

In Heywood's elaborate dramatization of [it] we are processionally led through a formal endorsement of all that Gresham stands for. And it is stressed that he stands for something enhancing....He represents the mercantile interest in Elizabeth's England, newly conscious of its potency, determined to be listened to and respected, but for all that heartily patriotic, and seeing its fortunes as tied in with and identical to those of the nation as a whole.[27]

One must not overstate the positive literary case for commerce. The optimistic case argued by Bacon, Dekker and Heywood was still the minority one, and for more than a hundred years to come the uncompromisingly hostile case was to dominate. 'For Jonson, Middleton, Marston, Massinger and the rest the merchant is a fool or a knave, or both, and his hopes and values are almost programmatically cursed and laughed at.'[28] Bacon's anonymous 'Merchants of Light' were cast into the shade by such memorably named villains as Ben Jonson's Sir Epicure Mammon and Sir Moth Interest,[29] Middleton's Quomodo, Falselight and Shortyard (also known as Blastfield),[30] Massinger's Luke Frugal and Sir Giles Overreach,[31] Mayne's Warehouse and Seathrift,[32] John Wilson's Suckdry and Squeeze,[33] Wycherley's Alderman Gripe, James Formal and Sir Jaspar Fidget,[34] Farquhar's Smuggler,[35] and Bunyan's Mr Badman.[36] It is a remarkable cast of villains and constitutes a formidable case against commerce and business in all its forms. Even unattractive characters such as Jonson's Volpone (himself seen as the incarnation of his age's characteristic hunger for wealth) gains a little credit and distinguishes himself from the grasping merchant Corvino by boldly declaring his superiority over the despised man of commerce:

> I gain
> No common way: I use no trade, no venture
>
> ...
> I turn no moneys in the public bank
> Nor usure private.[37]

[27] McVeagh, *Tradefull Merchants*, p. 17.
[28] *Ibid.*, p. 19.
[29] Mammon in Ben Jonson, *The Alchemist* (1610), Meercraft in *The Divell is an Asse* (1616), and Interest in *The Magnetic Lady* (1632).
[30] Thomas Middleton, *Michaelmas Term* (1606).
[31] Frugal in Philip Massinger, *The City Madam* (1632) and Overreach in *A New Way to Pay Old Debts* (1631).
[32] Both in Jasper Mayne, *The Citye Match* (1637).
[33] Both in John Wilson, *The Projectors* (1664).
[34] Gripe in William Wycherley, *Love in a Wood* (1671), Formal in *The Gentleman Dancing Master* (1672) and Fidget in *The Country Wife* (1675).
[35] George Farquhar, *The Constant Couple* (1699).
[36] John Bunyan, *The Life and Death of Mr. Badman* (1680).
[37] Ben Jonson, *Volpone* (1607), I, i, quoted in McVeagh, *Tradefull Merchants*, p. 21. Other important studies are L. C. Knights, *Drama and Society in the Age of Jonson* (London, 1937); John Loftis, *Comedy and Society from Congreve to Fielding* (Stanford, 1959).

They were mocked because they were feared. They were feared because they were seen as predatory, ambitious and aggressive, a threat to the established social order. The obsessive interest in them is testimony to how serious that threat was felt to be.

If one adds the familiar Victorian millocrats and swindlers to this cast of villains in Jacobean and Caroline satire and in Restoration comic drama the hostile literary case seems to be overwhelming. The nineteenth century's verdict seems to be as clearly advertised as the seventeenth century's verdict in such revealingly named characters as Disraeli's Shuffle and Screw, or Meredith's Major Strike, or George Eliot's Sir Gavial Mantrap, or Samuel Warren's Sir Sharper Bubble or Charles Lever's Davenport Dunn or indeed Dickens' Bounderby, Gradgrind, Merdle or Veneering.[38] If one adds to such a list the unappealing manufacturers depicted by Mrs Tonna, Mrs Trollope, Mrs Gaskell and Charles Kingsley in the 1840s, the case seems even stronger. The sense of uniform cultural condemnation seems clear if one then adds the *apparently* (and I stress that it is only apparent) unanimously hostile verdict provided by Charles Reade's Skinner in *Hard Cash* (1863), Anthony Trollope's Melmotte and Fisker in *The Way We Live Now* (1874–5), Thomas Hardy's Adner Power in *A Laodicean* (1881), G. B. Shaw's Andrew Undershaft in *Major Barbara* (1905) and Boss Mangam in *Heartbreak House* (1919), H. G. Wells' Uncle Ponderevo in *Tono Bungay* (1909) and D. H. Lawrence's Gerald Crich in *Women in Love* (1920) and Sir Clifford Chatterley in *Lady Chatterley's Lover* (1928).

This is familiar ground and to recall the tone of disdain, disapproval and even disgust in some of these authors one only needs to recall the string of adjectives used to describe Sir Matthew Dowling in Frances Trollope's *Michael Armstrong, The Factory Boy* (1840). He is described as abominable, wicked, low-born, brutal, treacherous, pitiful, cheating – in short a 'manufacturing savage'.[39] And that is his wife's verdict on his deathbed! If that is thought to be too specific consider Charlotte Brontë's summing up of the qualities of the British merchant as a class in *Shirley* (1849). They think, she wrote,

> too exclusively of making money: they are too oblivious of every national consideration but that of extending England's (i.e. their own) commerce. Chivalrous feeling, disinterestedness, pride in honour, is too dead in their hearts. A land ruled by them alone would too often make ignominious submission to Mammon. Many of them are extremely narrow and cold hearted, have no good feeling for any class but their own, are distant – even hostile to others; call them useless; seem even to question their right to exist; seem to grudge them the very air they breathe, and to think the circumstances of their eating, drinking, and living in decent houses quite unjustifiable. They do not know what others do in the way of helping, pleasing

---

[38] McKendrick, 'Enemies of...the Self Made Man', p. xix.
[39] Frances Trollope, *Michael Armstrong, The Factory Boy* (1840), p. 345.

or teaching their race; they will not trouble themselves to inquire; whoever is not in trade is accused of eating the bread of idleness, of passing a useless existence. Long may it be ere England really becomes a nation of shopkeepers.[40]

Faced with such ringing accusations and the condemnation implicit in Dickens' setpiece description of Coketown or Lawrence's description of Tevershall, it is perhaps little wonder that most businessmen remained convinced that the literary world viewed them with powerful disfavour. They had little doubt that the majority vote was hostile to them – as in fact it was – but they seem as blind as many historians to the widespread commendation of commerce of the early eighteenth century, unaware of the awe and admiration of industry which one finds in the late eighteenth century, and ignorant of the approving portrayal of individual businessmen which one can so easily find in Jane Austen, Mrs Stone, Mrs Gaskell, Mrs Craik and Charles Dickens even at the height of literary condemnation in the nineteenth century. There is admiration for the businessman to be found in the work of G. B. Shaw, H. G. Wells, E. M. Forster and Arnold Bennett in the early twentieth century when some of the fiercest literary salvos were being fired at the salesmen, the industrial magnates and the new managerial class.

Admittedly, the most vivid images are the hostile ones. In the bestiary of entrepreneurial analogies the businessman has been presented as 'the master spider of his race', as a predatory lobster, as a shark, as a bird of prey, a wolf, or even that master of disguise and deceit, the Black Grouper.[41] It hardly helps the standing of the businessman when the corrupt and immoral Skinner in *Hard Cash* (1863) justifies his actions, when he is caught out, with the reply, 'I'm not a viper; I'm a man of business.'[42]

Against this the more subtle affirmations of business virtue have been overpowered and the businessman has remained convinced of the hostility of literature. 'My bookshelves are crammed with volumes explaining what an evil creature I am. I possess numbers of books telling me how beautiful the world would be if only I and my class could be eradicated. The literary case against me is overwhelming.'[43] Sir Ernest Benn, who wrote this in *The Confessions of a Capitalist* (1925), revealingly gave examples to prove his case. Ruskin is quoted to the effect that 'to trade' is little more than 'the worst word for fraud...and trader, traditor and traitor are but the same word'.[44] Philip Snowden is quoted to the effect that the capitalist system is 'a war' in which 'unnumbered lives' are 'sacrificed' for 'commercial

---

[40] Charlotte Brontë, *Shirley* (1849), pp. 132–3.
[41] McKendrick, 'General Introduction to Business History', p. xxx.
[42] Charles Reade, *Hard Cash* (1863), ch. 51.
[43] E. J. P. Benn, *The Confessions of a Capitalist* (London, 1925; 13th edn 1936), p. 17.
[44] Ruskin, *Commerce: Munera Pulveris*, quoted in *ibid.*, p. 18.

gain', and the survivors are simply those 'most endowed with cunning and greed and audacity'.[45] Sidney Webb is quoted, simply equating 'the process of distribution' with 'blackmail'.[46]

These examples and all the others quoted by Benn are revealingly taken from literary critics[47] and political commentators rather than from novelists, poets and playwrights. They provide an important clue to the prevailing sense of literary condemnation. For the apparent unanimity of the adversary culture's response to businessmen owes more to the influential critics than it does to the record of imaginative writing alone. Those who have preached that a nation's culture resides in the best that has been thought and said have sometimes been rather selective in constructing their anthologies of the best thoughts and sayings. When Henry James praised the poetry of Matthew Arnold for 'its remarkable faculty for touching the chords which connect our feelings with the things that others have done or spoken' he was not only gracefully echoing Arnold's own definition of culture,[48] but offering further support for the culturally unifying effects of our literary heritage. When such claims are made for the influence of literary role models on the conduct and values of future generations it is important that the record is accurately represented. We need to recognize that even in the seventeenth century the poetry of Denham, Fanshawe, Weller, the early Dryden and Matthew Prior looked favourably on the merchant, whilst Pope in *Windsor Forest* (1713), Edward Young in *Imperium Pelagi* (1729) and John Gay in his eighth fable (1738) wrote panegyrics to commerce. Gay announces his belief that

> On trade alone thy glory stands
> That benefit is unconfin'd
> Diffusing good among mankind
> ....
> Be commerce then thy sole design
> Keep that, and all the world is thine.[49]

---

[45] Philip Snowden, *Labour and the New World*, quoted in Benn, *Confessions of a Capitalist*, p. 18.

[46] Sidney Webb, *A Constitution for the Socialist Commonwealth of Great Britain*, quoted in Benn, *Confessions of a Capitalist*, p. 19.

[47] He could have quoted many other critics using identical language. William Morris in his essay 'How We Live and How We Might Live' (1885) spoke of 'that other war called commerce' and equated exports with 'successful burglary'; May Morris, *The Collected Works of William Morris* (London, 1915), pp. xxiii and 5.

[48] The unifying force of English literature is frequently invoked in our culture, even if sometimes ironically. Winston Smith's comment 'The best books are those that tell you what you know already' lies at the ironic end of the spectrum in sharp contrast to the pieties of Matthew Arnold and Henry James: George Orwell, *Nineteen Eighty-Four* (1949), p. 161.

[49] Quoted in McVeagh, *Tradefull Merchants*, p. 69.

But Edward Young's *The Merchant* (1729) exceeds even his enthusiasm:

> Is 'merchant' an inglorious name?
> What say the sons of letter'd fame?[50]

he asks rhetorically, and provides his own ecstatic answer, comparing merchants favourably with heroes, priests, kings and even the heat-giving planets. His eulogy runs for forty pages but by 1729 its tone and content are almost representative. Pope sang the praises of harbours and public ways;[51] Richard Savage wrote of rivers that are taught a new commercial flow lest 'they flow in vain' – that is, without a commercial purpose and economic reward;[52] and James Thomson in *The Seasons* (1726–30) spoke of the benevolent consequences of 'generous Commerce' which binds nations in its 'golden chain'.[53]

In the theatre too the growing appreciation of the merchant is unmistakable. In the late seventeenth century they still had to compete with the hostile view but by the early decades of the eighteenth the benevolent verdict was clearly dominant. This is the period in literature's treatment of the businessman which John McVeagh has labelled 'The Merchant as Hero: 1700–1750'.[54] Even the names of the literary heroes proclaim their virtues as clearly as the villains of the earlier theatre proclaimed their vices. Wycherley's Manly in *The Plaindealer* (1676), Ravenscroft's Loveday in 1681,[55] Shadwell's Sir Edward Belfond in 1688,[56] Susannah Centlivre's Mr Freeman in 1718,[57] the *Spectator's* Sir Andrew Freeport and Richard Steele's Mr Sealand in 1722[58] are all inescapably men of business and self-evidently worthy of literary approval. The approbation of commerce and science and invention to be found in John Evelyn's diaries (1650-99) and Thomas Sprat's *History of the Royal Society* (1667) culminated in Steele and Addison's idealization of trade,[59] Mandeville's provocative justification of luxury and consumption,[60] and Defoe's idealization of the merchant.[61]

---

[50] Edward Young, *Poetical Works* (London, 1896), vol. II, p. 337.
[51] Alexander Pope, *Moral Epistles*, 'To Burlington', quoted in McVeagh, *Tradefull Merchants*, p. 71.
[52] Richard Savage, *Poetical Works*, ed. C. Tracey (Cambridge, 1962), pp. 221–2.
[53] James Thomson, *The Seasons* [1735], 'Summer', 138–9.
[54] McVeagh, *Tradefull Merchants*, ch. 3.
[55] Edward Ravenscroft, *The London Cuckolds* (1681).
[56] Thomas Shadwell, *The Squire of Alsatia* (1688).
[57] Susannah Centlivre, *A Bold Stroke for a Wife* (1718).
[58] Richard Steele, *The Conscious Lovers* (1722).
[59] See Jacob Viner, 'Satire and Economics in the Augustan Age', in Henry Knight Miller, Eric Rothstein and G. S. Rousseau (eds.), *The Augustan Milieu: Essays Presented to Louis A. Landa* (Oxford, 1971).
[60] Bernard Mandeville, *The Fable of the Bees: Private Vices, Publick Benefits* (1714, final version 1724).
[61] Michael Shinagel, *Daniel Defoe and Middle Class Gentility* (Cambridge, Mass., 1968).

To Steele in *The Englishman* (1713) the merchant was 'the greatest Benefactor of the English Nation';[62] to Mandeville in *The Fable of the Bees* (1714) the private vices of luxury, indulgence, vanity, fashion and conspicuous consumption had become public virtues as the subtitle to his insect allegory made clear;[63] while to Defoe in his *A Plan of English Commerce* (1727) and *The Compleat English Gentleman* (1729) the merchant reached his apotheosis as super-hero.[64] In Defoe's work the merchant's virtues almost define an Englishman's virtues. Whilst during our long period of relative economic decline during the last hundred years, the defining characteristics of the Englishman have been defensively reassessed and redefined to protect him from unfavourable comparisons with other national stereotypes, Defoe boldly characterized the Englishman not by his ability to invent but by his ability to develop other people's ideas – 'they are better to improve than to invent, better to advance upon the designs and plans which other people have laid down, than to form schemes and designs of their own'.[65]

But if Defoe's writing provided the high-water mark of approval of the man of business, he was to receive plaudits or at the very least recognition of his virtues in English literature for a very long time after him. His merits may have been anxiously debated by Fielding and Smollett and Goldsmith in the eighteenth century, and he had also to survive the doubts and fears created by the 'luxury debate'[66] of the mid-eighteenth century and the sharp literary response to the nabobs in the 1770s, but Dyer's merchants are still 'princely' in *The Fleece* in 1757, and to him 'all is joy' where 'trade and business guide the living scene'.[67] A sense of awe and admiration for the prime movers of the economy was still widespread.

In the poetry, painting and prints of this period one can clearly detect what F. R. Leavis called the 'sense of the Titanism and romantic sublimity in the works of man'.[68] Yet in this period of early dramatic economic growth, long before the disasters of the economic depression of 1839–42 which provoked the agonized beginning of the major literary debate over the contributory role of the manufacturer to what had gone wrong, one can already find clear evidence of a fierce and highly specific attack on the man of business. The overseas merchant of good birth and gentlemanly

---

[62] Richard Steele, *The Englishman* (1713), ed. R. Blanchard (Oxford, 1955), p. 320.

[63] See *The Fable of the Bees* (London, 1970 edition with an introduction by Philip Martin).

[64] Maximilian Novak, *Economics and the Fiction of Daniel Defoe* (Berkeley, 1962).

[65] Daniel Defoe, *A Plan of the English Commerce* (1727), p. 299.

[66] John Sekora, *Luxury, The Concept in Western Thought, Eden to Smollett* (Baltimore and London, 1977).

[67] John Dyer, *The Fleece* (1757), quoted in Margaret Drabble, *A Writer's Britain, Landscape in Literature* (London, 1979), p. 199.

[68] Leavis, *Nor Shall My Sword*, pp. 82–3.

accomplishment was still admired even in the late eighteenth century, but in the novels of the period 1760 to 1790 a sharp literary reaction against the lesser trader and the upstart businessman was already clear. No one has shown better than J. R. Raven how sharp a change from the literary approbation of the period up to 1760 can be seen in the next three decades of the eighteenth century.[69] Admittedly some novelists like Mrs Gomersall in *Eleonora* (1788) and *The Citizen* (1790) fought a spirited rearguard action. But Mrs Gomersall's defence of the businessman reflected the provincial sub-culture of Leeds,[70] just as Erasmus Darwin and Thomas Day and Anna Seward reflected the provincial sub-culture of the Midlands.[71] There were many such provincial sub-cultures. Just as the Lunar Society of Birmingham represented a different set of values[72] from those which dominated London culture, so Mrs Gomersall's Leeds businessmen were very different from those being depicted in the London literary world.[73]

Significantly Mrs Gomersall and others identified the novelist as the major force behind the anti-business sentiment of the late eighteenth century. Literature was already a formative influence and when Samuel Garbett and Jedediah Strutt and James Watt complained of their social reception and lowly status in this period,[74] they could legitimately point to the caricatures and stereotypes of the contemporary novel. The idealization of the merchant as gentleman continued in the merchant-prince tradition, but the self-made businessman was disdained as an upstart, a social parvenu, a mere mushroom who threatened the social order. Judged by the gentlemanly ideal he was consistently found wanting as society sought proof of its social ideals by the depiction in literature of those who

---

[69] J. R. Raven, 'English Popular Literature and the Image of Business, 1760–1790' (University of Cambridge Ph.D. dissertation, 1985).

[70] R. G. Wilson, *Gentleman Merchants: The Merchant Community in Leeds, 1700–1830* (Manchester, 1971).

[71] John Money, *Experience and Identity: Birmingham and the West Midlands, 1760–1800* (Manchester, 1977). For an examination of the cultural attitudes of Josiah Wedgwood and his Circle see Neil McKendrick, 'The Role of Science in the Industrial Revolution', in M. Teich and R. Young (eds.), *Changing Perspectives of the History of Science* (London, 1973), pp. 274–319, for the positive attitude to science and its economically purposeful use; and for the positive attitude to salesmanship, marketing and advertising see Neil McKendrick, John Brewer and J. H. Plumb, *The Birth of a Consumer Society: The Commercialization of Eighteenth-Century England* (London, 1982).

[72] Robert E. Schofield, *The Lunar Society* (Oxford, 1963).

[73] These regional subcultures are important. This type of cultural history is implicitly comparative, and the comparisons can be just as illuminating when made regionally as when made nationally. We would do well to heed not only Blaise Pascal's 'Verité en-deça des Pyrénées, erreur au-delà' (*Pensées*, 60, 294), but also the message of Mrs Gaskell's *North and South* that there are assumed truths in the South of England which would be falsehoods north of the Trent.

[74] McKendrick, 'Literary Luddism and the Businessman', p. xxix; Roy Porter, *English Society in the Eighteenth Century* (London, 1982), p. 87.

lacked them. The literary attack on the lack of gentlemanly characteristics of the nabob, the self-made manufacturer and the petty trader was merciless. Long before the literary attack of the 1840s and in a period of rapid economic growth, the literary onslaught on 'these sons and daughters of sudden opulence'[75] was already clearly evident. What novelists like Mrs Charlotte Lennox were attacking in novels like her *Euphemia* (1790) were not the business activities of their fictional victims but their failure to conform to the gentlemanly ideal. They lacked birth and social accomplishment. They did not know how to behave or how to conduct themselves. They were vulgar. Judged by standards of gentlemanly taste and manners and deportment they failed. The nabob failed because his ostentation was excessive, the petty trader failed because his social pretensions to gentility were open to ridicule. Both were seen as a threat to the established social order and were in consequence bitterly attacked. Those novelists who failed to attack them could look forward to sharp rebuke in the influential reviews of literary London.

Some of the doubts which afflicted those writing about the businessmen were relatively shortlived and highly specific to a contemporary concern. George Colman accurately reflects the changing response to the merchant in the 1770s when his merchant hero's cause is warmly espoused in *The English Merchant* (1767), while in his *The Man of Business* (1774), his merchants Golding and Tropick are of much more dubious worth. Samuel Foote's *The Nabob* (1772) and the anonymous *The Nabob: or, Asiatic Plunderers* (1773) also reflect the tensions posed by the enormous wealth of the returning nabobs who threatened the position of the landed classes by their wealth, their newly acquired possessions, their ostentatious free spending and their 'governing Spirit'. One of the first examples of condemnation of the businessman by use of previous literary authorities is cited by McVeagh when he quotes[76] from *The Nabob* (1773):

> Low-thoughted Commerce! heart-corrupting trade!
> So *Plato* thought, so *More*, and *Montesquieu*.[77]

But such a practice had a long way to go before it could achieve the cumulative condemnation which is held to be part of the present adversary culture. For many writers no single verdict was adequate to do justice to both their admiration and their doubts. Just as Colman's verdict is different in 1774 from that of 1767, so Blake's verdict changes dramatically from his eulogy of trade in 1783 to his condemnation in 1797, and the early

[75] Mrs Charlotte Lennox, *Euphemia* (1790), quoted in Raven, 'English Popular Literature', p. 150.
[76] McVeagh, *Tradefull Merchants*, p. 97.
[77] *The Nabob: or, Asiatic Plunderers* (1773), p. 42.

Wordsworth is much more optimistic than his later writing would suggest. Nor are the changes always in the pessimistic direction: Mrs Gaskell's verdict on Mr Carson in 1848 is very different from her approving verdict on Mr Thornton in 1855; H. G. Wells' verdict on Ponderevo in *Tono Bungay* (1909) is a startling contrast to his commendation of William Clissold in 1926. Nor are the verdicts consistent: Dickens after all produced his portrait of the impressive Mr Rouncewell, the ironmaster in *Bleak House* (1852–3), within eighteen months of his verdict on the appalling Mr Bounderby in *Hard Times* (1854); while Daniel Doyce, the 'genius of beneficent invention' in *Little Dorrit* (1855–7) coexists with the odious profiteer Merdle in the same book. Indeed those who label Dickens as a Luddite and who cite Dombey and Bounderby and Merdle and Veneering, plus Podsnap, Scrooge, Quilp, Montague Tigg and Carker (and unfairly add Gradgrind) to prove their point have to confront the fact that there is a balancing set of approving portraits of Dickensian men of business. Nicholas Nickleby is a virtuous and successful merchant, Rouncewell is an admirable and much admired manufacturer, Clennam is an approved business manager, Meagles is a benevolent banker, Daniel Doyce is an inventor of genius, the Cheeryble brothers are paragons of business and other virtues, and there are plenty of minor characters such as Solomon Gills and Jason Lorry to complete the alternative verdict of Dickensian approbation – all are generous and responsible, all are inescapably men of business and commerce.[78]

Many other writers display the same ambivalence. Charlotte Brontë's *Shirley* is often quite properly quoted for its condemnation of the British merchant and the British industrialist. It is the only major literary investigation of actual Luddism, and she displays real sympathy for the machine-breakers and the mill-burners. But she ends the novel with Gérard Moore, 'the man most abominated' at the beginning of the book,[79] and his brother Robert reformed and redeemed. Moore forgives the half-crazed weaver who shot him, and pays for his burial.[80] He presages his proposal of marriage with the sincere declaration that 'I can take more workmen, give better wages; lay wiser and more liberal plans; do some good; be less selfish.'[81] It is very much a businessman's proposal but his determination

---

[78] This period is well covered in A. Melada, *Captains of Industry in English Fiction, 1821–1871* (New York, 1955); Ivanka Kovecevic, *Fact into Fiction: English Literature and the Industrial Scene, 1750–1850* (London, 1975); John R. Reed, *Victorian Conventions* (Columbus, Ohio, 1975); Gertrude Himmelfarb, *The Idea of Poverty: England in the Early Industrial Age* (London and Boston, 1984); Sheila M. Smith, *The Other Nation: The Poor in English Novels of the 1840s and 1850s* (Oxford, 1980); Martha Vicinus, *The Industrial Muse: A Study of Nineteenth Century Working Class Literature* (London, 1974).

[79] Charlotte Brontë, *Shirley, A Tale* (1849), p. 22.

[80] *Ibid.*, p. 502.   [81] *Ibid.*, p. 506.

to do good is repeated over and over again (he will create work for 'the houseless, the starving, the unemployed'),[82] and Caroline's acceptance of him seals his redemption, as does Shirley's infatuated fondness for Louis Gérard Moore whom 'she will one day see as universally beloved as even *she* could wish: he will also be universally esteemed, considered, consulted and depended on...his advice will be always judicious, his help always goodnatured'.[83] The book ends on a nicely impartial note. The last page records that Robert Moore's promises and prophecies were 'partially, at least, fulfilled'.[84] Whether for good or ill is left unstated. What was once 'green, and lone and wild' was much altered – 'there I saw the manufacturer's day-dreams embodied in substantial stone and brick and ashes – the cinder black highway, the cottages, and the cottage gardens; there I saw a mighty mill, and a chimney, ambitious as the tower of Babel'. Charlotte Brontë contents herself with the simple judgment that it was 'different'. She refuses to draw a moral. 'It would be an insult to the sagacity' of her audience 'to offer directions' to 'the judicious reader putting on his spectacles' in search of one.[85]

The same balanced verdict can be found in E. M. Forster's *Howard's End* (1910), in Arnold Bennett's *Anna of the Five Towns* (1902) and *Clayhanger* (1910), while in *Major Barbara* (1905) Shaw explores a more complex set of ambivalent attitudes.[86] Given the fact that, in Jane Austen's Mr Gardiner, Mrs Gaskell's John Thornton, Mrs Stone's Mr Ainsley, Mrs Craik's John Halifax, Dickens' Cheeryble brothers, Bennett's Henry Mynors and Wells' William Clissold, the English novelist has supplied such a well-stocked cast of business heroes; given the fact that there is, in addition, a rich cast of dramatic commercial heroes depicted in Heywood and Dekker, in Wycherley and Shadwell, in Addison and Steele and Defoe (and indeed in so many other writers); one can reasonably ask why the business ideal is thought to be so ill represented in English literature.

Partly this arises from simple ignorance, which this study has tried to dispel. Partly it arises from the effects of selective anthologies which by sticking so resolutely to the 'from dark Satanic mill to D. H. Lawrence' tradition have telescoped the evidence and effaced from the record much of the approbation of the businessman and much of the endorsement of his values. Partly, too, it arises from the influence of powerful critical traditions which have interpreted the evidence 'to improve the moral

---

[82] *Ibid.*, p. 510. Significantly after his declaration and acceptance, he is recognized as a gentleman. 'You are a gentleman all through, to the bone', p. 508.
[83] *Ibid.*, p. 509.
[84] *Ibid.*, p. 510.   [85] *Ibid.*, p. 511.
[86] See J. M. Winter's examination of Shaw's *Major Barbara* in Chapter 9 below.

message' and produce a verdict which they find emotionally and politically sympathetic.[87]

There are many other contributory causes which help to explain the complex and subtle process by which the adversary culture has emerged. They involve what has been called 'the Luddite interpretation of History', 'the worship of inutility', the 'horror of the parvenu', 'the tyranny of technophobia' and many other factors which must be examined elsewhere.[88] The aesthetic critique, the environmental critique, the radical critique, the conservative critique, the anti-semitic critique and the xeno-phobic critique have all played their part along with the South's suspicion of the North, the arts' suspicion of science, even the Londoner's suspicion of the provinces. Given the space of a single chapter one can concentrate effectively on only one influence although it involves many separate strands and interacts with many others. That is the suspicion felt by the gentleman for the self-made man and the suspicion felt by the professional for the non-professional, which have joined to breed the suspicion felt by the twentieth-century mandarin, who usually regards himself as both gentleman and professional, for the practical man of business.

For many of the businessman's problems arise from the fact that he has rarely been judged against any acceptable business ideal. In the theatre and in the novel, he has almost invariably been judged by the criteria of the gentlemanly ideal in its various literary forms – the final twentieth-century version of which has absorbed much of the professional ideal.

Laura Caroline Stevenson in *Praise and Paradox*,[89] which deals with the depiction of the merchant in Elizabethan popular literature, has shown that the merchants are praised not by reference to their own class and achievements but in relation to the gentry and the existing social elite. The familiar image of the rapacious usurer can be transformed into that of the respected citizen, and the merchant can even achieve heroic status, but only in terms of the prevailing social values. As a result he is praised more for his civic virtues and political skills than he is for his actual business expertise.

John McVeagh in *Tradefull Merchants: The Portrayal of the Capitalist in Literature* has shown how often this is the case from the seventeenth century onwards. Mercantile characters, like Shadwell's Sir Edward Belfond and Ravenscroft's hero Loveday, are praised for their gentlemanly style,

---

[87] McKendrick, 'Enemies of...the Self Made Man', pp. xxix–xxxi; John Carey, *The Violent Effigy: A Study of Dickens' Imagination* (London, 1973), pp. 109–11.

[88] I have dealt with these in outline in the general introductions to the *Europa Library of Business History* (London, 1976 to 1979).

[89] Laura Caroline Stevenson, *Praise and Paradox: Merchants and Craftsmen in Elizabethan Popular Literature* (Cambridge, 1984).

2

not their business acumen. Shadwell describes Sir Edward as 'A Man of great Humanity and Gentleness and Compassion towards Mankind; well read in good Books, possess'd of all Gentlemanlike Qualities'.[90]

Robin Gilmour in *The Idea of the Gentleman in Victorian Fiction*[91] has described the anxious debate over who were and who were not gentlemen in Victorian fiction. Few problems caused more agonized discussion as Victorian society tried to come to terms with the social and economic upheaval caused by the Industrial Revolution. The influential makers of Victorian opinion – Ruskin, Arnold, Cardinal Newman and Samuel Smiles – all took the matter immensely seriously, and one cannot read far in Thackeray, Dickens or Trollope without realizing that they were fascinated by the image of the gentleman and its relations to the actual and ideal possibilities of the moral life in society. The idea of the gentleman is, as Asa Briggs has written, 'the necessary link in any analysis of Victorian ways of thinking and behaving',[92] and its importance was fully grasped in nineteenth-century fiction. For the moral component of gentlemanliness, and its social ambiguity, made it both open to debate and open to invasion in a way that the aristocracy was not. The problem was to widen the basis of qualification without sacrificing the exclusiveness which was the source of its esteem, and the different versions which evolved in literature faithfully reflected this paradox. Indeed it is a central thread in Victorian fiction and helps to explain why some groups succeeded and others failed to reach the goal of social acceptance. In this battle for status the businessman had to accept the ideals of other groups if he wished to be accepted. When Bertrand Russell wrote that 'the concept of the gentleman was invented by aristocrats to keep the middle classes in order'[93] he recognized that at least in the early stages the cultural hegemony of the aristocracy remained intact. But of far greater interest is the way in which the concept of the gentleman was later refined and developed greatly to the advantage of the professional middle classes and to the disadvantage of the industrial bourgeoisie.

Matthew Arnold recognized this division in the ranks of the middle classes very quickly. In 1868, in giving evidence to the Taunton Commission, he said,

So we have among us the spectacle of a middle class cut in two, in a way unexampled anywhere else; of a professional class brought up on the first plane with fine and governing qualities, but without science; while the immense business

[90] Thomas Shadwell, *The Squire of Alsatia* (1688), quoted in McVeagh, *Tradefull Merchants*, p. 33.
[91] Robin Gilmour, *The Idea of the Gentleman in Victorian Fiction* (London, 1981).
[92] Asa Briggs, *The Age of Improvement, 1783–1867* (London, 1959), p. 411.
[93] Quoted in Gilmour, *The Idea of the Gentleman*, p. 5.

class which is becoming so important a power in all countries, on which the future so depends and which in the leading schools of other countries fills so large a space, is, in England, brought up on the second plane, cut off from the aristocracy and the professions, and without governing qualities.[94]

Arnold perceptively noted that the business classes were cut off from both gentlemanly and professional ideals, and the development of those two ideals in literature helps to explain why this occurred – helps to explain why no acceptable business ideal evolved either in literature or in society.

In the eighteenth and nineteenth centuries the businessman continued to be judged as he had been in the sixteenth and seventeenth centuries not by his own merits but by those of the gentleman. If they wished to make him acceptable, the novelists must make him conform to the prevailing ideals. This was the fate of Jane Austen's admirable Mr Gardiner in *Pride and Prejudice* (1813). He easily rises above the snobbish disdain for trade of the odious Bingley sisters, he fully convinces Mr Darcy of his worth (that Mr Darcy whom Elizabeth thought would think 'a month's ablutions' insufficient 'to cleanse him from the impurities' of a visit to Mr Gardiner's place of work),[95] but he does so by behaving like a gentleman. He is one of the most admired characters in the novel but he is judged and accepted solely by the values of the gentlemanly ideal, not the business ideal. We are told nothing of the virtues and values which might make him a good businessman. Mr Darcy and Mr Knightley remain the real Austen heroes. They represent the dominant social ideal. They are rich, landed and of good birth. They are 'somebody without having to do anything'.[96]

The title of Mrs Craik's *John Halifax, Gentleman* (1856) proclaims how John Halifax's business successes were judged and against what standards. John Halifax was carefully distanced from the stereotype business figure of the Industrial Revolution and the 'Condition of England' novels by being placed in the rural West Country rather than the Industrial North, by being an Anglican not a non-conformist, and was allowed to escape environmental and aesthetic objections to industrial technology by careful choice of his business. But what made him most acceptable of all was that he was 'a born gentleman'. John Thornton in *North and South* was made acceptable by grafting on the values of the educated, socially acceptable southerner Margaret Hale to soften those characteristics which made him look like a northern businessman, and therefore unacceptable, at the beginning of the book. His transformation is represented by each step he takes towards the behaviour of a gentleman. Taking instruction in classics from Margaret Hale's father is the first revealing step towards social acceptability and

[94] Matthew Arnold, *Evidence to the Schools Inquiry (Taunton) Commission* (1868), vol. VI, pp. 626–7.
[95] Jane Austen, *Pride and Prejudice* (1813), p. 112.
[96] Ellen Moers, *Literary Women* (London, 1978), p. 66.

consequent literary approval. One can pick off one by one most of the list of business heroes in literature and find a similar explanation. Revealingly when one *cannot* do so (as with the Cheeryble brothers, who were northern, self-made manufacturers and were presented as such), they have been denounced as unacceptable, even unreal, by English critical opinion. For all their virtues and achievements, they jarred too much with the preferred values to earn anything more than dismissive disdain.[97] Even Samuel Smiles refused to admire money-making and chose to present his heroes as the exemplification of moral virtue rather than as an idealization of business skill and achievement.[98] Even as late as 1910 when E. M. Forster offered a functional justification of the wealth-creating Wilcoxes, on whom such cultivated, liberal-minded families like the Schlegels depended, he left his readers in no doubt as to which of the two was to be preferred.[99] If, as Oscar Wilde insisted, 'Life imitates Art more than Art imitates Life'[100] then its imitative instincts get little encouragement from business role models. In consequence 'In Britain today we all want to be Schlegels.'[101]

Perhaps most revealing of all is the fact that even Defoe qualified his enthusiasm for the men of business in one significant way. He goes further towards the formulation of a business ideal than any other writer. As a trader himself he knew what qualities were required for success, and he was fulsome in his recognition of the merchant's virtues and achievements. The creation of wealth posed no moral problems for Defoe. 'Wealth is wisdom, he that is rich is wise',[102] he wrote, and since the route to wealth ran via trade the gentleman should seek greater wealth by following the merchant's lead. He pays tribute too to the merchant's distinctive contribution to our national culture: 'a true-bred Merchant is a Universal Scholar, his learning excells the meer scholar in Greek and Latin, as much as that does that of the Illiterate Person, that cannot read or write'.[103]

But just when it seems that a well-formulated version of a possible business ideal is emerging, just when it seems that the businessman is being given precedence over the gentleman, Defoe's major qualification appears. 'Trade makes gentlemen', he wrote, and 'after a generation or two the tradesman's children come to be as good statesmen, judges or bishops as

---

[97] See Melada, *Captains of Industry*, pp. 107–8.
[98] See Aileen Smiles, *Samuel Smiles and his Surroundings* (London, 1978), p. 107.
[99] E. M. Forster, *Howards End* (1910).
[100] Quoted in Juliet and Rowland McMaster, *The Novel from Sterne to James: Essays on the Relation of Literature to Life* (London, 1981), p. vii.
[101] Noel Annan, 'The Path to British Decadence', *Sunday Times Weekly Review*, 22 May 1977, p. 324. Expanded in Noel Annan, '"Our Age": Reflections on Three Generations in England', *Daedalus* (Fall 1978), 81–109. There Lord Annan writes, 'In Britain we are all Schlegels now,' p. 106.
[102] Daniel Defoe, *The Compleat English Gentleman* (1729).
[103] *Ibid.*, p. 9: 'Thus tradesmen become gentlemen, by gentlemen becoming tradesmen.'

those of the most antient [*sic*] families'.[104] The assumption is that there is a higher calling above and beyond trade. Defoe's endorsement, like all the others, is qualified by the implicit acceptance of the superiority of another ideal. However beneficial trade is it is regarded as a transitional not a traditional mode of employment. Once the trader has made his legitimate and much valued fortune, he will be expected to seek to convert it into land or the pursuit of public service. It is not essential to buy land but there remains an overriding moral obligation for the merchant to place his or his children's talents at the call of his country's administrators and public servants. There could be no greater admission of the higher status of the superior ideal.

Whatever criteria were adopted (as the gentlemanly ideal was refined to meet the changing needs of society), the business ideal always remained subordinate to them. The social criteria of ancient land, ancient lineage and ancient wealth gave way (in the face of threats from those who looked likely to acquire at least mimic forms of those requirements) to behavioural criteria based on taste, manners and acceptable conduct – to a marked degree in the age of the Dandy.[105] This in turn gave way to the moral criteria of the Victorian ideal gentleman as Victorian authors sought to find worthier and more manly values than those discussed so avidly in the 'Silver Fork School' of novels of fashion.[106] When the institutional solution to the uncertainties of these moral criteria was found in the Victorian public schools with their insistence on duty before pleasure, service before self, public good before personal gain, those businessmen who gained acceptance for their sons by sending them to public schools saw them educated to resist and reject the profit-seeking, competitive individualism of the entrepreneurial ideal.[107]

Finally when the gentlemanly ideal was further refined to meet the needs of a more complex society – and professional criteria of acceptance were developed – the businessman ideal was once again downgraded in comparison with the professional ideal. The latter is the dominant ideal of contemporary English society and its emergence does more to explain the low status of the businessman than the overt hostility to the businessman which is claimed, erroneously, to flourish in contemporary fiction.

The rise of the professions in our society is a spectacular one – from 2.1 per cent of the male occupied population in 1881 to 11.6 per cent in 1971;

[104] 'The rising tradesmen swell into the gentry', Defoe, *A Piece of English Commerce* (1728), in *Defoe's Writings* (Oxford, 1927), p. 38.
[105] Ellen Moers, *The Dandy: Brummell to Beerbohm* (London, 1960).
[106] M. W. Rosa, *The Silver Fork School: Novels of Fashion Preceding Vanity Fair* (New York, 1936).
[107] 'The ultimate proof of success in business was the ability to leave it.' David Cannadine quoted in Porter, *English Society in the Eighteenth Century*, p. 87.

or, if we take a more inclusive definition and include professional administrators and managers, from 6.8 per cent in 1911 to 21.5 per cent in 1971.[108] 'At the same time', as Harold Perkin put it, 'there has been a veritable explosion of professional organisation'[109] – from seven such bodies in 1800 to twenty-seven in 1880 to 167 in 1970.

The professions have been remarkably successful not only in the growth of numbers but in the competition for status, authority and influence. In the battle for prestige they have been the most successful group in our society. Of three major forms of power (the economic, the political and the socio-ideological) the third 'socio-ideological persuasion' is the weapon of the professions. 'They live by persuasion and propaganda, by claiming that their particular service is indispensable...with the aim of raising their status and through it their income, authority and psychic rewards (deference and self-respect).'[110] In this the English professional classes have been notably successful, and in achieving their ends they fundamentally challenged the capitalist ideal and the ideal of the survival of the fittest through competition, because they put 'profits before people and salesmanship before social need and merit', self before service. As Perkin has persuasively argued,

although [the professional class] began in alliance with the capitalist ideal against the abuse of aristocratic power in government (parliamentary and administrative reform), taxation (the corn laws) and religion (tithes, church rates, control of education etc.) it rapidly turned against the abuse of capitalist power in children's employment, unsafe factories, insanitary industrial housing, adulteration of food, pollution of the environment, and so on. The so-called collectivist legislation of the nineteenth century can be read as one long assault on the irresponsibility of capital and competition by a public opinion moralized by the professional ideal.[111]

The professions were backed by a supportive ideology voiced by the most influential members of the educated middle class. They rapidly moved into a position of enormous strength in 'the intellectual aristocracy'.[112] As such, in Perkin's words, 'the professions have both the material self interest and the moral conviction to be...the vivisectionists of capital'.[113] Since they shared the same class, the same connections and the same ideals as so many of our most influential writers it is hardly surprising that literary fantasies of a world run by professional experts should flourish around the turn of the twentieth century. Sidney Olivier's 'League of Sane Men', George

---

[108] H. J. Perkin, 'Middle-class Education and Employment in the Nineteenth Century: A Critical Note', *Economic History Review* XIV (1961), 129.

[109] H. J. Perkin, *Professionalism* (Reading, 1981), p. 10.

[110] *Ibid.*, p. 11.   [111] *Ibid.*, p. 13.

[112] Noel Annan, 'The Intellectual Aristocracy', in J. H. Plumb (ed.), *Studies in Social History* (London, 1955), pp. 241–87.

[113] Perkin, *Professionalism*, p. 23.

Bernard Shaw's 'superman' in *Man and Superman* and 'elders' in *Back to Methuselah*, Sidney Webb's '2000 practical intellectuals' and H. G. Wells' 'platonic guardians' all represented the idea of a ruling clerisy, a class of learned scholars, a class of qualified experts. Little wonder that when H. G. Wells tried to produce an authentic business hero in *The World of William Clissold* in 1926, Clissold's virtues were judged as much by the values of the professional ideal as by those of the entrepreneurial ideal. Clissold was educated at Dulwich College, had a scientific training, wrote and published scientific papers and conformed in many ways to the professional ideal.

Inevitably as the professions have moved into positions of power, influence and authority, their ideals have been subjected to prolonged literary scrutiny. They have been criticized, satirized but ultimately endorsed. In literature as in society they won the propaganda battle. Nor is this surprising since they share the ideals and the educational experience of our most influential opinion-makers. They have received a constant flow of new talent because they fit so well the accepted English mode of social ascent – that is through sponsored mobility rather than the contest mobility of American society, which favours the thrusting business ideal.[114] Social mobility in England is greatly eased if the upwardly mobile are sponsored and approved by their schools, universities or government institutions. These are the corridors of power in which the professionals flourish. There was a homogeneity of cultural values among the educated elite of England – the professional values fitted in snugly, the values of the businessman were always felt to jar.

Literature in the twentieth century reflects this growth of power and prestige of the professional class at the cost of the business class. Just as nineteenth-century fiction was dominated by the ideals of the gentleman, so that of the twentieth century is dominated by a concern with the values of the professional ideal.

The literary record, in fact, provides evidential support to some very important recent findings. It supports and helps to explain the findings of W. D. Rubinstein, who has pointed to the significance of the divided Victorian middle class – with the much criticized industrialists coming from one distinct grouping and the much admired professional class dominating the other.[115] It supports Harold Perkin's claims in his Stenton lecture which described the dominance achieved in our society by the

---

[114] Ralph M. Turner, 'Modes of Social Ascent through Education: Sponsored and Contest Mobility' in R. Bendix and S. M. Lipset (eds.), *Class, Status and Power: Social Stratification in Comparative Perspective* (New York, 1966), pp. 449–58.

[115] W. D. Rubinstein, *Man of Property: The Very Wealthy in Britain Since the Industrial Revolution* (London, 1981); W. D. Rubinstein, 'Wealth, Elites and Class Structure in Modern Britain', *Past and Present* 76 (1977), 99–126.

professional ideal.[116] It supports one of the major conclusions of Lawrence Stone's *An Open Elite? England 1540–1880* which stresses that the route of successful businessmen was into the professions rather than into land.[117] It supports Michael Sanderson's view of the English university graduate's contribution to industry and the professions.[118] Finally, it confirms Donald Coleman's perception of the growing professionalism of English society[119] – a convergence towards a single ideal which made the 'Gentlemen vs Players' match such an anachronism after 1962 that the fixture was abolished after having been played since 1806.[120] It is in this phenomenon that we should seek the defeat and declining influence of the businessman. After the mid-1930s his ideals are not so much attacked as largely elbowed aside as another set of values dominated the literary stage.

For by then the world of literature shared one major assumption. 'That assumption', wrote Lord Annan,

is that the life of the professional classes is alone supportable and that of industry and commerce degrading...Whether it is Eliot or Forster, Lawrence or Leavis, Tawney or Herbert Read, the world of commerce, advertising, speculation, automation, management and enterprise, become so hateful that some of these sages praised those who wanted to return to the world of the wheelwright and the blacksmith...The life of pontificating, explaining, recommending, analysing and advising other men how to run their affairs rose in esteem, while the actual business of management was not so much denigrated as ignored and left to lesser fellows.

The shift in Britain out of business and industry and into the new bureaucracies of higher education, broadcasting, journalism, research organizations, social welfare, planning and the plethora of commissions, committees, boards, regulatory agencies designed to restrain evil and promote virtue, seems to be a direct response to what their sages have been telling the British since before 1914.[121]

It is a success story and a propaganda victory for the professional ideal that can, not surprisingly, be traced without difficulty in the novels of our major middle-class authors. D. H. Lawrence may have kept alive a vivid condemnation of industrialism in the 1920s, and Orwell may have led his readers to revisit the squalid consequences of industrialization to be found on *The Road to Wigan Pier* (1934), but they were the last major novelists to be preoccupied with the horrors of industrial society and the sins of those they held responsible for creating them. There has been a marked change in literary sensibilities since what one might call Orwell's 'Condition of England' novels of the 1930s.

[116] Perkin, *Professionalism*.
[117] Lawrence Stone and Jeanne C. Fawtier Stone, *An Open Elite? England 1540–1880* (Oxford, 1984).   [118] Sanderson, *Universities and British Industry*.
[119] Coleman, 'Gentlemen and Players', p. 116.
[120] *Wisden Cricketers' Almanack* (London, 1963), ed. Norman Preston, for details of the series.
[121] Annan, 'The Path to British Decadence', p. 3, and '"Our Age"', pp. 104–5.

Space does not permit a detailed survey of the literary treatment of the businessman in the past fifty years. But anyone familiar with the mainstream of English fiction since the mid-1930s will recognize the increasing preoccupation with the professional classes and the dwindling concern with the businessmen. Writers such as Elizabeth Bowen, L. P. Hartley, Rosamond Lehmann, Christopher Isherwood, Nancy Mitford and C. P. Snow have been described by a recent critic as having been 'all subjected to the educational pressures characteristic of this country', and thereby largely immune to any sustained interest in the industrialist or 'the industrial aspect of our society'.[122] The milieu they describe is that of the professional middle classes – the world of dons and bureaucrats, of doctors and barristers and solicitors, of architects and administrators. The characters in the novels of William Cooper, Angus Wilson, Kingsley Amis, Anthony Powell, Malcolm Bradbury, David Lodge, Iris Murdoch and Margaret Drabble – to offer only a sample – operate mainly in much the same professional society.

In this respect Anthony Powell's *A Dance to the Music of Time* (1951–75) and C. P. Snow's *Strangers and Brothers* (1940–70) – the two series of novels which offer a deliberately comprehensive view of their time – reflect the representative interests of the rest of the literary world. Businessmen do appear in these novels – 'Donner, the boring tycoon, Windmerpool the pushy businessman, and Bob Duport the rakish adventurer'[123] in Powell, and Lufkin and Timberlake in Snow – but they play a small and declining role. The titles of their novels – Powell's *A Question of Upbringing* (1951), *The Acceptance World* (1955), *The Kindly Ones* (1962) and *At Lady Molly's* (1957), and Snow's *The Masters* (1951), *The New Men* (1954), *The Conscience of the Rich* (1958) and *Corridors of Power* (1964) – reflect the academic world, the political world, the gentlemanly world through which the professional middle classes move with such accustomed ease.

It is striking, too, that both Snow and William Cooper, regarded by F. R. Leavis as the arch-Benthamite exponents of a technological utilitarian culture, largely ignore the businessman whilst they concentrate almost exclusively on the academic bureaucrats and politicians of the professional mandarin class. As a result the industrialists in their novels are allowed only incidental roles of minimum significance.[124]

There are, of course, occasional revivals of the traditional ogre figure such as Richard Portman, the unappealing tycoon in Doris Lessing's *The Golden Notebook* (1962), but after Evelyn Waugh's 'hard faced men who did well out of their war' or Basil Seal, who profited from chaos in *Black*

---

[122] John Atkins, *Six Novelists Look at Society* (London, 1977), pp. 62, 250.
[123] McVeagh, *Tradefull Merchants*, p. 191.
[124] McKendrick, 'Enemies of...the Self Made Man', pp. xxxvii–xxxix.

Mischief (1932), or Grahame Greene's Sir Marcus in *A Gun for Sale* (1936), it is difficult to find examples of major business characters who are thought to deserve extended or detailed treatment. Routine disdain is common, lofty unconcern is general. Only occasionally do English novelists focus now on those who manage, manipulate and profit from the business system, and in contemporary literature they are more often faceless symbols rather than the characteristic individual business ogres of the century from 1839 to roughly 1939.

Environmental contamination and pollution are still laid at the door of anonymous businessmen, but increasingly it is the state and the bureaucrats who are held to share responsibility. By the late 1940s George Orwell, too, had shifted much of his attack from industry to the state's manipulation of the possibilities of industrial technology. In *Nineteen Eighty-Four* (1949) he even felt able to parody the traditional figure of the evil businessman. He had long before admitted that the northern business ogre, so dominant in the literary hostility to industry in the nineteenth century, was 'nowadays pure anachronism' although his influence lived on like that of 'a tyrannical corpse'.[125] Only cant, he said, kept this legend alive. But in *Nineteen Eighty-Four* Orwell took a more detailed look at the stereotype of the evil capitalist. In his desperate search for truth in a world in which 'All history was a palimpsest, scraped clean and reinscribed exactly as often as was necessary', in which 'the past had not merely been altered it had actually been destroyed', in which it is 'a sign of madness to believe that the past is unalterable', Winston Smith keeps coming across the story of the wicked 'capitalists in their strange cylindrical hats', but he has no way of 'knowing how much of the legend was true and how much invented'.[126] Wherever he searches he comes back to the same legend. In oral history, in Rutherford's cartoons, even in children's history books, the stereotype is always the same.[127] The capitalist ruled in a 'dark dirty miserable' world in which the poor were hungry, shoeless and roofless, and in which children worked:

twelve hours a day for cruel masters who flogged them with whips if they worked too slowly and fed them on nothing but stale breadcrusts and water. But in among all this terrible poverty there were just a few great big beautiful houses that were lived in by rich men.... These rich men were called capitalists. They were fat ugly men with wicked faces.... [The capitalist] dressed in a long black coat... and a queer shiny hat shaped like a stovepipe, which was called a top hat.... The capitalists owned everything in the world, and everyone else was their slave. They owned all the land, all the houses, all the factories, and all the money. If anyone disobeyed them they could throw him into prison, or take his job away or starve him to death.[128]

[125] George Orwell, *The Road to Wigan Pier* (London, 1937), pp. 96–101.
[126] George Orwell, *Nineteen Eighty-Four* (1949; Penguin edn, Harmondsworth, 1978), pp. 35, 32, 67, 32.   [127] *Ibid.*, pp. 64–5, 75–6.   [128] *Ibid.*, pp. 61–2.

There are those who think that Orwell could parody the evil stereotype of
the capitalist in the certain knowledge that even by repeating the legend
he would reinforce it, but it is clear that in *Nineteen Eighty-Four* the
arch-propagandist was not aiming at the capitalist but at the new
aristocracy of the state bureaucracy. In the nightmare world of 1984 it
was the Ministry of Truth which rewrote past history and past literature
to prove that 'the centuries of capitalism...produced nothing of any
value'.[129] The enemies of truth are men like Ampleforth who spent their
lives 'producing garbled versions – definitive texts they were called – of
poems which had become ideologically offensive but which...were to be
retained in the anthologies';[130] or men like Syme whose function was to
destroy words offensive to the party; or men like Rutherford, the once
famous caricaturist, whose work was a tired 'rehashing of ancient
themes – slum tenements, starving children, street battles, capitalists in top
hats'.[131] All these men were serving the state. They were the new men who
had 'discredited the earthly paradise...at exactly the moment it became
realizable'.[132] 'The new aristocracy was made up for the most part of
bureaucrats, scientists, technicians, trade-union organizers, publicity
experts, sociologists, teachers, journalists, and professional politicians.'[133]
These were the people who ran the tyranny of 1984, compared with which
'all the tyrannies of the past were half-hearted and inefficient'.[134] In their
appallingly efficient way, by use of 'constant surveillance' and the
manipulation of print and public opinion they pursued the party slogan
'Who controls the past controls the future.'[135] To this end literature, that
most powerful form of propaganda, had to be rewritten to make it
ideologically acceptable. Significantly, the final paragraph of *Nineteen
Eighty-Four* is devoted to the efforts of the state to make literature
compatible with Newspeak.[136]

   The date set for this chilling literary Armageddon was 2050. It is in some
sense the greatest tribute to the power of literature to influence our
attitudes and values, to form opinion and to give legitimacy to social
aspirations and political ends. Judged against such state power over
thought and literature the industrial capitalist looks a puny target hardly
worth sustained attack, and George Orwell's last book signals a major
switch in the focus of literary concern. Often taken as the apotheosis of
literary Luddism, the last major writer to rework the old themes, the
culmination of cultural attack on the industrial capitalist, Orwell's two
great political allegories are in fact turning away from the industrialist to

[129] *Ibid.*, p. 82.   [130] *Ibid.*, p. 37.
[131] *Ibid.*, pp. 64–5.   [132] *Ibid.*, p. 164.
[133] *Ibid.*   [134] *Ibid.*, p. 165.   [135] *Ibid.*, p. 199.
[136] *Ibid.*, p. 251. For 'considerations of prestige' writers like Shakespeare and Dickens had
      to be brought 'into line with the philosophy of Ingsoc'.

deal with more powerful and more sinister forces – the power of the
totalitarian state. In this he is not unrepresentative of post-Second World
War fiction in England.

For most modern English writers there seems little need to make the case
against individual industrialists or even capital in general. Novelists seem
to feel that the theme is largely worked out. The pervasive acceptance of
the adversary culture makes literary condemnation of the businessman
almost unnecessary. In a society moralized by the professional ideal, it is
the mandarin class that needs detailed discussion and evaluation. The
businessman offers no threat, so attitudes to him as an individual can
become almost neutral – he can be charming or odious largely irrespective
of his choice of career in business.

So increasingly if businessmen appear at all it is as minor characters
whose career carries little significance. As John McVeagh has written of
the final volumes of the Anthony Powell series, 'minor surfacings apart,
capitalism is overlaid as a theme by literature, social change and counter-
culture.... In all this Powell suggests a receding of interest in the capitalist
issue felt by other contemporary imaginative writers in England generally,
and seems...to reflect accurately enough a gravitational shift in the
sensibility of British society at large during the last thirty years.'[137]

It is in fact very difficult to find widespread or substantial evidence of
that hostility to individual men of business in the fiction of the last fifty
years which it has been claimed explains the low esteem of the businessman
in our society. That is not to deny the social and economic consequences
of our literary culture. The accumulated verdict of the literature of the past
can still be profoundly influential, especially when selected and projected
by respected literary critics. Indeed much significance can be read into the
current literary silence on the businessman. The pervasive literary neglect
of the businessman in the mid-twentieth century can be as revealing as
the mid-seventeenth-century obsession and the mid-nineteenth-century
preoccupation with the dangers inherent in acceptance of commercial and
industrial values.

Whereas in Germany and the United States the businessman is still the
focus of serious literary debate because he is still seen as a central and
important member of society, the fact that he has faded from the English
literary scene need not betoken acceptance so much as the fact that he is
no longer regarded as needing attack. His modest and lowly role in the
social hierarchy is fixed and accepted in a world dominated by the educated
professional middle classes of England. Far from being the centre of debate
he has faded into obscurity. He is patronized and unheeded. In the Germany

[137] McVeagh, *Tradefull Merchants*, p. 192.

of the economic miracle Brecht and Grass and Böll have savagely criticized those in charge of industry. In the England of economic decline the silence is deafening, the neglect almost total. Some have argued that this itself can be profoundly damaging, since it breeds an ignorance which itself allows the prejudice of disdain to flourish. Unhindered by a real knowledge of the businessman's role or any deep understanding of his economic importance that prejudice can become more and more pervasive. As Sir Ezra Sterling (né Steimatstky) said in Anthony Blond's novel *Family Business* (1978), 'Prejudice is not just based on ignorance, it depends on it.'[138]

While the British businessman suffers the mild contempt reserved for those who lack status and prestige or real influence and power in our society; while he suffers the dismissive suspicion felt for those whose function is little understood but traditionally distrusted, the professional pundits and pontificators of the mandarin world now receive much more positive attention. They attract not only the respectful attention reserved for the successful but also the critical attack felt for those who seem to have such easy access to power and status and influence. Their role is implicitly accepted and endorsed in modern fiction but the literary sniping can easily be detected. The hypocrisy, the immorality, the cynical manipulation of power and position by politicians and dons and bureaucrats and the media Mafia are all increasingly coming under attack. The criticism is obvious in the work of Amis and Bradbury and Lodge and the like. John Arden's Butterthwaite in *The Waters of Babylon* (1957) invites the kind of attention a Victorian Bounderby deserved when he 'calls himself a Napoleon of local government' and boasts that his influence in affairs is much greater than those possessing industrial–commercial power. His was the bureaucratic route to power. And it is largely these routes to power and influence which inevitably now interest and provoke the novelist – not the old economic ones. John Fowles' hero delivers a memorable indictment of 'the policy makers and influence pedlars and attitude hucksters' in *Daniel Martin* (1977) when he records his

vision of a clogging spew of pundits and pontificators, editors and interviewers, critics and columnists, puppet personalities and attitude hucksters, a combined media Mafia squatting on an enormous dung heap of empty words and tired images, and conjoined, despite their private rivalries and jealousies, by one common determination: to retain their own status and importance in the system they had erected.[139]

This is an attack on the successful and the powerful and the influential of the 1970s just as the attack on the millowner was a recognition of his power and importance and success in the 1840s. They are criticized *because*

---

[138] Anthony Blond, *Family Business* (London, 1978), p. 19.
[139] John Fowles, *Daniel Martin* (New York, 1978), p. 277.

they are felt to be so generally admired and accepted and *because* their values seem so widespread in society. In consequence there are as many voices singing their praises and endorsing their professional values as there were then praising the Cheeryble brothers, or Mr Ainsley or Mr Rouncewell or John Thornton or John Halifax or the other Smilesian heroes of self-help and self-advancement over a hundred years ago. The controversy in literature reflects their central importance in contemporary society.

What is revealing today is *the way* in which the professional classes are praised and criticized, and *the way* in which their values are compared to those of the businessmen. For if literature is used as a guide to cultural assumptions and changing attitudes, then surely not only the past portrayals of the business and gentlemanly ideals should be discernible in English literary history, but contemporary values (such as the ideals and attitudes of the professional classes and the lack of interest of our elite core of graduates in a career in business, industry or commerce) should also be reflected in contemporary fiction. They are.

Anthony Keating, the major character in Margaret Drabble's *The Ice Age* (1977), illustrates perfectly the representative reaction of the typical Cambridge arts graduate of the late 1970s. The statistics of the Appointments Boards and the Careers Advisory Services record how few graduates were eager to seek a career in business, but Margaret Drabble precisely captures the set of attitudes which explains why.

Anthony Keating's was 'the usual story'. He came from a comfortable middle-class professional background of 'school masters, clergymen, doctors' –

His father had been a churchman and a school master, teaching in the cathedral school in an ancient cathedral city: he had sent his three sons...to a more distinguished public school, and had expected them to do well for themselves. He was a worldly man, who despised the more obvious ways of making money: throughout his childhood Anthony had listened to his father...speaking slightingly of the lack of culture of businessmen, of the philistinism and ignorance of their sons, of commercial greed, expense accounts, business lunches.[140]

From such a background Anthony Keating had predictably proceeded to Cambridge to read history. There the premature burdens of a baby, and a wife pregnant with another, complicated his further predictable progress into the professions which his family had expected.

His parents had always assumed that he would become a professional man of one sort or another: his two elder brothers were barristers. But to Anthony, with a baby and a large wife and another baby on the way, there did not seem to be enough time to train for a profession. He did not think that he would get a good enough degree to enter the Civil Service....So what was left? It must be said that it never

[140] Margaret Drabble, *The Ice Age* (London, 1977), pp. 19–20.

once crossed Anthony Keating's mind that he might get a job in industry. Rebel he was, but not to such a degree: so deeply conditioned are some sections of the British nation that certain ideas are deeply inaccessible to them. Despite the fact that major companies were at that time appealing urgently for graduates in any field, despite the fact that the national press was full of seductive offers, the college notice boards plastered with them, Anthony Keating, child of the professional middle classes, reared in an anachronism as an anachronism, did not even see the offers: he walked past them daily, turned over pages daily, with as much indifference as if they had been written in Turkish or Hungarian. He thought himself superior to that kind of thing....So Anthony got a job with the BBC.[141]

There, neatly encapsulated in half a paragraph, is the disdain, indifference and sheer ignorance exhibited by the professional English middle classes in their response to a career in industry.

Switching from the telescope of the long-term perspective of English literature to the microscope of attention to a single author can be justified by more than the exigencies of space. For an examination of a single novelist and concentration on a single novel allows one to capture the qualitative nature of the arguments and attitudes involved, which would be lost in a more panoramic and comprehensive survey. Margaret Drabble's *The Ice Age* provides an important illustration of the phenomenon of culturally influenced career choice not only because it implicitly discusses the survival of the gentlemanly ideal in its predominant twentieth-century form, and explicitly recognizes the social and educational expectations which underpin the professional ideal; but also because it is one of the few major examinations by a respected novelist of the businessman in contemporary English fiction. It provides a telling full stop to a survey of literary attitudes to the businessman in English literature which reaches back to Langland and Chaucer in the fourteenth century.

Margaret Drabble is a telling example, too, because she writes with a scholar's knowledge of the history of the changing literary response to industry and the industrial landscape. She is far more aware than most novelists of the history of *both* literary Luddism *and* literary eulogy of the businessman. She is as familiar with the admiration and even awe felt for industry and commerce by Defoe and Dyer and Dalton and Erasmus Darwin and Stephen Duck and Dr Johnson in the eighteenth century (to provide only an alliterative sample) as she is with the standard Victorian condemnation.[142] Her professional knowledge of both sides of the argument perhaps helps to explain the ironies and ambiguities of her own response to the businessman. Some contemporary authors reared on a selected diet of Blake, Dickens and D. H. Lawrence seem to be so imprinted with their

[141] *Ibid.*, pp. 21–4.
[142] Margaret Drabble, *A Writer's Britain* (London, 1979), ch. 2, 'The Pastoral Vision', and ch. 5, 'The Industrial Scene'.

sources as to be incapable of an independent view. Erica Jong's intrepid heroine, Isadora Wong, travelling the world in search of her ultimate 'zipless' experience, arrived in England so primed by the great tradition of literary condemnation that she summoned all her literary authorities to mind as soon as she arrived in Dover. She saw what she expected to see. She responded as literature had taught her to respond. 'The countryside was black and filmed with grime. I thought of Blake and Dark Satanic Mills. I knew I was in England by the smell.'[143] And that was the reaction to travelling through the fields of Kent!

Margaret Drabble has a more comprehensive list of literary sources to inform and influence her. Her judgments are less instinctively and spontaneously damning. Even before the major dissection of business attitudes in *The Ice Age* (1977) she allowed one of her main characters a passing retrospective defence of the merchant. In *The Realms of Gold* (1975), the heroine, Frances Wingate, the famous archaeologist, asks rhetorically, 'what is wrong with trade? Why should men not be merchants? Which is more civilized, a Roman legion or a caravan of merchandise?'[144] She spoke passionately because 'she had loved them, her traders, her merchants, her agents, she had loved and defended them, with their caravans and their date palms, their peaceful negotiations. Men of peace, not war, they had been, exchanging useful commodities and works of art.'[145]

But what could be defended in the past proves more complex in the present. The ambiguous reaction to, the ambivalent feelings towards, and the anxious assessments of, the moral role of modern business are what concerns *The Ice Age*. It is a subtle, ironic, carefully conducted debate in response to Frances Wingate's cry 'What is wrong with trade?' It is a response to businessmen seen not through the eyes of an archaeologist safely distanced from her traders, but through the eyes of worried and uncertain contemporaries – full of moral doubt about the businessman's role and full of dismay at England's declining economy and declining power. For what is so significant about the verdict on the man of business (as against the professional man and the gentleman) in *The Ice Age* is that it is offered in the context of a chilling analysis of the ills of contemporary England. Both the authorial voice and the individual characters speak of England in a state of almost terminal decline. The book is redolent with 'the sense of alarm, panic and despondency which seemed to flow loose in the atmosphere of England': 'England, sliding, sinking, shabby, dirty,

---

[143] Erica Jong, *Fear of Flying* (London, 1974), p. 274. She invokes Blake, Dickens and Lawrence as soon as she arrives in Dover.
[144] Margaret Drabble, *The Realms of Gold* (London, 1975), p. 38.
[145] *Ibid.*, p. 34.

lazy, inefficient, dangerous, in its death throes, worn out, clapped out, occasionally lashing out'.[146] Few groups escape clinical dissection. They are set out like a display of exotic specimens to be viewed with some distaste: 'The desperate comfortable lazy liberal folk'; 'The theatre-going elite of Britain', looking like a 'set for a Restoration comedy or a Weimar Republic drag-show'; 'drunk, idle, affluent, capitalist elitist' groups; 'the fashionable witty young men'; and 'the most depressing' of all, the embittered Oxford classics don corrupted not by success but by failure: 'having what seemed, initially, a well structured and secure career', he found himself trapped with a low salary and falling status – 'poor Linton had the historical misfortune to be gifted in a dying skill....Nobody wanted to do classics any more.'[147]

Such comments might seem no more than the predictable insights of an intelligent contemporary observer, but many reflect much of the current unease about the values and prestige which are attached to our accepted pattern of career choice. When Anthony Keating notes that 'the fate of classical studies might reflect something of a watershed in British history for who in a recession can afford the luxury of Greek, who can afford the luxury of a civil service staffed by those who have first class degrees in classics?'[148] he is voicing a common anxiety of our educated elite. When his mistress is given a copy of an American magazine carrying extended comment on 'British economic decline', 'the dismal fate of British industry', 'the failure of British firms to deliver goods', 'the inevitability of cut backs in public spending', she looks enviously at the American businessman who had offered it to her. She looks with new eyes at the breed that England failed to produce: 'there he sat, pleasant, solid, confident...civilised indeed, doubtless well informed, well travelled, well read. (He was reading a novel by Norman Mailer, she could see.)'[149] The contrast with the seedy, vulgar, crooked British businessmen who populate the pages of The Ice Age is striking. They offer ample justification for professional disdain. They even justify Anthony Keating's career in television which was based on revealing current swindles and business scandals and making each businessman interviewed 'look a greedy dishonest monster on the screen'.[150]

Yet it is his reaction to the falseness of such stereotypes which leads to Anthony Keating's conversion to the entrepreneurial creed. The conversion took place while Anthony was watching unedited film of an interview with Len Wincobank, the property whizz kid, produced by his bright young assistant Austin Jones:

---

[146] Drabble, The Ice Age, pp. 12, 93. See also pp. 52, 62–3.
[147] Ibid., pp. 209–10, 22, 74.
[148] Ibid., p. 75.   [149] Ibid., p. 153.   [150] Ibid., p. 27.

And it struck him, suddenly, with a dazzling flash: how could he not have noticed it before? The truth was that Len Wincobank was a genius, about ten times as intelligent, ten times as perceptive, ten times as clever as Austin Jones. Austin Jones, in comparison, was a boring somnambulist, a ventriloquist's dummy, mouthing without conviction or information or even any intelligence the obligatory provocative questions: questions which were based on an utterly false premise, the premise that he and the viewers lived in a society which disapproved of the profit motive and which condemned private enterprise....Elated, illuminated, he played the reels for a third time. Yes, here it all was. If you read the film correctly, with Wincobank as hero and Jones as villain, everything fell into place. He could not, of course, edit it that way: that was not his job.[151]

The conversion is not a prelude to an apologia for the contemporary businessman. Keating is certainly no John Thornton, John Halifax, Henry Myers or William Clissold. Indeed his portrait ultimately endorses more of the assumptions of the adversary culture than it condemns. But even by questioning some of the standard English attitudes, and by discussing the assumptions which support them, it reveals many of the reasons for the survival and spread of those cultural values.

The fate Keating suffers for his apostasy from his expected professional destiny is one which must satisfy the most extreme adherents to literary Luddism. He suffers a heart attack at the age of thirty-eight and is forbidden sex, butter, nicotine and alcohol. But worse is to come, for he finally finishes the book behind the Iron Curtain, imprisoned, mad, 'bitterly cold, usually hungry, and frequently afraid'. He is left without 'drink, sex, warmth and human affection', writing an ill-written unpublishable book on the nature of God. If he writes only for himself it matters little because ironically 'he has lost interest in any market'.[152]

He has suffered in fact the familiar fate of the social deviant in literature. Just as the rebellious wives of the 1860s scandal novels or the sexual deviants of the early twentieth century usually had to reaffirm the social and sexual orthodoxies by committing suicide or otherwise finding a conveniently miserable end, so the Luddite who lost his faith has to serve out his time in purgatory.

Like many deviants in literature before him, however, he is given a good run for his money before the old orthodoxies reassert themselves. He is allowed the excitement of a new life: the excitements of meeting 'a new world of people' – all the essential personnel of the financial and business world. These were the 'people who had once at best been fodder for his programmes, usually cast as villains'. They were 'The Other England. Where had they been all this time?'[153]

He is allowed, too, the excitements of making money, of creating wealth, of learning to understand the world of finance. He is allowed the

---

[151] *Ibid.*, pp. 26–7.   [152] *Ibid.*, p. 285.   [153] *Ibid.*, p. 34.

excitements of ownership, the excitements of success, the excitements of seeing his plans take concrete shape. He is allowed to enjoy a sense of euphoria. 'The activity made him immensely happy. He had never in his life been so fully committed, so deeply engaged, so deeply *interested* in what he was doing. He felt at times that he must have spent the first part of his life with his head in a bag, a bag which was taken off only when he got into some nice, safe, familiar, intellectual situation.'[154] But amidst all this excitement, exhilaration and euphoria, there are plenty of warnings of what is to come. The moral and cultural indicators are pointing to an inevitable and painful nemesis. 'The Other England' he so admired 'were only interested in money':

Some perhaps were villains, but they were all of them very interesting, and none of them paid any attention to all those things that had previously drifted idly round Anthony's mind – they did not read novels, or go to good films, or read the arts pages of newspapers, or listen to music or discuss the problems of the underprivileged.[155]

His newly acquired and much admired business partner, Len Wincobank, was as morally flawed as an individual as his new friends were morally and culturally flawed as a group. The admired entrepreneurial type had feet of clay: 'He had had energy, ambition, vision...he had also been a crook.'[156]

So when the crash comes one is morally and culturally prepared. And if the warning signals were missed, the post-mortem explanations make things brutally clear. Anthony was appalled at his folly: 'However had he got himself into this nightmare world?'. He had been 'seduced and corrupted'.[157]

Go for growth had been the slogan, and everyone had gone for it. Now some were bankrupt, some were in jail, some had committed suicide, and only the biggest survived unscathed. Casualties of slump and recession strewed the business pages of the newspapers, hit the front page headlines. Old men were convicted of corruption and hustled off to prison, banks collapsed and shares fell to nothing.[158]

Anthony Keating was 'not so ill placed as Stern, or Lyons, or Poulson' but his world had nevertheless collapsed and he regarded the ruins with horror: 'How had he been sucked into the gold rush?', 'Gold. Money. Ambition'. They had 'thrilled and corrupted' him. How had he – a gentleman and member of the professional middle class – got himself 'caught up in such a ludicrous world?'[159]

It was all right for the acceptable stereotypes in the business world to be involved. The self-made man from an impoverished background, the

[154] *Ibid.*, p. 31.   [155] *Ibid.*, p. 33.   [156] *Ibid.*, p. 167.
[157] *Ibid.*, pp. 14, 13.   [158] *Ibid.*, p. 14.   [159] *Ibid.*, p. 112.

Jewish businessman born into the world of commerce or the man born into industry – these the novel implies are the types one expects to find in business, not members of the professional middle classes:

It was easy to see how someone like Len Wincobank had got into it. Len's mother...had worked in a laundry. He had shared a bed with his brother. From rags to riches. Max Friedman was another sort: he had been born into the world of commerce...had a textile business anyway....Making money was natural to him: he had been brought up to it...Giles was one of the same.[160]

Here, in kernel form, are the English cultural and social expectations about where businessmen should come from. Anthony Keating was breaking ranks, rebelling, going against the expected behaviour patterns. His fate is an awful warning against others choosing the same path, being 'seduced and corrupted' by the spurious claims of business, being convinced by the spurious arguments of the entrepreneur, being attracted by the vulgar, the anti-intellectual, the philistine and the corrupt. The moral message is clear. Anthony Keating had sinned mightily and he must expect his punishment. He knew that 'it was all his own fault. He had brought it on himself.'[161] Not only did he choose to become a member of what Donald Coleman has called 'that curious but unloved species: the English businessman',[162] but he did so by quite explicitly rejecting his professional destiny and the career marked out for him by birth, school and university. His family past, his academic preparation, his father's expectations were all deliberately flouted.

It was them that, in his heroic stand, he rejected forever. Enough apology, enough politeness, enough self-seeking high-minded well-meaning, well-respected idleness, enough of quite-well-paid middle-status gentleman's jobs, enough of the Oxbridge Arts graduate. They had killed the country, sapped initiative, destroyed the economy. This was the new line of the new Anthony. Oxbridge Arts graduate turned [businessman].[163]

With these revealing words he announced his conversion from the prevailing ideals of his family and his class, and his apostasy from the prevailing cultural ideals of the dominant elite of Britain. He was born a gentleman and educated to be a professional. He had turned his back on both with the *cri de coeur* – 'I want to stop being a gentleman and become a businessman.'[164]

After such a declaration his fate was sealed. *The Ice Age* may be an atypical novel by an atypical author but it nevertheless ultimately reaffirms the prevailing cultural assumptions of the professional English middle classes towards the business class. The treatment is exceptional but the

[160] *Ibid.*   [161] *Ibid.*, p. 12.
[162] Coleman, 'Gentlemen and Players', p. 116.
[163] Drabble, *The Ice Age*, p. 34.   [164] *Ibid.*, p. 28.

verdict is representative. Miss Drabble may hold up for inspection the values of a child of the professional middle classes who was 'reared as an anachronism in an anachronism' but ultimately she reaffirms those values. The reaffirmation is all the more convincing for being questioned. The values are arguably all the stronger for being so critically scrutinized. Miss Drabble may recognize that some sections of the British nation are so deeply conditioned that certain ideas are inaccessible to them, but in the last resort she shares that conditioning and accepts it. *The Ice Age* is an unusual English novel in that it explicitly, rather than implicitly, judges business values against those of the gentleman and the professional. Neither side is allowed to escape unscathed and the effects on the economy are shown to be profoundly depressing, but the verdict is the usual one – a culturally predictable preference for the values and ideals of the professional middle class.

When one is seeking an explanation for the homogeneity of cultural values in England, and for the cultural assimilation of the upwardly mobile parts of our society (and in turn trying to explain the economic consequences of those cultural attitudes), one would do well to look to the pervasive influence of the gentlemanly and the professional ideal, both in our literature and in our society. The status anxiety of the businessman in England has been more easily soothed by his acceptance of those ideals than it has by any successful promotion of the business ideal. He has been consistently judged by their criteria of excellence and acceptability rather than by his own skills and achievements. Whatever the dominant criteria for judging social acceptance, whether the traditional social criteria of the landed gentleman of good breeding, or the behavioural criteria of the man of taste and culture and good manners, or the moral criteria of mid-Victorian novelists, or the institutional criteria of attending a public school, or finally the professional criteria of the educated English middle classes with their protective qualifications, the business ideal has never been able successfully to compete.

It is to the successful promotion and the cultural dominance of these attitudes (the origins of which long predate the mid-nineteenth-century debate on the businessman, and which incidentally long predate the English public schools) that the historian should turn his attention. Peaks of hostility to the businessman are of less significance. Such literary hostility has a very long pedigree. Its appearance in literature by no means coincides with or correlates with economic failure or entrepreneurial apathy – indeed the reverse correlation would be easier to justify. And the powerlessness of literary hostility alone (without the support of other influential and pervasive social attitudes) to influence career choice, and the quality of those recruited to particular careers, can be nicely illustrated, for example, by the failure of the swindle novels of the late nineteenth century to undermine the attractions of merchant banking and finance as a career. Such financiers appear in late Victorian fiction as a cue for public hostility,[165] like the demon king on stage, but because the City is still associated with aristocratic land and capital, because it is London-based, because it is not directly contaminated with the North, industrial pollution, environmental damage and all the other malign associations with industrial technology and actual manufacture, it has retained its career attractions. For all the moral doubts about the manipulation of capital, banking and the City have retained their gentlemanly image and associations. Such a career is still acceptable. It is much more compatible with our prevailing ideals than manufacturing or selling are. Those seeking to understand why, if cultural influences are so important in explaining Britain's entrepreneurial decline, those influences failed to affect Britain's financial dynasties,[166] will find much to aid them in the differential social evaluation of the industrialist and the financier. But that is another story which must be dealt with elsewhere.

[165] See Reed, *Victorian Conventions*, ch. 7, 'Swindles', pp. 172–92.
[166] See Clive Trebilcock, Chapter 7 below.

7

The City, entrepreneurship and insurance: two pioneers in invisible exports – the Phoenix Fire Office and the Royal of Liverpool, 1800–90

CLIVE TREBILCOCK

Convention has it that the institutions of the nineteenth-century City enjoyed unstinted financial and entrepreneurial success and that they prospered most dramatically over the period 1870–1914. This convention is not inaccurate but it is insensitive; it stands in need of much refinement.

Certainly the export of capital, insurance and shipping services from London in the half-century before the First World War constituted the greatest boom in invisible trade ever generated by an industrial economy. Its reputation is familiar and largely deserved. Moreover, that reputation has rubbed off on the bankers, underwriters and brokers who took the decisions about the loans, the policies and the cargoes. Whilst the manufacturing community of the late nineteenth century sits uneasily before a hung jury,[1] few doubts have been aired concerning the calibre of their financial colleagues, and fewer aspersions cast. The present status of the indictment against the manufacturer, very broadly, is that some (many?) late-Victorian industrialists may have failed while others (most?) probably did not; the 'some', 'many' or 'most' depends mainly on the strength of the historian's doctrine, the length of his dossier and the flexibility of his algebra. Yet the bankers, underwriters *et al.* have almost entirely escaped such probing discussion.

They have escaped so well that one recent and persuasive analysis of

---

[1] The literature is enormous and well known. Important examples are: D. H. Aldcroft, 'The Entrepreneur and the British Economy, 1870–1914', *Economic History Review* 17 (1964), 113; A. L. Levine, *Industrial Retardation in Britain, 1880–1914* (London, 1967); C. Erickson, *British Industrialists: Steel and Hosiery, 1850–1950* (Cambridge, 1959); P. L. Payne, *British Entrepreneurs in the Nineteenth Century* (London, 1974); M. Wiener, *English Culture and the Decline of the Industrial Spirit, 1850–1980* (Cambridge, 1981); C. H. Wilson, 'Economy and Society in Late Victorian Britain', *Economic History Review* 18 (1965), 183; D. N. McCloskey, 'Did Victorian Britain Fail?', *Economic History Review* 23 (1970), 446; also the exchange between McCloskey and Aldcroft in *Economic History Review* 27 (1974), 271. And see D. N. McCloskey and L. E. Sandberg, 'From Damnation to Redemption: Judgements on the Late Victorian Entrepreneur', *Explorations in Economic History* 9 (1971), 89; D. N. McCloskey (ed.), *Essays on a Mature Economy: Britain after 1840* (London, 1971); D. N. McCloskey, *Enterprise and Trade in Victorian Britain: Essays in Historical Economics* (London, 1981).

Victorian society has proposed that it contained not one middle class but two distinct middle classes: the familiar provincial bourgeoisie based largely on industrial and mercantile activity and a much less publicized metropolitan bourgeoisie drawing its substance from the professions, from contracting, from finance and the other invisible trades. W. D. Rubinstein thus partly resolves the conflict in performance between the suspect industrialists and the successful financiers by suggesting that they hailed from separate classes.[2] But he goes further, issuing the challenge that: 'Those who argue that sociological factors were of primary importance in explaining the decline of British entrepreneurship...must explain why this *failed to affect Britain's commercial and financial dynasties.*'[3] This of course is premature: it assumes *a priori* that there was an absence of entrepreneurial decline among the commercial and financial community. The necessary preliminary is to identify convincingly this absence, or, if the reverse is identified, to suggest that, after all, there may be more common ground between the industrial and financial middle classes than has so far reached the record.

The prospects for such a convergence at the outset do not look especially promising. Professor Coleman, in his influential and clear-sighted essay, 'Gentlemen and Players', noted a *divergence*: why was it that the public school education so often blamed for inculcating amateurism and technological innocence among industrial managers succeeded in producing for the City men fit to manage a world emporium of services?[4] That is a crucial question; but it is one to which an answer is perhaps available. In 1957 Professor Checkland drew attention to the rudimentary nature of the skills with which even the greatest financiers governed the City of the pre-1914 period, and scented traces of deterioration over the preceding century: the 'mind of the City' was neither trained nor scientific but baffled by 'all the difficulties of self-comprehension...afflicted by a demoralization of intelligence in sad contrast to the first two decades of the century'.[5] City man had become attached to a particular *practice*, a set of processes polished by usage but unexplained by theoretical analysis. Those who worked these processes were 'practical financiers' no more endowed with relevant intellectual training for their intricate task than the 'practical manufacturers' on the other side of the economy. Their confusion did not escape contemporaries. By 1916 the *Round Table* was clear that 'a large number of people regard our financial system as something which grows

[2] W. D. Rubinstein, 'Wealth, Elites and Class Structure in Modern Britain', *Past and Present* 76 (1977), 99–126.
[3] *Ibid.*, p. 115; my italics.
[4] D. C. Coleman, 'Gentlemen and Players', *Economic History Review*, 2nd Series 26 (1973), 111.
[5] S. D. Checkland, 'The Mind of the City', *Oxford Economic Papers* 9 (1957), 271, 277.

and *is not made* and which has by natural evolution grown almost to perfection'; and it harshly criticized the financiers themselves: 'It is unfortunately true that the Englishmen are few who have the thorough acquaintance which many Germans have of international banking, of languages and of other financial centres.'[6] Attachment to customary practice was widely diagnosed as the cause. It moved one critic from within the citadel to the satirical observation that 'If there is one term of reproach greater than another which can be levelled at a Lombard Street banker, it is to say that he is a theoretical man.'[7] These charges – traditionalism, insularity, anti-intellectualism, devotion to practical skills – are, of course, precisely those featured in the conventional indictment of the late Victorian or Edwardian manufacturer.

How then did the late Victorian or Edwardian City – or most of it – continue to succeed? Possibly because the lack of 'failure' in the pre-1914 City was nothing more than a lack of competitors. British industry faltered in the late nineteenth century only when its monopoly of world trade in manufactures was challenged by effective German and American rivalry. The financial sector did not confront any parallel threat to its international preeminence before 1914. Around 1870, London's loan fund, as measured by published bank deposits, was nearly twice that of New York, Paris and Berlin put together.[8] But when a competitive threat did arise in the inter-war period as these three cities graduated as fully mature financial capitals, the response of London's financiers was no more distinguished than that of Britain's industrialists a half-century earlier, and their adherence to out-moded solutions – the 'automatic' Gold Standard, the 'pre-war parity', the balanced budget – were quite as persistent.[9] Established custom, old tricks and institutional memory brought the City to grief as surely as they had caused distress among (some) British manufacturers; they merely took longer to do so.

But did they always take longer? Conventional understanding is that the great surge in Britain's 'invisible' marketings commenced in the 1860s and 1870s. Naturally, there had been overseas investment and insurance before, but in the last third of the nineteenth century conditions were ripe for bigger things. There was the surplus profit from a century and more

[6] Anon., 'Industry and Finance', *Round Table* 25 (1916), 62, 65. The author was probably Robert Brand (later Lord Brand), a partner in Lazards, the merchant bankers.
[7] Cited by Checkland, 'Mind of the City', p. 272.
[8] W. Bagehot, *Lombard Street*, 12th edn (London, 1906; first published 1873), p. 4, provides published bank deposits for December 1872 – February 1873 as follows: London, £120 million; Paris, £13 million; New York, £40 million; German Empire. £8 million.
[9] See, amidst an extensive literature, S. Pollard (ed.), *Gold Standard and Employment Policy Between the Wars* (London, 1970); D. Winch, *Economics and Policy* (London, 1972); E. V. Morgan, *Studies in British Financial Policy* (London, 1947); D. Moggridge, *British Monetary Policy, 1924–31; The Norman Conquest of $4.86* (Cambridge. 1972).

of industrial supremacy to dispose of and a need to make that surplus work as the country sank into what was to become a long-term economic addiction: purchasing from the foreigner a greater value of commodities than could be sold back to him. Moreover, the emergence of competing industrial economies between 1850 and 1914 generated a demand for British capital and services. Much of that demand expressed itself as a requirement for transportation and encouraged Britain to fund a revolution in steam traction. Finally, the pervasive spread of British imperial power and the vast expansion of the American economy provided markets for bankers, underwriters and brokers, seemingly without end. Such an interpretation provides well for both need and opportunity; it offers a neat world-view of the 'service economy' over the long term. For some sectors it is not only neat but also tolerably accurate. But not for all.

I

The export of fire insurance did not begin in the 1860s or 1870s, although many historians – while acknowledging earlier instances as 'isolated' or 'experimental' – strive to convey this impression. Thus Charles Jones writes, '*After 1860*, the major British insurance companies extended their business beyond the British Isles, setting up a far-ranging system of agencies and branches throughout America, South Africa, Australia and the East.'[10] The historian of the Royal Exchange Assurance concluded, similarly, that 'the distinctive feature of the fire insurance industry *in the second half of the century* was...the invasion of foreign and colonial markets by British fire offices', an expansion which he attributes to 'far-reaching changes in the pattern of fire insurance induced by *young and thrustful offices*'.[11] Even Professor Clayton, in his recent survey of the British insurance industry, confessed himself 'struck by the *essentially limited geographical development*'[12] of British interests before the 1850s, while the influential work of H. E. Raynes reassures us that any activity that did occur in the foreign market before the 1850s can safely be classified as 'initial experiments'.[13]

The geographical setting for this consensus is again comfortably settled by convention: the historian of the Sun Fire Office defines it well, 'Ties of fire insurance between Great Britain and the Continent never became so strong in the course of the last century as they did between Britain and the United States and the Dominions. Agency business in Europe was

[10] C. Jones in D. C. M. Platt (ed.), *Business Imperialism, 1840–1930* (Oxford, 1977), p. 53; my italics.
[11] B. E. Supple, *The Royal Exchange Assurance: A History of British Insurance 1720–1970* (Cambridge, 1970), pp. 213–14; my italics.
[12] G. Clayton, *British Insurance* (London, 1971), p. 79; my italics.
[13] H. E. Raynes, *The History of British Insurance* (London, 1964), p. 256.

hampered by government restrictions, backward social, political and economic conditions and the jealousy of native offices.'[14]

The emphasis created by these arguments is inaccurate. One large fire office – the third largest within the British economy in 1787, the second largest by the 1790s, temporarily the largest of all in the 1830s and 1840s – had invented the export of fire insurance in 1783. This was the Phoenix Fire Office. It was founded in 1781, wrote its first foreign policy in 1783, established its first foreign agency in 1786 and created its first American agency in 1804. The overseas activities of this office before 1860 were neither isolated nor experimental.[15] And they were certainly not small in scale. Phoenix was taking over 40 per cent of one of the largest incomes in fire underwriting from its foreign department by the 1810s and overseas premiums contributed an average share of 41.7 per cent to the company's total earnings in the seven decades between 1816–25 and 1876–85. Such cosmopolitan enthusiasms were not shared by the two offices which with Phoenix composed the ruling triumvirate of Britain's fire insurance business over the period 1800–70, the Sun (1710) and the Royal Exchange (1720). The Sun derived no more than 16.4 per cent of its total premiums from foreign insurances in the decade 1866–75 and on average earned no more than 13.5 per cent of its total takings from this source in the five decades between 1836–45 and 1876–85. Still more conservative, the R.E.A. gathered only 4.1 per cent of its total receipts from its foreign policies 1851–5, only 2.7 per cent 1861–5.[16] The level of real foreign earnings accepted at Phoenix 1806–15 was not matched by the Sun until 1866–75 and by R.E.A. not until the later 1890s.

Nevertheless, it could be argued that all these foreign insurance earnings were small beer when compared with the massive corporate insurance transactions of the late nineteenth century. That view may be proposed but it is not easily sustained. Even if comparison is widened to include an acknowledged specialist from the later era of invisibles exportation, the Commercial Union, Phoenix does not suffer by it. Before the late 1880s neither the Commercial Union, nor any other insurance company, surpassed the share of total U.K. invisible earnings controlled by Phoenix in the 1810s; eventually in 1889 the C.U. exceeded the share averaged by Phoenix for 1816–20.[17]

[14] P. G. M. Dickson, *The Sun Insurance Office, 1710–1960* (London, 1960), p. 187.
[15] For a comprehensive account of the Phoenix's foreign operation, see C. Trebilcock, *The History of Phoenix Assurance*, vol. 1:*1782–1870* (Cambridge, 1985), chs. 5, 6.
[16] Proportions are calculated from: Phoenix, Annual Analysis of Business of All Departments; Sun, Dickson, *Sun Insurance Office*, app. 1, pp. 304–5; Royal Exchange, Supple, *Royal Exchange Assurance*, pp. 155, 242.
[17] Calculated from: A. H. Imlah, *Economic Elements in the Pax Britannica* (Cambridge, Mass., 1958), table 4, p. 70; Phoenix Review of Foreign and Irish Agencies, I, 1787–1877; E. Liveing, *The Commercial Union Insurance Group* (London, 1941), p. 45.

Undoubtedly, then, Phoenix was a major pioneer in an exceedingly valuable invisible trade. Establishing this entails a comprehensive reversal of the conventional understanding: the surge in the export of fire insurance after 1860 was not the first but the second; the major perpetrator of the early-century surge was no casual experimentalist but a company controlling as large a share of the country's invisible earnings as any achieved by a single insurer at any time before 1880. It was no 'young and thrustful' company of the mid-nineteenth century but a veteran of the late eighteenth. Nor was it 'essentially limited' in its geographical development: by 1815 Phoenix possessed forty-seven agencies on the European, American and Asian continents. But Phoenix's 'strongest ties' were not the orthodox ones with the U.S.A.; for virtually the whole of the nineteenth century, Phoenix failed to share the underwriters' fabled suspicion of the home continent and specialized in Europe. Finally, at no stage but the very earliest did it travel alone. The big offices which have been closely studied were indeed reticent in formulating their foreign policies before 1850. However, a substantial group of lesser offices formed around the turn of the century – the British (1799), the Imperial (1803), the Globe (1803), the Albion (1805), the Atlas (1808) – advertised their intentions clearly enough in their choice of titles. Well before 1810, Phoenix foreign agents were reporting stiff competition from other British offices. As far afield as Bridgetown, Barbados, a Phoenix official reported in November 1807 that 'the Imperial and Albion would engross the applications coming to Europe...as I have found that they have the most active partisans here;[18] and in Jamaica the Imperial by March 1808 'has...already inundated [the island] with a proposal addressed to the sugar planters....I suspect it to have been intended as a stolen march upon us.'[19] Clearly there was a pre-history of exportation in fire insurance; and it was created not only by one large office but also by a flock of smaller imitators. The absence of this phase of insurance history from the orthodox account is a function solely of the archives so far exploited.

II

One inference from the foregoing is that the nineteenth-century financial sector cannot usefully be considered in the aggregate. Every undergraduate now knows that he must not write of 'late-nineteenth-century industry' in the lump. Should we not employ as much care in our handling of 'invisibles', 'high finance' or 'the City'? Were all entrepreneurs in these markets impeccable in skill and drive? Were there no financial pursuits

[18] Phoenix, Correspondence of Jenkin Jones, p. 6; 24 November 1807.
[19] Ibid., p. 28; 1 March 1808.

which displayed the symptoms of managerial 'failure' evident in some (or many) areas of manufacturing? Were there no signs of financial obsolescence? Was 'decline' an experience wholly escaped by the metropolitan bourgeoisie? The short answer appears to be that the late-nineteenth-century City contained old and new 'technologies', first- and second-generation 'pioneers', in quite as much abundance as manufacturing. In some financial sectors, institutions of the old technology had indeed existed for sufficiently long to have developed their own version of obsolescence. Certainly, some company histories suggest that introversion, conservatism and risk-avoidance formed the hall-mark of more than one insurance company.[20] If some of the offices were 'young and thrustful', others among the metropolitan bourgeoisie were hardly agog for enterprise. Again, some City professions, notably merchant banking or corporate insurance, were formidably capital-intensive and quite as difficult of entry as many types of heavy industry. In contrast, others, notably the varied forms of brokerage and real-estate services, offered lenient terms to newcomers and, frequently, quick returns. Thus the formidable Lloyds partnership of Hogg Robinson was launched in 1845 on a capital of only £2000, and, as late as 1910, a small broker specializing in non-marine risks, Charles E. W. Austin, earned a gross commission on his enterprise of barely £300 per year.[21] The City was in no way homogeneous in its contents: it housed old and new, durable and transitory, staid and sharp.

Even the assumption that the 'financial sector' was synonymous with the 'City' is erroneous. In one important area of invisible trade – insurance – some of the most important developments in the second half of the century occurred *outside* London. Just as, in the eighteenth century, British manufacturing underwent the vital diaspora northwards, so a hundred and more years later substantial portions of British finance gravitated towards the northern centres of wealth that commerce and manufacturing had created. This was not only true of insurance of course. The great surge in railway finance between 1840 and 1870 had been managed largely by a score of provincial stock exchanges created for that purpose.[22] But once the railway boom was spent, many of these outposts resorted to increasingly conservative lending policies or to closure. By contrast the urge towards non-metropolitan enterprise in insurance strengthened as the century progressed. The offices which boasted the fastest expansion of market shares in the 1850s and 1860s, those which

---

[20] This is an easily identified refrain in Barry Supple's history of the Royal Exchange.
[21] S. D. Chapman, 'Hogg Robinson: The Rise of a Lloyd's Broker', in O. M. Westall (ed.), *The Historian and the Business of Insurance* (Manchester, 1984), pp. 174–5, 177.
[22] See, for example, J. R. Killick and W. A. Thomas, 'The Provincial Stock Exchanges, 1830–70', *Economic History Review* 23 (1970), 96–111.

led the vast expansion in insurance exports from the 1860s and 1870s, were not London companies. They were the Royal of Liverpool, the Liverpool and London and Globe, and the Glasgow-based North British. Together these three offices accounted for almost one-fifth of the home fire market in 1869, the last year that fire duty, the tax that obligingly measured that market, was levied.[23] At this point two of the four largest British fire insurers were Liverpool companies. Their exploits in promoting the enormous insurance trade to the U.S.A. were far more dashing than anything achieved in London; the Royal, the Liverpool and London, and the North British were the first British companies to create American agencies in the revival of insurance exports around the mid-century.

Of course, there had been large provincial insurers before, notably the Norwich Union (1797), the West of England (1807) and the Manchester (1824), and one or two of these achieved the highest status. However, one great and successful provincial was still emphasizing in the 1860s that 'at the time the Royal Insurance Office was started, a very general opinion prevailed in London that no great Fire Insurance Company could be permanently established out of the Metropolis', and it confessed that one of its original intentions was 'to prove this opinion to be a fallacy'. Together with its Liverpool colleagues, the Royal supplied more than adequate proof, and had the grace to admit that 'no anticipation of so unheard of a progress, as had been attained was ever indulged or such a rapidity of advance ever thought practicable'.[24] Their gratified surprise can be readily understood. For in the late nineteenth century an entire set of Liverpool insurance companies escaped the confines of their local market to achieve not merely national but global significance. Four of them, the Royal (1845), the Liverpool and London and Globe (1836–64), the Queen (1857) and the London and Lancashire (1862), around the turn of the century controlled £6 million out of the £20 million in total takings earned by the British fire insurance business.[25] Even by 1863, the Royal of Liverpool claimed to be one of the largest fire insurers in the world, and thought that by then it might be the largest exporter of all: 'scarcely one company in existence does the same amount of business in Foreign parts as the Royal Insurance office'.[26] It was precisely the provincial bourgeosie who created this entrepreneurial success in the financial sector.

It thus becomes clear that two different kinds of insurance company proved important in developing the export of fire policies in the last century. One group, led by the Phoenix and London-based, pioneered entry

---

[23] Calculated from Phoenix Duty Book I.
[24] *Royal Insurance Almanac* (1863), pp. 28–9.
[25] Royal Insurance Co., *Fire Insurance and the City of Liverpool* (Liverpool, 1903), p. 19.
[26] *Royal Insurance Almanac* (1863), p. 37.

to the European and American markets at the remarkably early period 1783–1810. Another group, led by the Liverpool offices, pioneered re-entry to the American market from mid-century. We thus have an unusual opportunity for comparing the enterprise patterns of 'old' and 'new' financial technologies, first- and second-generation insurance pioneers. Comprehensive and compatible data in respect to total premium earnings, agency receipts and losses by market exist for two key companies: the Phoenix of London and the Royal of Liverpool.[27] The energy with which insurers approached the American market is often cited as a measure of enterprise, and that yardstick will be retained here. However, our data allow wider geographical coverage, and since it was possible to write enterprising insurance elsewhere, the larger span will be invoked when appropriate.

III

The attitude of Phoenix to the New World insurance markets was controlled by four main variables: the date of entry; the experience of disaster; the timing of the 'missions' sent by Head Office to sample the distant markets at first hand; and the incidence of political interruptions to trade, among them the American Civil War.

Phoenix's origins lay in the sugar trade; its founding shareholders of 1781–2 represented the major part of the refinery industry of London. Industrial expertise encouraged the refiners to look outside the capital for their insurances. So too did the comparative neglect of provincial fire business by the handful of metropolitan fire offices. Consequently the Phoenix's construction of a national agency structure was remarkably swift: it boasted as many agents after two years of business (121 in 1783) as the Sun could claim after more than seventy (123 in 1786), and twice as many as the Royal Exchange after sixty (60 in 1780). Industrial and provincial business provided Phoenix with a natural market niche. Other pressures encouraged the refiners to invent the exportation of fire insurance, widening the niche to international proportions. To begin with, the fire duty levied on all British (and colonial) policies from Phoenix's first year of trading did not apply to foreign insurance. Secondly, sugar expertise

---

[27] The comparable sources are: Phoenix Review of Foreign and Irish Agencies, books 1–3; Royal Results of Foreign Business, book 1, Liverpool City Library. I am most grateful to the Royal Insurance Co. Ltd for permission to use its foreign premium statistics and to the Phoenix Assurance Group for allowing me free access to the matching source, and to many others. Much of the retrieval and compilation of the premium numbers (see Tables 7.2 and 7.4) was carried out by my assistant, Pamela Judd; I am indebted to her for much painstaking work. The account of Phoenix's American dealings after 1870 also draws upon Robin Pearson's preparatory investigation for volume II of the Phoenix history.

could carry insurance further afield than the refinery centres of Bristol or Glasgow; a sugar house was much the same kind of risk whether it was located in Finsbury Park or in Finland. Insurances of this sort, founded upon secure knowledge of specific processes, could then be used to probe distant markets and to assess any other acceptable risks they might contain. Refinery policies could thus use familiar knowledge to break into new markets and form a base for the acquisition of new knowledge and diversified insurances. Finally, the experience of the refiners was cosmopolitan in a wider sense. They purchased their raw materials from the West and, sometimes, East Indies; they maintained contacts with plantation owners, consuls and shippers throughout the New World; they corresponded with their colleagues in the great European refinery centres; they imported labourers from Hamburg; many of their own number retained German names. They possessed access to a web of information which could place insurances with some precision across a transcontinental span. Insurance of course is a function of information.

It was entirely natural that Phoenix should favour initially the foreign sugar centres that it knew best, the closest ones, those linked to London by the most dependable lines of information. Accordingly, the office's first foreign agencies – six outposts created between April 1786 and December 1787, the first ever overseas appointments by any corporate insurer – were dominated by the refinery capitals of Nantes, Bordeaux and Hamburg. Among these, Hamburg, probably the largest sugar-processing centre in the world, said to contain some 700 refineries, was massively preeminent, accounting for over 90 per cent of Phoenix's agency earnings 1786–1805 and a still impressive 63.4 per cent 1816–25. For some seven decades Hamburg, Phoenix's clearing house for northern Europe insurances, was by far the most valuable single outpost in the office's entire organization. Unfortunately, however, Phoenix was not alone in cherishing European ambitions; continent-wide schemes seized the attention also of Revolutionary France, and, worse still, of Bonaparte's Grande Armée. Some of the best Phoenix agencies lay on French soil, others were cramped by French invasions. Even Hamburg's share of Phoenix agency earnings slid to 34.4 per cent over the war-torn decade 1806–15. Between Napoleon's introduction of the Continental System of blockade in 1806 and the Battle of the Nations outside Leipzig in 1813, Phoenix's net premium receipts from Europe fell from £30642 to a mere £17467; Hamburg's earnings plummeted by 48 per cent. Much like the British economy in general, Phoenix needed alternative export markets and it found them in much the same place. The new ground was broken in the spring and summer of 1804 with the appointment of Alexander Auldjo to the agency for Canada and Theophylact Bache to that for New York. 1805 saw the turn of the West

Table 7.1. *Phoenix North American premium receipts,*
annual averages by decade, 1806–75

	Current prices £	Constant prices[a] £
1806–15	20656	11117
1816–25	13472	9935
1826–35	8470	7583
1836–45	13180	11236
1846–55	12480	11762
1856–65	23727	19955
1866–75	54409	46188

[a] Constant prices are on a base year composed of an average of 1865 and 1885 (Rousseaux).

Indies: twenty-one new agencies were created, twelve of them in the islands and the rest scattered more widely from Oporto to St John's, Newfoundland. In 1806 the southern and eastern United States claimed five out of the ten foreign agencies created in that year, the residue being untidy afterthoughts strewn from Gibraltar to the Cape. By 1815 Phoenix had forty-seven overseas agencies, the R.E.A. had recently created one and the Sun was not to create its first for another twenty-one years.

The impact of the New World agencies on Phoenix earnings was immediate and dramatic. The West Indian locations did not amount to much, providing an average 3.5 per cent of total annual foreign premiums 1806–15 and exceeding 6 per cent in only one decade before 1875 (1846–55: 6.6 per cent). But North America proved an effective substitute for the European money-spinner confiscated by Bonaparte: the agencies of the U.S. and Canada generated an average 29.8 per cent of total annual foreign premiums 1806–15, their highest score for any decade 1806–75, a share closely approached only once more within this period (1866–75: 27.8 per cent). Moreover, the average decadal contribution of these agencies over the seven decades 1806–75 was a very useful 21.7 per cent. In money terms, the earnings of the mainland U.S. and Canadian agencies for 1806–15 were on average £20656 per annum and were not exceeded until 1856–65 and then, at £21948 per annum, not by much. Even in real terms the annual average takings for 1806–15 were only marginally exceeded in 1836–45 and 1846–55 before being handsomely passed in 1856–65 (see Table 7.1). Measured either way, Phoenix's North American agencies achieved a peak of performance in the 1800s very close to their level of attainment in a period when America was commencing its career as a generally popular attraction for British fire insurers. However, almost half a century separated these periods.

Nevertheless, the New World was no Arcadia for the precocious insurance man. If it was rich in pickings for the early underwriter, it was also fertile in inconvenience and disaster. It was inconvenient when the United States imposed sanctions on British trade between 1806 and 1810, but these did not prove effective. It was rather more disturbing when war flared briefly between the two transatlantic powers in 1812: the British bombarded Washington, and, in an act apparently contrived to make fire underwriters weep, set light to the White House. With rather precise logic – one British fire office for one British fire – some of the states retaliated against the largest foreign purveyor of insurance: Boston introduced a punitive insurance tax in 1822 and New York in the single definitive ban of 1814 threw the Phoenix out of the city and suppressed its valuable agency there. But, despite a few opinions to the contrary, New York does not constitute America. Quite apart from the important Phoenix annexe in Canada, Phoenix agencies were maintained for many more years within the United States, at provincial centres like New Orleans, Savannah and Norfolk, Virginia. At some points these agencies endured lean times but they did maintain an unbroken sequence of American premiums from 1804 – when Phoenix first arrived – until the mid-century – when the second generation of British exporters made landfall. By the time the newcomers wrote their first American policies, Phoenix had already earned more than £$\frac{3}{4}$ million from its various American agencies.

Disaster was not readily absorbed. Insurance, of course, trades in disaster but a long experience of calamity may not be an asset for the insurer; it hardens reflexes and skins and dulls the appreciation of new prospects. For Phoenix the special irony was that although Europe provided most of its foreign income (an average of 47 per cent for the seven decades 1806–15 to 1866–75 against 30 per cent for the New World), the Americas provided most of its disasters. With the exception of the Gothenberg fire of 1803 and the enormous blaze at Hamburg in 1842, the litany of horror was drawn exclusively from the West Indies, U.S.A. and Canada. Before the century turned, major fires struck at Tobago in 1790, Grenada in 1793, and both Charleston and Savannah in 1797; they continued after 1800 with catastrophe falling upon St Thomas in the Virgin Islands in 1806, Port of Spain in 1808, St Lucia in 1814, St John's, Newfoundland in 1816, and almost terminally in 1846, Norfolk, Virginia in 1817 and Savannah, for the second time, in 1819. After a brief respite of some twenty years, the flames took hold again in the 1840s. The decade began with an unusual demonstration from Europe: the 'conflagration which broke out on Thursday 5 May and continued burning until the following Sunday', in Hamburg in 1842, proved that tragedy was not restricted to the fiery extremities, to harsh climates or unproven markets. Within months however the New World had reasserted its primacy. In 1845 New York burned, although Phoenix, thanks to the state's ban upon the office, was not there to suffer. But in September and October there were conflagrations in both Quebec ('nearly 3000 houses totally destroyed... covering a space of about one mile in length and a half-mile in breadth, and the poor wretched inhabitants scattered about in all directions')[28] and Montreal; and in each of these Phoenix was deeply interested. Nevertheless, it was 1846 which proved the Year of the Fire with a vengeance. In June, St John's, Newfoundland suffered the worst inferno of the year, losing 'a burnt-out district comprising almost the whole of the Town' to 'one vast sheet of flame' and appalling firefighting.[29] In late summer Halifax, Nova Scotia, fought an equal blaze with far superior skill and resource. Lesser disasters were recorded by Phoenix within the same few months at La Praerie, Montreal, Nantucket, Lynn, Placentia Bay and Philadelphia. Their under-writers could have been forgiven for believing that for a two-year period a substantial proportion of the American continent was more or less permanently alight.

For the underwriter disaster is an ambiguous experience. Firstly, it encourages him to learn from past mistakes, and of course he will be lost if he does not do this. But precisely *what* he should learn is not so obvious. After cataclysm has struck, there is a natural tendency to shed risks, to contract the volume of insurances, to evacuate certain markets revealed as treacherous. However, this can easily go too far: the underwriter readily succumbs to a morbid fear of disasters past. The sequel is often excessive 'prudence', a puritanical insistence on limiting business to the 'best' risks, an over-vigorous selection which sacrifices volume of insurances to an often illusory concept of quality. Further this preoccupation with select lines is often insensitive to changes in the status of a market: street lighting, piped water and efficient policing turned many a frontier hell-hole into the acme of municipal probity within remarkably few years and it took alert and acquisitive insurers to keep track. Secondly, disaster was not in itself bad for business. True, in the short term it imposed punishing losses; but it also created opportunities. Smaller competitors were often swamped by the volume of claims while larger ones were more than usually amenable in agreeing higher rates. Tariffs and other collusive tactics were frequently forged among the embers of nineteenth-century towns. Certainly, with agreement or not, premiums could be pushed up to compensate for disaster

[28] Phoenix, Broomfield Correspondence, pp. 9–10; 11 September 1845.
[29] *Ibid.*, p. 86; 23 July 1846.

losses and the market would pay them. Finally, the market would itself expand as the nonchalant, the feckless or the over-confident were frightened into taking out first-time policies. The aftermath of disaster was no time for the underwriter to drag his feet.

For Phoenix, its ration of crises contained three which had powerful conditioning effects on the entrepreneurial performance of the office: St Thomas in 1806, Hamburg in 1842, and the American and Canadian blazes of the 1840s. In each case the company's response was the insurer's equivalent of sending a gunboat: they despatched a visiting fireman to adjust the claims, rake over the ashes and assess the market. These missions – Jenkin Jones to the West Indies and United States from 1807 to 1809; Thomas Richter to Hamburg in 1842; J. J. Broomfield to the New World again in 1845 and 1846 – became a Phoenix speciality. They brought mixed blessings. But then St Thomas cost the company over £200 000, Hamburg £250 000 and St John's, Newfoundland alone £114 575.

Each of these catastrophes left a special imprint on the corporate memory of the company. The first was very nearly fatal. Phoenix had not undertaken its diversification into the very distant transatlantic trade without hesitation. Almost the worst that could have happened, therefore, was a major loss within a newly created and not especially profitable part of the new agency system while the new initiative was still clearly on trial. St Thomas provided exactly that kind of loss. Moreover, it was so large because agents far removed from the control of Head Office had built up acceptances to irresponsible heights; it demonstrated all too clearly the difficulty of applying the reins to transatlantic agencies. The result was near bankruptcy: on the eve of the disaster in December 1806 Phoenix held an investment portfolio of £202 643; two years later the directors had nothing left but the property they stood up in, £28 298 worth of illiquid title deeds. Only the indulgence of their auditors bought them time and even then a further full-blown disaster in 1807 or 1808 would have brought the death blow. This had powerful implications for future managers. From the 1800s Phoenix greatly improved the capacity of its corporate memory; it maintained very exact and thorough analyses of business performance, premium receipts and losses. Any director of the 1820s, 1830s or 1840s, at the flip of a page, could admire the incisiveness and dash of his predecessors; and marvel at the devilish chances they took.

The first of the Phoenix missions, Jenkin Jones' trip to the Caribbean and the mainland United States, followed from one of these chances and was undertaken amidst bated breath. It was not helped by the fact that a second conflagration consumed Port of Spain in March 1808, within weeks of Jones leaving it. Fortunately, Phoenix was not heavily engaged in Trinidad but the second Caribbean blaze clearly raised questions as to whether it should be in this market at all. Jones learned of the 'deplorable calamity' with 'inexpressible pain' and, reduced temporarily to despair, saw it as 'terminating the utility of my Mission'.[30] Despite the company legend that Jones' embassy was an heroic sales tour, it is clear in fact that he had three main purposes: to bring agents under control; to improve information flows between London and the outstations; and to identify what Phoenix should *not* insure. Although he recovered some of his spirits, the main effect of his work was to 'purify our books'. Purification became a Phoenix watchword, a reflex solution to be applied in any crisis, a routine retreat into selectivity whenever the distant world became too threatening. In Jones' hands it was employed with discipline and precision but there was nothing he could do to prevent it assuming the aura of hallowed practice, the unquestioned status of holy writ for succeeding generations. The desperateness of the straits in which he applied it, and applied it successfully, naturally added to its sanctity as a company principle.

When the next catastrophe of comparable proportions occurred, the efficiency of the corporate memory and the institutionalization of the purification principle caused great problems for the more entrepreneurial of Jones' descendants. By the 1840s, the coherence of the original group of sugar refiners, the shared assumptions and expertise of a single commercial fraternity, had anyway undergone erosion and the quality of Phoenix management had suffered. But the company still contained bold spirits. They were certainly needed when the mercantile sector of Hamburg went up in smoke. Although this disaster befell one of the richest centres of traditional European trade, it had a much wider relevance. It was one of the worst blows to insurance confidence of the entire nineteenth century and provided an unpleasantly formative experience for those British ventures specializing in insurance exports at that time. Hamburg was no fiery trouble spot but a centre of excellence for the business; all three of the major British offices had established their earliest foreign agencies there. This conflagration affected profitable custom, commercial tradition and trusted friends. Had the City of London been put to the torch or the warehouses of Amsterdam ignited by a passing comet, the insurance community could scarcely have been more disturbed.

In May 1842 Hamburg burned to the tune of £5–7 million in current prices. One local office acknowledged nearly £¾ million of these claims, and went bankrupt. Many other German ventures followed suit. The British lasted better but suffered heavy injuries. The R.E.A. paid out £95 000 upon what had been one of its very few profitable overseas accounts. The Sun,

---

[30] Phoenix, Correspondence of Jenkin Jones, pp. 40, 51; 9 April 1808, 24 May 1808.

which had been in Hamburg only since 1836, shouldered losses of £117 000 and promptly vacated the market, its faith in affairs foreign all but extinguished. The Phoenix paid dearly for its premier status in European insurances: Hamburg proved more costly even than St Thomas, inflicting losses upon the pioneer exporter of around £¼ million.

Just as after St Thomas, Phoenix investments showed the strain: they plummeted from a pre-crisis peak of £600 103 in March 1842 to £376 152 by the year's end. Nevertheless the company did not face 1843 as it had 1808, on its beam end. Phoenix could afford rather more dash in responding to the crisis. Generally, Thomas Richter, who was sent on a five-week embassy to the ruined city, displayed such dash. By late June, with remarkable swiftness, he had adjusted over £200 000 worth of claims, settling most in bullion. Quick restitution is, of course, a major selling point in insurance and Richter made the most of it: the contrast between Phoenix and the ailing German offices was forcefully put. Bankruptcies had also greatly reduced the irritant of German competition and Richter wished to make the most of that as well. Furthermore, disaster had elicited the usual improved level of accord between the surviving offices: greatly increased, indeed doubled, premium rates for Hamburg were agreed between them and embodied in a formal tariff before the year's end. Misfortune, Richter saw, had created new opportunities for Phoenix in Hamburg: the only question was what level of risk the office should select. He pressed for extension, and K. D. Hodgson, a senior director sent out from England to add Board weight to Phoenix's loss adjustment, agreed with him. However, such robust tactics proved excessively strong meat for those back in Lombard Street. On 27 May the Board grudgingly sanctioned 'a modest increase in safe and prudent risks' but added, 'bearing in mind the experience furnished by the late calamity, the Board are not prepared as a permanent measure to increase the aggregate amount insured in the City'.[31] By 10 June their patience even with temporary increases was exhausted and they instructed that 'a gradual reduction of Risk at Hamburg should be immediately commenced'.[32] The reduction that they implemented was however neither gradual nor selective: in the ten years after 1842 receipts from Hamburg were taken down by a savage 62 per cent and the city's share in Phoenix total foreign income dropped from its customary preeminence of 34.3 per cent in 1842 to a mere 16.6 per cent by 1852. The long-term trend for Hamburg was fractured by the fire.

Clearly 'the experience furnished by the late calamity' was no simple matter: it told Richter and Hodgson to go forward and the rest of the Board to go back. The beneficial paradoxes of disaster, identified by Richter,

[31] Phoenix Directors' Minutes, Q16, p. 217; 27 May 1842.
[32] Ibid., p. 228; 10 June 1842.

appealed to the Board less than the rigorous enjoinder to 'purify the books'. This was a policy which attracted conservative minds too readily and in conservative hands could be pushed too far. There had been two views as to the proper treatment for Hamburg and the more pessimistic had prevailed. The mood of Phoenix's second-generation management was more subdued than that of the founders. They now had the full apparatus of business analysis to reveal how narrowly the founders had survived. The impact of Hamburg could not have come at a more unfortunate time. It acted as a terrible warning to those already warned. Subdued management was given every excuse for still more sombre assessments of its prospects. Any event that strengthened the desire for 'purification' at this juncture was bound to encourage the suppression of the enterprising option as the standard response to difficult choices.

This was evident in the Board's handling of the third Phoenix mission of the period: Broomfield's retracing of Jones' itinerary in the mid-1840s. Despite the miserable roll-call of pyres and bonfires he attended, Broomfield was far more content with Phoenix's agents and information flows than Jones had been. When it was not actually alight, he found Canada a thriving place and the Board followed his advice in pushing business here. By the early 1830s Canada contained the most valuable Phoenix agency system outside Hamburg and by the early 1850s the Canadian network had overtaken Hamburg. In contrast, Broomfield found only problems in the U.S.A.: they were composed equally of rapidly advancing competition and the inadequate responses of his Lombard Street masters to this threat. Where hazard levels were lower than in the Canadian north and a reputation for financial solidity counted for less, smaller offices could gain advantages. In particular, the native American offices could peddle their own speciality: rock-bottom premiums. Broomfield urged his superiors to retaliate with price reductions. Instead they stood on reputation, stuck by their rates and damned the consequences. These could be severe. In Norfolk, Virginia, in 1845 Phoenix's insistence upon a 1 per cent premium rate – when the local offices were proposing $\frac{1}{2}$ per cent – cost the British company an astonishing 65 per cent of its sums insured within twelve months.[33] Norfolk was no southern slum; if retired colonels, planters and merchants maintaining standards in an increasingly placid colonial-style town did not constitute sound fire risks, we may wonder what did. Broomfield did wonder. He warned that 'the parties would willingly pay us $\frac{3}{4}$ per cent as they prefer the security of the Phoenix Company, but they will not pay 1 per cent. Even those who have stayed with the Phoenix so far, say that they will leave if the 1 per cent rate is continued.'[34] Yet the

[33] Phoenix, Broomfield Correspondence, p. 116; 4 September 1846.
[34] *Ibid.*

Board appeared content that Phoenix commitments should be reduced: they assumed that the best risks would stay with the company at any price and that market forces could safely be left to purify the books without further managerial interference. Yet at Norfolk (as at Hamburg) Phoenix was not purifying the books of wastage and corruption; it was to Broomfield's (as to Richter's) considerable bafflement throwing away good risks.

The effect on the American trade, and the contrast with the Canadian, was marked. Premiums from Canada, Newfoundland and Halifax climbed sharply in the decade after Broomfield's visit, while American receipts followed a pattern similar to those at Hamburg, wobbled precariously and then toppled. In the decade 1836–45 the American agencies netted an annual average 9.3 per cent of the office's total foreign earnings against 8.6 per cent from the Canadian agencies. However, in the ensuing decade, which witnessed the acceleration of the new American manufacturing sector, the share of Phoenix's U.S. agencies fell to 5.3 per cent while that of the Canadian outposts advanced to 13.2 per cent. It was almost as if Phoenix directors felt happier in the backwoods.

There was some truth in this. The Board was just as likely to hand out purification to settled risks as to perilous ones, and this must have yielded better results where a good proportion of the risks *were* dangerous. By mid-century Jones' trusted mixture of purification and raised rates depressed business in some places more than could ever have been intended; the Board naturally preferred those places like Canada, where it did not. Furthermore, they chose to trade upon reputation, to emphasize reliability, rather than to compete in price, and this showed to best advantage in markets that were moderately *unreliable*. Behind such preferences lay a managerial perspective which featured traditional centres of commerce, established status, familiar risks and a fair price, innocent of special offers or sharp practice. This was an outlook that many later nineteenth-century manufacturers would have found familiar.

Broomfield perpetrated one final massive irony in Phoenix's history. He toured the New World at the right time for the mobilization of Canada and for warnings of American insurance competition. Yet in other respects he contrived disastrously to be in the wrong places at the wrong times. He travelled one of the world's strongest economies at the start of its industrial career yet detected no sweet music on the wind. In the 1850s British commissioners reported to the House of Commons on the gathering strength of American industry;[35] in the 1840s Broomfield reported nothing

[35] Sir T. Whitworth and G. Wallis, *The Industry of the United States in Machinery, Manufactures and Useful and Ornamental Arts* (London, 1854); *Report of the Commission on the Machinery of the United States* (Parliamentary Papers, 1854–5, L.). Both surveys were presented as reports to the House of Commons.

similar to Lombard Street. He was the classically misdirected tourist energetically appreciating the wrong attractions. He went mainly to the old economic capitals of the south – Savannah, Norfolk, Richmond – and to New York – from which Phoenix was still debarred – as well as to the pestilential Caribbean – which left him too ill to go anywhere else. It was an unfortunate selection, for few places on this map coincided with the centres of the new economic order. Around 1830 the cotton mills of Virginia and those of Massachusetts were much of a size; by 1860 the mills of New England were on average three times as big as those of the South. Yet in the middle of this process of growth, all Broomfield could do was muse wistfully that 'there are few manufactories of any kind in Savannah'. If he had dropped in on the industrial towns of Massachusetts or on Cincinnati or Chicago he would have found many more. He could have been luckier too with the premier industrial cities of the era, New York and Philadelphia: Phoenix could not get into New York and although Broomfield passed through Philadelphia he was in a hurry at the time; it was on fire and he did not report on it. If the United States achieved industrial 'take-off' between 1840 and 1860, Broomfield was not often in a position to notice. 'By 1860', writes Douglas North, 'the United States was second only to the United Kingdom as an industrial nation',[36] but of this developing potential Phoenix had received little inkling. Undoubtedly, as ill-luck would have it, the Broomfield mission encouraged Phoenix to underrate the American insurance market at precisely its most promising point. For the subdued impression conveyed by Broomfield was the most authoritative judgment upon America that Phoenix received in the mid-century period.

By the 1840s Phoenix was not well qualified to appreciate the enticing prospects of the American market. The company had pioneered the trade in overseas fire insurance and had built itself into one of Britain's largest fire offices on the proceeds. But the going had been hard and the experience of disaster chastening. Whatever the value of foreign insurances in general as money-spinners, too much of the hard going, too many of the catastrophes, had derived from the New World. There was nothing in Phoenix experience to suggest that America was synonymous with enticing prospects; its record 1804–45 was rather one of confusion, conflagration and competition. Although Broomfield was present when the record was changed, he came just too early either to notice or to report the fact. Finally, the Civil War, when it arrived, was particularly unkind to an agency system, the remnants of which were concentrated on the commercial capitals of the Old South. Phoenix's institutional memory, the

[36] D. North, 'Industrialization in the United States, 1815–60', in W. W. Rostow (ed.), *The Economics of Take-off into Sustained Growth* (London, 1963), pp. 46, 61.

lessons of one early financial 'technology', contained no pointers as to what the U.S. insurance market might become.

IV

Perhaps to exploit fully the opportunities of the mid-century world market in insurance it was necessary to *lack* the experience of St Thomas, Hamburg or St John's. The Royal of Liverpool, commencing in 1845, did miss all these. It developed from the commercial aftermath of the Industrial Revolution as directly as Phoenix had sprung from the initial industrial acceleration itself. Where the founders of the older office had been sugar-refining industrialists, those of the Royal were merchants, brokers and shipowners. Not only did they escape the early disasters in the foreign insurance business, they were also located at the centre of an extremely sophisticated structure of international intelligence. Where in the 1840s Phoenix sent its lone emissary to inspect the old centres of the American economy, the merchants and shippers of Liverpool were expert in the affairs of the new. They were the chief purveyors of the transatlantic trade. Their city boomed with it. New docks were going up at Birkenhead and the frantic activity in Liverpool's construction industry during the 1840s was a matter for national comment. The America trade was serviced by fleets of clippers, and steam passage to the United States had already been pioneered by the *Britannia*. The names which were prominent in this trade – Turner, Horsfall, Moore, Molyneux, Wainwright, Bouch, Booker, Maxwell – were also names which featured on the Royal's list of founding directors.

The men who launched the Royal comprised the Tory elite of Liverpool trade. Charles Turner was chairman of the Liverpool Dock Board and a merchant sufficiently eminent to stand for Parliament in 1852.[37] His colleague T. B. Horsfall descended from a line of plutocratic merchants, property-owners and charitable church-builders and was sufficiently eminent to get elected to Westminster: he was Mayor of Liverpool 1847–8 and M.P. 1853–68.[38] John Bramley Moore was another chairman of the Liverpool Docks and had one of the northern quaysides, built as part of the 1840s construction boom, named after him; he was also a famously dynamic mayor of the city, given to enormous fun fairs and virtuoso charity entertainments.[39] The Molyneux were long-established estate

[37] J. A. Picton, *Memorials of Liverpool* (London, 1873), vol. I, p. 475.
[38] *Ibid.*, vol. II, pp. 418–19, 565. Turner also, after sundry electoral difficulties, achieved his seat at Westminster by 1863.
[39] T. Baines, *History of the Commerce and Town of Liverpool* (London, 1852), p. 832; Picton, *Memorials of Liverpool*, vol. I. p. 597.

owners, but by the 1840s Edmund Molyneux, through the firm of Molyneux and Witherby, was one of Liverpool's leading importers of American cotton. George Wainwright was in the same line, the enterprise of Wainwright and Co. featuring prominently in the cotton trade from the 1820s and 1830s.[40] The remaining founders were brokers, shipowners, merchants or shipbuilders – like William Jones of the first board – sharing an elevated status in the commerce and society of Liverpool, and frequently sharing too a political persuasion. They formed a genuine provincial plutocracy drawing much of its wealth from that city's involvement with the sea.

No interest group was better placed to appreciate the attractions of the American insurance market. To its members this was so obvious that, irritatingly, they refrained from explaining it in their early promotional literature. Coyly their first prospectus says only, 'The advantages derivable to a commercial and populous town like Liverpool, from the establishment of an Insurance Company, composed of an extensive local proprietary mutually interested in its welfare and success, will be readily understood and appreciated by the public, without comment, especially at the present time.' It was left to a company publication of 1903 to add at least a little emphasis: 'The eminent position the Insurance Offices of Liverpool hold in their own field of commercial enterprise, and the prosperity and phenomenal development which they have experienced, may well be attributed in no small measure to the worldwide trade and influence of the Merchants and Ship-owners of Liverpool from whose ranks the Directors of its Fire Offices have been drawn.'[41] Here the connection is made: Liverpool's pattern of trade created rich prospects for Liverpool's insurers of foreign property.

Like the Phoenix, the Royal was very swift into the overseas market, almost as fast to Calcutta as to Cork, to Brazil as to Bury. By the end of its first year it had created foreign agencies in both of these places and in 1846 added Batavia, Demerara, Manila, Singapore and New Brunswick. By 1851 further outposts had been established in Chile, Peru, Sourabaya, Barbados, Gothenberg, St John's, Newfoundland, Montreal and Sydney. The invasion of the United States was approached somewhat more cautiously, but was well under way by 1852. Before it was fully launched, the Royal carried out its own version of the Jenkin Jones investigation: its manager, Percy Dove, toured the states in 1851 and in June personally appointed A. B. McDonald, secretary of the Knickerbocker Insurance Co.,

[40] D. M. Williams, 'Liverpool Merchants and the Cotton Trade 1820–5', in J. R. Harris (ed.), *Liverpool and Merseyside: Essays in the Economic and Social History of the Port and Its Hinterland* (London, 1969), p. 209.
[41] Royal Insurance Co., *Fire Insurance*, p. 11.

as the office's first American agent (for New York). Dove was more discriminating in 1851 than Broomfield had been in 1845: although Dove too inspected Savannah and Charleston and established agencies in both, he also looked carefully at Baltimore and Philadelphia, then the U.S.A.'s fourth largest city and a major industrial centre; and in each of those as well he left new agencies behind him. Further appointments were made at Boston, Cincinnati, Mobile and New Orleans in 1852 and at Louisville and San Francisco in 1853. In this Californian outpost the Royal was the second British insurer to arrive; it was beaten to the post by the Liverpool and London. Phoenix started to write San Francisco policies only in 1864.

The information that came into Liverpool with the crews and the cargoes and drew the city's insurers across the Atlantic concerned gold, new territories, railways and immigrants, as well as manufacturing. As the Royal settled into its new market, California was producing bullion to the tune of $50 million per year; Texas, Florida and Wisconsin had recently joined the Union and Oregon Territory opened for settlement; immigration produced an average one quarter of a million new citizens per year throughout the decade; and the recently constructed railway system exceeded 9000 miles of working track. News of such developments was music to insurers' ears and much of that news concentrated on Liverpool. Nevertheless, the city's new underwriters were careful to play to their skills. Just as Phoenix had initiated its overseas expansion by exploiting its connections in the sugar-refinery centres of Europe and America, so the Royal went first to the kind of places that Liverpool merchants and shippers knew best. Many of them were not unlike Liverpool. New York was itself the terminus for the Hudson River–Erie Canal route to the interior and a great seaport in its own right. Baltimore was the seaport for the mid-Atlantic states; Savannah and Charleston, among their other activities, were cotton-shipping centres; Boston was the maritime gateway for the mills of New England; Cincinnati was a flourishing Ohio River port as well as a major meat-packing centre; Mobile and New Orleans were the ports of the Gulf, San Francisco of the west. Where the first-generation Liverpool underwriters set up shop, the sea was never far distant. If for Phoenix it was the sugar refinery which formed the key to a wider world of insurance, the same service was provided for the Royal by the clippers and merchant-men which linked the dockside of its home town with the quays of much more distant ports.

As early as 1855, the Royal had found, in the market areas of Europe, North America, Latin America, the West Indies, Australasia and the Far East, no less than thirty-six such places. At this point the Phoenix foreign agency system had contracted to a complement of twenty-four outposts.

V

The policies adopted in the crucial mid-century decades by the old foreign pioneer and the new foreign pioneer could scarcely have been more different. True, the basic market structures were similar. Phoenix and Royal went, broadly, to the same geographical areas: in only one market area (Australasia) was the older company entirely absent while the younger one pocketed a substantial income. But then again the Royal made only a token showing in the African theatre while Phoenix drew a constant if unexciting return from this quarter. The real differences lay in the balance struck between the *same* markets by the two offices and in the very different levels of exploitation meted out to them (see Table 7.2).

Phoenix's line continued to be one of well-judged restraint, concentrating on a few strong points and trusting in 'purified' books to yield sufficient income. Towards the end of the period, even more cautiously, Phoenix trusted to other offices to yield its income; that is, it sought to address foreign markets not by direct agencies but by reinsurance, accepting surplus business from more thrusting competitors, primarily from the North British. The Royal did not believe that it was acting any more rashly. Charles Turner wrote in his chairman's report for 1862 that 'the Fire Revenue of the company, large as it is, might have been greatly enhanced by a slight relaxation of the cautionary rules which have invariably forbid [*sic*] any approximation to a laxity of principle in the conduct of the business. The Directors have consequently felt that the most injurious policy they could possibly adopt would be a reckless struggle for Revenue for the sake of Revenue alone, regardless of the main consideration that it should be a Revenue giving a fair promise of profit.'[42] This was scarcely throwing caution to the winds. However, the Royal managed to find a different form for what it still considered to be caution. To begin with, it was prepared to carry its most energetic efforts further afield. The Royal did conform enthusiastically with the orthodoxy that British exporters of insurance invisibles were attracted by transatlantic prospects, whereas Phoenix continued to exploit the inheritance derived from the neglected European phase of insurance exportation. Thus as early as 1854 the Royal had accumulated some seventeen agencies in North America; at the same date Phoenix had five. By contrast Phoenix maintained in Europe in 1854 nine major contact points; the Royal had only one.

The preponderance of Phoenix selling power in Europe persisted until the end of this period, although the Royal closed the gap somewhat over time (see Table 7.3). Phoenix maintained its lead towards the end of the

[42] Royal Insurance, Chairman's Annual Report, 7 August 1863.

Table 7.2. *Total foreign premiums by market area and shares of total premiums by market area, Phoenix and Royal: annual averages 1851–75*

	Europe		North America		West Indies		Australia and New Zealand		India and Far East		Africa and Islands		Middle East		Central and South America		'Home foreign' branch[a]		Total foreign premiums
	£ Prem.	% Share	£ Prem.	% Share	£ Prem.	% Share	£ Prem.	% Share	£ Prem.	% Share	£ Prem.	% Share	£ Prem.	% Share	£ Prem.	% Share	£ Prem.	% Share	£
1850 only																			
Phoenix	22326	40.0	12152	21.8	4225	7.6	—	—	1468	2.6	931	1.7	—	—	—	—	14707	26.4	55809
Royal	—	—	2201	26.9	1471	17.9	7	0.08	4429	54.0	—	—	—	—	88	1.1	—	—	8196
1851–5																			
Phoenix	24980	37.7	15756	23.8	4147	6.3	—	—	4175	6.3	1869	2.8	—	—	—	—	15401	23.2	66330
Royal	155	0.3	39849	72.1	4120	7.4	1910	3.5	7910	14.3	—	—	—	—	1321	2.4	—	—	55267
1856–60																			
Phoenix	32332	37.3	25348	29.2	5641	6.5	—	—	6667	7.7	3147	3.6	—	—	—	—	13580	15.7	86717
Royal	463	0.4	81322	70.3	9217	8.0	4541	3.9	11857	10.2	—	—	—	—	8353	7.2	—	—	115755
1861–5																			
Phoenix	44559	42.7	22721	21.8	6183	5.9	—	—	14269	13.7	1385	1.3	38	—	727	0.7	14455	13.9	104339
Royal	7466	3.9	92650	48.1	12393	6.4	9013	4.7	38291	19.9	—	—	1447	0.8	16069	8.3	15398	8.0	192730
1866–70																			
Phoenix	78815	50.2	34113	21.7	5988	3.8	—	—	18797	12.0	1067	0.7	384	0.2	5611	3.6	12275	7.8	157053
Royal	21866	7.7	114582	40.3	15900	5.6	17484	6.2	42156	14.8	10	—	6889	2.4	31383	11.0	33909	11.9	284180
1871–5																			
Phoenix	112083	47.7	74704	31.8	7335	3.1	—	—	17077	7.3	1559	0.7	893	0.4	9955	4.2	11214	4.8	234823
Royal	30957	5.2	417272	70.2	15807	2.7	18915	3.2	27860	4.7	—	—	2169	0.4	39803	6.7	41281	6.9	594067

[a] 'Home foreign' branch = Foreign business written 'unsighted' from London. All other foreign business was gathered on the spot by local agencies.
Source: Phoenix, Review of Foreign and Irish Agencies, I, 1787; Royal Insurance, Results of Foreign Business, Book 1.

Table 7.3. Numbers of agencies by market region, Phoenix and Royal 1850–75

	1850		1855		1860		1865		1870		1875	
	Phoenix	Royal	Phoenix	Royal	Phoenix	Royal	Phoenix	Royal	Phoenix	Royal	Phoenix	Royal
Europe	9	1	9	1	9	2	12	6	18	14	21	15
North America	5	1	5	15	5	15	6	13	8	26	7	27
West Indies	4	2	5	5	4	6	8	13	8	11	10	11
India and Far East	2	5	3	7	4	9	9	15	11	18	14	16
Africa	1	—	2	—	2	—	2	—	3	1	3	—
Central and South America	—	1	—	2	—	3	2	8	4	10	7	10
Australia	—	1	—	3	—	3	—	8	—	10	—	10
Middle East	—	—	—	—	—	—	2	2	2	2	2	2

period by a characteristic concentration on the more dangerous, frontier-like tracts of eastern and southeastern Europe. In two more distant regions – the West Indies and Middle East – there was not a great deal to choose between the sales efforts delivered by the two companies. Almost everywhere else, however, the Royal achieved much more striking levels of penetration. By 1870 its agents outnumbered those of Phoenix by ten to four in Central and South America, by ten to nought in Australasia and even in India and the Far East, another dangerous market which Phoenix approached with some determination, by eighteen to eleven. Yet it was in the most valuable area of all that the disproportion was most gross: in North America the Royal bested the Phoenix by twenty-six to eight, and if the comparison were restricted to the United States alone, by eighteen to two. In 1866, indeed, in the wake of the Civil War, Phoenix had not a single outpost in the United States to its name; and it recovered slowly from the experience. Again, in contrast, the Royal was represented by 1870 not only in New York, Boston and Baltimore but in such various industrious places as Cincinnati, Albany, Mobile, San Francisco, Cleveland, St Louis, New Jersey, Detroit and Milwaukee. In all locations, Europe not excepted, the Royal was faster to build up its sales force and, with the exception of Europe and Africa, more insistent on maintaining a *numerous* sales force.

The proof of this tactic lay in the counting of the premiums. The Royal's ability to delve more deeply into markets undeniably provided it with a superior income flow. Outside Europe the agents of the Liverpool company procured premiums that were frequently multiples of the Phoenix receipts. Inside Europe the Phoenix men retained their advantage, netting nearly four times the Royal's income even in 1871–5. Elsewhere the Royal's dominance was very marked. In its favoured territory, North America, it took anything between two and six times the Phoenix yield, achieving here a preeminence more emphatic than the London company's lead upon its favourite continent. However, the Royal did not restrict its energy to North America. In the West Indies it quickly built up to income levels between two and three times higher than Phoenix's, and, in the markets that were new to both offices, achieved clear advantages even more swiftly. In the Asian market, which each company placed among its most enticing prospects, the Royal characteristically bettered Phoenix by a factor of two throughout the period, while in Central and South America it both struck first and left Phoenix with the embarrassment of returns only one-sixth to one-quarter of its own takings by the late 1860s and early 1870s. The Royal approach also derived useful results from the growing Australasian market: while Phoenix ignored this demand entirely at the agency level, the Royal gathered from it an income in excess of Phoenix's gleanings from the African and Asian trades combined. This more than made up for the Royal's own uncharacteristic hesitations in Africa. The net result of these developments was that Phoenix total foreign income exceeded that of the Royal by nearly four times in 1851; that Royal foreign premiums stood virtually on a par with Phoenix foreign premiums in 1855; and that the Royal's overseas takings exceeded Phoenix overseas takings by a factor of 2.2 by 1875.

The Phoenix response to the more penetrating strategy of the Royal and its ilk was simple and deliberate: greater penetration was more dangerous because it brought in too many 'unpurified' risks, and should therefore be avoided. Safety, and a better percentage surplus, the Phoenix directors believed, were achieved by purification of the books and a more selective approach to distant risks. They were wrong. Or at least they were wrong outside Europe. Within the home continent Phoenix not only outsold Royal but achieved a much better claims record: the Royal reached a significant European income only around 1861 but in each of the subsequent three quinquennia suffered loss ratios well in excess of the Phoenix claims figure. 'Purification' won no other conquests.

In North America the Royal secured its massive income advantage on loss ratios that were sometimes similar to Phoenix results (1851–5), sometimes better (1856–60 and 1871–5) and rarely much worse (1861–5 and 1866–70) (see Table 7.4). Even when they were worse, the Royal emerged from trouble with more money in its pockets than the Phoenix: the Royal's 75.6 per cent average loss ratio on average annual North American earnings of £114 583 for 1866–70 still left a significantly better gross surplus (£27 917 p.a.) than the Phoenix's loss ratio of 47.8 per cent on takings of £34 113 (£17 795 p.a.).[43] In the West Indies the Phoenix's loss record was almost always better than the Royal's, but it did the office little good on the income side: in every quinquennium between 1851 and 1875, with the exception of 1861–5, the Royal extracted a larger surplus from the West Indies than did the Phoenix, whatever the level of its loss ratios. A similar pattern is evident in the Asian market: both companies achieved exceptionally good loss ratios, but, with the exception of 1871–5, those of the Phoenix were even better than those of the Royal. Again it hardly mattered: however selectively Phoenix trod, the Royal converted its two-fold superiority in gross premiums into a superiority in surplus receipts (premiums net of claims) that was usually very nearly twice as large as that of Phoenix. In Central and South America, Phoenix scarcely appeared at all until the very end of the period; by that time, the Royal was taking more than four times the Phoenix average annual premiums at significantly

---

[43] Gross premiums less total claims.

Table 7.4. Foreign premiums and loss ratios by market area, Phoenix and Royal: annual averages 1851–75

	Europe		North America		West Indies		Australia and New Zealand		India and Far East		Africa and Islands		Middle East		Central and South America		'Home foreign' Branch	
	£ Prem.	% Loss	£ Prem.	% Loss	£ Prem.	% Loss	£ Prem.	% Loss	£ Prem.	% Loss	£ Prem.	% Loss	£ Prem.	% Loss	£ Prem.	% Loss	£ Prem.	% Loss
1851–5																		
Phoenix	24980.8	44.0	15756.0	72.5	4147.0	29.1	1910.2	—	4175.8	1.6	1869.2	15.9	—	—	—	—	15401.0	32.4
Royal	155.6	—	39849.4	76.7	4120.0	14.9	—	46.7	7910	7.6	—	—	—	—	1321.6	0.1	—	—
1856–60																		
Phoenix	32332.0	68.2	25348.6	78.4	5641.4	28.1	—	—	6667.4	0.03	3147.4	43.7	—	—	—	—	13580.8	42.3
Royal	463.2	1.4	81322.4	54.5	9217.6	48.2	4541.0	57.4	11857.0	6.9	—	—	—	—	8353.8	140.2	—	—
1861–5																		
Phoenix	44559.4	34.7	22721.8	52.7	6183.2	29.9	—	—	14269.6	2.5	1385.0	1.6	38.2	—	727.6	—	14454.6	52.5
Royal	7466.4	53.0	92650.4	70.8	12393.6	110.1	9013.6	34.0	38291.0	19.6	—	—	1447.2	35.3	16069.4	29.9	15398.0	68.6
1866–70																		
Phoenix	78815.4	53.1	34113.0	47.8	5988.4	27.2	—	—	18797.4	29.8	1067.4	78.2	384.2	20.7	5611.0	36.3	12275.4	27.4
Royal	21866.0	97.6	114582.8	75.6	15900.2	32.9	17484.8	51.2	42156.0	43.9	9.6	—	6889.0	69.1	31383.8	54.3	33909.4	63.8
1871–5																		
Phoenix	112083.8	60.1	74704.4	94.5	7335.0	16.0	—	—	17077.8	15.9	1559.8	1.9	893.0	33.1	9955.2	87.0	11214.0	46.5
Royal	30957.2	88.8	417272.0	62.3	15807.0	33.1	18915.6	62.2	27860.0	2.7	0.4	—	2169.0	54.4	39803.8	52.7	41281.2	58.8

Note: % Loss = total fire claims as percentage of gross agency premiums.
Source: Phoenix, Review of Foreign and Irish Agencies, 1787–1877; Royal Insurance, Results of Foreign Business, Book 1.

better loss levels. In Australasia Phoenix did not yet venture while Royal achieved a very welcome income flow – equal to well over half its takings from Europe by the period's end – at very tolerable rates of loss.

VI

Caution clearly cost the Phoenix money, while the Royal's version of prudence earned a great deal more. However, selectivity and purification were not the only interpretations placed upon caution by Phoenix: it developed also an unusual leaning towards reinsurance, relying upon other offices to generate the initial premiums and accepting the surplus risks which they laid off. Other companies, notably the Alliance, had used foreign reinsurance much earlier in the century as a means of reconnoitring strange markets, gathering new skills by careful tracking of more experienced operators. But they were novices in overseas dealing; it was distinctly peculiar for the foreign pioneer to resort so widely to this tactic in the mid-century period.

However, the resort was very wide indeed. The great bulk of the rally in Phoenix's foreign trade between the later 1850s and the later 1860s derived from treaty reinsurance.[44] Overseas premiums improved between 1856–60 and 1866–70 by over 82 per cent, but almost three-quarters of this improvement came by way of treaty surpluses laid off by other companies. By 1870 Phoenix's treaties contributed almost exactly half the office's foreign takings and four of its top five overseas premium winners were treaty arrangements: Paris, St Petersburg, New York, Trieste. Only Canada with 8.8 per cent total foreign premiums, won mainly by direct trade, offered any competition. Even the premier European agency at Hamburg (5.0 per cent total foreign premiums) did not penetrate this top group, and apart from Yokohama (3.9 per cent) no other Phoenix direct agency managed better than 2.0 per cent of total foreign takings in 1870.

For its treaty earnings Phoenix relied upon a select group of specialist offices. Its Parisian remittances came from the Assurances Générales; these commenced in 1850 and were worth 14.4 per cent of all foreign earnings by 1855. The St Petersburg connection was achieved through the First Russian Company: the initial earnings were received in London in 1865, and they amounted to 11.4 per cent of all Phoenix's foreign takings by 1870. Trieste was broached by leave of the Azienda Assicuratice in 1869 and as early as 1871 its transfers to Phoenix were worth 7.1 per cent of

---

[44] Reinsurance may be sought on an *ad hoc* basis in respect to particular risks: this is facultative reinsurance. Or it may be negotiated for an entire market or even for a proportion of an office's entire business so that some share of the total obligation is automatically passed on to a second insurer: this is treaty reinsurance.

the latter's foreign trade. But the office's most revealing treaty arrangements by far concerned the American market.

Not until the very end of this period did Phoenix achieve any rectification
of its affairs in the U.S.A. Just before this, as other British offices were poised
for their richest market diversification of all, Phoenix earnings from the
states had dwindled to nothing. The southern remnants of the once
extensive U.S. agency network – only Savannah and Norfolk remained by
1860 – registered no returns for 1865 or 1866. The Civil War proved the
last straw for these outposts: Phoenix's reliance on the traditional south
had the cruellest of outcomes. What with the disasters of the 1840s, the
reports of Broomfield and the campaigns of Sherman, events conspired to
prejudice Phoenix against the United States. Its institutional experience
here was of the most adverse kind.

There was some recovery by 1870: both Savannah and Norfolk rallied
after 1867 even if they recorded only trivial receipts, while a new agency
entered at San Francisco in 1864 and was doing quite nicely by the end
of the decade. The U.S.A. trade advanced from its nadir of £481 in
premiums and 0.4 per cent total overseas earnings in 1865 to £22761
and 11.8 per cent total overseas earnings by 1870; but it did not do so
through these few agencies. The basis of the Phoenix's revival in the U.S.A.
lay in a single market: New York. After the Civil War, the state legislators
at last decided to let bygones be bygones and readmitted Phoenix to the
rich pickings of the metropolis. Yet here lay the final irony: for after having
been denied a New York agency for more than a half century, Phoenix
did not reenter America's richest market by direct agency trade. Just as it
had done in France, Russia and Austria–Hungary, Phoenix preferred the
longer spoon of reinsurance. This time, it took its surpluses not from a local
specialist but from a more forthright British office, the Glasgow-based
North British. The New York Treaty with the North British endured from
1867 until 1878 and brought both rich earnings and heavy losses. It was
anticipated in 1866 by smaller agreements with the North British covering
San Francisco, Nevada and Oregon and by several facultative transactions
with the Liverpool and London and Globe early in 1867. While the great
provincial underwriters of mercantile Britain, the Liverpool and London
and Globe, the North British and the Royal – the three largest British
exporters of insurance in the U.S. market by 1880 – were making their
fortune by direct agency trade, the office which had led the City's first
underwriting expedition across the Atlantic was content to follow in their
footsteps and collect their leavings. Not until the late 1870s and 1880s,
some twenty or thirty years behind the best British operators, did Phoenix
create a dozen or so new agencies in the U.S.A. and thus establish a
network appropriate to its international standing. Even then this initiative

stemmed from the state legislature of New York rather than the boardroom in Lombard Street: in 1879 the state forbade the ceding of reinsurance business to insurers who did not maintain financial reserves within state boundaries. The ruling made the North British–Phoenix treaty illegal and bounced Phoenix forcibly back into the direct agency business.

It is not difficult to find reasons for Phoenix's reticence in the U.S.A. This was the classic area in which Phoenix had been too much of a pioneer. In 1870 the yield from its American agencies was only slightly larger than the receipts of 1811. Phoenix had penetrated the transatlantic market far in advance of other City institutions only to encounter the region's pre-industrial teething troubles. The New World had generated one nearly lethal disaster in its earliest phase as a customer for fire insurance and maintained a steady stream of lesser catastrophes into the 1830s and 1840s. Examination of the reasons for this was preoccupied with fire losses and traditional economic centres, not with fresh prospects and new industrial concentrations. The institutional memory at Phoenix consequently carried, quite legitimately, a number of large black marks against the American account. This was corporate experience; and one is supposed to learn from experience.

VII

The Royal's experience of disaster was much less lurid. Only twice in its first quarter-century of foreign trading did its loss ratio for any given market over a five-year period exceed 100 per cent: for Central and South America 1856–60 (140.2 per cent) and for the West Indies 1861–5 (110.1 per cent). By contrast Phoenix's early losses were much more striking: for the West Indies 1806–10 (1326.7 per cent), for North America 1821–5 (106.4 per cent) and for Europe 1841–5 (195.3 per cent). Nor did Phoenix lose the habit: even the revival of its American business in the late 1860s was marred by disaster. The first five years of the treaty arrangement with the North British produced a loss ratio of 144 per cent. The cause of this sorry result was the great Chicago fire of 1871 in which Phoenix lost £99060. By comparison, the Royal walked with charmed footsteps. Its American operation suffered a 'destructive fire' at New Orleans in 1854 and closed the agency down; but the loss ratio for the city was no worse than 43.5 per cent. On Fourth of July 1866, Portland Maine was seared by a major blaze and that did drive Royal's loss ratio for its Boston agency up to 133.2 per cent for that year. But by 1870 when Philadelphia was losing more than £$\frac{1}{2}$ million in property per year to fire, the Royal still escaped with a loss ratio which, in the circumstances, was a modest 86.0 per cent. At Chicago it escaped rather more spectacularly. The conflagration of 1871 did close to £40 million worth of damage yet the Royal had established itself there only the year before: its loss ratio for Chicago in the year of the fire was a trifling 28.0 per cent. The Liverpool and London and Globe was unlucky to have been faster on its feet: it paid out over £600000 in claims. Not until the Boston blaze of 1872 was the Royal finally trapped by the flames; here it acknowledged liabilities of nearly £200000 and suffered a loss ratio of 219.6 per cent. But again the Liverpool and London and Globe fared worse and disbursed close to £300000. Until the turn of the century the Royal experienced nothing more damaging in the New World: a fire at St John's, New Brunswick cost it £75000 in 1877 and another at St John's, Newfoundland brought claims of £100000 in 1892. In contrast, the Phoenix had been paying out larger sums on transatlantic catastrophes in the 1800s and against an income many times smaller than the Royal's. From the vantage points of Phoenix's London and Royal's Liverpool the transatlantic market can scarcely have appeared to be the same place.

VIII

It is difficult to resist the suggestion that the institutional memory of the Phoenix was directly responsible for producing an entrepreneurial hiatus within this City-based insurance giant in the critical period 1850–90. The Company's resort to reinsurance is perhaps the best proxy for measuring its increasing conservatism during a period of expanding markets. In the U.S.A., Phoenix's interest remained suppressed until the Chicago fire. In the approved style for such events, that disaster encouraged a greatly increased demand for insurance cover. One major domestic office, the Insurance Co. of North America, recorded net profits of nearly $\frac{1}{2}$ million in 1873 and over $\frac{1}{3}$ million in 1874[45] and Phoenix itself managed a profit rate of 24 per cent on net U.S. premiums 1873–6. But Phoenix took the inheritance of Chicago entirely by reinsurance, quadrupling the average annual surplus accepted from other offices over the period 1866–70 to 1871–5. However, America was not the only market treated to Phoenix's most distant style of selling: the pattern imprinted by reinsurance on Phoenix's worldwide trade was more startling still (see Table 7.5). By contrast, the Royal of Liverpool took only 10–12 per cent of its foreign earnings from reinsurances even in 1871–5.

Clearly, Phoenix captured the prosperity of the mid-century international economy largely from the passenger's seat. Furthermore, the cyclical advance and retreat of reinsurance is sufficiently marked to suggest a distinct entrepreneurial phase; it provides a numerical monument to the

[45] M. James, *Biography of a Business, 1792–1942: The Insurance Company of North America* (New York, 1942), pp. 170–1.

Table 7.5. *Reinsurance earnings as a percentage of Phoenix total foreign premiums: annual averages*

	%		%
1856–65	23.2	1876–80	52.0
1866–70	48.8	1881–5	25.0
1871–5	57.8	1886–90	17.1

Table 7.6. *American premiums earned by British offices: rank order, 1890*

	$		$
1 London and Liverpool and Globe	4496999	9 Sun	1455217
		10 Norwich Union	1223029
2 Royal	3574840	11 Imperial	1103813
3 Commercial Union	2724387	12 Guardian	1103099
4 North British	2092754	13 Northern	1070766
5 London and Lancs	1740297	14 London	1021311
6 Lancs	1657056	15 Scottish Union	600083
7 Phoenix	1652698	16 Lion	436186
8 Queen	1576807	17 City of London	412408

effects of corporate memory upon export strategy. This phase ended when Phoenix was forced back into agency trade in the U.S.A. after 1879; the North American share of total reinsurance business declined from 31.5 per cent in 1871–5 to zero by 1881–5, and as the enthusiasm for reinsurance waned in the New World, so it moderated everywhere else. Within six years of the legal démarche of 1879 Phoenix had appointed sixteen direct agencies within the U.S.A., marking the company's return to a more forthright manner of exportation. By 1890 Phoenix ranked seventh among British exporters of fire insurance to the U.S.A. and virtually all of its improved income came from direct selling. Yet the true emphasis in the export of insurance invisibles from Britain to the richest underwriting market in the late-nineteenth-century world is provided by the titles of the six companies which ranked above Phoenix: only one of them, the Commercial Union, was a genuinely City-based development; the rest were financial offshoots from the commercial and industrial wealth of provincial, northern Britain (see Table 7.6). It is especially notable that the traditional great powers of early-nineteenth-century City insurance – the Sun,

Guardian, Imperial or London – achieved only modest rankings in this hierarchy, or, like the R.E.A., entirely failed to penetrate it.

The thesis of this chapter makes five claims: that in an important sector of Britain's invisible exports in the late nineteenth century the City was not the premier force; that northern insurance offices, foundations of the provincial bourgeoisie, were by this time dominant within the international affairs of the corporate underwriting business; that the New World insurance market was not 'pioneered' in the famous invisibles boom of the late nineteenth century but first broached in the middle of the industrial revolution period; that the City institutions which achieved this innovation were indeed displaying signs of entrepreneurial weakness by the time second-generation 'pioneers' reentered transatlantic markets; that the prime reason for this was the burden of institutional memory within the policy-making of the older insurance ventures.

Capitalistic enterprise is not simply a function of entrepreneurial personality, dominant social values or even of market opportunities. It is controlled also by institutional chronology and accumulated institutional experience. There is fair agreement that the different stages of a business venture's lifespan – infancy, adolescence, maturity, perhaps senility – have a powerful influence on the type of entrepreneurial decisions appropriate at a given point: aggressive behaviour may be necessary at one stage, conservation wiser at another. Less recognized is the premise that the experience of risk or disaster – or, of course, the experience of success, smooth innovation or simple good fortune – at particular stages in the growth pattern may condition decision-making in subsequent stages. If the institution possesses an efficient internal 'memory', this control will be reinforced. There is no capitalistic law which states that the opposing streams of market opportunity and accumulated experience shall conjoin at the moment most appropriate for maximum entrepreneurial effect.

Corporate memory is a constraint upon all kinds of business. But it has a special power in the dealings of insurers against fire and accident. For the industrial or commercial businessman, corporate memory may include unsuccessful products, misjudged advertising campaigns, contracting markets or inappropriate technologies. For the underwriting businessman it may include firestorm, earthquake, volcano or tidal wave. Life under-writing is, within limits, a predictable business but insurance against fire and accident deals with the raw material of disaster: unpredictable, massive, extravagantly costly and frequently outside the control of the best practice. Long acquaintance with such product characteristics can have very sobering effects on management.

Phoenix by its record-keeping reforms around 1810 had greatly augmented the power of its corporate memory. But the increasing weight of intelligence may not have been entirely healthy. Past experience offers lessons; but it also induces traumas. A Phoenix director of the mid-nineteenth century, as readily as the historian of the late twentieth, could place side by side on his desk the foreign premiums and losses for 1807 and the tally of the company's investments for 1807 and 1808. He could not but be impressed by the narrowness of the margin by which Phoenix had survived. Such risks, he might conclude, may have been acceptable when the Phoenix was being drawn from the shell but were better avoided once it had achieved some maturity. Moreover, the world in which it became mature was not all glowing opportunity. Much that glowed was spark and ember. If the trading settlements and commercial centres of the international economy were becoming ever more numerous, sophisticated and imposing, so in equal measure were the fires they fuelled. At this time, the insurer could be forgiven for believing that the march of trade and industry had as its prime consequence larger and more awesome conflagrations. Even the gilded cache of the American market was opened just as the older British offices completed their adjustment to an earlier selection of disasters.

Points of contact can be found between these managerial difficulties within the mid-century Phoenix and the managerial shortcomings associated with some manufacturing industries after 1870. The problem of institutional memory at Phoenix exerted an influence similar to that produced in manufacturing by technological obsolescence. Industrial firms which traced their ancestry to the early nineteenth century often clung too long to outmoded but still serviceable plant and to traditional methods of organization and workmanship; that is, they set an exaggerated store by experience. Institutional memory worked in much the same way: a particular disaster occurs; it is examined for salutary lessons; they are recorded; 'purification' of risks follows; any market tainted by association with the disaster is in future avoided, whatever the change in circumstances. Experience prevails over new opportunity; the obsolescence attaches to a piece of information and the method of assessing it. The office is held to this course by a respected piece of craftsmanship, by the often spurious rigorousness involved in 'purifying the books'. Old fears, remembered responses to crises past, can be as constraining to enterprise as the most venerable machines or the most antique working practices.

Yet, in any reasonable terms, Phoenix did not 'fail'. It remained one of the largest and most prosperous British insurance offices down to the mid-1980s: it ranked eighth by total premium income before its merger with the fifth-place Sun Alliance group in August 1984.[46] Yet it has long

---

[46] R. H. Carter and A. H. Godden, *The British Insurance Industry: A Statistical Review, 1983/4 Edition* (Brentford, 1983), p. 68. Calculated on 1982 trading results.

been an acknowledged feature of the company's record that it encountered a period of doldrums in the mid-Victorian decades. Like the British economy, Phoenix around 1870, indeed rather before 1870, underwent retardation, experienced deceleration. Nor was it alone among the long-established plutocrats of the insurance business, many of whom missed entrepreneurial opportunities around this time, surrendering large proportions of the City's control over the home insurance market and even larger segments of invisible exports to the underwriters of the Royal and its northern colleagues.

8

'At the head of all the new professions':[1] the engineer in Victorian society

W. J. READER

Donald Coleman published 'Gentlemen and Players' in 1973.[2] With its engaging blend of scholarship and love of cricket, it has moved well beyond the frontiers of economic history, and it must surely be his best-known essay. It develops the theme that in English business since the Industrial Revolution and especially over the last century or so there have been on the one hand 'educated amateurs' – the Gentlemen – and on the other hand 'practical men' – the Players.[3] The Gentlemen have had a liberal education at or nearly at public schools, the Players vocational training elsewhere; and the gap in social standing, though not uncrossable, has yawned wide between them.

The engineer may be taken as a representative 'practical man', and this is particularly true of the nineteenth century, when higher education in engineering was neglected in English universities and regarded with suspicion by engineers themselves. In 1871, there were only twelve professors of engineering in the United Kingdom, and only twice as many twenty years later.[4] It may be worth while, therefore, with 'Gentlemen and Players' in mind, to consider how engineers stood in Victorian society, especially since at the present day professional engineers in Great Britain are sorry for themselves, being neither so highly regarded nor so handsomely rewarded as their colleagues elsewhere.

Sir Monty Finniston, an engineer himself, has a characteristically brisk explanation for the engineers' plight. 'At one time, 150 or so years ago', says the official summary of the Finniston Report,

there were two distinct groups in the engineering industry – the engineers who were, roughly speaking, professional men albeit somewhat lowly in the pecking order of professionals, and the mechanics who were not on it at all.... Today, the word 'engineer' is used to describe both groups indiscriminately, and the not

---

[1] T. H. S. Escott, *England, its People, Polity and Pursuits*, 2 vols. (London, n.d.), vol. II, p. 451.
[2] *Economic History Review*, 2nd Series 26 (1973), 92–116.
[3] *Ibid.*, p. 102.
[4] *The British Almanac of the Society for the Diffusion of Useful Knowledge* (London, 1871). See also Michael Sanderson, *The Universities and British Industry 1850–1870* (London, 1972), pp. 23–4.

uncommon headline 'Engineers on strike again' helps to sustain the low level of esteem into which professional engineers have fallen, even if they toil manfully on, come strike or high water.[5]

Such disdain for these noble fellows, Finniston says, is not good for the competitiveness of British industry. 'A new statutory Engineering Authority' should therefore be set up to act as a 'champion of change' in 'the engineering dimension', a phrase coined by Finniston's committee 'as a shorthand way of describing the philosophical outlook toward industry that the British people must acquire.... This involves a complex of attitudes towards industry which is lacking in Britain's culture and which must be fostered.'[6] In other words: 'Love your engineers, or else....'. This demand for a whoesale change in public attitudes, as Finniston suggests, has strong historical undertones. It has affinities with critical studies over the last ninety years or more, of which Martin Wiener's *English Culture and the Decline of the Industrial Spirit* is a recent example, and on which 'Gentlemen and Players' is a commentary.

As far as attitudes towards engineers are concerned, dissatisfaction with engineers' status is a theme which can be followed for over sixty years through the pages of the *Journal of the Institution of Electrical Engineers*, giving rise to the assertion in 1919 that 'the status of the engineer is still a dubious one; at least it is so in this country' and to the complaint, seven years later, that 'a properly trained engineer is of as good a mental calibre as, say, a doctor...and one of the reasons why he does not get the same recognition is because he is poorly paid'.[7] The status of engineer officers in the Royal Navy, long a cause of complaint, was made worse in 1925 by Fleet Order 3421 which deprived them of executive rank.[8] Yet British engineers had not always been so discontented, so much inclined to consider themselves undervalued.

Victorian engineers were part of the burgeoning professional class which was conspicuous in the social scenery of nineteenth-century England. Along with the doctors, the solicitors, the architects and others they were trying to bring to their occupation a blend of high technical competence and genuine concern for the client's interest. That, armoured in commercial shrewdness and guarded by a sharp eye for job protection, would, they hoped, raise them socially above 'trade' and provide a secure and worthwhile livelihood for anyone with sufficient staying power – and money – to fight his way to qualification and establishment in practice.

The professional man in his nineteenth- and twentieth-century form

[5] *Engineering our Future* (London, 1980), p. 10.
[6] *Ibid.*, p. 4.
[7] *J[ournal of the] I[nstitution of] E[lectrical] E[ngineers]* 57 (1919), 225; 64 (1926), 879.
[8] Reports of I.E.E. Council in *J.I.E.E.* 64 (1926), 661; 66 (1928), 646.

emerged to meet the demands of the increasingly wealthy and complex society created by the Industrial Revolution. Of the engineers it might be said, without gross oversimplification, that the Industrial Revolution was created by them. Samuel Smiles thought so. 'Our engineers', he wrote,

may be regarded in some measure as the makers of modern civilisation....For what were England without its roads, its bridges, its canals, its docks, and its harbours? What were it without its tools, its machinery, its steam-engine, its steam-ships, and its locomotive? Are not the men who have made the motive power of the country, and immensely increased its productive strength, the men above all others who have tended to make the country what it is?[9]

Just as, amongst doctors, physicians ranked higher socially than surgeons, and amongst lawyers barristers stood above attorneys, so amongst the engineers of the early – and not so early – nineteenth century some members of the profession could more confidently claim gentility than others, for their professional ancestors were the designers of fortifications and siege-works who served the King in his armies: the Royal Engineers. Until 1772 the Corps of Royal Engineers consisted of officers only and all officers were by convention gentlemen, even though the cavalry might not think so. During the eighteenth century, therefore, the designers of public works for peaceful purposes – docks, harbours, canals, bridges, lighthouses – began to call themselves civil engineers, partly to distinguish themselves from their military colleagues but partly, there can be little doubt, to lay claim to the coveted rank of a gentleman, which in the nineteenth century became an essential ingredient in professional standing.

Throughout the nineteenth century the designers of great public works were considered by themselves and acknowledged by others to stand at the head of the engineering profession. These were men, in the earlier years, such as John Smeaton (1724–92), Thomas Telford (1757–1834), John Rennie (1761–1821) and his son Sir John (1794–1874); in the next generation, Sir John Hawkshaw (1811–91), Edward Woods (1814–1903) and Sir James Brunlees (1816–92). Their works included Smeaton's Eddystone lighthouse in the mid-eighteenth century; Telford's highland roads and bridges and his Holyhead road; the Thames bridges by the two Rennies (Waterloo Bridge by the father, London Bridge by father and son); Avonmouth docks by Brunlees; Hawkshaw's Severn Tunnel; many miles of railway in many countries by Woods.[10] The laying out of railways, first in the United Kingdom and then throughout the world, surpassed even the construction of canals in the opportunities offered to the engineer, though to win the battles which were fought over the passing of railway acts he

[9] Samuel Smiles, *Lives of the Engineers*, new and revised edn, 5 vols. (London, 1874), *Brindley and the Early Engineers*, p. xxiii.
[10] D[ictionary of] N[ational] B[iography] and *Supplements* (Oxford, various dates).

needed to be at least as pugnacious and skilful in the arts of parliamentary persuasion as in his own technology.

To such redoubtable personages none would have denied the highest professional standing nor the rank of a gentleman, though few had been born to it. Telford's father, for instance, was a shepherd; the elder Rennie's, a farmer; Brunlees', gardener and steward to the agent of the Duke of Roxburgh. All these were Scots, as were many engineers. Hawkshaw's father was also a farmer, but in Yorkshire.[11] It is notable, however, that although a few of the great constructors might be knighted, none in the nineteenth century was ennobled. The only Victorian engineer raised to the peerage was William Armstrong (1810–1900), chiefly celebrated as a builder of heavy guns.

Peerages were bestowed very sparingly on professional men, except lawyers and soldiers – indeed only on three: a poet (Tennyson) in 1884; a painter (Leighton) in 1896 (on the day before he died); and a doctor (Lister) in 1897. It is hardly necessary, perhaps, to point out that professional employment, created by the middle classes for the benefit of the middle classes, was far beneath the dignity of the Victorian aristocracy. Their sons might serve in the more expensive regiments of the army, but to have called them 'professional soldiers' would have been taken as an insult.

'Civil engineer' was a term much more widely applied in the nineteenth century than at the present day. Thomas Tredgold, in 1824, defining 'the profession of a Civil Engineer', called it:

the art of directing the Great Sources of Power in Nature...as applied in the construction of roads, bridges, aqueducts, canals, river navigation and locks, and in the construction of ports, harbours, moles, breakwaters and lighthouses and in the art of navigation by artificial power for the purpose of commerce; and in the construction of machinery; and in the drainage of cities and towns.[12]

Through Tredgold's luxuriant verbiage the steam engine is visible. It had already been important, when he wrote, for half a century or more and it was well on its way to becoming the prime mover at the heart of industrial society. There could be no question that the designers of steam engines were civil engineers of the highest consequence, for theirs above all was the art of directing one of the 'Great Sources of Power in Nature'.

The engineers who designed steam engines, however, could not claim the same professional ancestry as the designers of great public works. Just as in medicine the surgeons arose from the ranks of the barbers, so in engineering the machine designers came from amongst blacksmiths,

---

[11] *Ibid.*
[12] Sir Robert Wynne-Edwards, 'Civils', in T. L. Dennis (ed.), *Engineering Societies in the Life of a Country* (London, 1968), p. 29.

millwrights, instrument makers and other skilled craftsmen: in other words, from amongst the only people in an agricultural society who were likely to know much about tools, metals or machinery. The numerous nineteenth-century engineers of the Napier family descended from a blacksmith employed by the Dukes of Argyll. Joseph Bramah (1748–1814) was apprenticed to a carpenter. Henry Maudslay (1771–1831) worked in the blacksmiths' shop at Woolwich Arsenal. George Stephenson (1781–1848) was a colliery engineman. He did not learn to read and write until he was seventeen.[13]

In Coleman's terms, the designers of public works could make a colourable claim to be Gentlemen, but the machine designers were indisputably Players. Moreover the difficulty soon arose which still plagues Sir Monty Finniston: How could you distinguish between mechanical engineers and mechanics?

Henry Robinson Palmer (1795–1844), speaking in January 1818 at the meeting which founded the Institution of Civil Engineers, was in no doubt:

An Engineer is a mediator between the Philosopher and the working Mechanic ....The Philosopher searches into Nature and establishes her laws, and promulgates the principles on which she acts. The Engineer receives those principles and adapts them to our circumstances. The working Mechanic, governed by the super-intendence of the Engineer, brings his ideas into reality. Hence the absolute necessity of possessing both practical and theoretical knowledge.[14]

The distinction between the engineer and the mechanic was easily drawn on paper: less easily in working life. Nor is it clear that all mechanical engineers had any great wish to draw it. As practical men they gloried in their practicality and had little or no respect for 'Philosophers' or for 'theoretical knowledge', of which in the early nineteenth century little was in any case available in engineering. They expected aspiring engineers to be apprenticed as they had been apprenticed and to go, as they had gone, 'through the mill' alongside the mechanics. Some of them may have shared with George Stephenson a determination to reject social or intellectual honours with an outspokenness amounting to inverted snobbery. In 1847 Stephenson said he had been offered a knighthood 'several times', and he had been invited to become a Fellow of the Royal Society and of 'the Civil Engineers Society, but I objected to these empty additions to my name'.[15]

The meeting at which the Institution of Civil Engineers – the 'Civil Engineers Society' which Stephenson so emphatically scorned – originated was a meeting of young men, whose average age is said to have been about twenty-five, in the Kendal Coffee House opposite St Bride's Church in Fleet Street. 'It is a remarkable fact', said Palmer at the meeting,

[13] D.N.B.
[14] *A Brief History of the Institution of Civil Engineers* (London, 1928), pp. 10–11.
[15] W. O. Skeat, *George Stephenson: The Engineer and His Letters* (London, 1973), p. 247.

that notwithstanding the extensive advancement of science and the general increase of means for an acquaintance with it, while the principles of systematic education for most of the learned and scientific professions have been and still are actively encouraged, not even an attempt seems to have been made towards the formation of any special source of information or instruction for persons intending to follow the profession of a Civil Engineer.

Those present at the meeting resolved to make good this deficiency, so far as they could, by forming 'a Society consisting of persons studying the profession of a Civil Engineer'.[16] This modest students' discussion group, for it was at first little more, increased in stature when Telford accepted the Presidency in 1820 and it achieved the final dignity of a professional association by the grant of a Royal Charter in 1828.

'The profession of a Civil Engineer' was intended from the first to cover engineers concerned with machinery as well as the designers of public works. Palmer himself had been apprenticed to Bryan Donkin (1768–1855), who developed machinery for paper-making and other purposes, but when Palmer addressed the Fleet Street meeting he was working for Telford. It was for many years possible for an able engineer to distinguish himself in many fields, as the career of I. K. Brunel (1806–59), above all, triumphantly demonstrated, and the Institution of Civil Engineers was intended to be the institution for all engineers.

Nevertheless a breach opened between those uncouth fellows the mechanical engineers, typified by George Stephenson, who built railway locomotives and presumed to lay out railway routes, and engineers of the older type, civil engineers in the modern sense, who built public works. Perhaps, as L. T. C. Rolt suggested, the 'mechanicals' represented the thrust of a new technology which the 'civils' resented.[17] There seems also to have been a good deal of provincial jealousy of London, with which the 'civils', fairly or not, were identified.

For whatever reason, the two branches of the engineering profession did not consort easily in the Institution of Civil Engineers, and in 1847, with the hearty approbation of George Stephenson, the Institution of Mechanical Engineers was set up – in Birmingham. It was established, according to the promoters' circular, 'to enable Mechanics and Engineers' – no mention of Philosophers – 'engaged in the different Manufactories, Railways and other Establishments in the Kingdom to meet and correspond'. Here is no suggestion of any hard-and-fast distinction between engineers and mechanics – indeed, quite the reverse. A month after the inaugural meeting Stephenson wrote: 'I have...consented to become President to I

[16] *Brief History of the Institution of Civil Engineers*, pp. 10–11 and *passim*.
[17] L. T. C. Rolt, *The Mechanicals* (London, 1967), p. 16.

believe a highly respectable mechanics' Institute at Birmingham.'[18] Presumably he meant the new professional Institution.

Since the early mechanical engineers seem to have been anxious to set themselves so low, it is hardly surprising to find outsiders taking them at or below their own valuation. H. Byerley Thomson (1822–67), a lawyer of some distinction, in 1857 defined a profession as a calling in which 'a man for reward places at the public service his intellectual labour, and the fruits of intellectual knowledge, and experience'. 'Machine engineers', he said,

are not strictly civil engineers, nor are they in the sense of our original definition professional men, but they are so mixed up with the operations of the other engineers, that it is impossible not to refer to them. They are the makers of machines, engines, or machinery, on a large scale, and occupy an important feature in the manufacturing industry of the country.[19]

Certainly the Admiralty, for many years, did not look upon mechanical engineers as gentlemen. They were graded even lower than surgeons. When they first went to sea, in the 1820s, they were no more than grimy mechanics employed by the firms who made the engines which they tended, and they did not achieve commissioned rank until 1847, four years later than the surgeons. Amongst executive officers, prejudice against the engineering branch did not die out until well into the twentieth century.[20]

After the mechanical engineer the next sub-species of engineer to emerge, in the 1840s and 1850s, was the telegraph engineer, basking in the glow of the newest and most miraculous technology, comparable perhaps with the information technology of the present day, and presented to a public not yet disposed to be sceptical about the wonders of science. The electric telegraph was first brought to success in Great Britain, and for a period of about thirty years it gave Britain a long lead in the applications of electrical science.

The telegraph engineer was a new kind of engineer altogether because he could not practise his profession without some approach to a scientific education. That, as Palmer had observed to the civil engineers at their inaugural meeting, was not easily available from the established institutions of the day, but, as the telegraph system spread, educational entrepreneurs set up 'telegraph schools', such as the School of Telegraphy established by Thomas Evans Lundy in the City Road, London, which, it was reported

[18] R. H. Parsons, *A History of the Institution of Mechanical Engineers* (London, 1947), p. 11; Rolt, *Mechanicals*, pp. 14–18; Skeat, *Stephenson*, ch. 7.
[19] H. Byerley Thomson, *The Choice of a Profession* (London, 1857), pp. 2, 301.
[20] Michael Lewis, *The Navy in Transition* (London, 1965), pp. 197–8, 201, 205. Oral information from the late Engineer-Vice-Admiral Sir Harold Brown.

180   W. J. READER

in 1873, 'still exists' although Lundy was by then dead.[21] Little is known of these schools, but scattered references in electrical engineers' obituaries make it certain that Lundy's was not unique.

The telegraph engineer, at the leading edge of the most advanced technology of his day, was a 'man of science' – even a 'savant' – with connections in the most admired scientific circles. He unquestionably earned his living by placing at the public service 'the fruits of intellectual knowledge, and experience'. He ran no risk at all of being confused with mechanics in grubby overalls, and a considerable number of early telegraph engineers were officers of the Royal Engineers and therefore incontrovertibly gentlemen. In short, both technically and socially the telegraph engineer was a professional man ready-made, with none of the ambiguities which flawed the image of the mechanical engineer.

The first President of the Society of Telegraph Engineers was the naturalized Prussian William Siemens (1823–83), one of those German immigrants who contributed so much to the success of Victorian England. His address to the Society's first General Meeting, in 1872, radiates professional confidence:

The great network of international telegraphy extends already to every portion of the civilised and semi-civilised world; it traverses deserts and mountain chains, it passes over the deep plateau of the Atlantic and over the more dangerous bottom of tropical seas; what would be good practice in one country or under one order of climatic influences would be objectionable, insufficient, or wholly impracticable under another; but all these systems are intimately linked together, and the knowledge of the Telegraph Engineer must apply equally to all.[22]

The telegraph engineers were self-conscious scientists, anxious to understand and extend the theory as well as the practice of their profession. The Society of Telegraph Engineers, ancestor of today's Institution of Electrical Engineers, was founded not only as a professional association but also as a learned society, with the intention of filling a gap in the ranks of those which already existed. 'Considering', said William Siemens, 'that electricity is not represented at present by a separate learned society, ranking with the Chemical or Astronomical Societies, I am of opinion that we should not exclude from our subjects questions of purely electrical science.'[23]

The founders of the S.T.E. therefore did their best to attract the leading 'electricians' of the day including not only practising engineers but, as one early President put it, 'that large body of private scientific workers who love and pursue the science of Electricity without any thought of regarding it as a profession'.[24] The Society's earliest membership list, of 1872, shows 12 Fellows of the Royal Society amongst a total of 278. By 1891 there

[21] J[ournal of the] S[ociety of] T[elegraph] E[ngineers] 1 (1872–3), 139.
[22] Ibid., pp. 22–7.
[23] Ibid.   [24] Latimer Clark, 13 Jan. 1875, quoted in J.S.T.E. 4 (1875), 21.

were 35 F.R.S.s among 1978 members of what had by then become the Institution of Electrical Engineers, and of the first 35 Presidents of the Society and the Institution (1872–1914) 20 were F.R.S. (of 35 Presidents from 1947 to 1981, 5 were F.R.S.).

Many of the early telegraph engineers were officers of the army, chiefly of the Royal Engineers, or of the navy. Captain Dawson R.N. startled the President, at the first Annual Meeting, by asking whether the Society proposed to discuss the application of electricity to 'the uncivilized purposes of civilized war', by which he probably meant harbour defence schemes relying on electrically fired 'torpedoes' (sea mines).[25] Field telegraphs, however, were more important. They were used in the Crimea in the 1850s; by the 1860s no war between European powers could be run without them; and during the 1870s and 1880s the telegraph systems set up for colonial campaigns were regularly described at meetings of the S.T.E. by returned officers. A great deal of telegraph wire was stolen by Pathan tribesmen during the Afghan operations of 1878–9, and some of it was cut up and fired back at the British forces.[26] Officers and other ranks of the R.E. telegraph service were well qualified, after they left the army, for employment by the Post Office or, later, in the emergent electrical industries. Major-General Charles Webber, President of the S.T.E. in 1882, became chairman of one of the early electric-light companies, Anglo-American Brush Electric Light Corporation.

The telegraph engineer, like the civil engineer, went all over the world in the practice of his profession. International telegraph routes needed thousands of miles of cable which could only be laid along the seabed from steamships, since no sailing ship could be manoeuvred accurately enough. The *Great Eastern*, in her day the largest ship afloat, found her only profitable employment as a cable layer. Nevertheless telegraph engineering, fundamentally, was a matter not of massive equipment but of delicate apparatus worked by light current, far removed from the embankments, cuttings and masonry of the civil engineer or the mechanical engineer's heavy machinery.

When electric lighting and electric traction began, during the last twenty years of the nineteenth century, and when electricity began to be used as a driving force in factories, demand arose for high voltages, heavy current and the ponderous plant needed to generate and distribute power over wide areas. The telegraph engineer came to be overshadowed by the electrical engineer, who was a mechanical engineer with a scientific education. In particular, he was a steam engineer.[27]

[25] *J.S.T.E.* 1 (1872–3), 35.   [26] *J.S.T.E.* 10 (1881), 234.
[27] R. E. B. Crompton, *Reminiscences* (London, 1928); Brian Bowers, *R. E. B. Crompton: Pioneer Electrical Engineer* (London, 1969); James Grieg, *John Hopkinson: Electrical Engineer* (London, 1970); *D.N.B.*

With important reservations in the case of mechanical engineers, it seems fair to say that in late Victorian England engineers were well thought of and thought well of themselves. Why not? They shared the general satisfaction with the country's immediate past and the general optimism for its future, based very largely on scientific and technical progress. They had only to look around them at home and abroad, particularly in the growing British Empire, to see how large a part engineers had played and were playing in building the nation's power and prosperity while at the same time building very satisfactory careers for themselves.

Engineering, like other growing professions, offered a solution to the perennial problem of Victorian middle-class parents: what shall my son be? Unless there was a vacancy in a business or professional practice owned by the family or their friends, the problem was serious. Salaried employment at any level, even the level of the meanest clerkship, was scarce, and for any job with good prospects the competition was ferocious. Professional training, provided the family could pay for it and, if necessary, support a young man through his first uncertain years, would provide an advantage that might be decisive. Telegraph engineering and electrical engineering had also the advantage, setting them apart from medicine and the law, that they did not usually involve the uncertainty and expense of launching into private practice. There were opportunities in the public service or with large companies, such as the overseas cable companies and the greater railways, which did not depend on the goodwill of owning families.

'At the head of all the new professions', wrote T. H. S. Escott in the late 1870s,

> must be placed that of the civil engineer. The calling is pre-eminently that created by the most distinctively characteristic achievements and aspirations of the age, while it opens up a vista of rich rewards....There is reason to believe that the profession of the civil engineer...appeals with peculiar force to the imagination and ambition of the youth of the day. It is the pioneer of progress and civilisation, moral and material, all the world over; it gratifies the adventurous spirit which is the heritage of the English race. The civil engineer who spans rocky defiles, pierces mountains, unites continents, and by designing new schemes of railway and telegraphic extension annihilates space and time, is the modern representative of the navigator of the Elizabethan era...who sailed over remote seas in quest of new lands and fresh enemies to subjugate. The headmaster of a large public school recently observed to the present writer that three out of every four of his pupils would, if polled, declare for engineering.[28]

There is plenty of supporting evidence for Escott's view that engineering, about 1880, was a profession much favoured in the public schools and among the upper-middle classes generally. Whatever classically educated

[28] Escott, *England*, vol. II, pp. 451–2.

clerical headmasters may have thought about it, parents and their sons wanted it, and what parents wanted they generally got. F. W. Sanderson (1857–1922) established engineering workshops at Dulwich College and later, as headmaster, at Oundle School. Under Sanderson's rule, from 1890 to 1922, numbers at Oundle rose from 92 to 500.[29] Other headmasters were less enthusiastic for engineering than Sanderson, but many Victorian engineers went to public schools. The list includes Eton, Harrow, Rugby, Clifton, Rossall, Merchant Taylors', City of London and University College School, and a systematic survey of available records would no doubt reveal many more.[30]

That engineering was neglected in Victorian higher education, especially at the ancient universities, is notorious, but so was professional education generally, because professional training in England was thought of, until very recently, chiefly in terms of apprenticeship. Sir John Rennie, writing in 1867, set out a formidable list of subjects which an intending engineer should study at school – arithmetic, algebra, geometry, natural philosophy, geography, geology, astronomy, chemistry, land and hydrographical surveying, as well as grammar, English composition, history, French, German and Latin. This he called a sound elementary education, adding that 'every youth of ordinary talents has a tolerably fair knowledge of these at seventeen or eighteen'. After that he should be apprenticed for two or three years to 'some good steam engine and machinery manufacturer' to become a practical as well as a theoretical mechanician which is the soundest basis for good engineering'. His training should be rounded off with three or four years with 'some well known civil engineer' to get experience of railways and public works.[31]

The premiums demanded for apprenticeship by the kind of firms Rennie had in mind would have strained many middle-class parents' resources, and comparatively few young engineers, perhaps, would have been able or willing to spend quite so long as Rennie recommended in gaining unpaid or poorly paid experience. Nevertheless a glance at the careers of numerous engineers, as set out in obituary notices, shows that the kind of programme Rennie sketched, adapted according to circumstances, represented the accepted Victorian method of training for engineering as a profession, rather than as a skilled trade.

In spite of the intensely practical nature of this professional training – its bias towards 'Players' rather than 'Gentlemen' – there seems to have been little or no social prejudice (except in Her Majesty's Navy) against engineering as a profession for gentlemen. R. E. B. Crompton came of a Yorkshire county family, had influential connections, and used them to

[29] *D.N.B.*   [30] Chiefly from obituary notices.
[31] Sir John Rennie, *Autobiography* (London, 1875), p. 430.

considerable effect. Sir John Swinburne (1858–1958) and A. A. Campbell Swinton (1863–1930), two eminent electrical engineers, belonged to the Scottish gentry. Even the aversion of the aristocracy to professional employment, where engineering was concerned, was not absolute. Lord Sackville Arthur Cecil (1848–98) ('odd and peculiar...but very popular')[32] trained in railway workshops, served as chief electrician on a cable-laying expedition under Sir Charles Bright (1832–88), and became general manager of the Metropolitan District Railway. He was half-brother to the third Marquess of Salisbury. The Hon. Sir Charles Parsons (1854–1931), who invented the steam turbine, belonged to the family of the Earls of Rosse.

All in all, up to the 1880s English engineers showed no sign of the uneasiness which afflicts them today, even though since the 1850s there had been warnings of the advance of foreign competition, particularly from Germany. Then during the last twenty years or so of the nineteenth century German and American competitors left British firms decisively behind in the newer branches of electrical engineering: a particularly bitter blow since in submarine telegraphy, one of the great mid-century technical marvels, British firms led all the rest. 'We have not been pioneers in any great advance in the application of electricity', lamented Professor G. F. Fitzgerald, of Trinity College Dublin, in 1900, 'since the development of submarine telegraphy.'[33]

There had long been misgivings about the superiority of German over British technical education.[34] Unfavourable comparisons followed, in the newspapers and in the technical journals, between electrical engineering abroad and at home. 'What a revelation it was to almost all of us, that visit of a year ago to Switzerland!' said John Perry, President of the I.E.E. in 1900. 'We were very much like what engineers of 1870 would have been if suddenly brought into a generating station.'[35]

In spite of Charles Parsons' steam turbine, English engineers' self-confidence, round about the turn of the century, was badly dented, especially perhaps amongst the electricals. It is not the purpose of this chapter to explore that dent in detail, but with time, as Finniston suggests, it has grown deeper and wider, and with reason. 'It is not all smoke', said Professor Perry in the Presidential address quoted above, 'there is a real danger in this foreign competition unless we mend our ways.'[36] Finniston's complaint, eighty-odd years later, is that we haven't mended them yet, and perhaps Donald Coleman, in 1973, hinted at some of the reasons why.

[32] *J.I.E.E.* 27 (1898), 667.   [33] *J.I.E.E.* 29 (1899–1900), 402–3.
[34] 'Electrotechnics', Presidential Address of W. E. Ayrton, 28 Jan. 1892, *J.I.E.E.* 21 (1892), 5.
[35] *J.I.E.E.* 30 (1900–1), 64.   [36] *Ibid.*, pp. 57–8.

9

Bernard Shaw, Bertold Brecht and the businessman in literature

J. M. WINTER

The cultural context of business activity is a time-honoured theme in the study of economic and social history. A vast and varied literature on this subject has emerged, ranging from the celebrated essay published by Max Weber in 1905 on *The Protestant Ethic and the Spirit of Capitalism* to R. H. Tawney's *Religion and the Rise of Capitalism* (1926) and to more recent sociological explorations of attitudes to entrepreneurship and profit-making.[1] Most such works are concerned with general perceptions of wealth and the wealthy rather than with the ways businessmen themselves have reflected on their careers and their place in society. But recently there has been an upsurge in interest in business history, in part stimulated by the publication of a number of widely respected histories of firms, such as Donald Coleman's three-volume account of Courtaulds, or of biographies of men of wealth, such as Gerson Bleichröder, Bismarck's banker and confidant.[2] As a result, it has become possible to broaden our understanding both of the process of wealth-creation and of the multiple meanings given to it by different generations in different societies.

Even a cursory glance at a fraction of the writings of critics and defenders of businessmen in the past century and a half of English (let alone European) history will suffice to warn the reader against any single interpretation of attitudes to entrepreneurship and commerce. And yet one historian recently has had the courage to cut through the knot of scholarly caution to offer a distinctive reading of English cultural history with respect

---

[1] D. C. Coleman, 'Gentlemen and Players', *Economic History Review*, 2nd Series 26 (1973), 92–116. For other examples, see D. C. McClelland, *The Achieving Society* (London, 1961); E. E. Hagen, *On the Theory of Social Change* (London, 1962).

[2] D. C. Coleman, *Courtaulds: An Economic and Social History*, 3 vols. (London, 1969, 1979); F. Stern, *Gold and Iron: Bismarck, Bleichröder and the Building of the German Empire* (London, 1977); and the elegant remarks in Stern's 'Capitalism and the Cultural Historian', in D. B. Weiner and W. B. Keylor (eds.), *From Parnassus: Essays in Honor of Jacques Barzun* (London, 1968); and his 'Money, Morals and the Pillars of Society', in Stern, *The Failure of Illiberalism: Essays on the Political Culture of Modern Germany* (New York, 1972). Other examples of the variety of business history published on European subjects are: P. Fridenson, *Histoire des usines Renault* (Paris, 1977); and J. Kocka, *Unternehmensverwaltung und Angestelltenschaft am Beispiel Siemens, 1847–1914* (Stuttgart, 1969).

to business activity. In *English Culture and the Decline of the Industrial Spirit, 1850–1980*, M. J. Wiener has provided an account of what he sees as 'a century of psychological and intellectual de-industrialization' following immediately upon the stabilization of the English economy in the 1850s. Inculcated through the public school system and 'reflected in the literary culture', a 'cultural counterrevolution', he tells us, occurred in England, with deleterious consequences for the performance of the English economy. Adopting 'a conception of Englishness that virtually excluded industrialism' and which praised the pastoral ideal, the children of businessmen fled from the field of their fathers' achievements, and thereby discarded 'the distinctive, production-oriented culture shaped' during the Industrial Revolution. English society as a whole, and English businessmen in particular, were, in Wiener's view, rendered incapable of 'the conscious and committed pursuit of economic growth', since they were the victims of a profoundly ambivalent attitude to the making of money, amounting in effect to 'a collective inferiority complex'. Thus, in the field of cultural history, Wiener believes he has located the missing key to 'the leading problem of modern British history...the explanation of economic decline'.[3]

Wiener's thoughtful study raises important problems related not only to the thorny question of the retardation of economic growth in late-Victorian Britain but also to the motivation of individual businessmen and their location within the communities in which they lived. These issues must be examined against the growing body of archival evidence about business behaviour. But it is as important to test Wiener's hypotheses in the realm of cultural history as it is to find out if they illuminate the history of the firm or the entrepreneur. It is the intention of this chapter to begin to do so and to suggest that the Victorian and post-Victorian debate about 'industrialism' was never so anti-industrial or anti-business as Wiener suggests. Indeed, I shall try to establish the *relatively* mild nature of cultural criticism of industrial society in Britain by comparing the work of two writers who directly addressed the theme of the morality of business practice: the playwrights Bernard Shaw and Bertold Brecht.

It must be stated at the outset that no one could possibly claim that either Shaw or Brecht are representative figures in British or German cultural history. For a start both were socialists, although of very different kinds. But since it is the antagonists of the 'business ethic' who are of the greatest interest to Wiener, and since it would be a very odd cultural history of Britain or Germany which excluded these two writers, we must surely attend to precisely what they had to say about capitalists and capitalism. The contrast between them, I shall argue, is a revealing one.

---

[3] M. J. Wiener, *English Culture and the Decline of the Industrial Spirit, 1850–1980* (Cambridge, 1981), pp. 157, 158, 145, 5, 13, 96, 145, 3.

But the problem of representativeness cannot so simply be brushed aside. Indeed, it plagues all cultural history, and Wiener's is no exception. He offers no principle of selection of the sources he cites, and leaves anyone who disagrees with him with the unsatisfactory option of aligning one set of references describing favourable attitudes to business alongside another set with a less rosy disposition to businessmen and their doings. For this reason, it is perhaps wise to adopt an inductive method, in which particular attitudes to industry and wealth are examined carefully before we reach any grand conclusion about the nature of a culture taken as a whole, however that be done. After all, the character of the evidence must be established before considering how widely held were the notions imbedded in it.

To be fair, Wiener's research has gone well beyond the record of literature, which is, of course, only one vehicle for the propagation of ideas about business activity. But fiction, poetry and plays, both the critically acclaimed and (perhaps even more so) the second-rate, have served as carriers of images and prejudices, and the historian ignores them at his peril. This Wiener does not do, but his treatment of literary evidence is somewhat cavalier. He does not spend much time elucidating the complexities of the stance taken by specific writers – with the possible exception of Dickens – to social questions. In fact his principle of selection of literary comment is impossible to detect. The only reference to Shaw in his book is in terms of Shaw's attitude to Dickens.[4] D. H. Lawrence, an author whose work might very well provide material to confirm Wiener's hypothesis, is mentioned once, and Orwell not at all. Perhaps what matters is which novels businessmen (or prospective businessmen) have read, but on this point, too, silence prevails. But most importantly, the overall effect of Wiener's synthetic sweep is to obscure or distort the record of what, over a period of 150 years, individual writers have found wanting in industrial society and what they proposed to do about it. To describe it all as features of 'the decline of the industrial spirit' is to offer a caricature of social criticism, which is as deserving of correction as is any other which creeps into historical writing.

In the context of this argument, the comparative mode has distinct advantages. First of all, Wiener's hypothesis is implicitly comparative over time, suggesting a waning of earlier 'pro-industrial' values, without either proving that there was a more vigorous pro-business culture before the 1850s or establishing that there was less suspicion of money-making and greed before the Crystal Palace Exhibition than after it. Secondly, his thesis is comparative in another way, in suggesting that Americans benefited

---

[4] *Ibid.*, p. 82.

from a more unambiguously 'pro-industrial culture'.[5] Surely the comparative method is the essence of cultural history; the only relevant question is what is an appropriate comparison to make.

I hope to suggest that two kinds of comparison are most useful in elucidating the point of Shaw's theatrical social criticism. The first is to measure his position against that of mid-Victorian writers who addressed social questions; the second is to explore the commentary on Shaw imbedded in a German play derived in part from his work.

It is the purpose of this chapter, therefore, to adopt an inductive approach simply to clarify the nature of one important and well-known literary text concerning businessmen and their values. Although not in the same category as Dickens in terms of readership or popularity, Shaw's work, both on the stage and in later film adaptations, has had a wide and enduring appeal.[6] Aside from *Pygmalion*, this is nowhere more the case than in his famous comedy, *Major Barbara*, which is the central text to be examined in this chapter. This masterly meditation on money and morality was written in 1905 and first performed in that year.

The structure of this chapter is straightforward. First, we examine a number of older literary themes and resonances to which Shaw refers in this play. Secondly, we take a look at Shaw's attitude to businessmen and the world they live in as expressed in this, perhaps his most celebrated, drama. We then try to highlight the essential features of Shaw's viewpoint by reference to a remarkable and little-known reworking of some of the same themes by the German playwright Bertold Brecht, in his play *St Joan of the Stockyards*, written in 1931 but first performed on the stage in 1959.

Shaw's *Major Barbara* is, on one level, a play about conversion, a struggle between Barbara's Christianity and her munition-maker father's 'Undershaftianity'.[7] As such, it echoes, and intends to echo, aspects of Victorian literary responses to industrialization. Shaw's treatment of them is never unambiguous, but part of the power of his art is that through aphorism and irony his plays reopen the mid-Victorian literary debate about money and morality.

It may be useful to outline part of this earlier literature, in order to set the stage, as it were, for Shaw's ironic handling of some of its central themes. For we must appreciate that it was Shaw's intention not only to lampoon capitalists and Christians, but also to send up the tradition of earnest literary comment on them which can be dated from the 1830s and

[5] *Ibid.*, p. 6.
[6] D. Costello, *The Serpent's Eye: Shaw and the Cinema* (Notre Dame, Ind., 1965).
[7] J. Frank, '*Major Barbara*: Shaw's "Divine Comedy"', *Publications of the Modern Language Association* 71 (1956), 65; reprinted in R. Zimbardo (ed.), *Twentieth Century Interpretations of Major Barbara: A Collection of Critical Essays* (Englewood Cliffs, N.J., 1970), pp. 28–41.

1840s. That body of literature constituted a powerful response to the social problems associated with the dynamic phase of British industrialization. While no two writers who commented on social problems in literary form adopted the same tone or precisely the same emphases in their work, it is still true that the novels of Dickens, Mrs Gaskell, Disraeli and Kingsley, as well as the essays of Carlyle, Ruskin and even of Engels, came to be seen as part of one phase of literary and cultural history.[8]

At the same time, it is important to note that this body of writing is sufficiently multi-faceted to defeat attempts to label it as 'anti-industrial' or 'anti-industrialist'. It is perhaps better to characterize it as a three-part bill of indictment of English industrial society in the early nineteenth century.

On one level, it was an indictment of the venality, arrogance and inhumanity of individual businessmen in general, and *not* of industrialists in particular. The *locus classicus* of this position is Dickens' *Dombey and Son* (1848), a devastating portrait, not of an industrialist at all, but rather of a London merchant bereft of decency or straightforward paternal senti-ment, returned to humanity by the accident of bankruptcy and his daughter's loyal affection. The figure of Bounderby in *Hard Times* (1854) is a lesser version of the same theme, but even this Lancashire charlatan appears more as a banker than a cotton master. A decade previously, Carlyle had published in *Past and Present* (1845) a clarion call for businessmen to become captains of industry, true heroes of their nation, rather than mere worshippers of wealth. Such a 'working aristocracy' was, in his view, the hope of the future. Here too the concept of 'anti-industrial' attitudes among writers seems utterly inapplicable.[9]

On another level, the literature of the 1830s and 1840s can be seen as an indictment of the mechanical and unChristian philosophy of 'industrial-ism'. In the hand of Carlyle, and in the Dickens of *Hard Times*, to excoriate 'industrialism' was not to reject industry *per se* but rather to condemn the worship of industry as a form of paganism, which reduced individuals to cogs in a machine. The famous portrayal of 'Gradgrindery' at the opening of *Hard Times* was intended to suggest that wicked or egotistical individuals were much less of a menace than was the regimentation of society according to rigid utilitarian principles. After all Gradgrind, the hardware merchant-turned-M.P., himself escapes from Gradgrindery, in a classic

---

[8] The literature on this subject is vast. See, for a beginning, K. Tillotson, *Novels of the Eighteen-forties* (Oxford, 1954); L. Cazamian, *Le Roman social en angleterre, 1830–1850* (Paris, 1935); R. Chapman, *The Victorian Debate: English Literature and Society 1832–1901* (London, 1970); A. H. House, *The Dickens World* (London, 1941); R. Williams, *Culture and Society, 1780–1950* (London, 1958).

[9] T. Carlyle, *Past and Present* (London, 1845), book IV, ch. 4; see also F. Kaplan, *Thomas Carlyle: A Biography* (Cambridge, 1983).

conversion scene, touched by his daughter's despair, but the unredeemed features of Bounderby and Bitzer suggest that the onward march of Gradgrindery would not be so easily stemmed.

A third component of literary comment on industrialization presents different emphases. In Mrs Gaskell's *Mary Barton* (1848), in Charles Kingsley's *Alton Lock* (1846), and in Friedrich Engels' *Condition of the Working Class in England in 1844*, published in German the following year, and in English not until 1892, the indictment is that industrialization was not worth the suffering it entailed for the mass of the population. These writers claimed that for those trapped in the industrial maze, or enclosed in the ugliness of urban squalor in industrial towns, poverty was effectively a life sentence, with no hope of remission. Much has been written about whether these writers presented an accurate view of the social costs of industrialization,[10] but what is of greater importance is their belief that deprivation was not an accidental result of temperament or character, but was built into the economic system. Furthermore, they held that such poverty was not the fault of any one individual or set of individuals, but rather a seemingly unavoidable part of the process of economic growth.

Much of this three-part literary bill of indictment of English society in the early-Victorian period had a distinguished literary history behind it. To write of the yawning gap separating the rich and the poor, or to decry the existence of the 'two Englands', in the phrase associated with Disraeli's novel *Sybil* (1846), was to recall some Shakespearean images;[11] and to portray the venality of wealth was to invite the obvious comparison with Shylock and a host of other characters in Jacobean and Restoration comedy.

But we must attend to what is new in Victorian writing to appreciate Shaw's point of departure in *Major Barbara*, and indeed in much of his other work. The first innovation in what may be called Victorian 'social problem' literature is the emphasis it placed on the workings of a new economic

[10] As one might expect, Engels has drawn the most severe fire on this point. Compare the W. H. Chaloner and W. O. Henderson edition (London, 1958) of Engels' 1844 essay with S. Marcus, *Engels, Manchester and the Working Class* (London, 1974).

[11] For example, *King Lear* act III, scene iv, lines 28–36:

> Lear:
> Poor naked wretches, whereso'er you are,
> That bide the pelting of this pitiless storm,
> How shall your houseless heads and unfed sides,
> Your loop'd and window'd raggedness, defend you
> From seasons such as these? O, I have ta'en
> Too little care of this. Take physic, Pomp;
> Expose thyself to feel what wretches feel,
> That thou mayest shake the superflux to them,
> And show the Heavens more just.

system, which was explosive, much more creative of wealth than the older agricultural or commercial modes of production, and much more unpredictable in its vicissitudes. Most writers recognized that industry in mid-nineteenth-century Britain generated more wealth than this country had ever known, but it seemed to them (and not only to them) to do so more irregularly, with wilder fluctuations and their attendant consequences for the mass of the population. It is no accident that much of this writing (though not all of it) appeared in the wake of the severe depression of 1839–42, or that it occasioned fears, expressed in literary form, of a possible collapse of the edifice of Victorian society.

What also distinguished the new economic order of industrial capitalism was the fact that it was manned by two new classes. The first was a class of industrialists, and here we must attend to Professor Crouzet's observation that while there was industry galore in eighteenth-century England, it was industry by and large without industrialists.[12] By the 1840s and 1850s few could doubt that a new elite had appeared, although its relation to older elites was and remained a problematic matter.[13]

Equally troubling was its relation to the new working class or, as some Victorians preferred, working classes. However homogeneous in outlook or aspiration the labouring population was, no one writing in the 1840s was unaware that some of their spokesmen claimed to speak for a working class and to assert its right to full participation in the political life of the nation, and occasionally even to the full fruits of its labour. This is not the place to review the vast literature on class formation in Victorian Britain; it is sufficient to note that the language of class antagonism described what many contemporaries saw in front of their eyes – a divided industrial nation and, as such, one with a very uncertain future.[14]

The solutions writers offered to these problems varied substantially, but broadly speaking they were more confident about what would not work than they were about what would improve the lot of the poor and create a more just society. What nearly all shared, though, was an emphatic belief in the impossibility of progress through collective working-class action. From the portrayal of the trade unionists in *Mary Barton* or *Hard Times* to the Chartists in *Sybil*, or (to take a later example) the riotous miners in George Eliot's *Felix Holt the Radical* (1866), the strategy of working-class solidarity or mass action is shown as the way of despair and disaster.

[12] In the 1982 Ellen MacArthur lectures, University of Cambridge.
[13] See J. Foster, *Class Struggle and the Industrial Revolution* (London, 1974); R. S. Neale, *Class in English History, 1680–1850* (Oxford, 1981); W. D. Rubinstein, *Men of Property: The Very Wealthy in Britain Since the Industrial Revolution* (London, 1980); D. Cannadine, *Lords and Landlords: The Aristocracy and the Towns, 1774–1967* (Leicester, 1980).
[14] See A. Briggs, 'The Language of Class', in A. Briggs and J. Saville (eds.), *Essays in Labour History* (London, 1960).

Instead it is possible to identify in popular literature a central concern with individual salvation as the brightest hope for the alleviation of social problems. The contradictions inherent in this view – so mercilessly exposed by Shaw – need not concern us at this point. What is more important is the pervasiveness of this fundamentally religious imagery, regardless of the author's denomination or belief, in the body of writing under review.

The first major form this individualist approach to the resolution of social conflict took was the portrayal of the classical path of salvation through suffering. The Way of the Cross, in this context, meant melodrama, not theology. In Mrs Gaskell's *Mary Barton* it described the plight of the industrialist Henry Carson, whose son was murdered by a starving working man, but who came to see the need to forgive, and without fanfare to improve social conditions sufficiently to ensure that desperate acts of the kind that ended his son's life would not occur again. In the case of Dickens, it appeared as the triumph of decency, however hard-pressed or ill-treated; in the final clearing of the good name of Stephen Blackpool in *Hard Times*, in the tearful reconciliation of the virtuous Florence Dombey with her father, or in the peaceful passing of Smike in the care of Nicholas Nickleby, to choose but three of dozens of Dickensian moments celebrating the triumph of a kind of doctrineless Christianity.

The theme of personal salvation leads directly to a second motif of Victorian writing which had a special resonance in Shaw's plays. It is that conversion to decency and recognition of human values, however belated, tended to come about, in much Victorian fiction, through the intercession of the purity of womanhood in an impure world.[15] Be it in the inexplicable devotion of Rachel to Stephen Blackpool or the unassailable goodness of Sissy Jupe in *Hard Times*, in the ethereal presence of Sybil in Disraeli's novel of that name, in Florence Dombey's unshakeable daughterly dedication to her evil father, or in numerous other cases of feminine virtue in fiction, Victorian writers seem to have suggested that whatever the mess that men created in the world of social affairs, women – mysteriously, perhaps biologically – had the power to cleanse and to purify.

Of course the special place of women in Victorian fiction is highlighted still further by the regular appearance of the polar opposite of the female heroine – the fallen woman or girl of the streets. Either as prostitute or paragon, in the gutter or on a pedestal, women played a vital role in the literature of social comment. They announced the virtues of family, decency, loyalty and sacrifice which had the potential to undermine the egoism, vanity and venality of men and even at times to rescue them from the predicaments they created. There are, no doubt, exceptions to this rule; the impressive portrait of Mrs Transome in George Eliot's *Felix Holt the*

[15] N. Auerbach, *The Woman and the Demon: The Life of a Victorian Myth* (Cambridge, Mass., 1982).

Radical springs to mind. But on the whole, if caricature be a characteristic Victorian literary device, it applies to women much more firmly than to businessmen. Here, too, we find an important point of reference for many of Shaw's plays, and for *Major Barbara* in particular.

While the themes of salvation through suffering and the purifying power of womanhood are the central motifs in Victorian literature to which Shaw alludes in this play, there is yet another Victorian literary convention upon which he draws in interesting ways. It is the notion of salvation through escape, which frequently served as a useful device to resolve the dramatic tension of Victorian melodrama. Three examples should suffice to illustrate this theme. After the truth about Tom Gradgrind comes out in *Hard Times*, he makes his remorseful getaway through the circus folk who spirit him out of the country. Secondly, after the crimes and tribulations of *Mary Barton*, we learn that the heroine embarks on a new life, not in England, but in Canada. And thirdly, after being banished from her father's presence, Florence Dombey finds a new life with the seafaring folk who are her (and ultimately her father's) salvation.

What we should note here is that departure to another world was not only a well-advertised fact in mid-Victorian England, but that it signalled a veiled recognition by many writers that in industrial England itself there might *not* be a solution to the problems of living a decent life. Wiener has noted how this feeling found expression in the elevation of the pastoral in literature, and in this he is following the earlier lead of Raymond Williams, whose *The Country and the City* is a sure guide to this part of the literary landscape.[16] But for our purposes what is relevant is the extent to which Dickens provided his characters with a haven of safety among transient workers, not rooted or trapped in the routines of factory life; consider the circus troupe in *Hard Times*, the sailing men in *Dombey* and the actors in *Nicholas Nickleby*, just for a start. Perhaps it is not too fanciful to suggest that such figures hint at a degree of pessimism in the writings of Dickens and his contemporaries as to the likelihood of finding a way through the moral, political and personal maze of industrial society. To a degree, this tempered the optimism and the images of hope offered by compassion and femininity in Victorian literature. But equally, the theme of salvation by escape to a new world provides a third point of reference to earlier writing which Shaw explores in his inimitable fashion in *Major Barbara*, as indeed in other plays.

Shaw's play *Major Barbara* succeeds as a comedy by turning upside down virtually every major feature of the literature of conversion we have outlined above. The author made no bones about this in his preface to the play. It was precisely because conventional Christian morality sanctioned

[16] R. Williams, *The Country and the City* (London, 1973).

and idealized the lonely struggle of the individual against temptation and evil as the path of righteousness that Shaw would have none of it. Salvation through suffering, repentance and forgiveness – so fond a theme in Victorian literature – is completely rejected by Shaw as the false doctrine of 'Crosstianity'. Shaw claims to loathe the Cross 'as I loathe all gibbets'. But his real objection was to its symbolic appeal. 'Forgiveness, absolution, atonement are figments', declares Shaw:

> punishment is only a pretence of cancelling out one crime by another; and you can no more have forgiveness without vindictiveness than you can have a cure without a disease. You will never get a high morality from people who conceive that their misdeeds are revocable and pardonable, or in a society where absolution and expiation are officially provided for us all.[17]

This was available in literary form as much as in religious life, for what they shared was what was to Shaw the discreditable aim of 'making a merit of such submission'.[18] In the preface to *Major Barbara*, Shaw even went further, in his characteristically provocative manner, and claimed that:

> Churches are suffered to exist only on condition that they preach submission to the State as at present capitalistically organized....Indeed the religious bodies, as the almoners of the rich, become a sort of auxiliary police, taking off the insurrectionary edge of poverty with coals and blankets, bread and treacle, and soothing and cheering the victims with hopes of immense and inexpensive happiness in another world when the process of working them to premature death in the service of the rich is complete in this.[19]

Here Shaw was clearly following in an older tradition of socialist ethics. In the preface to the postwar play *Back to Methuselah* (1921), he stated explicitly that it was not Marx's economics or history which appealed to him; it was his moral indignation.[20] The Marx that Shaw had in mind was the man who offered a one-word reply to the question as to what vice he abhorred most. That reply was, 'Servility'.[21]

When Shaw wrote that 'there is no salvation...through personal righteousness, but only through the redemption of the whole nation from its vicious, lazy, competitive anarchy' called capitalism,[22] he was certainly announcing the collectivist's creed. But he was also repudiating a whole set of Victorian literary conventions about moral conflicts and their resolution by the individual.

Shaw repeatedly illustrated these conflicts by examining the theme of

---

[17] G. B. Shaw, *Major Barbara* (paperback edn, London, 1981), Preface, p. 32 (hereafter cited as *M.B.*).

[18] *Ibid.*, p. 29.

[19] *Ibid.*, p. 39.

[20] G. B. Shaw, *Back to Methuselah* (London, 1921), Preface, pp. lviii–lix.

[21] As cited in Stern, *Gold and Iron*, p. 96.   [22] *M.B.*, Preface, p. 27.

tainted money.[23] In *Mrs Warren's Profession* (1894), Vinnie Warren is shocked by the recognition that her mother was once forced by poverty into prostitution; this revelation she gets over. But what she cannot accept is that her entire upbringing was financed by her mother's remaining in brothelkeeping long after her own security was assured. This is precisely the form of Barbara Undershaft's dilemma, but in her case, the play does not end with her walking *out* on her father, but rather in running *into* his factory town and accepting the challenge of his world.

This reconciliation of father and daughter is unlike anything else in Victorian or Edwardian literature. The typical trajectory of the drama of conversion is reversed, when Barbara understands that to reject money and industry is to enter a cul-de-sac. She ultimately yields to the argument that the only way to keep her ideals is to accept the challenge of money, rather than to ignore its power. That meant to give up high-minded charitable good works, which never got to the root of the problem: which was, simply, that too many people had too little money to live decent lives. This was a fact which all the Hosannas in Christendom wouldn't alter.

Major Barbara, we should remember, opened at precisely the time that a Royal Commission on the Poor Laws was beginning its deliberations. One of its Commissioners was Shaw's fellow Fabian, Beatrice Webb, whose origins and asceticism were, for her, uncomfortably close to those of Shaw's heroine. The play was written, and first staged, against the background of a strenuous Fabian campaign to break up the Poor Law, and to eliminate the principle of 'less eligibility' on which workhouses were intended to operate. One of the purposes of the play is thus to show the irrationality of philanthropy and relief under conditions of mass destitution in many of Britain's urban centres.

This Shaw demonstrates in two ways. The first is by introducing us to 'the Poor'. These we meet in Act II in the West Ham shelter of the Salvation Army. There are two kinds of working men portrayed here. The first is the ultimate Utilitarian, Bronterre O'Brien Price, also known as Snobby. He is a man who recognizes that the surest way to the heart of the Salvation Army (and its handouts) is through confession, and the gaudier the better. He is, Shaw tells us, 'a workman out of employment...young, agile, a talker, a poser, sharp enough to be capable of anything in reason except honesty or altruistic considerations of any kind'.[24] What he is best at is playing 'the game as good as any of em'; that is, the conversion game, requiring deep blackness of past behaviour (concocted on demand) to contrast with the radiant whiteness of his newly saved soul.

The other sort of working man is altogether a different type. Bill Walker

[23] B. F. Dukore, *Money and Politics in Ibsen, Shaw, and Brecht* (Columbia, Mo., 1980), esp. chs. 2, 5, 7.   [24] *M.B.*, p. 75.

is a drunken brawler, who comes to the shelter to find the culprit who made his girlfriend into what we would now call a 'born-again Christian'. Instead, he finds one of the Salvation Army girls, Jenny Hill, and one of her charges, Rummy Mitchens. After punching and manhandling both of them, he is trapped by Major Barbara into feeling the rudiments of guilt about his brutality. His instinct is to be punished 'like a man', and after failing to receive the treatment he clearly believes he deserves at the hands of a free-for-all wrestling champion turned Soldier of the Lord, he tries to salve his conscience by a pound's donation to the Salvation Army.

Barbara's refusal to accept this man's money sets up the turning-point of the play, which is the second part of Shaw's case against the philanthropic impulse. If Shaw's first point is that most working men were sufficiently degraded by poverty to have little or no chance to conform to middle-class notions of decency or improvement, his second is that those who did the improving were merely pawns in the hands of the men responsible for poverty in the first place. Thus Bodger the whisky king offers a large donation, dwarfing Bill Walker's pound which Barbara had already refused. But the catch is that Bodger's beneficence stands only on condition that some other worthy soul matches his generosity. Who better than Andrew Undershaft, fortunately just at hand? Barbara's father, after all, wouldn't stoop to small gestures. When *this* donation is accepted by Barbara's superior, Mrs Baines, Bill Walker's cynicism is restored, since he was a witness to the proof that every man and woman had his or her price. From Barbara's standpoint, his soul is thereby 'lost', and her house of cards collapses all around her. She gives up the Salvation Army, disillusioned by its willingness to sup with the devil.

This highlights a second profound irony in Shaw's play. Unlike much of Victorian fiction, it is the man of business, a veritable captain of industry, who converts the woman of virtue, and not the other way around. As we noted above, the woman's redeeming love was a frequent, if not essential, ingredient in the Victorian drama of personal redemption. As Shaw notes in the preface to *Major Barbara*, it was his intention to 'violate the romantic convention that all women are angels when they are not devils...'.[25] But since Barbara is her father's daughter – and hence a bit of both – she is incapable of remaining defeated for very long.

This brings us to the third unusual feature of Shaw's play. We have noted the prominence of the motif of escape in Victorian social fiction. We find this theme in *Major Barbara* as well, but in the form of a Utopia. If few hopes can be placed in the capacity of the respectable middle class, housed in Wilton Crescent (the setting of Act I), to change for the better, little more can be expected from the urban poor of West Ham (the setting of Act II).

[25] *Ibid.*, Preface, p. 12.

But in Act III we are presented with the kind of world the American writer Lincoln Steffens later responded to in the memorable terms, 'I have seen the future and it works'.[26] Undershaft's conventional son Stephen is similarly thunderstruck. Perivale St Andrews is, he enthuses,

magnificent. A perfect triumph of modern industry. Frankly, my dear father, I have been a fool: I had no idea of what it all meant: of the wonderful forethought, the power of organization, the administrative capacity, the financial genius, the collosal capital it represents.[27]

The fact that Stephen is indeed a fool does not detract from the truth of what he says. This is a perfect example of the need to separate Shaw's playfulness from the serious intention of the play.

For what Perivale St Andrew represents is the embodiment of the Shavian form of the Fabian dream.[28] It is emphatically an industrial world, but one without a single pauper or a single dark satanic mill. Shaw tells us that Undershaft's factory town is 'an almost smokeless town of white walls, roofs of narrow green slates or red tiles, tall trees, domes, beautiful campaniles, and slender chimney shafts, beautifully situated and beautiful in itself'.[29] It is graced by not one but two Methodist chapels, a William Morris Labour Church, and an Ethical Society, but the last is not well frequented, since the men who work in the explosives sheds – 'all strongly religious' – 'object to the presence of Agnostics as unsafe'.[30] Indeed Adolphus Cusins, the Greek scholar, whose 'confession' as to the facts of his parents' somewhat dubious marriage – his mother is his father's deceased wife's sister – enables him to inherit the entire enterprise, tells Barbara that 'It only needs a cathedral to be a heavenly city instead of a hellish one.'[31] And its priest is a man of benevolence, who never gives orders, but rather enquires as to the welfare of his workers and their families.[32]

The fact that what they produce is munitions is, of course, one of Shaw's classically wicked ironies. But by dissociating the form of the ideal industrial life from its product, Shaw permitted his audience to see that to be opposed to capitalism, and the poverty it inevitably produced, was

---

[26] J. Kaplan, *Lincoln Steffens: A Biography* (New York, 1974), p. 250.

[27] *M.B.*, p. 131.

[28] This is not to be confused with Beatrice Webb's Fabianism; see her (predictable) annoyance at *Major Barbara* in her diary entry for 2 December 1905, in *Our Partnership*, ed. M. I. Cole (London, 1948), pp. 314–15. Indeed, Beatrice Webb may well have been the model for Major Barbara. See N. and J. Mackenzie. *The First Fabians* (London, 1977), pp. 308–9. On Fabianism in general, see A. McBriar, *Fabian Socialism and English Politics, 1884–1918* (Cambridge, 1962); on Shaw's Fabianism, the most penetrating remarks are still to be found in E. J. Hobsbawm's unpublished Cambridge Ph.D. dissertation on Fabian thought, 'Fabianism and the Fabians' (1950).

[29] *M.B.*, pp. 128–9. [30] *Ibid.*, p. 126.

[31] *Ibid.*, p. 129. [32] *Ibid.*, p. 127.

in no sense to be opposed to industry. What Undershaft had created for
one purpose could be used for any other. All that was needed for the
transformation is the collective recognition that the destruction of the
possibilities of human life by poverty was no less an obscenity than the
destruction of human life in war. Indeed, Shaw seems to suggest that, in
some respects, the slow death of primary poverty was worse than to die
on the field of battle. Fallen soldiers are the nation's heroes and receive
the nation's gratitude and honour; even their families receive a pension.
But fallen workers are the nation's shame, to be shunted aside when they
cannot be forgotten.

The absence of poverty is the essence of Shaw's Utopia in *Major Barbara*.
Undershaft is a twentieth-century Robert Owen, but Perivale St Andrews
went one large step beyond New Lanark. Both were new communities, but
only Shaw's prepared the ground for revolution. 'Come and make explosives
with me', Undershaft says to his new-found successor Cusins. 'Whatever
can blow men up can blow society up. The history of the world is the
history of those who had the courage to embrace this truth.' And then
posing the question to his daughter, Undershaft completes her conversion:
'Have you the courage to embrace it, Barbara?'[33] Embrace it she does, and
dedicates herself to the saving of souls, even in 'the Valley of the Shadow'.
'Major Barbara', she proclaims triumphantly, 'will die with the colours.'[34]

In 1931 Bertold Brecht wrote a play centring on the encounter of Joan
Dark, a spirited lady of the Salvation Army (here called the Black Straw
Hats) and a captain of industry, J. Pierpont Mauler, the meat king of
Chicago. The echoes of *St Joan* (1924) as well as of *Major Barbara* are
deafening. Of course, Shaw was not the only author to go through a
Brechtian overhaul here: Schiller, Goethe and Shakespeare are also
parodied in this play.[35] But the existence of a parallel text, written in an
entirely different theatrical and political environment, helps us to see more
clearly the nature and limits of Shaw's position.

[33] *Ibid.*, p. 144.   [34] *Ibid.*, pp. 152–3.
[35] The literature on Brecht and his forays into German and non-German literary history
is vast. Here is a tiny sample of the literature available in English, which throw light on
this aspect of Brecht's work. K. A. Dickson, *Towards Utopia: A Study of Brecht* (Oxford,
1978); E. Bentley, *The Brecht Commentaries 1943–1980* (London, 1981); E. Bentley, *The
Theatre of War* (London, 1970); R. Brustein, *The Theatre of Revolt* (London, 1966);
J. Willett, *The Theatre of Bertold Brecht* (London, 1977); M. Esslin, *Brecht: The Man and
His Work* (London, 1959); R. Gray, *Brecht the Dramatist* (Cambridge, 1976); W. Benjamin,
Understanding Brecht, trans. A. Bostock (London, 1973); I. Fetscher, 'Bertold Brecht and
Politics', in B. N. Weber and H. Heinen (eds.), *Bertold Brecht, Political Theory and Literary
Practice* (Manchester, 1980), pp. 11–40; G. Bartram and A. Waine (eds.), *Brecht in
Perspective* (London, 1982); K. Volker, *Brecht: A Biography*, trans. J. Nowell (London,
1979); P. Demetz (ed.), *Brecht: A Collection of Critical Essays* (Englewood Cliffs, N.J.,
1962).

On some matters, the distance between Shaw and Brecht is not great. Brecht was clearly influenced by his reading of *The Jungle* (1906), Upton Sinclair's novel of the appalling life of workers in the Chicago meat trade, and although *Major Barbara* was written just before the appearance of Sinclair's novel, Shaw refers to it on three occasions in the preface to the play.[36]

Furthermore, both presented the Salvation Army in a similar light, although, as one might expect, Brecht's treatment of the subject is harsher and much more sharply drawn than Shaw's. Joan Dark's first speech shows clearly the thematic parallels between the two plays as well as the contrast in the sheer violence of language and imagery between *St Joan of the Stockyards* and *Major Barbara*:

> In a gloomy time of bloody confusion
> ordered disorder
> planned wilfulness
> dehumanized humanity
> when disturbances are unending in our cities:
> into such a world, a world like a slaughterhouse
> summoned by rumored threats of violence
> to stop the brute strength of the dim-sighted people
> from smashing its own tools and
> crushing its own bread-basket underfoot
> we wish to bring back
> God.
> Of little fame these days
> almost disreputable
> not admitted now
> among realities:
> but, for the lowest, the one salvation.[37]

Initially her advice to the poor is 'Strive upward, not downward. Get in line for a good job up above, not here below.'[38] And, above all, avoid the temptation of resorting to brute force, 'As if force ever caused anything but destruction. You believe that if you rear up on your hind legs there'll be paradise on earth. But I say unto you: that way not paradise but chaos is created.'[39]

The structure of the play, superficially like that of *Major Barbara*, is the story of Joan Dark's conversion from spirituality to reality, from a fixation on the other world to a clear understanding of this one. But her fate is not that of Major Barbara, but of Shaw's (and Schiller's and Shakespeare's) St Joan. She must die in order that her beliefs may be buried beneath the

---

[36] M.B., Preface, pp. 26, 28, 40.
[37] Bertold Brecht, *St Joan of the Stockyards*, trans. F. Jones (Bloomington, Ind., 1969), pp. 30–1 (hereafter cited as *Joan*).
[38] *Ibid.*, p. 33. [39] *Ibid.*, p. 34.

sanctity of sainthood. She winds up, in her dying moments, committed not to saving souls in a purified factory, but to destroying the entire capitalist system.

Even before she offers her parting aphorisms, which we shall look at in a moment, she had an outlook different from that of Shaw's Barbara. She not only wanted to help the poor; she also wanted to know why there was poverty in the midst of wealth. To find out whose fault was the suffering of the poor she seeks out Mauler, who shows her the true face of poverty. The squalidness and degradation she sees among the poor do not surprise her, and she rejects the view that the depravity of the poor is the source of their tribulations. She tells a group of wholesalers and packers something which Major Barbara in her missionary days did not express:

My dear sirs, I keep hearing that the poor have not enough morals, and it's true. Immorality breeds down there in the slums, and revolution goes along with it. I ask you: Where are their morals to come from, if morals are all they have? Where can they get anything without stealing it? My dear sirs, there is such a thing as moral purchasing power. Raise that and you'll get morality too. And by purchasing power I mean something very simple and natural: money. Wages. And that brings me back to the facts of the matter. If you go on like this you'll end up eating meat yourselves, because the people out there lack purchasing power.[40]

Indeed, these are precisely Undershaft's sentiments, and occupy a position remote from Barbara's until virtually the end of the play.

Well before her 'conversion', Brecht's Joan is also endowed with a much greater sense of curiosity about the connection between riches and poverty, or, in Brecht's terms, about how capitalism works. As a result of her enquiries, she begins to see that poverty *must* exist in order that the accumulation of wealth can go inexorably on. Just before she expires, already beatified by the capitalists as 'St Joan of the Stockyards', she leaves the Black Straw Hats some very unbeatified sentiments, which they refuse to hear. She tells them:

> But those who are below are kept below
> so that those above may stay above
> and the vileness of those above is measureless
> and even if they get better that would be
> no help, because the system
> they have built is peerless:
> exploitation and disorder, beastly and therefore
> past understanding.[41]

And because the capitalist system cannot be softened by appeals to sentimentality, the only hope for the poor is in the acceptance of precisely the means Joan had repeatedly refused to accept throughout the play. She

[40] *Ibid.*, p. 59.   [41] *Ibid.*, p. 121.

is approached by workers with a letter to alert their comrades about an imminent general strike; this letter she does not pass on, an act of omission she comes to regret. Only when she fully appreciates the force of necessity in economic life, can she accept the necessity of force. Her parting words are:

> So anyone down here who says there is a God
> although there's none to be seen
> and He can be invisible and help them all the same
> should have his head banged on the pavement
> until he croaks.[42]

Joan Dark emphatically does *not* die with the colours. Shaw, in contrast, lets Major Barbara off the hook. She needn't enquire into the causes of poverty, or to ponder the uses of violence; she can march in step with her Greek philosopher, Adolphus Cusins, in his (and her father's) Platonic Republic, where philosophers are kings and kings, philosophers. In this respect, we can perhaps see better how Shaw escaped from the more difficult dilemmas posed by Brecht.

The contrast between the approach of the two playwrights is perhaps most clear-cut in their portrayal of the two businessmen, Undershaft and Mauler. Here too, we can see the relative mildness of Shaw's characterization. Thus, Undershaft, in Shaw's stage directions:

Andrew is, on the surface, a stoutish, easygoing elderly man, with kindly patient manners, and an engaging simplicity of character. But he has a watchful, deliberate, waiting, listening face, and formidable reserves of power, both bodily and mental, in his capacious chest and long head. His gentleness is partly that of a strong man who has learnt by experience that his natural grip hurts ordinary people unless he handles them very carefully, and partly the mellowness of age and success.[43]

We have no similar notes about Mauler, but everything about him suggests vulgarity and brutality. His one redeeming feature would seem to be a mawkish sentimentality, which makes him want to puke when he sees what goes on in the stockyards. As a result, he claims he is 'ready to become a decent man and not a butcher', a notion he repeats to Joan when they first meet.[44]

When Joan brings some poor people to the Stock Exchange, Mauler faints at the sight of them. When he comes to, he agrees to buy enough meat to put them all back to work.[45] He tells his agent Slift why he fainted: because he saw that one day he would pay for his crimes. Anyone wishing to explore the limitations in Shaw's critique of capitalism should consider this set of completely unShavian remarks, in Brecht's *St Joan of the*

[42] *Ibid.*, p. 122.   [43] *M.B.*, pp. 65–6.
[44] *Joan*, pp. 28, 42.   [45] *Ibid.*, pp. 59–60.

Stockyards. Referring to Joan's visiting delegation of the poor, Mauler wonders:

> What was she talking about? I didn't
> hear, because at her back
> there stood such people with such ghastly faces
> of misery, the very misery
> which comes before a wrath that will sweep us all away
> that I saw nothing more. Now, Slift
> I'll tell you what I really think
> about this business of ours.
> It can't go on like this, nothing but buying and selling
> and one man coldly stripping off another's skin;
> there are too many people bellowing with pain
> more of them all the time.
> What falls into our bloody cellars
> is past all comfort:
> when they get hold of us
> they'll toss us out
> like rotten fish. Not one of us
> will die in bed. Before
> we come to that they'll stand us against walls
> mob after mob and clean the world of us and
> our hangers-on.[46]

This brief discussion of some of the dramatic ideas of Bernard Shaw and Bertold Brecht in no sense exhausts the possibilities of comparison between their work.[47] Interesting affinities exist between *Major Barbara* and other Brecht plays, such as *The Good Woman of Setzuan* (1938–42), and much could be made of Brecht's repeated borrowing of English themes, from *Edward the Second* (1924) to *A Man's A Man* (1924–6) and *The Threepenny Opera* (1928).

But our primary purpose here is not comparative literature but rather the elucidation and development of ideas stated in works of English literature on the subject of businessmen and the world over which they preside. In this context, to read Brecht alongside Shaw is to appreciate the futility of applying to the latter the label 'anti-industrial' or 'anti-industrialist'. Indeed, the positive features of Andrew Undershaft are essential to the purpose of Shaw's play, which was to show that it is just as absurd to construct a demonology of business activity as it is to conjure up a hagiography of entrepreneurship. Shaw's Undershaft is *both* demon and hero, both the destroyer and the creator, the cynic and the idealist, and as such he presides over a marvellous parody of Victorian caricatures of businessmen as unalterably evil or unassailably beneficent.

[46] *Ibid.*, pp. 63–4.
[47] Dukore, *Money and Politics*; D. R. Sauvageau, 'Shaw, Brecht, and Evolution: The Early Plays' (University of Minnesota Ph.D. dissertation, 1977).

Shaw's point surely is that businessmen will take on the character of the society they serve; change the society and businessmen will be transformed overnight. It was no accident that Shaw joined the Webbs in setting up the London School of Economics, just on the edge of the City of London, to teach businessmen, civil servants and others the truths of the new social sciences. They had an essential part to play in society; the only question was whether their contribution would be restricted to the generation of private profit or opened up to the more important realm of public service.

The second key distinction which emerges from a comparison of *Major Barbara* and *St Joan of the Stockyards* is the mildness of Shaw's attack on the capitalist system, when compared to that of Brecht. It is true that Undershaft invites Cusins to join him in making explosives to blow up society. But, as in most of Shaw's plays, the suspicion remains that those projectiles will contain a nasty shower of words.

Of course, nearly three decades separated the writing of these two plays, decades of war, revolution and economic crisis.[48] By the 1930s, Shaw, like the Webbs, had come to adopt a much more extreme political position, but it was a change which left most of his dramatic ideas intact. In addition, we must note the different effects of humour in these men's work, for in Shaw's hands it served to blunt the message; in Brecht's, to sharpen it. But, overall, the distance between the outlook of these two writers is less a function of time or style, and more a function of the political culture in which each wrote.

It is not just that the politics of the streets, with all its attendant violence, which was the background to much of Brecht's writing,[49] was virtually unknown in Britain at the time Shaw wrote *Major Barbara*. Nor is it solely that the socialist movement in this country, then as now, was incurably and immovably committed to democratic traditions. It is also that Shaw operated in an intellectual community that was conspicuously different from what Europeans call an 'intelligentsia', a group of writers and thinkers fundamentally at odds with their society and its mores. Such was the world of Brecht's Munich and Berlin in the postwar years, an artistic and intellectual world very remote from Shaw's London.

Noel Annan has claimed that one way of resolving 'the paradox of an intelligentsia which appears to conform rather than rebel against the rest of society' is to note that many of them married each other or their relations.[50] In the case of Shaw, this explanation simply will not do. But

---

[48] A more contemporary text in German literature is, obviously, Thomas Mann's *Buddenbrooks* (Munich, 1902). An interesting comparison could be made between Thomas Buddenbrooks and Undershaft, but this would go well beyond the confines of this paper.

[49] See E. Rosenhaft, *Beating the Fascists?* (Cambridge, 1983).

[50] N. G. Annan, 'The Intellectual Aristocracy', in J. H. Plumb (ed.), *Studies in Social History: A Tribute to G. M. Trevelyan* (London, 1955), p. 285.

however we account for it,[51] it is the very character of English intellectual life that is an essential part of the explanation as to why the cultural critique of business in this country, from Dickens to Shaw and beyond, was so relatively mild. The essential reason was that, either in the form of the literature of conversion in the novels of the 1840s or in the parody of that literature in the work of George Bernard Shaw, English writers, even the renegade Irish Protestant among them, never fully repudiated the values of their society. Of course, to establish this argument rigorously, careful study would have to be made of the works of each of the writers in question. But, when that is done, I believe it will show the error of interpreting their work as forming part of the 'counterrevolutionary' 'anti-industrial' crusade which Martin Wiener has identified as the source of England's industrial decline. To judge by literary evidence, the crusade never took place. English writers, and even the iconoclast Shaw among them, were too close to the culture they criticized really to leave it behind. As such they were very much like Major Barbara, who never really gave up the colours of her very English faith.

[51] See E. J. Hobsbawm, 'The Fabians Reconsidered', in *Labouring Men* (London, 1964), for the view that the Fabians expressed the aspirations of a *nouvelle couche sociale* of brainworkers, who hoped to run British society, and not to overthrow it. As such the Fabians were the last people you would expect to form an 'intelligentsia'.

10

~~~~~~

Lost opportunities: British business and businessmen during the First World War

B. W. E. ALFORD

Donald Coleman has provided us with a characteristically succinct account of Courtaulds' war:

> Despite the involvement of this country in four years' grim and expensive warfare, Courtaulds were able, during this time, to sell all the artificial silk they could make: and sell it, moreover, at prices which rose more than did the general level of prices.... Such weakening as there was in the support which the monopoly derived from its patents was amply balanced by the circumstances of war. What the second international consortium failed to do when it collapsed, the war achieved by narrowing, in some places completely shutting off, the channels of trade.[1]

Such a description appears somewhat heretical when compared with more general accounts of the impact of the First World War on the British economy; though it is important to note that most attention has been given to the immediate postwar period while discussions of the war years themselves have tended to concentrate on the ways in which extraordinary financial, production and manpower needs were met.[2] As to the economic effects of the war, two main lines of argument emerge from the literature. One concludes that it had powerfully damaging consequences which continued well into the 1920s and even beyond. The other seeks to show that the war exacerbated longer-term problems affecting the British economy through the scale, nature and speed of its demands, and through the distortions it caused in international trade and finance; altogether, it is alleged, this made it much more difficult to achieve necessary structural changes, in particular in the industrial sector.

---

[1] D. C. Coleman, *Courtaulds: An Economic and Social History*, vol. II: *Rayon* (Oxford, 1969), pp. 126, 128.

[2] The major works which deal with this subject are: William Ashworth, *An Economic History of England, 1870–1939* (London, 1960); W. Arthur Lewis, *Economic Survey 1919–1939* (London, 1949); Alan S. Milward, *The Economic Effects of the World Wars on Britain* (London, 1970); Sidney Pollard, *The Development of the British Economy 1914–1950* (London, 1962); Ingvar Svennilson, *Growth and Stagnation in the European Economy* (Geneva, 1954). An interesting contemporary analysis was made by E. M. H. Lloyd, *Experiments in State Control* (Oxford, 1924). An excellent select bibliography of works on war and economic development generally will be found in J. M. Winter (ed.), *War and Economic Development* (Cambridge, 1975), pp. 257–92.

The difference between these views is less important than what they hold in common, which is that the war was bad for British business and industry. So, was Courtaulds' experience a rare exception to the rule, or does it indicate that in some areas at least the war had beneficial economic effects, and, if so, how did businessmen respond to them? The purpose of this chapter is to address the question in terms of both the broad business environment and the experiences of major British firms. It must be emphasized, however, that it concentrates on the industrial sector, mainly on manufacturing industry, while recognizing that the economic and other effects of the war went wider than this. In no sense does this study seek to justify the war.

In 1930, Bowley surveyed the main attempts which had been made over the 1920s to measure the losses resulting from the war, and he added his own calculations which reckoned that if the war had not occurred Britain would have benefited to the equivalent of up to four years' capital accumulation.[3] This order of magnitude has been corroborated by more recent estimates by Svennilson and Lewis.[4] And in the latest and most exhaustive refinement of national income data, the war period has been defined statistically as 1913 to 1924 and described as follows: 'The absolute fall in G.D.P. across the war, not made good until the late 1920s, is one of the most spectacular features of recent British economic history.'[5] While there is some acknowledgment of other factors which might have influenced economic performance outside the war, the message is clear and unequivocal: the war broke the rhythm of compound growth. Losses of production and investment translate, by implication, into subsequent industrial stagnation and business difficulties. The problem with this analysis, however, is that statistical abstraction is no substitute for historical investigation and thus statements which refer to the period 'across World War I' are little more than literal translations of pre-defined arithmetical relationships. No attempt is made, for example, to incorporate into this analysis the work of business historians. It is by no means clear, therefore, what the rate of growth was over the war itself, or, even more important for our purpose, how it was distributed between sectors and industries.

The bewitching identities of factor input analysis or the simpler counterfactual calculations of foregone income and capital accumulation can be treacherous guides to historical explanations of the process of economic

[3] A. L. Bowley, *Some Economic Consequences of the Great War* (London, 1930), pp. 87–8.
[4] Svennilson, *Growth and Stagnation*, pp. 18–19; W. Arthur Lewis, 'World Production Prices and Trade', *The Manchester School* 20 (1952), 127.
[5] R. C. O. Matthews, C. H. Feinstein and J. Odling-Smee, *British Economic Growth 1856–1973* (Oxford, 1982), p. 543.

change. Moreover, they tend to encourage an approach which focuses primarily on rates of economic motion which are seen to be disturbed by troublesome events such as the First World War, whereas it is the very mixture of uneven development, growth, stagnation, contraction and random shocks which is the historical reality. To take an extreme hypothesis, but one bearing directly on this subject, it could have been that the war caused a loss of production through the run-down of large sectors of industry, but that subsequently this led to their rapid modernization through the need for capital reequipment and thence to higher rates of growth than would have been achieved through 'uninterrupted' development. Indeed, from what is known of the pre-1914 performance of British industry, it is clear that it was already flagging both in relation to its nineteenth-century record and in comparison and competition with its foreign counterparts. Much paper and ink has been expended in efforts to explain why this was so; and, necessarily, in ways which do not enlist the First World War as part of the explanation. A crucial element in the challenge to British industry was the changing nature of market opportunities.

Part and parcel of the advance of industrialization and the attendant rise in real *per capita* incomes was an alteration in the range of goods traded in international markets. The application of new, especially science-based, technologies caused 'net value added' (as against the cost of raw materials) to account for a growing proportion of the final value of output of manufactured goods. In turn, this broke the large element of complementarity in international trade in terms of the exchange of primary products and raw materials for manufactured goods and led to a growing distancing effect, in terms of income and trading relationships, between the advanced and less advanced economies. Obversely, industrialized nations were brought increasingly into competition with one another and the accompanying growth in tariff protection was substantially a symptom of this.[6] Various studies have shown how British industry was unable to adapt to these fundamental changes: a high proportion of its exports was made up of a narrow range of staple goods going to relatively low-income countries – a pattern which was intensified by increasing exports of coal and, more broadly, by a steady swing to Empire markets.[7] And when

[6] S. B. Saul, *Studies in British Overseas Trade 1870–1914* (Liverpool, 1960), pp. 134–65. See also M. E. Falkus, 'United States Economic Policy and the "Dollar Gap" of the 1920s', *Economic History Review* 24 (1971), 599–623, for an analysis of a central part of the longer-term development of these pre-war changes in the structure of international trade.

[7] A succinct analysis of this is provided by Forrest Capie, *Depression and Protectionism: Britain between the Wars* (London, 1983), pp. 12–39. More detail is available in Saul, *Studies in British Overseas Trade*; and for the longer-term perspective in an international framework Svennilson, *Growth and Stagnation*, pp. 168–202, 294–303, is unsurpassable.

compared with its American and German counterparts, British business showed up weakly in chemicals, electrical engineering and modern types of metal manufacture.

The war had an immediate and direct impact on the export trades of firms in the staple industries. Naval hostilities shut off foreign markets and allowed neutral foreign competitors and indigenous producers to step in. And in the case of coal, the war indirectly weakened demand for it by promoting more rapid technical change based on oil. In immediate terms, however, loss of overseas demand was compensated for by buoyant war needs.[8] But, it can be argued, this was merely small and temporary compensation against the speed and scale of the loss. Is it the case, however, that the accelerated loss was necessarily a bad thing?

One way of defining the extent of Britain's outmoded industrial structure by 1914 is in terms of proportions of capital and labour employed in various industries. It is well known that the upshot is that against broad criteria of what was required for good competitive performance in international terms, there was an overcommitment to the staple industries, which were in decline through the permanent loss of comparative advantage, and, taking it a stage further, factor combinations were yielding too low rates of productivity growth in a whole range of industries.[9] In relation to this, the answer to the question posed could be that the concentrated impact of the war was, potentially, a most effective means of breaking the narrow and limited expectations of businessmen – individuals who have been portrayed so frequently as unenterprising and inherently resistant to change – and, more generally, of facilitating investment strategies which would have forced the pace of change in an atmosphere of flexibility, mobility, even of compulsion. Yet when the evidence is examined, it can be shown that the loss of markets did not bring about such a change of attitudes and, partly as a consequence, businessmen did not respond successfully to the opportunities which appeared.

In assessing the reactions of the staple industries there is the problem of a lack of detailed studies of individual businesses but, nevertheless, a large amount of evidence is available from other sources. In the coal industry the war had little effect on the owners' legendary obscurantism and they

[8] The Ruhr conflict, a direct consequence of the war, indirectly provided some postwar assistance to the industry.
[9] E. H. Phelps Brown with Margaret H. Brown. *A Century of Pay* (London, 1968), pp. 113–26, 174–96; and for broad aggregate analyses see R. C. Floud, 'Britain 1860–1914: A Survey', in Roderick Floud and Donald McCloskey (eds.). *The Economic History of Britain since 1700* (Cambridge, 1981), pp. 1–26, and Matthews, Feinstein and Odling-Smee, *British Economic Growth*, pp. 21, 33.

were well matched by the miners, as postwar events were to show.[10] In cotton, iron and steel, heavy engineering and shipbuilding, businessmen prepared for peace in a decidedly bullish mood.[11] The financial aspects of this will be considered a little later, but it is clear that businessmen's assessments of future demand led them to invest heavily in plant and equipment. These attitudes were summed up by the Sheffield correspondent of *The Economist* as early as 1916:

British steel trade prospects [after the war] are exceedingly bright....the bulk of an enormous export trade in iron, steel and engineering products will stand to be shared between Britain and the United States at highly profitable prices. Our works will be taxed to their uttermost capacity, with the overflow of orders going to America.[12]

Much similar evidence could be cited. However, in none of these industries was such optimism matched by anything approaching careful attention to the full range of possibilities of technical innovation. Had it been so, businessmen would have been brought up against crucial issues of plant layout. Here is the response of the director of the British Engineers' Association representing 440 firms in the industry to a line of questioning on this subject by the Balfour Committee:

Have you any actual experience of workshop conditions in the United States? – I have been in the United States twice, but I have not been there for a good many years now. I cannot speak of most recent conditions.

[10] A valuable survey which contains detailed references to other work on the industry is provided by M. W. Kirby, *The British Coalmining Industry 1870–1946: A Political and Economic History* (London, 1977). Of particular interest in this respect is Barry Supple, Chapter 11 below. See also W. H. B. Court, 'Problems of the British Coal Industry Between the Wars', *Economic History Review* 15 (1945), 1–24.

[11] There is a large literature from which evidence can be drawn to support this statement but it is too voluminous to be cited here. Among the more important studies are: P. W. S. Andrews and Elizabeth Brunner, *Capital Development in Steel: A Study of the United Steel Companies Ltd* (Oxford, 1951); D. L. Burn, *The Economic History of Steel-making, 1867–1939: A Study in Competition* (Cambridge, 1940), pp. 350–92; J. C. Carr and W. Taplin, *History of the British Steel Industry* (Oxford, 1962), pp. 299–360; Peter L. Payne, *Colvilles and the Scottish Steel Industry* (Oxford, 1979), pp. 125–50; L. Jones, *Shipbuilding in Britain Mainly Between the Two World Wars* (Cardiff, 1957); G. W. Daniels and J. Jewkes, 'The Post-war Depression in the Lancashire Cotton Industry', *Journal of the Royal Statistical Society* 91 (1928), 153–92, especially pp. 165–82; W. Lazonick, 'Industrial Organization and Technological Change: The Decline of the British Cotton Industry', *Business History Review* 57 (1983), 195–257; L. C. Sandberg, *Lancashire in Decline: A Study in Entrepreneurship, Technology, and International Trade* (Columbus, Ohio, 1974) – it is important to note that while the author presents a persuasive case that entrepreneurs were not responsible for the decline he ignores the extent to which they were responsible for failing to adjust to it; J. H. Bamberg, 'The Government, the Banks and the Lancashire Cotton Industry, 1918–39' (University of Cambridge Ph.D. thesis, 1984), pp. 8–33; G. C. Allen, *British Industries and their Organization* (London, 1951 edn).

[12] Cited by Andrews and Brunner, *Capital Development in Steel*, p. 78.

Have you gone through the workshops of the United States? – At that time I went through some workshops.

Might I ask how long ago that is? – 1899.[13]

And this was in 1925! It was an outlook, moreover, which was characteristic of witnesses representing a range of industries.

Firms in iron and steel were undoubtedly subjected to heavy wartime demands which to some degree forced them into developments that they might not otherwise have chosen, but this was by no means an overriding factor, as evidence provided by steelmen themselves reveals.[14] In short, it has to be seen as something to be discounted at the margin against the large investment commitments which were made by firms in anticipation of buoyant postwar markets. Leading firms embarked on a course of acquisition and amalgamation. United Steel is an example *par excellence* of a company brought into being in this way, and by 1919 it had achieved a capitalization of £13.2 million which placed it as the tenth largest manufacturing company in the U.K.[15] Other steel firms which achieved rankings in the top fifty – in significant part by similar means – were G.K.N., Consett, Dorman Long, Richard Thomas, Stewarts and Lloyds, Ebbw Vale, and John Lysaght.[16] And to these have to be added the amalgamations involving the takeover of virtually the whole of the Scottish steel industry by leading shipbuilders and centring on the firms of Colvilles and Beardmores.[17] Scottish shipbuilders were totally convinced that this was crucial to ensuring supplies of steel plate for what they judged would be the heavy demand for British ships of traditional type once peace returned.

One possible indication of a change in business attitudes towards international competition is the wartime attitude to protection.[18] Calls for protection were led by iron and steel manufacturers who lobbied the government through their trade association. In part, these were stimulated by a general upsurge of xenophobia. In part, also, they reflected genuine concern over shortages of strategic war supplies, and for this reason they

---

[13] Committee on Industry and Trade (Balfour Committee), *Minutes of Evidence*, vol. I (London, 1930), p. 637, paras. 9559–61. The three volumes of evidence published by this committee (volumes II and III appeared in 1931) are a major and underused source of evidence on business opinion on a wide range of matters affecting British industry over this period.

[14] *Ibid.*, e.g. vol. I, paras. 6230–1, 6370, 6376–8, 9451–9, 14578–83; moreover, it is significant that a number of witnesses did not refer to the war at all as a source of their current problems. See also Andrews and Brunner, *Capital Development in Steel*, pp. 104–7, 111–13.

[15] Leslie Hannah, *The Rise of the Corporate Economy*, 2nd edn (London, 1983), p. 189.

[16] *Ibid.*, pp. 189–90.

[17] Payne, *Colvilles*, pp. 139–50; John R. Hume and Michael S. Moss, *Beardmore: The History of a Scottish Industrial Giant* (London, 1979), pp. 152–79.

[18] Capie, *Depression and Protectionism*, pp. 7, 61–5.

were met with some positive response from the government. But on the major issue of permanent protective measures there is no evidence that these demands sprang from a new understanding of the changed and changing nature of world trade in relation to which tariffs could be a means of facilitating industrial reorganization. On the contrary, there is considerable evidence of a view among British businessmen that they suffered from international competition because foreign businessmen enjoyed special advantages, not because they were more efficient. The fear was that German firms would revert to aggressive, state-assisted economic warfare once the military conflict was over. For a time this dominated official thinking in the Ministry of Reconstruction and was reinforced by lobbying on behalf of business interests through individuals, trade organizations and government committees. The demand was clear: existing staple industries had to be protected and assisted, not modernized and restructured. Moreover, when the fear and subsequent alarm about potential postwar raw material and shipping shortages receded and disappeared, so too did support for protection, and the abolition of wartime controls also came quickly. When the possibility of protection was raised some eight years later during the Balfour Committee enquiries it received very little support, and the same basic attitudes to international competition were still much in evidence even after years of considerable trading difficulties. Witnesses stressed the advantages which foreigners gained from more favourable tax regimes, lower wages and indirect state assistance of various kinds, and stoutly denied that British industries were inherently less efficient than, say, their German or U.S. counterparts; and they did not accept that there had been fundamental long-term shifts in demand for staple goods.[19]

The impact of war on markets and expectations in other sectors of industry was somewhat different from that in the staples. Indeed, our discussion began with a leading example, Courtaulds, and to that record of domestic success during the war it is necessary to add that its U.S. subsidiary – The American Viscose Corporation – surged ahead on a high tide of consumer demand in that vast, lush market, and, as will be seen, the offspring yielded a rich return to the parent firm.[20]

[19] For the war period see Peter Cline, 'Winding Down the War Economy: British Plans for Peacetime Recovery, 1916–19', in Kathleen Burk (ed.), *War and the State: The Transformation of British Government, 1914–19* (London, 1982), pp. 157–81. Cline emphasizes that concern arose from government fears about national security and that there was no change in basic economic orthodoxy. For the latter period see Balfour Committee, *Minutes of Evidence*, vols. I–III, which contain many comments on the lines described above. These views were summed up in the *Final Report of the Committee on Industry and Trade*, Cmd 3282 (1929), pp. 267–8.
[20] Coleman, *Courtaulds*, vol. II, pp. 138–40.

212   B. W. E. ALFORD

Lever Brothers was the second largest manufacturing company in the U.K. in 1919, and it dominated the soap, edible oil and fats industry. Initially, the war brought problems: 'The loss of several continental businesses, the shortage of capital, labour and raw materials, the growth of government interference in industrial affairs...'.[21] But the clouds soon parted and the first substantial increase in the soap market for many years came as a result of 'the increase in employment and purchasing power as well as the social changes which resulted from these things'.[22] Exports boomed, especially to the U.S.A. Over and above this the war brought Levers into margarine production because of the impossibility of securing adequate supplies from the Continent. In the short run it required changes in the organization of production, with the establishment of new factories in Britain; in the longer run the consequences of this were more profound since it strengthened the position of the British industry against its Dutch rival.[23]

Other companies to benefit from similarly based wartime consumer demand were Imperial Tobacco, which by 1920 accounted for 72% of the U.K. market for cigarettes and tobacco, and which was ranked third among the fifty largest U.K. manufacturing companies,[24] and Boots, which was a combination of manufacturing and retailing in the pharmaceutical and allied industries.[25] Both firms produced mass-market goods and benefited immediately from rising wages and full employment. Moreover, the war accelerated the swing from pipe tobaccos to cigarettes, and also created opportunities for Boots to exploit demands for specifically wartime goods for civilians and servicemen. Smaller, but well-known, companies operating in similar markets were Allied Suppliers, Huntley and Palmers, and Crossfields: all experienced a sharp boost to sales.[26]

Parallel evidence on a broader front is provided by an analysis of changes in the operation of the labour market over the war years.[27] 'Dilution and the enormous expansion of the munitions industries and allied trades

[21] Charles Wilson, *The History of Unilever: A Study in Economic Growth and Social Change*, vol. I (London, 1954), p. 216.
[22] *Ibid.*
[23] *Ibid.*, vol. II, p. 175.
[24] B. W. E. Alford, *W. D. & H. O. Wills and the Development of the U.K. Tobacco Industry, 1786–1965* (London, 1973), p. 324; Hannah, *The Rise of the Corporate Economy*, p. 189.
[25] Stanley Chapman, *Jesse Boot of Boots the Chemists: A Study in Business History* (London, 1974), pp. 82–102.
[26] Peter Mathias, *Retailing Revolution: A History of Multiple Trading in the Food Trades Based Upon the Allied Suppliers Group of Companies* (London, 1967), pp. 216–24; T. A. B. Corley, *Quaker Enterprise in Biscuits: Huntley and Palmers of Reading, 1822–1972* (London, 1972), pp. 180–202; A. E. Musson, *Enterprise in Soap and Chemicals: Joseph Crossfield and Sons, Limited, 1815–1965* (Manchester, 1965), pp. 265–85.
[27] J. M. Winter, 'Aspects of the Impact of the First World War on Infant Mortality in Britain', *Journal of European Economic History* 11 (1982), 713–38.

increased working class incomes';[28] and the indirect but sensitive measure of this effect is the sharp reduction in infant mortality over the period. The process involved the virtual elimination of unemployment and under-employment (including that among women and young people), the upgrading of jobs, war bonuses and wage advances, the narrowing of differentials, minimum wage regulations, overtime working, and piece-rate payments, together with improved social provisions. All of this worked particularly to the advantage of those industries producing goods and services for the material improvement of the mass of the population, which was movement in the direction necessary for overall improved economic performance.

Less directly connected with mass markets was the chemical industry, which in 1914 had been lagging well behind its German and American counterparts, and the full seriousness of this was exposed during the war when there were shortages of crucial materials. But over the war the industry gained a useful edge on competitors. 'Brunner Mond and Nobel's Explosives both did extremely well...and to these wealthy, efficient, and ambitious firms the wartime demand for enormous expansion, far from being a cause of muddle and resentment, was welcome and stimulating.'[29] The German industry was excluded from the U.K. market so that 'by 1918 the chemical firms of Great Britain and the U.S.A., if not level with the great German groups, had at least gone a long way towards shortening the German lead, which for many years before 1914 had been long and growing longer'.[30]

The electrical industry in Britain paralleled the chemical industry in the sense that on the eve of war it was an area of technology dominated by the Americans and Germans. However, the leading U.S. companies of General Electric and Westinghouse had recognized the potential of the U.K. market before 1914 and had established U.K. subsidiaries to exploit it; a move which provided them with the added insurance of being able to circumvent any tariff barriers which might be erected.[31] The leading British company was the General Electric Company though, significantly, it had been founded and was being run by the Bavarian-born Hugo Hirst. The commercial peregrinations of these companies over the war years is as fascinating as it is complex, but one fact is clear: they did well out of the war. G.E.C. (U.K.) was enabled to buy out the German half-share in Osram,

[28] *Ibid.*, pp. 727–8.
[29] W. J. Reader, *Imperial Chemical Industries: A History*, vol. I: *The Forerunners 1870–1926* (Oxford, 1970), p. 253.
[30] *Ibid.*, pp. 317–18.
[31] Robert Jones and Oliver Marriott, *Anatomy of a Merger* (London, 1972), pp. 7–95, give a detailed account of these developments. On the more general subject of U.S. subsidiaries see Frank A. Southard Jr, *American Industry in Europe* (Boston, 1931).

the electric lamp bulb manufacturer and, together with British Thomas Houston (the British subsidiary of General Electric (U.S.)) and Westinghouse, it was benefiting from wartime demands for a range of electrical equipment which was at the heart of technological change in modern warfare.

Of all the new technologies the one which perhaps was to be the most ubiquitous in its effects was motor-car manufacture. Before the war it was substantially a form of handicraft industry serving a bespoke market. But the pace and nature of development was being set in the U.S.A., where by 1910 annual production of cars was running at nearly 200000 and, as with many other consumer goods and services, this influence spread to Britain and Europe. Ford established an assembly plant at Trafford Park in 1912 and, it has been claimed, 'the catalyst which provided the spur to British manufacturers was not war, but Henry Ford, who provided W. R. Morris with the model for assembly production, and later helped to modify Herbert Austin's conservative views on methods of manufacture'.[32] Even so, the war stimulated potential demand through increasing public consciousness of the utility of motor vehicles and by directly increasing the number of trained drivers.[33] The industry gained in efficiency from the stimulus which war production gave to the adoption of interchangeable parts, and the way was prepared for Austin and Morris.

Motor-vehicle production was one element in the buoyant wartime demand for glass, and it was boosted in the immediate postwar years directly as a result of attempts to honour wartime pledges to provide 'homes for heroes' through various housing schemes. Pilkingtons dominated flat-glass production and it could barely match the pressure of wartime demand; this more than compensated for the loss of export markets in South America and Canada to U.S. suppliers.[34] The other industry to benefit in this connection was tyre production. Dunlop was Britain's leading company and over the period even its 'loss-making French company became profitable'.[35]

Finally in this regard, an industry which became enmeshed with a whole new range of goods and services was that of petroleum. The two leading U.K. companies were British Petroleum (B.P.) and Shell and they mush-

[32] Roy Church, *Herbert Austin: The British Motor Car Industry to 1941* (London, 1979), p. 194.

[33] P. W. S. Andrews and Elizabeth Brunner, *The Life of Lord Nuffield: A Study in Enterprise and Benevolence* (Oxford, 1955), p. 96.

[34] T. C. Barker, *The Glassmakers: Pilkington: The Rise of an International Company, 1826–1976* (London, 1977), pp. 242–6. See also *Final Report on the Glassware Trade Prepared by a Sub-Committee appointed by the Standing Committee on Trusts*, Cmd 1385 (1921), pp. 6–9; despite its title this report contains interesting information on the flat glass industry.

[35] Geoffrey Jones, 'The Growth and Performance of British Multinational Firms Before 1939: The Case of Dunlop', *Economic History Review* 37 (1984), 41.

roomed in size as a consequence of war demands. B.P., in particular, 'emerged from the war incomparably, almost unrecognizably, stronger' than it had been in 1914.[36] The aggregate significance of the firms which have been surveyed in relation to markets and demand can be gauged from the fact that in 1919 they accounted for approximately 50 per cent of the capitalization of the fifty largest companies and for slightly more than this by 1930, which indicates their continued importance.[37] This, of course, implies nothing about the absolute level of investment in manufacturing industry, which in fact grew slowly over the inter-war years.[38] More directly, our analysis leads to the question of whether war demand was translated into profits and profitability. Care has to be exercised in assessing this because, as is well known, prices roughly doubled over the period and rose by a further 23 per cent by 1920.

Big profits and profiteering certainly became a cause for public concern as the war developed, and in 1915 the Excess Profits Duty was introduced in an endeavour to deal with the problem. But while this did something to create an impression of public probity and responsibility, all the indications are that in financial terms it was very ineffective. The state of company law meant that those who were determined could relatively easily evade substantial liability; and those less determined or plain honest benefited from the backward state of accounting practice. Moreover, the manner in which costs were estimated and prices fixed not only allowed many loopholes but ensured that efficient firms did well anyway; and official investigations both during and immediately after the war were somewhat naive in their approach to the matter.[39] The profits bonanza was

[36] R. W. Ferrier, *The History of the British Petroleum Company*, vol. I: *The Developing Years 1901–1932* (Cambridge, 1982), pp. 202, 295; Robert Henriques, *Marcus Samuel: First Viscount Bearsted and founder of 'Shell' Transport and Trading Company 1853–1927* (London, 1960), p. 650.

[37] Hannah, *The Rise of the Corporate Economy*, pp. 102–3, 189–90.

[38] At between 20–25 per cent of the pre-war rate. Moreover, investment as a proportion of gross domestic product fell sharply. See Matthews, Feinstein and Odling-Smee, *British Economic Growth*, pp. 140, 378; and for a detailed analysis of capital formation, C. H. Feinstein, *Domestic Capital Formation in the United Kingdom 1920–1938* (Cambridge, 1965).

[39] For some discussion of this issue see Jonathan S. Boswell and Bruce R. Johns, 'Patriots or Profiteers? British Businessmen and the First World War', *Journal of European Economic History* (1982), 423–45; evidence from major company histories which supports their broad line of argument is more extensive than they recognize and, moreover, they give too much credence to the final judgments of certain postwar committees set up under the Profiteering Acts of 1919 and 1920. A number of these committees recorded that firms did not appear to keep proper financial accounts so that it was impossible to do more than estimate costs, prices, profits and return on capital. On a number of occasions, however, the confident tone of their conclusions betrays a failure to heed their own

experienced across a wide range of industry and, effectively, it most probably amounted to a redistribution of profits away from such sectors as services, building and construction, and internal transport, to those industries directly supplying war materials or meeting the demands arising from growing working-class incomes.[40] The ways in which firms applied these windfall gains, however, varied considerably.

Such financial buoyancy matched the bullish outlook of U.K. steel makers and helped them to pursue their orgy of acquisition and amalgamation.[41] The other staple industries could, potentially, have applied some of their high monetary profits as powerful solvents to deadweight capital liabilities. Instead, to varying degrees these funds were used in the war and immediate postwar years to expand capacity for supplying traditional markets and, once again, to promote amalgamations in the largely false belief that this would produce good profits through a system of regulated competition.[42] The depth of this belief was revealed time and time again and by a wide range of witnesses from these industries when they appeared before the Balfour Committee some seven or eight years later. The following comments from a leading representative of the cotton spinners referring to the immediate postwar years are typical;

It has been reported to us that one of the great difficulties is that many mills are now over-capitalized.... – A good many spinning mills were capitalized on a much higher basis.

warnings. See, for example, *Report into the Prices, Costs, and Profits at all Stages of the Biscuit Trade*, Cmd 856 (1920); *Report on Agricultural Implements and Machinery*, Cmd 1315 (1921); *Report on Iron and Steel Products*, Cmd 1360 (1921); *Report on Pottery*, Cmd 1360 (1921). This list could easily be extended. The whole series of these reports not only contains much indirect evidence of high profits in a number of industries over the war period but also it collects together much interesting evidence on a range of topics connected with the industries. D. H. Aldcroft, *British Railways in Transition: The Economic Problems of Britain's Railways Since 1914* (London, 1968), pp. 32–6.

[40] Comprehensive statistical analysis of these changes over the war years is not available. For an excellent discussion of wage data see J. A. Dowie, '1919–20 is in Need of Attention', *Economic History Review* 28 (1975), 429–50. Matthews, Feinstein and Odling-Smee, *British Economic Growth*, pp. 160–97, provide an analysis of factor shares, but because they use the sub-period 1913–24, which combines the period of high wartime employment with the years of sharply rising unemployment which followed, it is of limited value for our purposes. Even so the shift to real wage income is clear: see table 6.5, p. 171. Direct evidence on the cut-back in the building industry will be found in the reports of sub-committees set up under the Profiteering Acts of 1919 and 1920, see *Interim Report on the Prices, Costs and Profits of the Brick Trade*, Cmd 959 (1920), which shows that output in 1918 was one-fifth the level of 1913; *Report on Cement and Mortar*, Cmd 1091 (1920); *Report on Light Castings*, Cmd 1200 (1921).

[41] Andrews and Brunner, *Capital Development in Steel*, pp. 77–9, 102–18; Burn, *Economic History of Steelmaking*; Carr and Taplin, *History of the British Steel Industry*; Hume and Moss, *Beardmore*, pp. 332–44; Payne, *Colvilles*, pp. 139–50.

[42] The tolerance of the British legal system to such arrangements is an important factor in these developments. The Committee on Trusts (1918) was ineffective in this regard partly because, in a general sense, it felt that large-scale organizations were economically necessary and it did not question their nature very closely.

...Our view is that it was an improvident scheme of finance, in which were dissipated large reserve funds which would have been very useful later on when trade fell away.[43]

Shipping companies suffered enormous losses of tonnage through sinkings – amounting to 40 per cent of the pre-war merchant marine at their peak – but a combination of new building and convoys had reduced overall losses to 12 per cent by 1918.[44] Government control was exercised through the system of Blue Book rates, and this industry was in the forefront of the official mind when the Excess Profits Duty was conceived in 1915. Nevertheless, the major groups, including Royal Mail, Elder Dempster, Harrisons and Holts, did well, and with large accumulated profits tucked away in secret reserve accounts, they applied their efforts to match their optimism.[45] Flotation was the central principle in both their yards and boardrooms. Companies were acquired and merged and $2\frac{1}{2}$ million tons of ceded German ships were purchased for fear that they might fall into competitive hands; yet this was regardless of their low technical efficiency.[46] In sum it amounted to a collective failure to understand the shifting distribution of international shipping and the need to make adjustments accordingly.

For many firms in a range of industries, profligate use of war profits was compounded with the easiest of easy credit from the clearing banks. Some years ago, Pigou ascribed to the banks major responsibility for the postwar inflation, and other commentators have similarly drawn attention to it.[47] One of the most vivid accounts of these events was provided by the financier, Lord Brand, writing of his own experiences as a director of Lloyds Bank in 1919:

My impression of Board meetings...at that time was that we ladled out money; we did it because everybody said they were making and were going to make large profits, and while you had an uneasy feeling yet you thought that while they were making large profits there could be nothing said about ladling out the money.[48]

But the fact remains: the clearing banks were not compelled to lend, they chose to do so. What is more, they were technically lending short, in the

[43] Balfour Committee, *Minutes of Evidence*, vol. I, paras. 7699–700.
[44] S. G. Sturmey, *British Shipping and World Competition* (London, 1962), p. 36.
[45] Sturmey, *British Shipping*, pp. 36–60, 94–7; P. N. Davies, *The Trade Makers: Elder Dempster in West Africa 1852–1972* (London, 1973), pp. 187–208; Edwin Green and Michael Moss, *A Business of National Importance: The Royal Mail Shipping Group 1902–1937* (London, 1982), pp. 35–52; Francis Hyde (with J. R. Harris and A. M. Brown), *Shipping Enterprise and Management 1830–1939: Harrisons of Liverpool* (Liverpool, 1967), pp. 123–78.
[46] Sturmey, *British Shipping*, pp. 57–8.
[47] A. C. Pigou, *Aspects of British Economic History 1918–1925* (London, 1947), pp. 169–83.
[48] Cited by Susan Howson, *Domestic Monetary Management in Britain 1919–38* (Cambridge, 1975), p. 10. For another good example of this see Bamberg, 'The Government, the Banks', p. 79.

218   B. W. E. ALFORD

form of overdrafts, without seemingly realizing that they were providing the cash flow to support long-term commitments, the success of which would determine whether they would ever see their money back. This reveals both the nature of the relationship between finance and industry and the narrow competence of financial entrepreneurship itself, something which became an issue somewhat later on in the investigations of the Macmillan Committee. Over the 1920s the banks' incompetence brought its nemesis from which they were extricated by Montagu Norman and the Bank of England.[49] In this context, however, the important point is that this evidence warns against the danger of seeing British businessmen of the period – as many themselves did – as in some way the victims of postwar inflation which was caused by international dislocations; in all probability businessmen in industry and finance were themselves substantially the guilty parties.[50]

Outside the staple industries Courtaulds' experience was not untypical. Donald Coleman has shown how the company's financial success, especially that derived from its American subsidiary, was garnered through the medium of capital gains rather than trading profits. Precisely how much this amounted to it is impossible to say because detailed accounts are not available, but a good indicator is provided by Courtaulds' share capital, which rose from £2 million to £12 million between 1914 and 1920.[51] In the soap and edible fats industry, Unilever led the way with booming profits – especially from its U.S. operations where an annual loss of £20000 was transformed into an annual profit of £300000 over the period. Its overall capitalization rose from £12 million to £47 million between 1913 and 1920.[52] Imperial Tobacco in tobacco, Brunner Mond and Nobel's in chemicals, Boots in pharmaceuticals, Pilkingtons in glass, Dunlop in rubber, G.E.C., British Thomson Houston and Westinghouse in electrical engineering, Shell and B.P. in petroleum: all made large profits which well outpaced inflation over the period and placed them in a substantially stronger position in 1920 than in 1914.[53]

[49] For an account of this see R. S. Sayers, *The Bank of England, 1891–1944* (Cambridge, 1976), vol. I, pp. 314–30.
[50] Cf. this view with Dowie, '1919–20 in Need of Attention'. There are important points of difference in terms of focus and explanation, but the important similarities are the emphasis on 'cost–push' rather than 'demand–pull' factors and a recognition that industrialists probably bore a major responsibility for real wage rises.
[51] Coleman, *Courtaulds*, vol. II, p. 153, and Coleman's comments suggest that his figures were probably conservative.
[52] Wilson, *Unilever*, vol. I, pp. 244–5, app. 3.
[53] Imperial Tobacco Company private archives; Reader, *Imperial Chemical Industries*, pp. 303 et seq.; Chapman, *Jesse Boot*, pp. 135–6, 205–9; Barker, *The Glassmakers*, pp. 255–6; Jones, *Shipbuilding in Britain*; Jones and Marriott, *Anatomy of a Merger*, pp. 22, 58, 69, 84–6, 144–5 – English Electric was easily floated in 1919 with a capital of £5 million, which made it larger than any other British electrical company at that time; Henriques,

And, once more, these performances were matched by smaller, related companies.[54] The thrust of this evidence is that in financial terms the war provided the means for firms in the staple industries to make structural adjustments which took account of their long-term prospects, and it opened the way for the exploitation of new sources of demand in the expanding industries. The evidence relates, moreover, to a substantial proportion of the core of manufacturing industry together with important parts of other major sectors of the economy. It is recognized that other economic activities suffered, though precisely how and to what extent must await further investigation. Indeed, the potential gain from such a shift is at the centre of our analysis. Hence, the focus here is on manufacturing industry because it was at the core of the chronic economic problems of the inter-war years. Probably the most serious error was the manner in which those industries facing long-term decline threw away the financial advantages which the war gave them. This was not simply a loss: it turned an enormous advantage into a crippling handicap. There is the possibility, of course, that the war itself in some way caused these misjudgments, but before this is considered it is necessary to examine in a little more detail changes in business structure and organization, in particular in those industries in the potential growth sectors of the economy.

The business reorganization which occurred in iron and steel, cotton, shipbuilding, shipping and heavy engineering was of a kind which included little alteration in business practices, since the primary objective was to achieve greater concentration of ownership and an increase in production along existing lines.[55] Characteristically, amalgamated companies operated as loose federations and were controlled by some form of holding company arrangement, structures which were tailor-made for a strategy of meeting declining markets by means of output sharing and quota arrangements, rather than through the adoption of modern techniques of business organization which, for comparison, were already well established in the U.S.A. Ironically, over the postwar years the U.K. began to catch up with

Marcus Samuel, p. 650; Ferrier, *History of the British Petroleum Company*, pp. 220–35. A number of these sources refer to the incompleteness of the available accounts, implying that profits were understated.
[54] See for example Mathias, *Retailing Revolution*; Musson, *Enterprise in Soap and Chemicals*, pp. 315–16; Charles E. Harvey, *The Rio Tinto Company: An Economic History of a Leading International Mining Concern 1873–1954* (Penzance, 1981), pp. 362–3; Boswell and Johns, 'Patriots or Profiteers?'
[55] Apart from the studies of particular firms and industries cited above, a very useful survey analysis is provided by Alfred D. Chandler Jr, 'The Development of Modern Management Structure in the U.S. and the U.K.', in Leslie Hannah (ed.), *Management Strategy and Business Development* (London, 1976), pp. 23–51.

the U.S.A. in terms of the degree of concentration in manufacturing industry, but it was a perverse achievement.[56]

During the war the backward state of accounting practices was an advantage, but from a company's standpoint this was a reward to omission. For the longer run the need was for careful and more comprehensive accounting if sensible investment decisions were to be made. Failure to recognize this was a major shortcoming of British business over the 1920s. Cost accounting was virtually unknown in British companies, to say nothing of discounting methods of evaluating investment projects.[57] Even the practice of depreciation of fixed assets was handled in a hit-and-miss way; an interesting consequence of which is that attempts to calculate capital formation at either industry or economy level for these years are necessarily subject to very wide margins of error.[58]

In the expanding industries the bounties of war were not squandered, not least because it was inherently more difficult to do so than in the staple industries. Yet in major respects their reactions to the pressures and demands of war fell a long way short of justifying an accolade for enterprise. Courtaulds, once again, provides a classic case. Its huge success with rayon had made it easily the world's largest producer of artificial silk by 1920. This proved to be a high point, however. Some falling away was the natural accompaniment to the entry of new foreign producers but it is quite clear that this by no means accounted for the full extent of it:

The mistakes made [in the inter-war years] arose again from the continued influence in the 1920s and '30s of attitudes of mind which belonged to an earlier era, and an inflexibility of approach in recognizing the questions at issue.[59]

During the war and inter-war years the company engineered no major changes in structure and organization and it was backward in its approach to industrial relations. All this contributed to what, as late as 1952, the chairman could describe as 'a Gentlemen's Club atmosphere in the Board Room [which]...I believe it is true to say that over the years...has spread to all the Departments of our business'.[60]

[56] For a statistical analysis see Leslie Hannah and J. A. Kay, *Concentration in Modern Industry: Theory, Measurement and the U.K. Experience* (London, 1977), p. 3 and *passim*.

[57] An interesting and, it would seem, rare exception to this is provided by a group of major mining companies including Rio Tinto Zinc and Rhodesian Anglo-American. See B. W. E. Alford and C. E. Harvey, 'Copperbelt Merger: The Formation of the Rhokana Corporation, 1930–32', *Business History Review* 54 (1980), 334–5.

[58] The major study here is Feinstein, *Domestic Capital Formation in the United Kingdom 1920–1938*. In the light of company histories which have been published since these estimates were made, it is very questionable whether even the author's careful qualifications go far enough in indicating the potential degrees of error involved: pp. 18–20, 236–7.   [59] Coleman, *Courtaulds*, vol. II, p. 497.

[60] D. C. Coleman, *Courtaulds: An Economic and Social History*, vol. III: *Crisis and Change 1940–1965* (Oxford, 1980), p. 24.

The persistence of existing forms and traditional attitudes was matched by other major companies. William Lever remained in dictatorial control of his firm and it took a major commercial misjudgment, the collapse of international primary product prices and, ultimately, the intervention of the Almighty – none of which were consequences of the war – before even the beginnings of reorganization were attempted.[61] Imperial Tobacco did nothing to take stock of its loose federal organization or to look for new areas in which it might employ its hugely accumulating financial resources and undoubted marketing skills.[62] The evidence could be multiplied by examples from the other firms already referred to. Probably the most serious deficiency which is revealed was the lack of understanding of the nature of marketing as distinct from the narrower and traditional techniques of selling. Marketing is concerned with deciding market objectives and then integrating research, production, advertising, selling and distribution into a policy and programme designed to secure these objectives. In a significant sense, the emphasis on selling reflected an approach which had been conditioned by the experience of industrializing under highly competitive conditions. Against this British industry was now rapidly promoting monopolistic organization, but was not matching it with understanding of the more sophisticated marketing techniques required to develop it successfully. Even in the quasi-public industry of electricity supply, although the war exposed the need for coordination between companies if gains in efficiency were to be achieved, it was nothing like enough to overcome traditional management attitudes. It took years' more experience of supply difficulties and inefficiencies, together with growing concern about international companies, before changes were made.[63] It may well be that there is a sense in which over the 1920s a form of corporate economy emerged in Britain. If so, it was surely one populated with types which on an international time scale belonged to an earlier stage of corporate evolution.[64]

A major part of the explanation as to why the pressures and opportunities of the war were not enough to overcome company inertia is bound up with the relationship between business and government. Total war presented a wholly new order of demand on resources. In a preliminary barrage before a big battle, for example, British artillery would regularly use $1\frac{1}{2}$ million shells – a figure which can be compared with an annual output of

[61] Wilson, *Unilever*, vol. I, pp. 243–312.
[62] Bernard W. E. Alford, 'Strategy and Structure in the U.K. Tobacco Industry', in Hannah, *Management Strategy*, pp. 73–84.
[63] Leslie Hannah, *Electricity before Nationalization* (London, 1979), pp. 53–104, 170.
[64] Cf. A. D. Chandler Jr, *Strategy and Structure: Chapters in the History of the Industrial Enterprise* (Cambridge, Mass., 1962); A. D. Chandler Jr, *The Visible Hand: The Management Revolution in American Business* (Cambridge, Mass., 1977).

0.5 million shells in 1914.[65] Yet despite the fact that at a very early stage the government had taken large powers of requisitioning and control by decree, it persisted in meeting its enormous requirements by purchasing through the market. Gradually, specific shortages forced it to adopt more direct methods of acquisition and once this process was begun it spread as one need impinged on another. Even so shortages proliferated. The details could be recounted but the central issue here is the impact this had on the relationship between government and business. In formal terms there was a major change, in that the traditional free-enterprise economy was overtly superseded by central control. Yet in reality the manner in which these controls were operated did not in any way supplant private enterprise. Businessmen were drawn into government to direct the new agencies which were set up, and the implementation of particular policies was commonly effected through boards and committees made up of those industrialists directly affected. Big companies initially feared *dirigisme*; they quickly learned that the spectre had not materialized. In important respects top businessmen made a heavy commitment to the war effort, but it was one in which patriotism and self-interest could be nicely combined.[66]

The politics of this period have recently attracted detailed attention which has revealed that neither before nor during the hostilities did the government commit itself to planning for total war.[67] Failure to understand the need for such a thing was a characteristic of politicians and generals alike: in each case a curious mixture of gentlemen and players, who seemed to suffer from the worst defects of either type when it came to waging successful warfare. The alternative subsequently provided by Lloyd George and his ilk, aided by recruits from the boardroom, solved the immediate crisis of 1915/16, but it was a solution based on pragmatism and laced with meretricious slogans and rhetoric. In short, the war did not precipitate a change in economic orthodoxy, not least because the war was not seen as in any way resulting from a failure in the existing economic order – it was seen as an aberration from it.[68] No clear alternative economic

---

[65] W. K. Hancock and M. M. Gowing, *British War Economy* (London, 1949), p. 6.
[66] Cf. Boswell and Johns, 'Patriots or Profiteers?', pp. 439–41.
[67] See David French, *British Economic and Strategic Planning 1905–1915* (London, 1982); but see also the comments by A. Milward in a review of this book in *Journal of Economic History* 43 (1983), 511–12, where he argues, convincingly to my mind, that French does not go far enough in his criticisms of Asquith and his colleagues. In addition, there is much useful material in Burk, *War and the State*, though the sub-title of the book, *The Transformation of British Government, 1914–1919*, together with its brief introduction, does not match the content, which generally emphasizes the transitory nature of wartime changes.
[68] Cf. this view with A. Marwick, *The Deluge: British Society and the First World War* (London, 1973). Furthermore, the thrust of my analysis does not, by implication, agree with certain aspects of K. O. Morgan, *Consensus and Disunity: the Lloyd George Coalition Government, 1918–1922* (Oxford, 1979), especially pp. 367–75. Insofar as Morgan deals with the

rationalization existed or seemed to be called for. Indeed, there was no pressing need to plan for peace: in strong contrast to the post-1945 period, the years immediately after 1918 were not years of basic shortage. In 1919 British imports were 88 per cent of their 1913 level and the balance of payments was in healthy surplus.[69] And the attitude of leading businessmen to the government's capacity for directing industry can be sharply illustrated by the comments of Sir Alfred Mond, who had considerable experience of Whitehall:

as a Minister and businessman [I am convinced] that it is impossible to carry on the industries of this country from a Government Department....A curiously paralysing influence seems to come over everybody as soon as they begin to work for the State.[70]

For a while, it is true, businessmen in government had challenged the orthodox fiscal stance because of fears of postwar German competition. Yet even in this, representatives of the business community took care to guard against direct government interference in industry. Their attitude was unchanged and unchanging and because of it the abandonment of reconstruction plans was easily accepted once the German threat was thought to have been removed. Thus the quick abolition of controls which followed the war meant that insofar as government involvement was a necessary condition for promoting changes in industrial structure it would require factors quite different from the war to bring it about.[71]

One other relationship which has to be considered is that between business and organized labour. Unions, as is well known, come to play a central role in economic matters between 1914 and 1918. Their pre-war radicalism – even extremism – was submerged under a tide of patriotism tinged with xenophobia. In cooperating with governments at the national level unions became less rigid and extreme in their organization and objectives; in terms of workshop practices concessions were more limited and somewhat transitory.[72] The policy of labour dilution was most

economic impact of the First World War it appears to me to involve certain inconsistencies which stem, in part, from a confusion of short- with long-term factors, and this has consequences for his political analysis.

[69] Interesting comments on this theme were made by J. R. Hicks in a review article of Pigou, *Aspects of British Economic History*, which appeared in *the Manchester Guardian*, 11 June 1947, p. 4. Pigou's book had been prepared 'at the request of the Government for departmental use in 1941–2' and clearly Hicks saw little practical value in it: 'This is a new task to which we are called, which needs new methods; for it the experience and even the ideas of "last time" offer little guidance.'

[70] Cited by Sheila Marriner, 'Sir Alfred Mond's Octopus: A Nationalized House-Building Business', *Business History* 21 (1979), 40. Lloyd George said of Mond that 'No better business brain has ever been placed at the disposal of the State in high office...', *ibid.*, p. 27.   [71] Cf. Cline, 'Winding Down the War Economy'.

[72] A characteristically perceptive analysis on aspects of this is provided by Henry Phelps Brown, 'A Non-Monetarist View of the Pay Explosion', *Three Banks Review* 105 (1975), 3–24.

extensive in the multifarious engineering industry, yet it did not produce a durable transformation in workshop organization.[73] In the manufacture of munitions a new order of division of labour was achieved (especially through the use of female labour) but it proved to have little lasting effect because it was largely confined to those areas which bore the least relevance to peacetime production. Nevertheless, in general businessmen and union officials were brought into a new relationship. An interesting example is provided by Imperial Tobacco, which prior to the war had little experience of unionism. In 1918 the Board decided, by a majority vote, to recognize trade unions; the main argument advanced in favour of doing so was that wage fixing would be standardized and that unions would effectively deal with any potentially recalcitrant workers.[74]

In sum, however, little was done to develop more up-to-date labour relations.[75] This failure was revealed clearly somewhat later in the aftermath of the breakdown of the Mond–Turner discussions.[76] It remains an open question as to where responsibility for this inertia lay. The indications are that it varied from industry to industry, though the situation in the expanding industries is in many ways the most striking. Samuel Courtauld and William Morris both directed companies producing the most up-to-date consumer goods and yet both behaved like enlightened, late-Victorian paternalistic employers in their dealings with their workmen.[77]

In returning to the question posed at the outset of this discussion, it is necessary to repeat that our analysis focuses mainly on the manufacturing core of the British economy. As to the war itself, it has been argued that its domestic economic impact has to be assessed within a broader, international framework and over a longer-term time-scale, which take account of the spread of industrialization and its consequent effects on the nature and pattern of world trade, the operation of international financial institutions, and domestic industrial structures. Among the major econo-mies Britain, by virtue of its early industrial start, was mostly on the receiving end of these developments by the early twentieth century and,

[73] See Jonathan Zeitlin, 'The Labour Strategies of British Engineering Employers, 1890–1922', in H. F. Gospel and C. R. Littler (eds.), *Management Strategies and Industrial Relations* (London, 1983), pp. 25–53.
[74] Imperial Group Ltd, private archives.
[75] Devotees of the 'work process' approach to labour history see things somewhat differently and for the flavour of their analysis see A. L. Friedman, *Industry and Labour: Class Struggle at Work and Monopoly Capitalism* (London, 1977).
[76] M. Jacques, 'Consequences of the General Strike', in J. Skelley (ed.), *The General Strike* (London, 1976), pp. 375–404.
[77] Coleman, *Courtaulds*, vol. II, pp. 157–9, 437–49; R. Church, 'Myths, Men and Motor Cars: A Review Article', *Transport History* N.S. (1979), 105.

as a result, began to suffer from what might be termed an advanced form of economic backwardness.

The war undoubtedly accelerated these trends, especially in relation to the staple industries. But this is not to say that it was therefore even more difficult for firms to adapt themselves to these trends, or that the war transformed the trends into major causes of subsequent industrial decline. To the contrary, it has been argued in this chapter that the war indirectly offered a new basis for longer-term adjustments in industrial structure through protected markets, real rises in profits and the potential solvent of inflation for clearing away accumulated over-capitalization in the form of fixed-interest debt. The records of a wide range of individual businesses and businessmen provide no significant evidence of wartime shock and despair. The overall response was a mixture of optimism and complacency.

Donald Coleman has written persuasively about British business culture in terms of 'gentlemen and players', and although his concern is mainly with the years before the war, he alludes to the persistence of these attitudes well into the twentieth century.[78] The striking feature for which our analysis provides support is that the war did little, if anything, to alter this outlook or, interrelatedly, the business organizations within which it was nurtured.

It might be argued that the nature of businessmen's responses to the opportunities of war was sharply constrained by factors beyond their control. There is the view, for example, which seeks to explain Britain's growing industrial problems of this time in terms of structural rigidities within the economy which were unique to Britain's form of capitalism.[79] The most pernicious blocks are seen to be competitive market structures promoting short-run profit maximization rather than long-run growth, family firms, financial institutions which operated within short time horizons, conservative trade unions and the political economy of Liberalism. The worst-affected industries were the staples, but even growth industries such as motor-car manufacture were thus inhibited. These rigidities, it is claimed, blocked the emergence of corporate capitalism in the manner and to the extent which was required to promote more rapid growth through the imposition of the visible hand of monopolistic control over production and markets. There are a number of reasons, however, why such an argument is less than compelling. Not only does it require much more careful definition and analysis in terms of the precise nature and operation

[78] D. C. Coleman, 'Gentleman and Players', *Economic History Review*, 2nd Series 26 (1973), 92–116.
[79] The best example is provided by Lazonick, 'Industrial Organization and Technological Change', and this article contains references to other similar work relating to other industries.

of institutional rigidities, including the relationships between them, it simply does not match the available evidence. Opportunities for company reorganization were real and, indeed, changes were made which in a number of cases cut across the alleged rigidities of market structure and family ownership and which were aided and abetted by the clearing banks. The flaw was the failure of businessmen to incorporate into these changes innovative forms of organization and commercial practice.

More generally, it is unnecessary to adopt an all or nothing position on the issue of structural and institutional rigidities. In the explanation of the slow pace of industrial change in Britain over the early twentieth century there are good grounds for giving considerable weight to such factors as heavy commitments of capital (especially social overhead capital) and labour to staple industries; to the special disadvantages which Britain suffered through the want of quite new forms of international economic institutions; and to the limitations of the domestic market for new goods within the existing pattern of income distribution. In major respects these were obstacles beyond the 'power of the market' to overcome; and in order to break through them a new form of political economy was required in which government and business were brought into a new relationship. How much weight should be attached to these factors as against that of the responsibility of individual firms and businessmen is not an issue here. Correspondingly, it is not claimed that these elements in any particular combination fully explain Britain's subsequent economic problems, which in industrial terms crystallized into three million unemployed in 1932. But the attitudes and commercial practices of businessmen bore *some* responsibility for what developed during the 1920s, particularly in relation to the domestic potential for economic growth. Alternative investment decisions and strategies of diversification had not suddenly and necessarily become things which could only be effected through the centralized agency of the state. And in comparative international terms the relatively poor performance of the U.K. economy during these years is an important point to be borne in mind.

It might be claimed that the war, far from having little or no shock effect on British business, in some areas had a direct impact: wartime profits and the defeat of Germany lulled the senses and led to the belief that somehow peace would deliver to Britain the kind of economic ascendancy she had enjoyed in late-Victorian years. In this way responsibility can be shifted from individual businessmen to the war itself. In truth, however, to the extent that this was a factor it would be a case not of what the war caused but of what it revealed of the poor judgment of British entrepreneurs. As has been shown, moreover, there is clear evidence that over the latter years of the war, when many misguided investment decisions were being made, businessmen were worried about the prospect of postwar German competition.[80]

British businessmen in a range of major industries failed to exploit the benefits and opportunities which the war gave them. It may well be too harsh to say that they learned nothing and forgot nothing as a consequence of the First World War; but at all events they demonstrated clearly their natural liking for 'business as usual'.

[80] Cline, 'Winding Down the War Economy'.

11

Ideology or pragmatism? The nationalization of coal, 1916–46*

BARRY SUPPLE

From some viewpoints, coalmining seems a quintessential nationalized industry – troubled by powerful economic and social forces, directly dependent on public support and subsidy for the maintenance of harmony and the enhancement of productivity, plagued by lagging efficiency. Yet the transfer of the country's collieries to public ownership on 1 January 1947 was envisaged as a *solution* to many of these problems, which had been troubling the industry since the First World War. Indeed, public ownership can be represented as an end as well as a beginning – as the culmination of a political and economic controversy that had dogged the mining industry for at least thirty years.

When it finally came, nationalization was a victory for a surprising variety of interest groups and opinions. It was also surprisingly uncontentious. Quite apart from the miners' and the Labour Party's commitment, the Liberal Party were wavering and the Conservatives favoured a substantial increase in public control. Indeed, according to *The Economist* in April 1945, 'Support for the principle of public ownership of the mines is now very wide indeed, extending probably to two and a half of the three parties.'[1]

More than this, there were businessmen and engineers in the industry – fervent advocates of structural change and technical modernization – who had abandoned any hope that the traditional patterns of ownership and control could be reformed on a voluntary basis.[2] Most of these favoured some form of collective industrial self-management. But even among the coal owners (that is, the leading shareholders and managers of colliery firms) there was undoubtedly a large minority who acknowledged the

* Research for this chapter was undertaken as part of a history of the coal industry sponsored by the National Coal Board. I am grateful to the Board for its generous support and to Sonia Supple, Stephanie Tailby and Nick Tiratsoo for their help with the gathering of data and the formulation of ideas. I alone am responsible for the conclusions.

[1] 18 April 1945, p. 220 (quoted in A. A. Rogow, *The Labour Government and British Industry, 1945–51* (London, 1955), p. 155).

[2] See, for example, 'A Charter for Coal', March 1944, in Durham Coal Owners' Association Records, vol. 63 (Durham County Records Office).

inevitability of public ownership because they were despondent about economic prospects under private enterprise. Twenty-seven years earlier, David Lloyd George, in a weary response to the political pressures of 1919, had predicted that sooner or later the nationalization of the troublesome coal industry would have to take place. By 1945–6 this political insight seemed justified by events: nationalization had been stripped of the acrimony and disagreement that had surrounded it in 1919. It had become a pragmatic as well as an ideological step, reflecting enthusiastic or resigned acceptance of the need for public ownership, and reflecting even more widespread exasperation with the failure and obduracy of the owners, who for a generation had appeared incapable of running their industry successfully or harmoniously.

To historians, public ownership appeared to have been inevitable because there was no viable alternative policy for technical modernization. There is also, however, another strand to the accepted story: although an article of faith that had been accepted and discussed for decades, nationalization seemed a singularly badly prepared step. For this we have the word of the man who, above all others, ought to have known – Lord Shinwell:

> For the whole of my political life [he later wrote] I had listened to Party Speakers advocating state ownership and control of the coal mines....I had believed, as other members had, that in the Party archives a blue-print was ready. Now, as Minister of Fuel and Power, I found that nothing practical and tangible existed.

And another Cabinet Minister, Jim Griffiths, subsequently claimed that the new Minister had been given two pamphlets – one a Welsh translation of the other![3]

In fact, the preparation for nationalization consisted less in the drawing-up of detailed plans than in the experience of industrial processes and the vicissitudes of government intervention over the previous generation. The origins of public ownership were to be found neither in pamphlets nor in ideologies.

The winter of 1916–17 is the most convenient starting-point for the modern history of coal nationalization, since it was the juncture at which the stresses of war produced a fundamental reconsideration of the structure of the economy and the allocation of its resources. In the case of coal mining it was a particularly fateful moment because of the decision – antedating Lloyd George's displacement of Asquith – to take the industry into public control.

This control of coal mining was undertaken in order to ensure an

[3] E. Shinwell, *Conflict Without Malice* (London, 1955), pp. 172–3; Lord Wigg, *George Wigg* (London, 1972), pp. 123–4.

adequate and steady supply of one of the war's essential raw materials. But the threat to coal supplies came not from any straightforward deficiencies in the working of market forces. Rather, it came – as it was often to do – from manpower shortages and the notorious turbulence of labour relations in the industry, especially in South Wales (where over 200000 men had successfully initiated an outright strike in July 1915). Various expedients (including the nationalization of the pits producing coal for the navy) were discussed in 1915–16, but the deep-seated resentments between miners and owners, the miners' suspicions of the owners' presumed profiteering, and the unprecedented bargaining strength that had accrued to them because of wartime shortages, continued to threaten a breakdown in production. By the early winter of 1916 – and not for the last time – the owners' refusal to compromise lost them sympathy where they might have expected to retain it: 'their own management', argued the President of the Board of Trade, 'was leading straight to a general strike'. The Welsh district's 'recurrent disputes and unrest' threatened strategic supplies every three months and could only be ended by the government 'assuming control over the coalfield in the national interest'.[4] To this the Cabinet agreed without demur. By February, control had been extended to all British coalfields.

As with public ownership in 1946, control in 1916–17 was either welcomed or acknowledged to be inevitable. In the last resort, however, it was introduced to purchase the wartime cooperation of the labour force – to reassure the miners that the owners would not benefit from shortages. It therefore related far more to the problems of labour than to the mechanics of production.

'Control' was far removed from 'nationalization' however; and the mines continued to be managed by their owners. Nevertheless, by the standards of the pre-1913 world, it looked like a major piece of at least 'socialization'. Wages were for the first time settled nationally; prices were controlled. During the war the allocation of supplies was based on administrative not competitive decisions, and transport was centrally coordinated and merged. Above all, however, the material positions and aspirations of the miners were enhanced, while the varying profits of different districts were pooled, allowing the super-profits of exports to subsidize the pricing of inland supplies, and, more significantly, enabling the less productive districts to pay higher wages. Indeed, as long as the shortage of coal persisted (in effect, until the end of 1920), the miners achieved an extraordinary accretion of effective power. In spite of the existence of a Coal Mines Department, on most of the really important

---

[4] Runciman Papers, University of Newcastle: WR147, 'The South Wales Coalfield. November 1916'.

issues (wage negotiations, for example, or the privileged treatment of miners in relation to conscription) the miners insisted on *direct* access to the highest ministerial levels.[5]

In fact, even under public control, the miners' union preferred the ways of collective bargaining to any elaborate corporate consultation. Indeed, they quite explicitly rejected the idea of a formalized advisory role in a bureaucratic structure, in favour of a more remote possibility – namely direct workers' control, preferably within a nationalized industry. In their annual conference of 1918 they adopted a motion urging public ownership of the mines 'with joint control by the workmen and the State' and demanded that, pending nationalization, the existing joint advisory committee 'should be vested with direct power jointly with the Coal Controller' since 'the present form of Government control of the mines tends to develop into pure bureaucratic administration, which is in itself as equally inimical to the interests of the workmen and of the industry as was the uncontrolled form of private ownership'.

These developments were psychological and institutional preludes to the perturbations of 1919. In the summer of 1918 the Miners' Federation of Great Britain had formulated its prospective postwar claims – notably, a substantial increase in wages, a reduction in hours, and nationalization combined with participation in management. And it was the formal submission of these demands, backed by the threat of a national strike early in 1919, which precipitated the crisis enquiry of the Sankey Commission. More than this, the initiative of the miners' representative on the Commission transformed it, in Beatrice Webbs' words, into a 'revolutionary tribunal' and elevated its proceedings into 'a state trial of the coal owners and the royalty owners, culminating with the question, "why not nationalize the mines?"'[6]

The Sankey hearings were themselves an amazing phenomenon.[7] In public and much publicized disputation, the coal owners were completely outclassed and humiliated. The miners and their allies (Sidney Webb, R. H. Tawney and L. G. Chiozza Money) drew attention to the social miseries of mining communities, the wartime profits of colliery companies, and the cost-saving supposedly derived from the central control of the industry. They demanded joint control and public ownership. On the other

---

[5] For the history of the industry during the First World War, see R. A. S. Redmayne, *The British Coalmining Industry During the War* (London, 1923).

[6] Margaret I. Cole (ed.), *Beatrice Webb's Diaries, 1919–1924* (London, 1952), p. 152 (12 March 1919).

[7] In its early stages the Sankey enquiry was mentioned by *The Times* as a precedent to be followed (18 March 1919, p. 11b: 'it has thrown much light on dark places'). However, the newspaper was much less impressed with the later proceedings.

side, the owners were at first reduced to bluster and fragile assertions. Caught unawares by events and moods, they had not appreciated how far the circumstances of control and shortages had given the initiative to the miners and the advocates of continued state intervention. Decontrol, competition and the restoration of 1913 might not, after all, be inevitable. However eccentric the composition of the Royal Commission (the miners controlled 50 per cent of the membership) a majority came to favour some form of nationalization. Indeed, even before it had considered the issue of public ownership in detail, its chairman and businessmen members (other than the coal owners) had pronounced unanimously that 'on the evidence already given, the present system of ownership and control...stands condemned, and some other system must be substituted for it, either nationalization or a method of unification by national purchase and/or by joint control'.[8]

Although this – the Sankey Commission's most important recommendation – came to nothing, the enquiry was an outstanding event in the industrial politics of coal. For a few months it made the unprecedentedly radical step of nationalization seem feasible. There were even many members of the local coal owners' associations who felt that public ownership was inevitable, and some who welcomed it as a way of realizing on their assets.[9] More generally, business anxieties about the economic consequences of sharing control with a militant union anxious to increase its members' share of the industry's proceeds led to an expressed preference for outright nationalization, albeit wrapped in a veiled threat to sabotage the industry by abandoning it. In a notorious statement Lord Gainford said:

I am authorized to say, on behalf of the Mining Association, that if the owners are not to be left complete executive control, they will decline to accept the responsibility of carrying on the industry, and though they regard nationalization as disastrous to the country, they feel that they would, in such event, be driven to the only alternative – nationalization on fair terms.[10]

What is clear is that in 1919, in the face of threatened social upheaval, there was an important if transitory shift in public opinion. Nationalization, it was hoped, would solve a crisis of labour relations. This was Sir John Sankey's argument. Public ownership, he reported, was necessary in the main because it was likely to be the best way to dispel 'the present atmosphere of distrust and recrimination'. Harmony in industrial relations

---

[8] *Coal Industry Commission Act. Interim Report by the Honourable Mr Justice Sankey, C.B.E., (Chairman), Mr Arthur Balfour, Sir Arthur Duckham, K.C.B., M.I.C.E., and Sir Thomas Royden, Bart., M.P., 20th March*, P.P. 1919 xi, Cmd 84 (1919), p. 5.

[9] See Barry Supple, '"No Bloody Revolutions but for Obstinate Reactions"? British Coalowners in their Context, 1919–20', in D. C. Coleman and Peter Mathias (eds.), *Enterprise and History: Essays in Honour of Charles Wilson* (Cambridge, 1984), pp. 223–4.

[10] P.P. 1919 xii, p. 810.

therefore presupposed the elimination of private enterprise. It was a widely shared view.

In the last resort, then, nationalization in 1919 – as with government control in 1916 – was seen, not as a technical, nor even as an ideological, step; but as an emollient to the grievances of the workforce. The owners went even further. The recommendation, they claimed, was extorted from a Commission (whose chairman had lost his nerve) by the threat of a national strike in an atmosphere of national panic. At every private sitting, their representative claimed, Sidney Webb, 'the stage manager for the other side', reminded the Commissioners 'that all we had to do was prevent a strike'. This was a jaundiced but nevertheless accurate view. For it is well known that Cabinet spokesmen urged Sankey and the 'independent' businessmen to make a recommendation that went some way towards public ownership. If they did not, argued Tom Jones, 'there would be a Strike...of such magnitude as might lead to something like a social revolution'.[11] There was certainly little discussion of the practical implications or likely consequences of nationalization.

Yet all this was a flurry in the spring and summer of 1919. As things turned out – in spite of the miners' bargaining strength, the owners' apprehensions and the public's expectations – the structure and ownership of the coal industry remained unchanged. Part of the reason for the union's failure lay in the monolithic character of existing political forces: once the owners had pulled themselves together and developed their publicity machine, they were able to muster sufficient support among Conservative M.P.s to block the Cabinet's serious consideration of public ownership.[12] But the campaign for nationalization also foundered on other obstacles: on the Cabinet's purposeful prevarication, which allowed time to elapse and the crisis atmosphere to abate; on the considerable and speedy concessions to a large part of the miners' case in the way of higher wages, lower hours and the promise of severe profit-restrictions; and above all, perhaps, on the loss of enthusiasm for structural reform among the rank and file of the miners, and certainly among their trade union allies, once their material aspirations had been met.

In retrospect, the Sankey episode can easily be interpreted as the slick betrayal of idealistic miners by a cynical government playing for time. But this is too facile a judgment. First, because the miners were defeated by dint of their own strategy: they 'lost all because they would not be content with less than all'.[13] Second, because the government's attitude was not,

[11] Transcript of meeting between representatives of the Mining Association and Lloyd George, 14 November 1919 (N.C.B. Library, P622:338); Tom Jones to David Lloyd George, 14 and 18 March 1919: House of Lords Records Office, F23/4/34 and 38.
[12] See Supple, '"No Bloody Revolutions"', p. 229.
[13] Baldwin to Lloyd George, 30 January 1922: P[ublic] R[ecords] O[ffice], POWE 221/13.

234 BARRY SUPPLE

and could not be, utterly negative. The fact is that after much pained heart-searching, the Cabinet was apparently prepared to accept a far-reaching programme of industrial reform. In rejecting outright national-ization, Lloyd George proposed three main departures: a welfare programme (to be financed by a levy on coal); the public ownership of mineral royalties; and the restructuring of the coal-mining industry into large, regional corporations with strong representation of the miners on their boards.[14] Historians have sometimes implied that this last proposal was also cynical – that it was made on the assumption that the miners would reject it. And certainly the government appeared relieved when the miners' union declined to compromise over its doomed campaign for full-blooded nationalization. Nevertheless, the Cabinet records show perfect-ly serious discussions of these alternative systems, and of quasi-public companies. What is interesting is that the official proposals foundered on the miners' opposition to what would have been an embryonic form of 'corporatism'. As had happened during the war, the Miners' Federation declined to cooperate in tripartite 'crisis management'. In the words of their President, they preferred the old system of private enterprise 'to setting up trusts which might be trusts between the miners and the mineowners …against the general public'.[15]

After the events of 1919, the return of the coal-mining industry to private enterprise became inevitable. Nevertheless, when the international market for coal collapsed in the winter of 1920–1, thus obliging the government to relinquish financial responsibility (and therefore control), political extrication did not prove easy. As the owners attempted to reduce wages and the miners attempted to prolong the pooling of profits to cross-subsidize earnings, the state was drawn into wage negotiations. Admittedly, the miners were beaten in their three-month strike; but they did secure a national wages agreement providing for an embryonic form of profit-sharing within districts, and the government gave a large subsidy to mitigate the speed at which wages were reduced. By the summer of 1921, the coal industry had finally returned to the basic system of ownership and control that it had known before 1914. It was, however, old-fashioned private enterprise with a difference. For the slump opened a period of some two decades of almost universal and continuous stagnation.*

---

[14] *Hansard*, Commons Debates, 18 August 1919.

[15] P. B. Johnson, *Land Fit for Heroes: The Planning of British Reconstructions, 1916–1919* (London, 1968), p. 477.

* In the rest of this chapter, the coal industry is considered as if it were a single industry, uniformly affected by economic and political vicissitudes. Although convenient, this approach is misleading, since 'coal' was represented by a variety of products (i.e. markets) and the circumstances, prosperity and relationships of its production varied markedly

Overseas competition, industrial retardation, economies in the use of coal and substitute fuels – all transformed the booming industry of 1913 into the first of Britain's lame ducks. The capacity of the mines was simply too large for available or prospective markets. By the late 1930s (themselves years of relative buoyancy) output and employment were still 20 per cent below the levels of 1913.

Obviously, when the extent and implications of this long-run decline were appreciated after 1926, they gave rise to wide-ranging discussions of policies and expedients designed to cushion the blow or revive the industry's fortunes. At the time, however, the earlier vigorous debate about nationalization was not renewed. On the one hand, the union was in no position to force the issue back onto the political agenda. (Its gesture in that direction at the Samuel Commission's enquiries in 1925–6 had a desperate frailty, for its real, and doomed, preoccupation was to defend existing wages and hours.) On the other hand, and more tellingly, in the atmosphere of the 1920s and 1930s, nationalization never appeared a realistic solution for the problems of an industry beset by chronic unemployment, falling sales, a lack of investment incentives and surplus capacity. Reorganization was constantly recommended; public ownership hardly at all.

However, the absence of any serious consideration of formal public ownership did not by any means preclude the active pursuit of elaborate government intervention in the industry's affairs. After the failure of wage repression in 1926, the pressure of circumstances was inevitably towards voluntary and then compulsory reform. From 1927 the industry seemed on the slope to devastation. By June 1928 unemployment in coal mining had reached 25 per cent of the labour force (wholly and temporarily out of work) and it was to get much worse. And the coal owners (even in South Wales, where the class war had been at its fiercest) accepted the fact that wages could not be forced any lower and that such reductions were in any case not the solution to the industry's problems.[16]

Instead, the industry began to experiment with output restrictions and rationing on a district basis. Local cartels were formed to assign production quotas and, hopefully, to control prices. Although the purely voluntary character of these selling schemes undermined their effectiveness, they

from area to area – and even from mine to mine within regions. However, the economic trends and political pressures did (very broadly) apply to the great bulk of the industry, and its parts had sufficient in common to be perceived and to act, for most purposes, in a common framework – even though the variety made coherence or unity of action, whether by miners or owners, difficult to attain.

[16] See the records of the Scottish Coal Owners Association (in the Scottish Records Office) for 9 May and 9 July 1927, and of the Monmouthshire and South Wales Coal Owners Association (in the National Library of Wales) for 19 August and November 1927.

were really remarkably radical for such an individualistic industry. Meanwhile, radicalism was also stirring – however feebly – in government circles. In October 1928 the Minister of Labour, Steel-Maitland, wrote to the Prime Minister: 'Imagine our charge sheet on the Day of Judgement: "The greatest material evil of your day was worklessness. Did you try to diagnose it?" What could we say?' To a large extent, of course, this was a cry of desperation. But Steel-Maitland was also toying with grandiose schemes for coal and steel rationalization as part of a new Unionist industrial policy. In particular, he was exploring means by which the state might provide financial aid or even exert direct compulsion to oblige colliery firms to merge in order to streamline their capacity and to modernize their equipment.[17] But what the advocates of rationalization had not yet fully appreciated (quite apart from the ideological and financial obstacles to such a programme) was the paradox of reorganization amid unemployment – the impossible attempt to combine higher productivity with the maintenance of employment in a stagnant market.

The pursuit of a policy for the mining industry in the last months of Baldwin's Unionist administration – although unproductive – was a final acknowledgment of the failure of market forces or traditional remedies to touch the problem of chronic unemployment. Even so, when the Labour government attempted to reform the industry in 1929–30 it had little to do with the crisis of worklessness. Instead, as in 1919, the attempt was a response to pressure from the miners' union to improve the conditions of those in work. Still smarting from their defeat in 1926, the miners now insisted that the Labour Party should carry out its pledge to reduce the length of the underground working day. But the government realized that, in order to do this without precipitating a renewed round of wage cuts, it would have to increase the net proceeds of the industry. And it did this through the Coal Mines Act of 1930, which provided for the compulsory formation of cartels in each of the coal fields. As a result, and without any rending controversy, the distributive side of the coal industry moved – with manifest relief – into a web of social control. At the same time, however, the Liberal Party (on whose votes the Labour government depended) was reluctant to accept state-sponsored monopoly arrangements without some reassurances about greater efficiency. Hence the 1930 Act included a provision creating the Coal Mines Reorganization Commission. This body was charged with the encouragement of colliery amalgamations and with the more productive grouping of coal mines. It reflected (however unsuccessful its efforts turned out to be) that official impulse towards 'rationalization' which was the nearest that inter-war governments came to systematic industrial intervention.

[17] Cambridge University Library, Baldwin Papers, 130/10 (22 October 1928).

In the event, neither 1930s governments nor the Reorganization Commission had any noticeable influence on the structure of coal mining. Superficially, this was due to the Commission's practical powerlessness in the face of a badly framed law and to determined non-cooperation from the owners. But there was also a deeper reason for the Commission's innocuousness.

The advocacy of rationalization in the staple industries had originated in the pursuit of efficiency in the 1920s. But by the 1930s it was based on the widespread realization that their capacity was hopelessly in excess of any feasible market. In these circumstances, rationalization (as with much industrial policy today) was envisaged as a means of closing factories and mines, reducing manpower needs, and streamlining the industry to reduce excessive supply and costs. At the core of the process, therefore, lay the reduction of the labour force in the basic industries. With unemployment rates running at 20 per cent and more – and in the coal industry at 30 and 40 per cent – a government would have had to have been peculiarly foolhardy or insensitive to pursue a policy of rationalization in any determined way. In 1930, for example, Sir Oswald Mosley, rejecting 'the economics of the last Century', argued that it was inconceivable that any increase in the productivity of the staple industries would increase sales sufficiently to outweigh the reduction in employment which would result from greater efficiency.[18] And in the winter of 1933–4 the Secretary for Mines resisted proposals that the amalgamation provisions of the 1930 act should be enforced, on the grounds that regular employment in the industry had fallen by more than 20 per cent since it had been passed. Further, he defended the continued cartelization of the industry even though it perpetuated inefficiency: to abolish the marketing controls would be to create a further 150000 unemployed; the Coal Mines Act was, in his words, 'a buffer between the Community and economic and social strife in the coal industry'.[19] But if, during the early 1930s, the government was inhibited from pursuing ruthless reform, it was in no one's private interest to bear the cost of buying up and closing down excess or inefficient capacity. The industry was too large, but the benefits of reducing it – even the benefits in terms of profits – could not be captured by those who might choose to invest in the reduction.*

[18] P.R.O. CAB 23/209/220–59 (23 January 1930); CAB 24/211/460–5 (1 May 1930).
[19] P.R.O. PREM 1/172 (12 December 1933); CAB 24/247/40–52 (1 February 1934). The owners – determined to resist the C.M.R.C. – made political capital out of the social costs of any extensive amalgamations: COAL 12/171 (15 March 1933); POWE 22/55 (24 and 31 March 1933).
* The coal industry's instability was notorious. Marginal firms constantly hovered over the market for coal and the immobility of capital once invested meant that collieries rarely went out of business on a decisive or permanent basis. By the same token, ostensibly uneconomic firms could continue operations for long periods, or become quiescent only to reappear on the market if prices increased.

It was a classic case of social (i.e. general) benefits justifying public action – but of social costs immobilizing political initiatives. As Sir Ernest Gowers (chairman of the Coal Mines Reorganization Commission) put it – with some exasperation:

the real question is not whether concentration shall take place or not; it is whether the process shall be left to the haphazard forces of sporadic bankruptcies and casual purchases or brought about designedly by the industry's being so organized as to give the power to those who control it to adopt this policy as they think fit.[20]

Rational as this sort of observation was, it was a counsel of unrealistic perfection. In the depth of the slump, no administration could possibly create even more derelict communities. The most powerful political argument against a policy of industrial rationalization was then, as it remains today, precisely that it might be successful.

Once again, therefore, considerations of social harmony determined the main thrust of industrial policy. There was, however, this difference: in 1919 the government had been brought to the verge of nationalization by the fear of social unrest generated by the power of the miners during a boom in demand; thirteen or fourteen years later it was constrained to accept a policy of inaction by the fear of social unrest generated by a collapse of demand. By the early 1930s the miners were, essentially, placated by a shoring-up of a somewhat ramshackle capitalism.

Yet a policy of complete inaction was hardly feasible. Once the very worst of the unemployment had passed, the government began a more vigorous exploration of ways in which the industry might be reformed. It so happened that some senior coal owners were beginning to worry about their political vulnerability. In 1933, for example, a leading Scottish owner (Sir Adam Nimmo) warned his colleagues that:

Whatever Government may be in power...behind this great basal industry...there is always a great pressing social problem which the country cannot neglect...It is my sincere conviction...that unless we do take the common problems of the industry into our own hands...there will be an increasing amount of [government interference]...Every Government, it does not matter which ticket it may hold, is a Government that cannot have regard...for the *individual* interests within an industry.[21]

And in the winter of 1935–6 the owners proved remarkably conciliatory in accepting a national wage claim on behalf of the miners and in participating in a national consultative scheme. On the other hand, however, they remained adamant in their resistance to any externally imposed restructuring of the industry. Over the years, therefore, the feeling

---

[20] P.R.O. POWE 16/517II (21 December 1933).
[21] *Mining Association of Great Britain, Annual Report for 1933* (London, 1934), pp. 10–11.

grew – even in the most orthodox of official circles – that the owners would not change unless they were forced to change. This was certainly Sir Ernest Gowers' opinion. Writing in 1935 and referring to the miners' arguments of 1926 (that if wage cuts were conceded the owners would postpone industrial reform indefinitely), Gowers said:

They were right. They made their sacrifice under duress, and for the next ten years the owners gave themselves over to an orgy of cutting their own and one another's throats, threw away with both hands the opportunities given to them by Parliament to reorganize themselves, and obstructed by every means in their power the attempts of the Coal Mines Reorganization Commission to do it for them.[22]

The fact was that the owners were ready enough to accept the benefits of a regulated market. But this only made their continued resistance to official pressure to reorganize the mines the more obnoxious to their critics. 'Bourbonism of the type deployed by the mineowners', said *The Economist* in 1938, 'invites a campaign to end "economic royalism" once and for all.'[23] And even *The Times* exploded against what it called the owners' 'unmeasured language' which was 'ill-suited to the mouths of those whose industry was rescued from suicide by the action of the State'.[24]

The occasion of these outbursts was the controversy surrounding a fairly startling departure by the Tory Party. After discussions which had begun in 1932 and legislative proposals which went through a variety of forms in 1935–8, the government, by the Coal Act of 1938, nationalized the country's coal royalties and provided that control of those royalties (which would take effect in 1942) was to be exercised by a strengthened Coal Commission. More than this, the Commission was to have enlarged powers to initiate and enforce official schemes of colliery amalgamation. In conjunction with the royalty owners, the Mining Association mounted an elaborate publicity campaign against these measures. It failed, of course, to prevent the nationalization of royalties; but in spite of its counter-productive effect on the owners' reputation, the vigour of their opposition succeeded in retaining severe restraints on executive action to secure colliery mergers.

Nevertheless, by 1938 public intervention in the affairs of the coal industry had progressed a long way from the reluctant tinkering of the early 1920s. Its marketing and pricing policies were subject to systematic regulation; its raw material was to be brought into public ownership; the government was constantly sensitive to its political and social implications (as well as to its broad economic needs); and a state commission – with real if modest powers – was preparing to mount an assault on the

[22] P.R.O. CAB 27/597 (1 July 1935).
[23] 5 February 1938, p. 277.   [24] 3 February 1938, p. 13b.

independence of colliery companies, thereby, in the words of its chairman, testing the 1938 legislation 'to destruction'.[25] As a wartime civil servant pointed out in 1943, 'no other industry had so nearly brought about a revolution in the structure of industry as a whole as the coal mining industry did in the period between the two wars'.[26]

What is striking is how much of this had been brought about not by 'corporatism' but by 'industrial politics' – that is by confrontation and (occasionally) compromise – rather than by the creation of harmonious institutions incorporating the state, labour and capital. Much of the time, of course, the industry had been left to its own devices. But insofar as intervention had taken place, it had been stimulated by crisis – by the threat of strike or lockout, by the collapse of markets and prices, by the need to pay a 'social wage'. More than this, the industry had successfully resisted economic reform either because its interest groups had succeeded in entrenching their material ambitions, or because official anxiety about social instability had taken precedence in policy-making. Even the legislation of 1938 – which to some observers seemed to promise a new industrial order – was hedged by legal and procedural difficulties which filled its original supporters with gloom. In the event, the validity of neither viewpoint was tested. In 1939, as the international atmosphere deteriorated, the coal owners became less accommodating in their discussions with the Coal Commission, and the Commission itself brought its enquiries to a halt.

The Second World War proved to be a powerful if temporary barrier to any fundamental reorganization of the industry.[27] At the same time, however, the crisis of production which punctuated the years 1941–5 greatly sharpened the controversy about the structure of coal mining, and focused it quite decisively on the possible role of public control and ownership.

The wartime problem of coal was obviously quite different from that of the inter-war years. No longer was there a burden of surplus capacity; now, the perennial anxiety was over coal shortages. Government intervention was therefore mustered to encourage higher productivity, to increase the labour supply and mitigate problems of industrial relations, to maintain and coordinate output, and to secure the cooperation of a labour force which was resentful of its past experiences and relative standing. Yet the

---

[25] Sir Ernest Gowers, 'The Coal Industry after the War' (16 January 1942): P.R.O. POWE 26/429.
[26] J. S. Fulton, 'Organization of the Coal Mining Industry' (Spring 1943): P.R.O. POWE 26/420.
[27] For the detailed history of the industry in 1939–45, see W. H. B. Court, Coal (London, 1951).

coalition government was inhibited from any drastic reorganization by the political and administrative risks of innovation. And just as the control of labour was rendered impossible by the sensitivity of the miners, so the public control of industrial structures was ruled out by the possible threat to the morale and the cooperation of the owners.

In 1941, for example, Sir Ernest Gowers requested permission for the Coal Commission to recommence the collection of statistical information – so that, when the time came, the Commission would be ready to press for schemes of reorganization (in his words) 'before comfortable people have time to sit back with the idea that they can just go on in the old ways'. But even this data-gathering exercise was forbidden. The President of the Board of Trade said that he 'was particularly anxious not to have the Coal Owners upset'. Indeed, Gowers' arguments (he talked of the owners' 'right wing' arming themselves for 'the tactics of obstruction that have served the die-hards so well in the past') were hardly reassuring on the point of controversy.[28]

An even more urgent and controversial issue came to the surface in the spring and summer of 1942. By then it seemed very likely that the output of coal would be insufficient to ensure adequate supplies in the winter of 1942–3 – with very serious consequences for the war effort and civilian morale. At the same time (and clearly related to the problem of production) the miners were beginning to protest about their wages, which were lower than those in many munitions factories, and were falling even further behind because of the operations of pre-war agreements. As Hugh Gaitskell warned Hugh Dalton (President of the Board of Trade) in February 1942, 'Politically, the fuel position is...full of dynamite.'[29] This judgment was soon confirmed when it proved politically impossible to introduce fuel rationing. On the other hand, it was obvious that the existing situation could not be allowed to continue. A much greater measure of public control was judged necessary in order to concentrate production, improve technical standards and encourage mechanization. Even so, the coalition government rejected not merely nationalization (which the miners had advocated) but any direct government control of the running and finances of the mines. Instead, a Ministry of Fuel and Power was established. In principle, the new ministry could order mine managers to pursue specific policies. But in practice the managers were still employed by, and in the long run dependent on, coal owners. This was the so-called 'dual control' system – an ambiguous and unsatisfactory arrangement.

At the same time that these halting steps towards a centrally directed industrial policy were taken, there was a more fundamental move towards

[28] P.R.O. POWE 22/127 (1941).
[29] London School of Economics, Dalton Papers, 7/4/lv.

a national scheme of wage determination – something that had been the miners' aim ever since the First World War. By 1942 the relative harmony which had characterized national industrial relations throughout the war was beginning to break down. In the case of the coal industry, with its profoundly unsatisfactory inter-war history, the unsettled and anxious state of the labour force was particularly enfeebling to the war effort – impairing both productivity and the willingness of miners to stay in the industry. The situation was seriously aggravated by the apparently ineradicable suspicion of private ownership and the relatively low pay which was a sour and continuing grievance. As a result the coalition government granted extensive concessions. On the one hand, it attempted to reassure the miners by giving an undertaking that the new controls would last until Parliament had come to a definite conclusion about future organization. On the other hand, it created an independent tribunal which – as is the way of such tribunals – was very generous to the miners' claims: wages were substantially increased, a national minimum established and the tribunal rejected the owners' plea that these flat-rate increases should be made conditional on improvements in output and attendance. More than this – although it took a longer enquiry to achieve – a national system for future wage determination was created. Power and necessity had at last helped the miners realize their long-cherished ambition.

The framework of control and labour relations established in 1942 lasted throughout the rest of the war. But within it, and on the basis of the long-lasting exasperation with the coal owners, pressures were engendered which led not simply to nationalization – but nationalization without tears. Those forces operated at three levels: the unwavering support of the miners for expropriation and the growing commitment of the Labour Party to the same end; the more covert but in the end more influential discussions among civil servants and technocrats; and the unresolved difficulties of coal production and the resulting tensions within the coalition.

In 1942, when the miners accepted the compromise of a Ministry of Fuel and Power, Hugh Dalton wrote that they had at least learned that their traditional policy of '"all or nowt" always ends in nowt', and that, in agreeing to dual control, they had followed the best political advice: 'keep on nibbling at the cheese, boys.'[30]

In fact, however, the Miners' Federation maintained their claim for public ownership throughout the war – a case which was based on some

---

[30] Dalton Papers, Diary, 12 June 1942. This echoed opinion which, certainly throughout the 1920s, had blamed the miners' obstinacy for the comprehensive nature of their defeats.

rather vague claims concerning organizational efficiency and on seemingly more cogent reasoning about the deleterious effects of a system of private profit on the morale of the labour force. For its part, the Labour Party, while its leading members were committed to nationalization as a principle, could not publicly press for public ownership except as a long-run goal. But the issue was kept alive by back-bench arguments and by a Labour Party Coal and Power Sub-Committee (one of thirteen on postwar reconstruction). The Sub-Committee, which met between October 1941 and March 1944, recommended a 'unified industry under public ownership and control', and envisaged a public corporation.[31]

The miners' position was equally clear. But although they continued to advocate nationalization, they used their enormous industrial power (as they had done in the First World War and then in 1919) not to pursue a reform of the industry's structure but, rather, to defend their autonomy and improve their material position. They pressed hard and successfully for better services, for easier labour controls and for improved wages. They utterly refused to contemplate not merely increased hours but also those marginal adjustments at the end of shifts that would have improved the smooth operations of mines. They resisted most attempts at managerial or bureaucratic disciplines – most dramatically at Betteshanger in 1942 when 1600 men went on strike and the government ensured that their fines were withdrawn. And early in 1944, as the war reached a critical stage, they initiated extensive strikes in support of wage claims, thereby losing much of the sympathy of civilians and soldiers that they had earlier gained. Even so, the government was again obliged to give in: wages were once more increased, and the existing levels were guaranteed until December 1947 – an undertaking which both reassured the labour force about an otherwise uncertain future, and obliged the state to continue its financial intervention and control.

In spite of all this, however, the performance of the industry, and its labour productivity, deteriorated throughout the war. The government, by its generous intervention on the miners' behalf, succeeded in keeping the industry going and just about maintaining supplies. But it was a precarious process. For neither full employment nor high wages and bonus schemes stimulated higher output. The miners had succeeded in reversing their material deprivation. They had become one of the highest-paid groups in the country (on an hourly basis, perhaps the highest). But their memories and prejudices remained disconcertingly long, their industrial cooperation disconcertingly grudging. In the end, it was that intransigence, rather than

[31] Labour Party Archives, RDR 157 and 255. Printed as *Coal and Power Report by the National Executive Committee of the Labour Party to be presented to the Annual Conference to be held in London from May 29th to June 2nd 1944* (1944).

any cogent argument or technical reasoning, which was the miners' main contribution to the securing of public ownership.

As far as nationalization was concerned, the activities and opinions of civil servants were much more directly influential than those of the miners and the Labour Party. I have already mentioned Sir Ernest Gowers' exasperation with the owners in the 1930s and 1941, and the efforts of the Coal Commission to oblige the industry to reorganize itself. Early in 1942 – even before the discussion of the production crisis which led to the creation of the Ministry of Fuel and Power – Gowers had produced a memorandum arguing that in the long run industrial reform would have to be forced on the owners. Large-scale reorganization was needed – and might only be acceptable with a large amount of public control. A public-corporation solution was the most reasonable aim.[32]

That was in January 1942. By the spring, the new President of the Board of Trade, Hugh Dalton, had replaced the chief civil servant at the Mines Department (described by Gaitskell as a real enemy of the war effort and a puppet of the coal traders)[33] with Lord Hyndley – who, like Gowers, advised Dalton 'that the coal industry should be run on Public Corporation lines', although they doubted if it would be feasible to introduce such a change in wartime because of the likely opposition and disruption.[34]

Gowers and Hyndley – together with more junior wartime civil servants, including John Fulton and Harold Wilson – formed the active core and principal entrepreneurs of a secret committee, established by the Minister of Fuel and Power in the autumn of 1942, to discuss the postwar organization of the coal-mining industry.

Such a step was not, of course, unique to coal. For example, in 1942 and 1943 reconstruction in the electricity supply industry was also subject to confidential enquiry. There, too, the outcome pointed in the direction of forceful public management and intervention.[35] But the Gowers Committee was operating in a much more sensitive area and its conclusions were therefore more dramatic, albeit less publicized. Indeed, only the need to placate the Committee's two businessmen members (neither of whom was from the coal industry) prevented an outright advocacy of nationalization. As it was, the agreed report recommended that the owners be given one more – strictly limited – chance to reorganize their firms into bigger, more efficient and more responsible amalgamations. If progress were not achieved within two years, then a public corporation should be forced on

[32] P.R.O. POWE 26/429 (16 January 1942); Memorandum for Coal Commission.
[33] Dalton Papers, 7/4/1 (? April 1942).
[34] Dalton Papers, Diary, 27 March 1942.
[35] Leslie Hannah, *Electricity Before Nationalization: A Study of the Development of the Electricity Supply Industry in Britain to 1948* (London, 1979), pp. 336ff.

the industry. In fact, the logic of all the arguments used pointed inescapably in this latter direction: the economies of operation demanded integrated and concentrated management, and in order to sustain it there would have to be unified financial control. But managerial and financial amalgamations could not be imposed on reluctant owners and shareholders (who in any case had 'made a terrible mess of things' in the inter-war years). In effect, public ownership was necessary because the civil servants had lost confidence in the industry's private enterprise. More than this, they recognized that it was politically impossible to return to 'undiluted private enterprise' after the war; that Parliament would 'not consider any step considered by public opinion to be retrograde' so that some element of public control was inevitable; and that such a step was needed because of 'the fundamental importance of labour in the industry, and the need to win its cooperation'.[36]

The Gowers Committee (the existence of which was concealed from the rest of Whitehall as well as from the industry) reported to the Minister, Gwilym Lloyd George, in the summer of 1943. Its report never surfaced into the decision-making reaches of government. But its arguments were rapidly becoming public property through the sheer force of circumstances. By the summer of 1943 it was becoming clear that the wartime problems of coal production had not been solved by the creation of a ministry and the imposition of 'dual control'. In June, Major Lloyd George confessed his frustrations to the War Cabinet and by October he advocated a drastic solution: the complete requisition of the mines by the state for the duration of the war, so that the government would have sole managerial and financial control.[37]

Nothing came even of this ministerial initiative. Yet Lloyd George's doubts about existing policy coincided with a renewed plea by the miners for public ownership as the only solution for the problem of low production. The result was a political crisis which could only be resolved by the personal intervention of the Prime Minister in one of his rare Commons performances on a matter relating to the civilian economy. And it was resolved in favour of the *status quo*. Churchill articulated the principle which maintained temporary unity of the coalition government: 'Everything for the War, whether controversial or not, and nothing controversial that is not *bona fide* needed for the War'.[38] And that, he argued, precluded coal nationalization. It was a masterly piece of imprecision (which in 1944 was also to fend off a political crisis in relation to the electricity supply industry that threatened the harmony not merely of the government but also of the

[36] Files in P.R.O. POWE 26/420 and POWE 20/429.
[37] P.R.O. PREM 4/9/5/524 (2 October 1943).
[38] *Hansard*, Commons Debates, 13 October 1943.

Conservative Party, where there were important fissures on the subject of a 'middle way' and a 'mixed economy').[39] The Prime Minister was no doubt influenced by all sorts of ideological as well as quite mundane political considerations. But the issue was also a pragmatic one. Churchill's *éminence grise*, Lord Cherwell, asserted that there were no practical arguments in favour of immediate public ownership, while even the suggestion that it might be possible would induce a disruptive wave of strikes to force the issue.[40]

In spite of the Commons' overwhelming support for a policy of caution, the short- and long-run anxieties which had produced the debate on nationalization did not disappear. Late in 1943 the Ministry of Fuel and Power was obliged to devise a more stringent form of regional control and intervention. In 1944, Gowers again activated the Coal Commission's statistical enquiries with the aim of preparing the ground for postwar reorganization – and was again ordered to stop.[41]

By this time, however, the discussions had moved onto a new plane. The relative failure of the control devised in 1942, the increase in the costs implied in the various wages awards, and the exposure of British mining to an embarrassing scrutiny by experts from both sides of the Atlantic, had all combined to focus attention on the industry's technical inefficiency. Even officially, wartime needs were no longer the only preoccupation. In September 1944, therefore, the Minister appointed a high-powered Technical Advisory Committee of mining engineers, the Reid Committee. Their report (in March 1945) was a devastating critique of British mining and its practices and organization. The significance of the report was two-fold. First, in the coal industry more than any other, questions of technique could not be dissociated from questions of organization and industrial relations. Hence, the Reid Committee's fundamental criticism and proposals extended beyond technology to the need to overhaul the industry's structure, so as to maximize investment and economies of scale; and to reform its labour relations, so as to eliminate the principal obstacles to improvement. Secondly, the report had a prodigious effect on public and political opinion. Both its explicit conclusion (that the industry needed a vast programme of modernization and reform) and its implicit arguments (that public initiative, compulsory amalgamation and some form of official control were necessary) were widely accepted. Indeed, they reinforced and solidified a very powerful public mood, which was exemplified by a parallel

[39] On the frailty of unity among Conservatives in relation to the role of the state in the electricity supply industry, see Hannah, *Electricity Before Nationalization*, pp. 345–6.
[40] P.R.O. PREM 4/9/5 (7 October 1943).
[41] It took him a further five months to get the Minister to make a public statement that it was the Ministry and not the Commission which had decided not to proceed: P.R.O. COAL 17/179 (25 January 1944 – 12 March 1945).

report from the Tory Reform Committee,[42] and echoed in widespread approval in the press. The Reid Report was a symbol that in coal, as in so many other fields, the road to 1945 was coming to an end.

In the winter of 1944–5, therefore, a sense of the need for radical reorganization was beginning to prevail. This applied even to the owners, among whom a minority of dissenters had already proposed enforced reform. Even before the Reid Report was produced, the Mining Association had published the result of its own enquiry, undertaken by its new President, Robert Foot, a distinguished businessman untainted by coal ownership. The Foot Report was a large squib, but a damp one. Its proposals for a voluntary and autonomous control board to oversee the whole industry, but manned exclusively by coal-owners, were rightly viewed as an unsatisfactory death-bed repentance – an apparent revolution that had come a decade too late. Now, even permanent civil servants allowed themselves to condemn the owners' proposals as 'half-baked', its presentation as 'absurd and repulsive', and its intent as 'sinister' and 'dangerous'.[43]

The bureaucrats were, however, unduly anxious, presumably because they could not sense which way the political winds were blowing. A Conservative victory in the General Election would no doubt have introduced confusion and hesitancy into industrial policy for coal. But given the climate of opinion (technical as well as lay), together with the political and economic realities of the industry, a return to conventional private enterprise was by now inconceivable. The industry was fragmented and its structures antiquated; wartime commitments concerning wages and structures, and the vital significance of coal supplies in reconstruction, precluded decontrol; the state could no longer even pretend to be indifferent to the industry's management and development policies. Most important of all, however, and underlying most other considerations, the industry's labour force – enjoying unparalleled power, as well as prosperity – would be decisively reluctant to accept, and certainly unwilling to cooperate in, any system other than a form of public ownership. The war seemed to have demonstrated beyond argument that the sullen opposition of the miners to the owners could and would sabotage any hopes for technical modernization and productivity increase under private enterprise. Nor was this just a question of work habits and wage claims. Among the *New Statesman & Nation's* arguments against the owners' plan and in favour of national-

---

[42] Q. Hogg *et al.* for the Tory Reform Committee, *A National Policy for Coal* (London, 1944).
[43] R. N. Quirk to Nott-Bower, 8 March 1945: P.R.O. POWE 23/108. Just over a year later Quirk was writing to Gowers urging him to make the case publicly that the industry would not be able to achieve a large output under private enterprise (POWE 28/108: 3 April 1946).

ization was the assertion that reorganization was essential, and that the workers' cooperation would be withheld from any regime of private enterprise – especially one which might dislodge considerable numbers of miners.[44] Given the desire to create a single large firm, or even a number of large firms, public ownership was probably the easiest way to curb the abuse of private monopoly and to ensure the ready provisions of substantial investment funds. But the most common reason for seeking it on pragmatic grounds was that which had led Sir John Sankey to advocate it in 1919: it was seen as a means (perhaps the last and only means) to improve human relations in an industry that was constantly liable to be crippled by labour unrest. For a generation, almost every departure in terms of organization and social control had derived from the same pressure. Now, the wheel had come full circle at a time when the opposition to public ownership had become innocuous.

It remains true, of course, that nationalization was attained by a Labour government which had a principled as well as a practical commitment to public ownership. But in the case of coal, the step was taken as smoothly and decisively as it was because of the experience of thirty years of industrial history, during which the Labour Party's clause IV principles and its analyses of the economic system were fairly marginal to events. More than this, when it came, nationalization was not based on any very detailed consideration of forms and structures: Shinwell's subsequent complaint that a generation of discussion had left him no specific guidance was essentially true. On the other hand there had been plenty of formal enquiries into coal mining. In fact Shinwell himself had chaired a joint committee of the Labour Party and the unions as recently as the spring of 1945. And the new Minister could, and did, benefit from the advice of well-informed and committed civil servants who were cooperative, even enthusiastic, on the subject of public ownership in coal mining. At the same time, however, it was unreasonable to imagine that much detailed planning for nationalization could have been undertaken before 1945. Rather, the problem was that the Labour government's legislative pro-gramme allowed too little time for careful preparation in 1945. Yet even if there had been much more time, it is doubtful if the two major weaknesses of the National Coal Board – the continuance of labour resentment and excessive centralization – could have been overcome.

Given the themes of this chapter, it is the former – the deficiencies of labour relations in the public corporation – that are historically the more interesting, for they echo so much of the industry's early history.

---

[44] *New Statesman & Nation*, 7 April 1945, p. 220.

It has, of course, been argued that nationalization failed to solve the problem of labour relations because it precluded workers' control or direct participation – just as the failure of the campaign for nationalization in 1919–20 has been blamed on the abandonment of syndicalist ideals.[45] But on any realistic consideration it is very difficult to see how more intensive and elaborate participation in management could have provided anything other than an aggravation of the industry's economic problems, either in the inter-war period or since 1946. Throughout the 1920s and 1930s the industry was incapable of generating sufficient employment for those notionally attached to it. The pursuit of efficiency would have worsened that problem, while the pursuit of short-run improvements in wage rates or conditions (which always took precedence for the miners) would have threatened even more jobs. As the mining trade journal pointed out in 1945, throughout the 1930s a 'degree of inefficiency was tolerated rather than face a formidable social problem'.[46]

Of course, superficially, and certainly compared with private enterprise in the 1930s, nationalization worked in one very important respect; for much of the 1950s and 1960s it proved possible simultaneously to run down the industry and modernize its technology. But the financial cost was enormous – and it was potentially easy largely because (unlike the 1930s) full employment cushioned the effects of the reduction in capacity.

A more telling comparison must therefore be (as in so many other aspects of British economic history) between the 1980s and the 1930s. Once again, the industry has excessive and expensive capacity – made the more excessive and expensive by virtue of the subsidies derived from public ownership. Hence once again, there is pressure to rationalize a declining industry. And once again there is nowhere for the excess labour to go – although now there are, at least, generous arrangements for redundancy and early retirement.

But the essential point remains that, in spite of early goodwill, nationalization did not produce industrial harmony. Rather, it ultimately institutionalized the potential conflicts in industrial relations and to that extent it has not solved the industry's economic problems. Further, the major economic and commercial decisions have frequently been made in relation to the stresses and crises of labour relations – as, at a quite different level, they were between 1919 and 1939. Fifty years on, the industry's economic position (although not its technology or its wage levels) would be familiar to the bitter adversaries of the 1920s and 1930s. Contrary, then, to the hopes and predictions of those who advocated public ownership from the

---

[45] M. G. Woodhouse, 'Mines for the Nation or Mines for the Miners? Alternative Perspectives on Industrial Democracy, 1919–21', *Llafur* 2, 3 (Summer 1978), 92–109.

[46] *Colliery Guardian*, 26 January 1945, p. 114.

First World War onwards, it was not a remedy for the sickness of the industry's labour relations. With the disappearance from the scene of the owners, the miners' suspicions, resentments and economic ambitions found other points of focus. And (as happened with intervention in the inter-war period) the public corporation ushered in not so much an era of 'corporatism' as a renewed bout of industrial politics. The obstacles to industrial reforms, and the costs of overcoming them, have remained disconcertingly familiar.

Perhaps the most telling explanation of why this should be so came from Gwilym Lloyd George in the debate on the Nationalization Bill.

On the date when the State takes over, what will be the effect on [the miner]? He will go to the same pit and get the same lamp from the same man; he will go into the same cage, will probably be lowered by the same man, and when he gets to the bottom, he will, if he is in certain parts of the country, see the same expression on the face of the pony. He will see the same manager, the same deputy, the old roadway, the same coalface, and, on the Friday, he will probably be paid by the same man.[47]

Lloyd George was right – just as his father had been right in predicting the inevitability of nationalization in 1919. Nothing essential had been changed. The problems of productivity, size and costs still had to be tackled – and they were still tackled in the context of destabilized labour relations that only full employment elsewhere could ameliorate. Nationalization was in many ways simply the latest form taken by enforced state interventions designed to resolve or avert industrial strife and a declining industry. The pressure of that strife, the temptation to cushion it, the decline of the industry, have all continued or reappeared. The material ambitions and structural resentments of the labour force are still the most important determinants of policy. To optimists on 1 January 1946, nationalization may have appeared the 'End of History' and the 'Beginning of Nowadays'. It was neither. It was the continuation of industrial politics by other means.

[47] Quoted in R. A. Brady, *Crisis in Britain* (London, 1950), p. 119.

Bibliography of D. C. Coleman's published works

The British Paper Industry, 1495–1860 (Oxford, 1958; reprinted Westport, Conn., 1975).
Sir John Banks, Baronet and Businessman (Oxford, 1963; reprinted Westport, Conn., 1975).
Courtaulds: An Economic and Social History, 3 vols. (Oxford, i and ii, 1969; iii, 1980).
Industry in Tudor and Stuart England (London and Basingstoke, 1975).
The Economy of England, 1450–1750 (1977; reprinted 1978).

The Domestic System in Industry (London, Historical Association, 1960).
What Has Happened to Economic History? (Cambridge, Inaugural lecture, 1972).

Part 2 (1485–1700) and (with S. Pollard) Part 3 (1760–1850), in *A Survey of English Economic History*, ed. M. W. Thomas (London, 1957; 2nd edn 1960; 3rd edn 1967).
'Economic Problems and Policies', in *New Cambridge Modern History*, vol. v, ed. F. L. Carsten (Cambridge, 1961).
'Sir John Banks, Financier', in *Essays in the Economic and Social History of Tudor and Stuart England*, ed. F. J. Fisher (Cambridge, 1961).
Introduction to and editing of K. Samuelsson, *Religion and Economic Action* (translated from the Swedish by E. G. French, Stockholm, 1961).
'Economic History: General' and 'English Economic History, 1500–1750', in *Handbook for History Teachers*, W. H. Burston and C. W. Green (London, 1962; 2nd edn 1972).
'Industrial Revolution' and 'Industrialization', in *A Dictionary of the Social Sciences*, ed. Julius Gould and William L. Kolb (London, 1964).
Introduction to and editing of *Revisions in Mercantilism* (London, 1969).
'Countryside and Industry: The Economics of an Age of Change', in *The Eighteenth Century: Europe in the Age of the Enlightenment*, ed. Alfred Cobban (London, 1969).
'English History: Economic and Social Development, 1603–1789', in *Encyclopaedia Britannica*, vol. viii (Chicago, 1970).
'Textile Growth', in *Textile History and Economic History*, ed. N. B. Harte and K. G. Ponting (in honour of Julia de Lacy Mann, Manchester, 1973).

251

'War Demand and Industrial Supply', in *War and Economic Development*, ed. J. M. Winter (Cambridge, 1975).

'Politics and Economics in the Age of Anne', in *Trade, Government and Economy in Pre-industrial England*, ed. D. C. Coleman and A. H. John (London, 1976).

'Courtaulds and the Beginning of Rayon', in *Essays in British Business History*, ed. Barry Supple (Oxford, 1977).

'Thomas Southcliffe Ashton, 1889–1968', in *Dictionary of National Biography, 1961–70* (Oxford, 1981).

'Ralph Davis: An Appreciation', in *Shipping, Trade and Commerce*, ed. P. L. Cottrell and D. H. Aldcroft (Leicester, 1981).

'Historians and Businessmen', in *Enterprise and History*, ed. D. C. Coleman and P. Mathias (Cambridge, 1984).

ARTICLES

'London Scriveners and the Estate Market in the Later Seventeenth Century', *Economic History Review* (1951).

'Naval Dockyards under the Later Stuarts', *Econ. Hist. Rev.* (1953).

'Combinations of Capital and Labour in the English Paper Industry, 1789–1825', *Economica* (1954).

'Labour in the English Economy of the Seventeenth Century', *Econ. Hist. Rev.* (1956). Reprinted in *Essays in Economic History*, vol. II, ed. E. M. Carus-Wilson (1962).

'Industrial Growth and Industrial Revolutions', *Economica* (1956). Reprinted in *Essays in Economic History*, vol. III, ed. E. M. Carus-Wilson (1962); in *The Rise of Capitalism*, ed. D. S. Landes (New York, 1966); and in *Genoza nowozytnej Anglii*, ed. A. Maczak (Warsaw, 1968).

'Eli Heckscher and the Idea of Mercantilism', *Scandinavian Economic History Review* (1957). Reprinted in *Economic Thought: An Historical Anthology*, ed. James A. Gherity (New York, 1965); and in *Revisions in Mercantilism*, ed. D. C. Coleman (London, 1969).

'The Early British Paper Industry and the Huguenots', *Proceedings of the Huguenot Society of London* (1957).

'Premiums for Paper', *Journal of the Royal Society of Arts* (1959).

'Museums in the Eighteenth Century: the Economic Background', *Museums Journal* (1959).

'Growth and Decay During the Industrial Revolution: The Case of East Anglia', *Scand. Econ. Hist. Rev.* (1962).

'An Innovation and Its Diffusion: The New Draperies', *Econ. Hist. Rev.* (1969).

'Gentlemen and Players', *Econ. Hist. Rev.* (1973).

'Ralph Davis, 1915–78', *Proceedings of the British Academy* (1979).

'Mercantilism Revisited', *Historical Journal* (1980).

'Ken Ponting: An Appreciation', *Textile History* (1983).

REVIEW ARTICLES

'Technology and Economic History, 1500–1700', *Econ. Hist. Rev.* (1959).

'Review of Periodical Literature: Great Britain, 1500–1700', *Econ. Hist. Rev.* (1959–62).

'The New Age of Technology, 1750–1900', *Economica* (1960).

'The "Gentry" Controversy and the Aristocracy in Crisis, 1558–1641', *History* (1966).
'Early Modern Economic England', *Econ. Hist. Rev.* (1972).
'The Model Game', *Econ. Hist. Rev.* (1977).
'Texts for Pre-industrial Times', *Historical Journal* (1978).
'The Local and the Global in Early Modern Society', *Historical Journal* (1982).
'Proto-industrialization: A Concept Too Many', *Econ. Hist. Rev.* (1983).

COMMENTS AND REJOINDERS

'Rejoinder: G. R. Hawke on – What?', *Econ. Hist. Rev.* (1971).
'The Coal Industry: A Rejoinder', *Econ. Hist. Rev.* (1977).
'Philanthropy Deflated: A Comment', *Econ. Hist. Rev.* (1978).

BOOK REVIEWS

The Enforcement of English Apprenticeship, 1563–1642 by M. G. Davies, *Journal of Political Economy* (1957).
The Royalists During the Puritan Revolution by P. H. Hardacre, *Econ. Hist. Rev.* (1957).
The Royal African Company by K. G. Davies, *Economica* (1958).
Cultural Foundations of Industrial Civilization by J. U. Nef, *British Journal of Sociology* (1958).
A History of Industrial Chemistry by F. S. Taylor, and *The Chemical Industry During the Nineteenth Century* by L. F. Haber, *Victorian Studies* (1958).
Profit and Power by C. H. Wilson, *Econ. Hist. Rev.* (1958).
The County Committee of Kent in the Civil War by A. M. Everitt, *Econ. Hist. Rev.* (1958).
Philanthropy in England, 1480–1660 by W. K. Jordan, *Econ. Hist. Rev.* (1960).
The Strutts and the Arkwrights by R. S. Fitton and A. P. Wadsworth, *History* (1960).
The Stages of Economic Growth by W. W. Rostow, *Bankers Magazine* (1960).
Commercial Crisis and Change in England, 1600–42 by B. E. Supple, *History* (1960).
British Industry: Change and Development in the Twentieth Century by J. H. Dunning and C. J. Thomas, *Economica* (1961).
The Brewing Industry in England, 1700–1830 by P. Mathias, *English Historical Review* (1961).
A History of Labour in Sheffield by S. Pollard, *Eng. Hist. Rev.* (1961).
Marshall's of Leeds: Flax Spinners, 1788–1886 by W. G. Rimmer, *Times Literary Supplement* (30 June 1961).
Carron Company by R. H. Campbell, *Economica* (1962).
The Industrial Revolution on the Continent by W. O. Henderson, *History* (1962).
The Century of Revolution, 1603–1714 by C. Hill, *Econ. Hist. Rev.* (1962).
Guinness's Brewery in the Irish Economy, 1759–1876 by P. Lynch and J. Vaizey, *Journal of Economic History* (1962).
People and Industries by W. H. Chaloner, *History Today* (1963).
Men of Iron: The Crowleys in the Early Iron Industry by M. W. Flinn, *British Journal of Industrial Relations* (1963).
American and British Technology in the Nineteenth Century by H. J. Habakkuk, *Economica* (1963).
The Wool Trade in Tudor and Stuart England by P. J. Bowden, *Eng. Hist. Rev.* (1964).

Calendar of Treasury Books, vol. xxxi, pt I (1717), *Econ. Hist. Rev.* (1964).
Contemporary Printed Sources for British and Irish Economic History, 1701–1750, ed. L. W. Hanson, *Jour. Econ. Hist.* (1965).
The Fleming-Senhouse Papers, ed. E. Hughes, *Econ. Hist. Rev.* (1965).
Kentish Sources, iv: *The Poor*, ed. E. Melling, *Econ. Hist. Rev.* (1965).
Herbert Correspondence, ed. W. J. Smith, *Econ. Hist. Rev.* (1965).
The World We have Lost by P. Laslett, and *An Introduction to English Historical Demography*, ed. E. A. Wrigley, *History* (1967).
Cambridge Economic History of Europe, vol. iv, ed. E. E. Rich and C. H. Wilson, *History* (1968).
Invention and Economic Growth by J. Schmookler, *Journal of the Royal Society of Arts* (1968).
Land, Labour and Population in the Industrial Revolution, ed. E. L. Jones and G. E. Mingay, *Eng. Hist. Rev.* (1969).
Calendar of Southampton Apprenticeship Registers, ed. A. L. Merson, *Econ. Hist. Rev.* (1969).
The Royal Forests of Northamptonshire, ed. P. A. J. Pettit, *Econ. Hist. Rev.* (1969).
The Rise of the Entrepreneur by J. W. Gough, *Business History* (1970).
Science and Technology in the Industrial Revolution by A. E. Musson and E. Robinson, *Econ. Hist. Rev.* (1970).
Scarcity and Choice in History by W. H. B. Court, *Econ. Hist. Rev.* (1971).
A Theory of Economic History by J. R. Hicks, *Eng. Hist. Rev.* (1971).
The Family Life of Ralph Josselin by A. Macfarlane, *History* (1971).
Partners in Science: Letters of James Watt and Joseph Black ed. E. Robinson and D. McKie, *Econ. Hist. Rev.* (1971).
The Lancashire Textile Industry in the Sixteenth Century by N. Lowe, *Business History* (1973).
Three Generations in a Family Textile Firm by Jocelyn Morton, *Textile History* (1973).
Poverty and Progress by R. G. Wilkinson, *Guardian* (8 March 1973).
W. D. & H. O. Wills and the Development of the U.K. Tobacco Industry, 1786–1965 by B. W. E. Alford, *Econ. Hist. Rev.* (1974).
Essays in Kentish History ed. M. Roake and J. Whyman, *Econ. Hist. Rev.* (1974).
Family and Fortune by L. Stone, *History* (1974).
England and the Baltic by H. Zins, *Slavonic and East European Review* (1974).
The Fontana Economic History of Europe, vol. ii: *The Sixteenth and Seventeenth Centuries*, ed. C. M. Cipolla, *Econ. Hist. Rev.* (1975).
Rural Change and Urban Growth, 1500–1800, ed. C. W. Chalklin and M. A. Havinden, *Agricultural History Review* (1976).
The Paper Industry in Scotland by A. G. Thomson, *Eng. Hist. Rev.* (1976).
The Economy of Europe in an Age of Crisis, 1600–1750 by J. De Vries, *T.L.S.* (22 July 1977).
Comparative Aspects of Scottish and Irish Economic History, 1600–1900, ed. L. M. Cullen and T. C. Smout, *Irish Economic and Social History* (1978).
The Social Thought of Bernard Mandeville, by T. A. Horne, *History* (1979).
New Cambridge Modern History, vol. xiii, ed. P. Burke, *Econ. Hist. Rev.* (1980).
Economic Thought and Ideology in Seventeenth Century England, by J. O. Appleby, *Journal of Modern History* (1981).
Mercantilism as a Rent-seeking Society by R. B. Ekelund Jr and R. O. Tollison, *Business History* (1982).

Structure and Change in Economic History by D. C. North, *T.L.S.* (15 January 1982).
The Past and the Present by L. Stone, *Econ. Hist. Rev.* (1982).
Ireland and Scotland, 1600–1850, ed. T. M. Devine and D. Dickson, *Scottish Economic and Social History* (1984).
Manufacture in Town and Country Before the Factory, ed. M. Berg, P. Hudson and M. Sonnenscher, *T.L.S.* (11 May 1984).
Greene King: A Business and Family History by R. G. Wilson, *Econ. Hist. Rev.* (1984).

Index